Relational Database Design and Implementation

Third Edition

Relational Database Design and Implementation: Clearly Explained

Third Edition

Jan L. Harrington

ELSEVIER

AMSTERDAM • BOSTON • HEIDELBERG • LONDON
NEW YORK • OXFORD • PARIS • SAN DIEGO
SAN FRANCISCO • SINGAPORE • SYDNEY • TOKYO

Morgan Kaufmann Publishers is an imprint of Elsevier

MK®

MORGAN KAUFMANN PUBLISHERS

AN IMPRINT OF ELSEVIER SCIENCE

Morgan Kaufmann Publishers is an imprint of Elsevier.
30 Corporate Drive, Suite 400, Burlington, MA 01803, USA

This book is printed on acid-free paper.

Library of Congress Cataloging-in-Publication Data

Harrington, Jan L.
Relational database design and implementation : clearly explained / Jan L. Harrington.—3rd ed.
p. cm.
Rev. ed of: Relational database design clearly explained, 1998.
Includes bibliographical references and index.
ISBN 978-0-12-374730-3
1. Relational databases. 2. Database design. I. Harrington, Jan L. Relational database design clearly explained. II. Title.
QA76.9.D26H38 2009
005.75′6—dc22 2009022380

ISBN: 978-0-12-374730-3

For information on all Morgan Kaufmann publications,

visit our Web site at www.mkp.com or www.elsevierdirect.com

Printed in the United States of America

09 10 11 12 13 5 4 3 2 1

Contents

PART II DATABASE DESIGN THEORY

Preface to the Third Edition

My favorite opening line for the database courses I teach is "Probably the most misunderstood term in all of business computing is *database,* followed closely by the word *relational.*" At that point, some students look a bit smug because they are absolutely, positively sure that they know what a database is and that they also know what is means for a database to be "relational." Unfortunately, the popular press, with the help of some PC software developers, long ago distorted the meaning of both terms, which led many businesses to think that designing a database is a task that could be left to any clerical worker who had taken a one-week course on using database software. As you will see throughout this book, however, nothing could be further from the truth.

> *Note:* The media has given us a number of nonsense computer terms such as *telephone modem* (we're modulating an analog signal, not a telephone), *software program* (the two words mean pretty much the same thing), and *cable modem* and *DSL modem* (they're not modems; they don't modulate and demodulate analog signals; they are more properly termed *codecs* that code and decode digital signals). It's all in an attempt to make computer jargon easier for people to understand, but it has generally had the effect of introducing misunderstandings.

This book is intended for anyone who has been given the responsibility for designing or maintaining a relational database. It will teach you how to look at the environment your database serves and to tailor the design of the database to the environment. It will also teach you how to design the database so it provides accurate and consistent data, avoiding the problems that are common to poorly designed databases. In addition, you will learn about design compromises that you might choose to make in the interest of database application performance and the consequences of making such choices.

If you are a college instructor, you may choose to use this book as a text in an undergraduate database management course. I've been doing that for a number of years (along with *SQL Clearly Explained,* this book's companion volume) and find that students learn from it quite well. They appreciate the straightforward language rather than a text that forces them to struggle with overly academic sentence structures. They also like the many real-world examples that appear throughout the book.

Changes in the Third Edition

The core of this book—Parts II and III, the bulk of the content of the previous editions—remains mostly unchanged from the second edition. Relational database theory has been relatively stable for more than 30 years (with the exception of the addition of sixth normal form) and requires very little updating from one edition to the next, although it has been seven years since the second edition appeared. The major changes are the discussions of fifth and sixth normal forms. The first two case studies in Part III have been updated; the third case study is new.

The chapter on object-relational databases has been removed from this edition, as well as object-relational examples in the case studies. There are two reasons for this. First, support for objects within a relational environment has largely been provided as a part of the SQL standard rather than as changes to underlying relational database theory. Second, the direction that SQL's object-relational capabilities have taken since the second edition appeared involves a number of features that violate relational design theory, and presenting them in any depth in this book would be more confusing than helpful.

By far the biggest change, however, is the addition of the new Parts I and IV. Part I contains three chapters that provide a context for database design. Database requirements don't magically appear at the point an organization needs a database, although looking at the previous editions of this book, you might think they did. Chapter 1 presents several organizational aspects of database management, including the hardware architectures on which today's databases run, and a look at service-oriented architecture (SOA), an information systems technique in which databases, like other IT functions, become services provided throughout an organization.

Chapter 2 provides an overview of several systems analysis methods to show you how organizations arrive at database requirements. In Chapter 3 you'll discover why we care about good database design. (It really *does* matter!)

Part IV provides an overview of a variety of database implementation issues that you may need to consider as you design a relational database. The topics include concurrency control (keeping the database consistent while multiple users interact with it at the same time), data warehousing (understanding issues that may arise when your operational database data are destined for data mining), data quality (ensuring that data are as accurate and consistent as possible), and XML (understanding how today's databases support XML).

The addition of Parts I and IV also make this book better suited for use as a textbook in a college course. When I used the second edition as a text in my classes, I added supplementary readings to cover that material. It's nice to have it all in once place!

The material about older data models that was presented in Chapter 3 in the second edition has been moved into an appendix. None of the material in the body of the book depends on it any longer. You can read it if you are interested in knowing what preceded the relational data model, but you won't lose anything significant in terms of relational databases if you skip it.

What You Need to Know

When the first edition of this book appeared in 1999, you needed only basic computer literacy to understand just about everything the book discussed. The role of networking in database architectures has grown so much in the past decade that in addition to computer literacy, you now need to understand some basic network hardware and software concepts (e.g., the Internet, interconnection devices such as routers and switches, and servers).

Note: It has always been a challenge to decide whether to teach students about systems analysis and design before or after database management. Now we worry about where a networking course should come in the sequence. It's tough to understand databases without networking, but at the same time, some aspects of networking involve database issues.

Acknowledgments

As always, getting this book onto paper involved an entire cast of characters, all of whom deserve thanks for their efforts. First are the people at Morgan Kaufmann:

- Rick Adams, my editor of many years. (His official title is Senior Acquisitions Editor).
- Heather Scherer, Rick's capable assistant
- Marilyn Rash, the project manager. We've worked together on a number of books over many years and it's always a pleasure.
- Eric DeCicco, the designer of the wonderful cover.
- The folks who clean up after me: Debbie Prato, copyeditor, and Samantha Molineaux, proofreader.
- Ted Laux, the indexer.
- Greg deZam-O'Hare and Sarah Binns who pulled it all together at the end.

A special thanks goes out to my colleague, Dr. Craig Fisher, who is a well-known expert on data quality. He provided me with a wealth of resources on that topic, which he thinks should be a part of everyone's IT education.

JLH

Part I

Introduction

The first part of this book deals with the organizational environment in which databases exist. In it you will find discussions about various hardware and network architectures on which databases operate and an introduction to database management software. You will also learn about alternative processes for discovering exactly what a database needs to do for an organization.

Chapter 1

The Database Environment

Can you think of a business that doesn't have a database that's stored on a computer? Maybe you can't, but I know of one: a small used paperback bookstore. A customer brings in used paperbacks and receives credit for them based on their condition and, in some cases, the subject matter of the books. That credit can be applied to purchasing books from the store at approximately twice what the store pays to acquire the books. The books are shelved by general type (for example, mystery, romance, and nonfiction), but otherwise they are not categorized. The store doesn't have a precise inventory of what is on its shelves.

To keep track of customer credits, the store has a 4 × 6 card for each customer on which employees write a date and an amount of credit. The credit amount is incremented or decremented, based on a customer's transactions. The cards themselves are stored in two long steel drawers that sit on a counter. (The cabinet from which the drawers were taken is nowhere in evidence.) Sales slips are written by hand, and cash is kept in a drawer. (Credit card transactions are processed by a stand-alone terminal that uses a phone line to dial up the processing bank for card approval.) The business is small, and their system seems to work, but it certainly is an exception.

Although this bookstore doesn't have a computer or a database, it does have data. In fact, like a majority of businesses today, it relies on data as the foundation of what it does. The bookstore's operations require the customer credit data; it couldn't function without it.

Data form the basis of just about everything an organization that deals with money does. (It's possible to operate a business using bartering and not keep any data, but that certainly is a rarity.) Even a Girl Scout troop selling cookies must store and manipulate data. The troop needs to keep track of how many boxes of each type of cookie have been ordered and by whom. They also need to manage data about money: payments received, payments owed, amount kept by the troop, amount sent to the national organization. The data may be kept on paper, but they still exist, and manipulation of those data is central to the group's functioning. In fact, just about the only business that doesn't deal with data is a lemonade stand that gets its supplies from Mom's kitchen and never has to pay Mom back. The kids take the entire gross income of the lemonade stand without having to worry about how much is profit.

Data have always been part of businesses. Until the mid-twentieth century, those data were processed manually. Because they were stored on paper, retrieving data was difficult, especially if the volume of data was large. In addition, paper documents tended to deteriorate with age. Computers changed that picture significantly, making it possible to store data in much less space, to retrieve data more easily, and, usually, to store it more permanently.

The downside to the change to automated data storage and retrieval was the need for specialized knowledge on the part of those who set up the computer systems. In addition, it costs more to purchase the equipment needed for electronic data manipulation than it does to purchase some file folders and file cabinets. Nonetheless, the ease of data access and manipulation that computing has brought to business has outweighed most other considerations.

DEFINING A DATABASE

Nearly 30 years ago, when I first started working with databases, I would begin a college course I was teaching in database management with the sentence "There is no term more misunderstood and misused in all of business computing than *database*." Unfortunately, that is still true to some extent, and we can still lay much of the blame on commercial software developers. In this section we'll explore why that is so and provide a complete definition for a database.

Lists and Files

A portion of the data used in a business is represented by lists of things. For example, most of us have a contact list that contains names, addresses, and phone numbers. Businesspeople also commonly work with planners that list appointments. In our daily lives, we have shopping lists of all kinds, as well as "to do" lists. For many years, we handled these lists manually, using paper, day planners, and a pen. It made sense to many people to migrate these lists from paper to their PCs.

Software that helps us maintain simple lists stores those lists in files, generally one list per physical file. The software that manages the list typically lets you create a form for data entry, provides a method of querying the data based on logical criteria, and lets you design output formats. List management software can be found not only on desktop and laptop computers but also on our handheld computing devices. Unfortunately, list management software has been marketed under the name "database" since the advent of PCs. People have therefore come to think of anything that stores and manipulates data as database software. Nonetheless, a list handled by a manager is not a database.

> *Note:* For a more in-depth discussion of the preceding issue, see the first section of Appendix A.

Databases

There is a fundamental concept behind all databases: There are things in a business environment, about which we need to store data, and those things are related to one another in a variety of ways. In fact, to be considered a *database*, the place where data are stored must contain not only the data but also information about the relationships between those data. We might, for example, need to relate our customers to the orders they place with us and our inventory items to orders for those items.

The idea behind a database is that the user—either a person working interactively or an application program—has no need to worry about how data are physically stored on disk. The user phrases data manipulation requests in terms of data relationships. A piece of software known as a *database management system* (DBMS) then translates between the user's request for data and the physical data storage.

Why, then, don't the simple "database" software packages (the list managers) produce true databases? Because they can't represent relationships between data, much less use such relationships to retrieve data. The problem is that list management software has been marketed for years as "database" software, and many purchasers do not understand exactly what they are purchasing. Making the problem worse is that a rectangular area of a spreadsheet is also called a "database." As you will see later in this book, a group of cells in a spreadsheet is even less of a database than a stand-alone list. Because this problem of terminology remains, confusion about exactly what a database happens to be remains as well.

DATA "OWNERSHIP"

Who "owns" the data in your organization? Departments? IT? How many databases are there? Are there departmental databases, or is there a centralized, integrated database that serves the entire organization? The answers to these questions can determine the effectiveness of a company's database management.

The idea of data ownership has some important implications. To see them, we must consider the human side of owning data. People consider exclusive access to information a privilege and are often proud of their access: "I know something you don't know." In organizations where small databases have cropped up over the years, the data in a given database are often held in individual departments that are reluctant to share that data with other organizational units.

One problem with these small databases is that they may contain duplicated data that are inconsistent. A customer might be identified as "John J. Smith" in the marketing database but as "John Jacob Smith" in the sales database. It also can be technologically difficult to obtain data stored in multiple databases. For example, one database may store a customer number as text, while another stores it as an integer. An application will be unable to match customer numbers between the two databases. In addition, attempts to integrate the data into a single, shared data store may run into resistance from the data "owners," who are reluctant to give up control of their data.

In yet other organizations, data are held by the IT department, which carefully doles out access to those data as needed. IT requires supervisor signatures on requests for accounts and limits access to as little data as possible, often stating requirements for system security. Data users feel as if they are at the mercy of IT, even though the data are essential to corporate functioning.

The important psychological change that needs to occur in either of the preceding situations is that data belong to the organization and that they must be shared as needed throughout the organization without unnecessary roadblocks to access. This does not mean that an organization should ignore security concerns but that, where appropriate, data should be shared readily within the organization.

Service-Oriented Architecture

One way to organize a company's entire information systems functions is *service-oriented architecture* (SOA). In an SOA environment, all information systems components are viewed as services that are provided to the organization. The services are designed so they interact smoothly, sharing data easily when needed.

An organization must make a commitment to implement SOA. Because services need to be able to integrate smoothly, information systems must be designed from the top down. (In contrast, organizations with many departmental databases and applications have grown from the bottom up.) In many cases, this may mean replacing most of an organization's existing information systems.

SOA certainly changes the role of a database in an organization in that the database becomes a service provided to the organization. To serve that role, a database must be designed to integrate with a variety of departmental applications. The only way for this to happen is for the structure of the database to be well documented, usually in some form of *data dictionary*. For example, if a department needs an application program that uses a customer's telephone number, application programmers first consult the data dictionary to find out that a telephone number is stored with the area code separate from the rest of the phone number. Every application that accesses the database must use the same telephone number format. The result is services that can easily exchange data because all services are using the same data formats.

Shared data also place restrictions on how changes to the data dictionary are handled. Changes to a departmental database affect only that department's applications, but changes to a database service may affect many other services that use the data. An organization must therefore have procedures in place for notifying all users of data when changes are proposed, giving the users a chance to respond to the proposed change and deciding whether the proposed change is warranted. As an example, consider the effect of a change from a five- to nine-digit zip code for a bank. The CFO believes that there will be a significant savings in postage if the change is implemented. However, the transparent windows in the envelopes used to mail paper account statements are too narrow to show the entire nine-digit zip code. Envelopes with wider windows are very expensive, so expensive that making the change will actually cost more than leaving the zip codes at five digits. The CFO was not aware of the cost of the envelopes; the cost was noticed by someone in the purchasing department.

SOA works best for large organizations. It is expensive to introduce because typically organizations have accumulated a significant number of independent programs and data stores that will need to be replaced. Just determining where all the data are stored, who controls the data, which data are stored, and how those data are formatted can be daunting tasks. It is also a psychological change for those employees who are used to owning and controlling data.

Organizations undertake the change to SOA because in the long run it makes information systems easier to modify as corporate needs change. It does not change the process for designing and maintaining a database, but it does change how applications programs and users interact with it.

DATABASE SOFTWARE: DBMSS

A wide range of DBMS software is available today. Some, such as Microsoft Access[1] (part of the Windows Microsoft Office suite), are designed for single users only.[2] The largest proportion of today's DBMSs, however, are multiuser, intended for concurrent use by many users. A few of those DBMSs are intended for small organizations, such as FileMaker Pro[3] (cross-platform, multiuser) and Helix[4] (Macintosh multiuser). Most, however, are intended for enterprise use. You may have heard of DB2[5] or Oracle,[6] both of which have versions for small businesses but are primarily intended for large installations using mainframes. As an alternative to these commercial products,

---

[1]*http://office.microsoft.com/en-us/access/default.aspx*

[2]It is possible to "share" an Access database with multiple users, but Microsoft never intended the product to be used in that way. Sharing an Access database is known to cause regular file corruption. A database administrator working in such an environment once told me that she had to rebuild the file "only once every two or three days."

[3]*www.filemaker.com*

[4]*www.qsatoolworks.com*

[5]*www.306.ibm.com/software/data/db2/alphablox*

[6]*www.oracle.com*

many businesses have chosen to use open source products such as MySQL.[7]

For the most part, enterprise-strength DBMSs are large, expensive pieces of software. (The exception to the preceding sentence, of course, is open-source products.) They require significant training and expertise on the part of whoever will be implementing the database. It is not unusual for a large organization to employ one or more people to handle the physical implementation of the database along with a team (or teams) of people to develop the logical structure of the database. Yet more teams may be responsible for developing application programs that interact with the database and provide an interface for those who cannot, or should not, interact with the database directly.

Regardless of the database product you choose, you should expect to find the following capabilities:

- A DBMS must provide facilities for creating the structure of the database. Developers must be able to define the logical structure of the data to be stored, including the relationships among data.
- A DBMS must provide some way to enter, modify, and delete data. Small DBMSs typically focus on form-based interfaces; enterprise-level products begin with a command-line interface. The most commonly used language for interacting with a relational database (the type we are discussing in this book) is SQL (originally called Structured Query Language), which has been accepted throughout much of the world as a standard data manipulation language for relational databases.
- A DBMS must also provide a way to retrieve data. In particular, users must be able to formulate queries based on the logical relationships among the data. Smaller products support form-based querying, while enterprise-level products support SQL. A DBMS should support complex query statements using Boolean algebra (the AND, OR, and NOT operators) and should also be able to perform at least basic calculations (for example, computing totals and subtotals) on data retrieved by a query.
- Although it is possible to interact with a DBMS either with basic forms (for a smaller product) or at the SQL command line (for

[7] *See www.mysql.com*. The "community" version of the product is free but does not include any technical support; an enterprise version includes technical support and therefore is fee-based.

enterprise-level products), doing so requires some measure of specialized training. A business usually has employees who must manipulate data but don't have the necessary expertise, can't or don't want to gain the necessary expertise, or shouldn't have direct access to the database for security reasons. Application developers therefore create programs that simplify access to the database for such users. Most DBMSs designed for business use provide some way to develop such applications. The larger the DBMS, the more likely it is that application development requires traditional programming skills. Smaller products support graphic tools for "drawing" forms and report layouts.

- A DBMS should provide methods for restricting access to data. Such methods often include creating user names and passwords specific to the database and tying access to data items to the user name. Security provided by the DBMS is in addition to security in place to protect an organization's network.

DATABASE HARDWARE ARCHITECTURE

Because databases are almost always designed for concurrent access by multiple users, database access has always involved some type of computer network. The hardware architecture of these networks has matured along with more general computing networks.

Centralized

Originally network architecture was centralized, with all processing done on a mainframe. Remote users—who were almost always located within the same building or at least the same office park—worked with dumb terminals that could accept input and display output but had no processing power of their own. The terminals were hard-wired to the mainframe (usually through some type of specialized controller) using coaxial cable, as in Figure 1.1. During the time that the classic centralized architecture was in wide use, network security also was not a major issue. The Internet was not publicly available, the World Wide Web did not exist, and security threats were predominantly internal.

Centralized database architecture in the sense we have been describing is rarely found today. Instead, those organizations that maintain a centralized database typically have both local and remote users connecting using PCs, LANs, and a WAN of some kind. As you look at

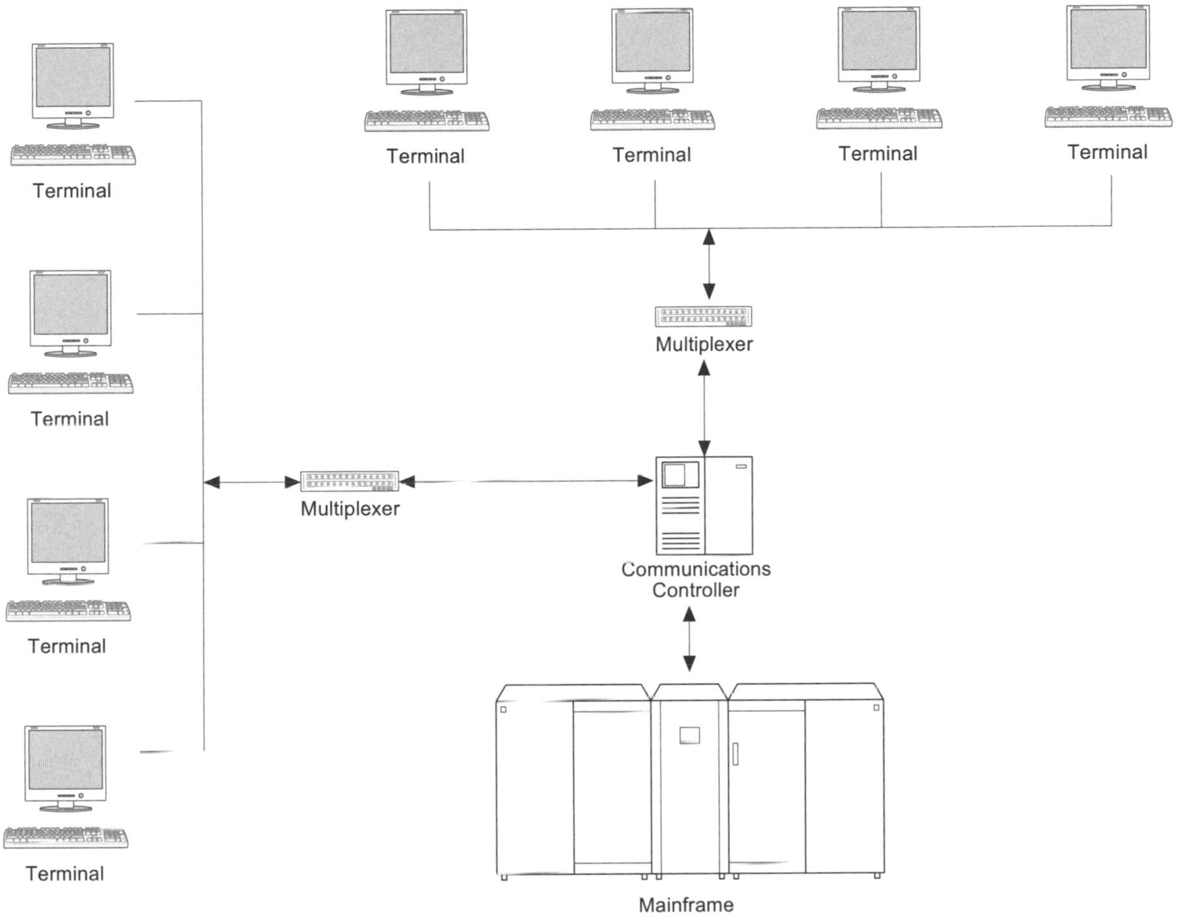

■ **FIGURE 1-1** Classic centralized database architecture.

Figure 1.2, keep in mind that although the terminals have been replaced with PCs, the PCs are not using their own processing power when interacting with the database. All processing is still done on the mainframe.

From the point of view of an IT department, the centralized architecture has one major advantage: control. All the computing is done on one computer to which only IT has direct access. Software management is easier because all software resides and executes on one machine. Security efforts can be concentrated on a single point of vulnerability. In addition, mainframes have the significant processing power to handle data-intensive operations.

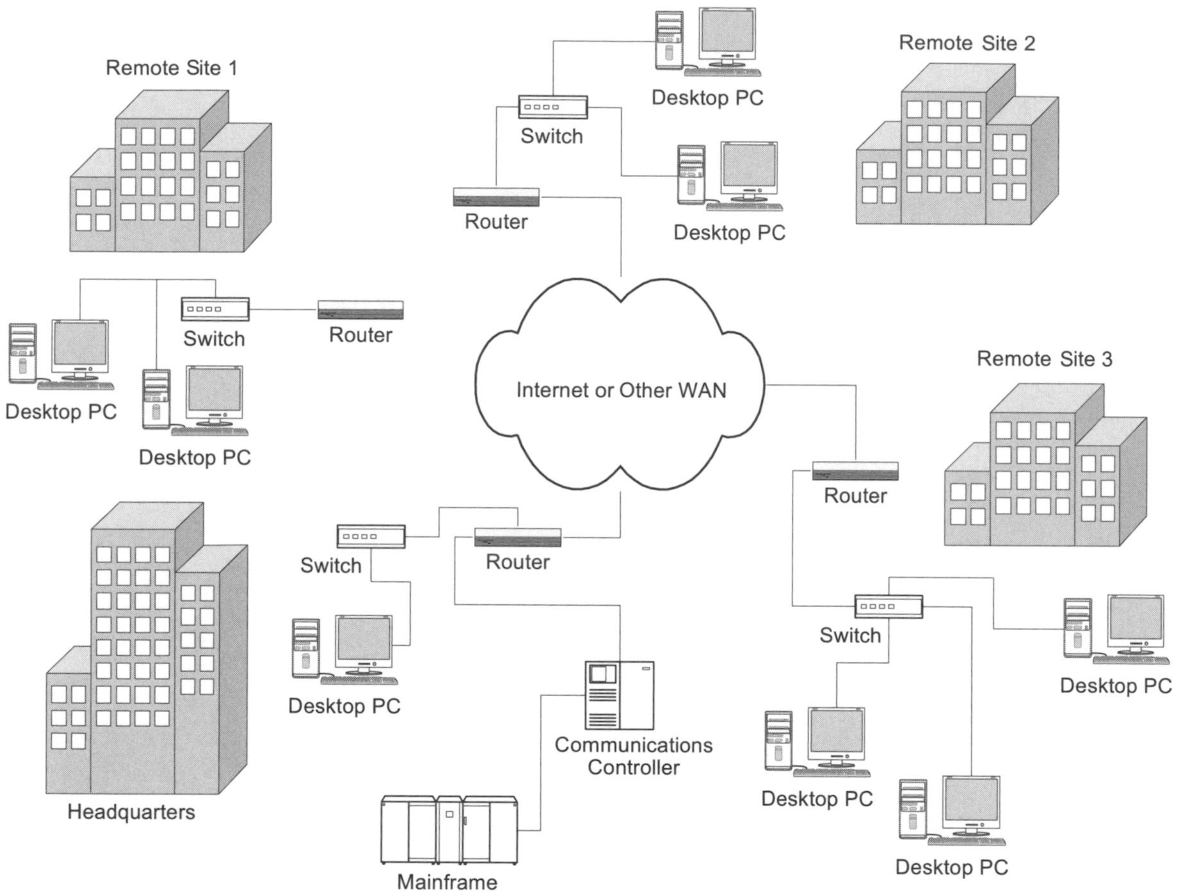

■ **FIGURE 1-2** A modern centralized database architecture including LAN and WAN connections.

One drawback to a centralized database architecture is network performance. Because the terminals (or PCs acting as terminals) do not do any processing on their own, all processing must be done on the mainframe. The database needs to send formatted output to the terminals, which consumes more network bandwidth than would sending only the data.

A second drawback to centralized architecture is reliability. If the database goes down, the entire organization is prevented from doing any data processing.

The mainframes are not gone, but their role has changed as client/server architecture has become popular.

Client/Server

Client/server architecture shares the data processing chores between a server—typically a high-end workstation—and clients, which are usually PCs. PCs have significant processing power and are therefore capable of taking raw data returned by the server and formatting it for output. Application programs are stored and executed on the PCs. Network traffic is reduced to data manipulation requests sent from the PC to the database server and raw data returned as a result of that request. The result is significantly less network traffic and theoretically better performance.

Today's client/server architectures exchange messages over local area networks (LANs). Although a few older Token Ring LANs are still in use, most of today's LANs are based on Ethernet standards. As an example, take a look at the small network in Figure 1-3. The database

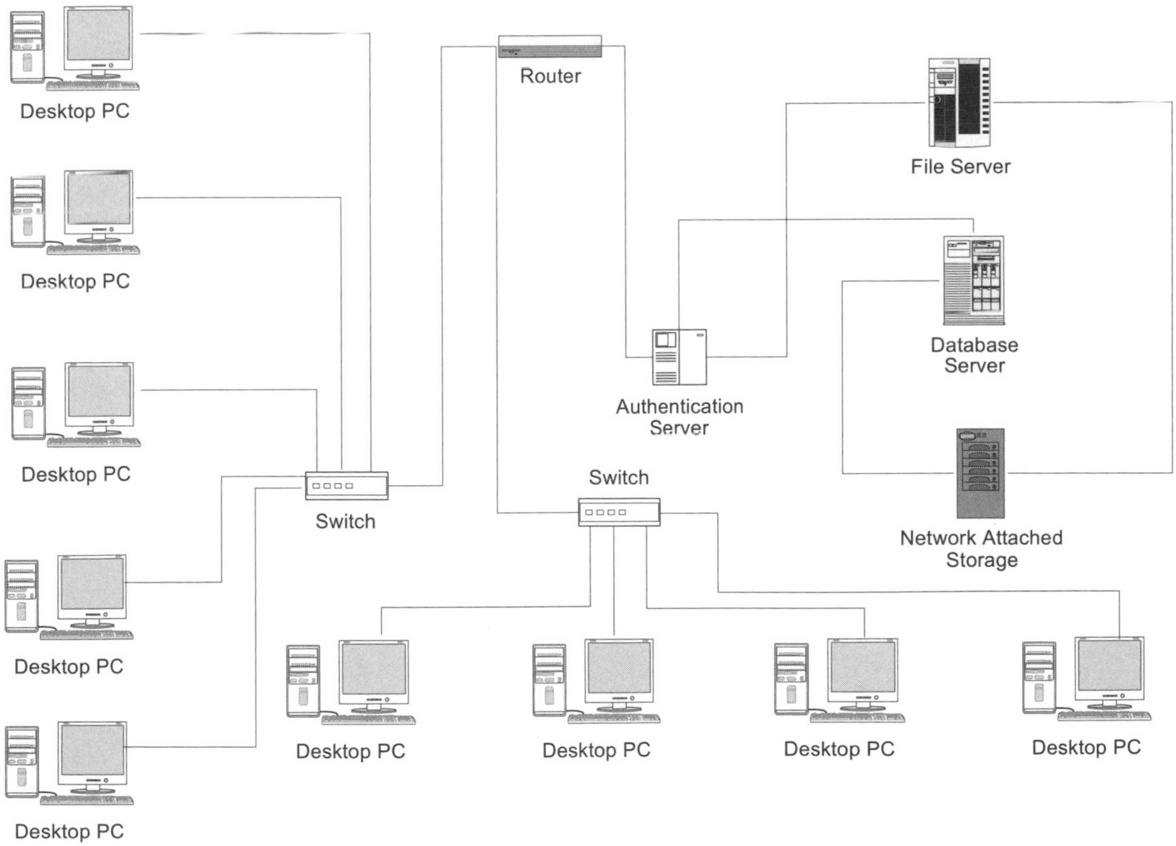

■ **FIGURE 1-3** Small LAN with network-accessible database server.

runs on its on server (the database server), using additional disk space on the network attached storage device. Access to the database is controlled not only by the DBMS itself but by the authentication server.

A client/server architecture is similar to the traditional centralized architecture in that the DBMS resides on a single computer. In fact, many of today's mainframes actually function as large, fast servers. The need to handle large data sets still exists, although the location of some of the processing has changed.

Because a client/server architecture uses a centralized database server, it suffers from the same reliability problems as the traditional centralized architecture: If the server goes down, data access is cut off. However, because the "terminals" are PCs, any data downloaded to a PC can be processed without access to the server.

Distributed

Not long after centralized databases became common—and before the introduction of client/server architecture—large organizations began experimenting with placing portions of their databases at different locations, with each site running a DBMS against part of the entire data set. This architecture is known as a *distributed database*. (For an example, see Figure 1-4.) It is different from the WAN-using centralized database in Figure 1-2 in that there is a DBMS and part of the database at each site as opposed to having one computer doing all of the processing and data storage.

A distributed database architecture has several advantages:

- The hardware and software placed at each site can be tailored to the needs of the site. If a mainframe is warranted, then the organization uses a mainframe. If smaller servers will provide enough capacity, then the organization can save money by not needing to install excess hardware. Software, too, can be adapted to the needs of the specific site. Most current distributed DBMS software will accept data manipulation requests from any DBMS that uses SQL. Therefore, the DBMSs at each site can be different.
- Each site keeps that portion of the database that contains the data that it uses most frequently. As a result, network traffic is reduced because most queries stay on a site's LAN rather than having to use the organization's WAN.

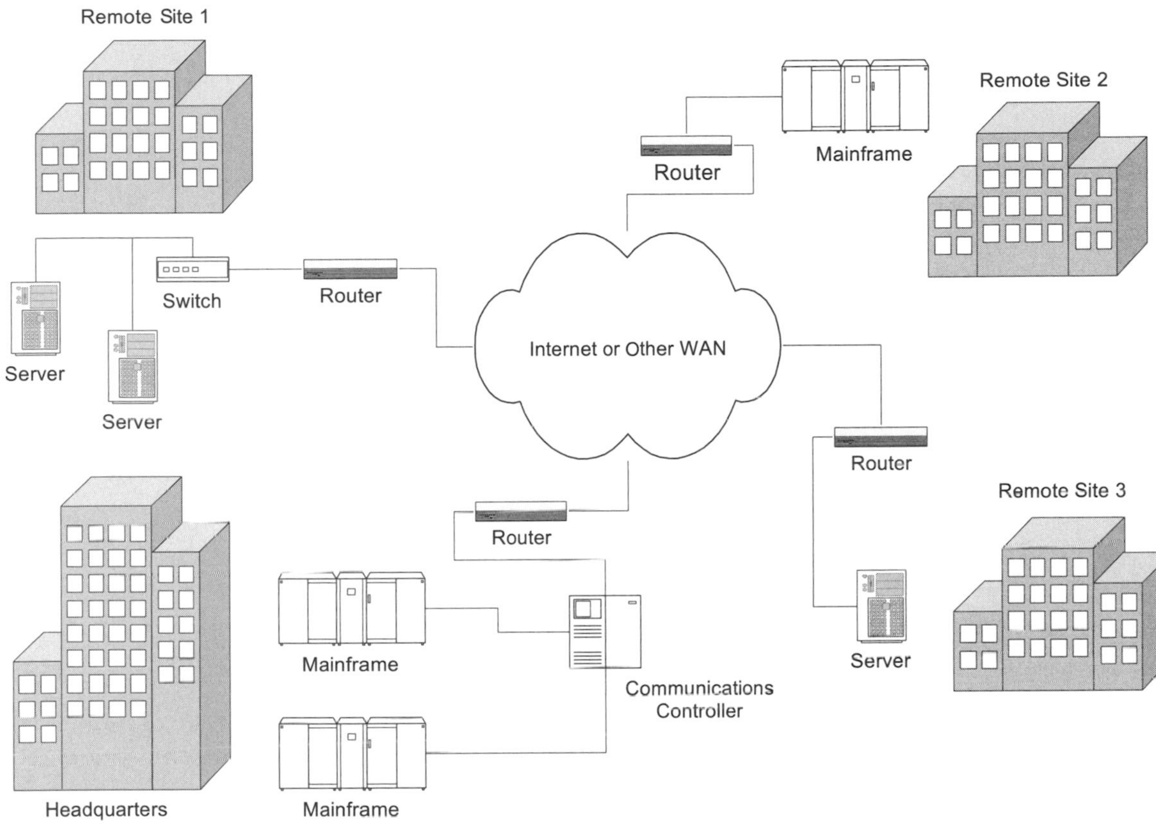

■ **FIGURE 1-4** Distributed database architecture.

- Performance for local queries is better because there is no time lag for travel over the WAN.
- Distributed databases are more reliable than centralized systems. If the WAN goes down, each site can continue processing using its own portion of the database. Only those data manipulation operations that require data not on site will be delayed. If one site goes down, the other sites can continue to process using their local data.

Despite the advantages, there are reasons why distributed databases are not widely implemented:

- Although performance of queries involving locally stored data is enhanced, queries that require data from another site are relatively slow.

- Maintenance of the data dictionary (the catalog of the structure of the database) becomes an issue: Should there be a single data dictionary or a copy of it at each site? If the organization keeps a single data dictionary, then any changes made to it will be available to the entire database. However, each time a remote site needs to access the data dictionary, it must send a query over the WAN, increasing network traffic and slowing down performance. If a copy of the data dictionary is stored at each site, then changes to the data dictionary must be sent to each site. There is a significant chance that at times the copies of the data dictionary will become out of sync.
- Some of the data in the database will exist at more than one site. This introduces a number of problems in terms of ensuring that the duplicated copies remain consistent, some of which may be serious enough to prevent an organization from using a distributed architecture. (You will read more about this problem in Chapter 15.)
- Because data are traveling over network media not owned by the company (the WAN), security risks are increased.

The Web

The need for Web sites to interact with database data has introduced yet another alternative database architecture. The Web server that needs the data must query the database, accept the results, and format the result with HTML tags for transmission to the end user and display by the user's Web browser. Complicating the picture is the need to keep the database secure from Internet intruders.

Figure 1-5 provides an example of how a Web server affects the hardware on a network when the Web server must communicate with a database server. For most installations, the overriding concern is security. The Web server is isolated from the internal LAN, and a special firewall is placed between the Web server and the database server. The only traffic allowed through that firewall is traffic to the database server from the Web server and from the database server to the Web server.

Some organizations prefer to isolate an internal database server from a database server that interacts with a Web server. This usually means that there will be two database servers. The database server that interacts with the Web server is a copy of the internal database that is inaccessible from the internal LAN. Although more secure than the architecture in Figure 1-5, keeping two copies of the database means

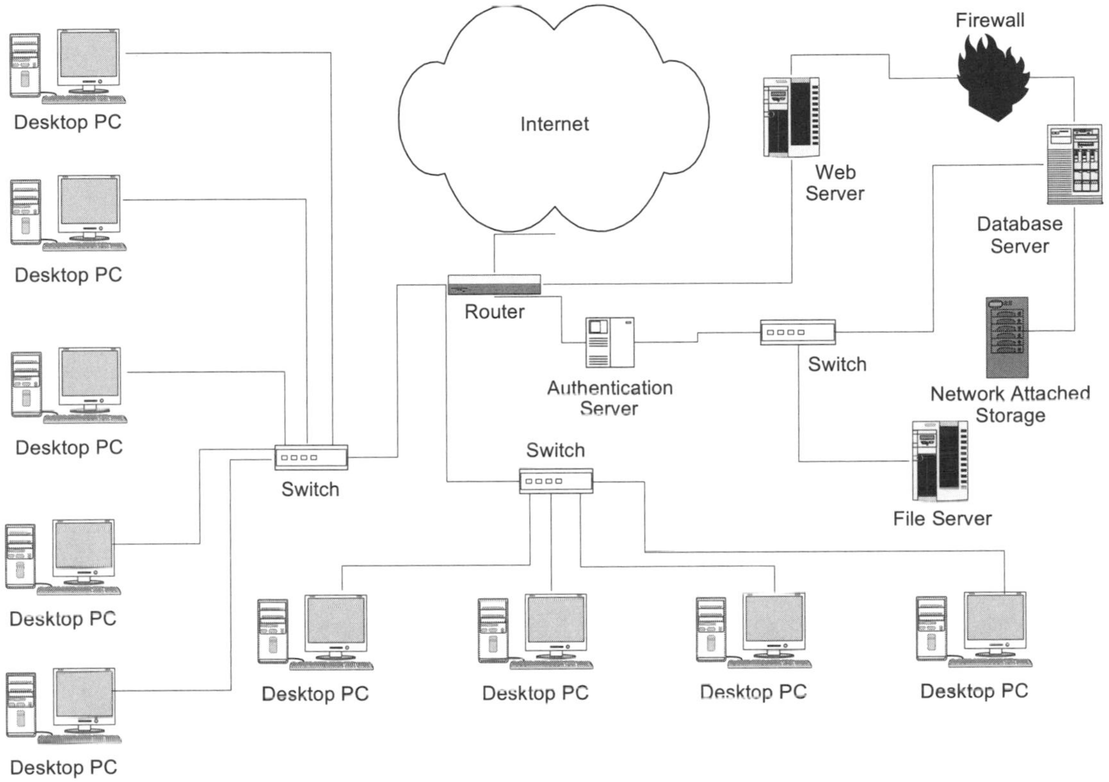

■ **FIGURE 1-5** The placement of a database server in a network when a Web server interacting with the database is present.

that those copies must be reconciled at regular intervals. The database server for Web use will become out of date as soon as changes are made to the internal database, and there is the chance that changes to the internal database will make portions of the Web-accessible database invalid or inaccurate. Retail organizations that need live, integrated inventory for both physical and Web sales cannot use the duplicated architecture. You will see an example of such an organization in Chapter 14.

Remote Access

Adding to whatever architecture we've chosen for our database hardware, we often have to accommodate remote users. Salespeople, agents in the field, telecommuters, executives on vacation—all may have the need to access a database that is usually available only over a LAN. Initially, remote access involved using a phone line and a modem to dial into the office network. Today, however, the Internet (usually with the help of a VPN—a virtual private network) provides cheaper and faster access, along with serious security concerns.

As you can see in Figure 1-6, the VPN creates a secure encrypted tunnel between the business's internal network and the remote user.[8] The remote user must also pass through an authentication server before being granted access to the internal LAN. Once authenticated, the remote user has the same access to the internal LAN—including the database server—as if he or she were present in the organization's offices.

OTHER FACTORS IN THE DATABASE ENVIRONMENT

Choosing hardware and software to maintain a database and then designing and implementing the database itself was once enough to establish a database environment. Today, however, security concerns loom large, coupled with government regulations on the privacy of data. In addition, a new database is unlikely to be the first database in an organization that has been in business for a while; the new database may need to interact with an existing database that cannot be merged into the new database. In this section, we'll briefly consider how those factors influence database planning.

Security

Before the Internet, database management was fairly simple in that we were rarely concerned about security. A user name and password were enough to secure access to a centralized database. The most significant security threats were internal—from employees who either corrupted data by accident or purposely exceeded their authorized access.

Most DBMSs provide some type of internal security mechanism. However, that layer of security is not enough today. Adding a database server to a network that has a full-time connection to the Internet means that database planning must also involve network design.

[8]To be totally accurate, there are two kinds of VPNs. One uses encryption from end-to-end (user to network and back). The other encrypts only the Internet portion of the transmission

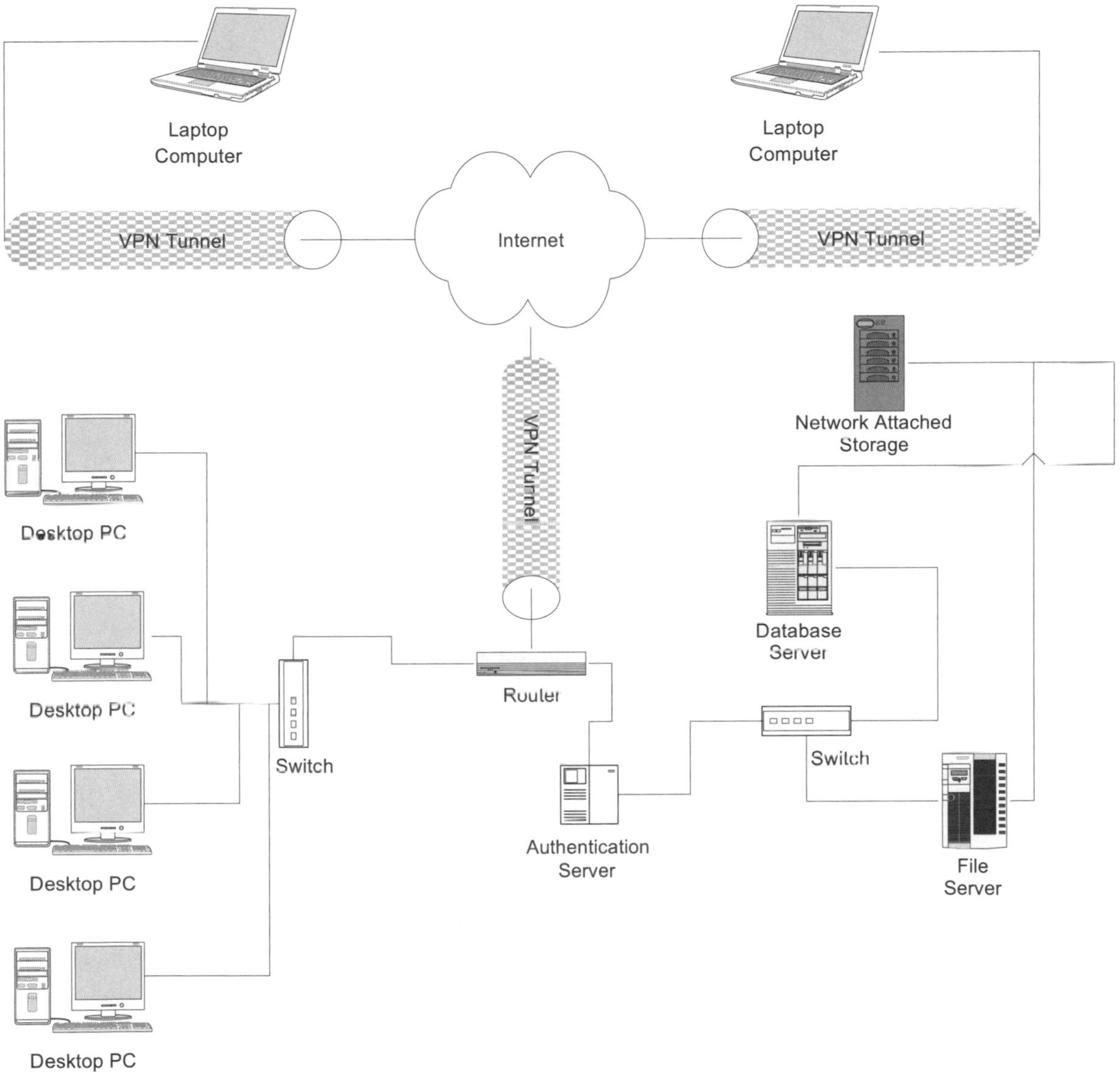

■ **FIGURE 1-6** Using a VPN to secure remote access to a database.

Authentication servers, firewalls, and other security measures therefore need to be included in the plans for a database system.

There is little benefit to the need for added security. The planning time and additional hardware and software increase the cost of implementing the database. The cost of maintaining the database also increases as network traffic must be monitored far more than when we had classic centralized architectures. Unfortunately, there is no alternative. Data is the lifeblood of almost every modern organization, and it must be protected.

The cost of a database security breach can be devastating to a business. The loss of trade secrets, the release of confidential customer information—even if the unauthorized disclosure of data doesn't cause any problems, security breaches can be a public relations nightmare, causing customers to lose confidence in the organization and convincing them to take their business elsewhere.

Note: Because database security is so vitally important, Chapter 16 is devoted entirely to this topic.

Government Regulations and Privacy

Until the past 10 years or so, decisions about what data must be secured to maintain privacy has been left up to the organization storing the data. In the United States, however, that is no longer the case for many types of data. Government regulations determine who can access the data and what they may access. The following are some of the U.S. laws that may affect owners of databases.

- *Health Insurance Portability and Accountability Act (HIPAA):* HIPAA is intended to safeguard the privacy of medical records. It restricts the release of medical records to the patient alone (or the parent/guardian in the case of those under 18) or to those the patient has authorized in writing to retrieve records. It also requires the standardization of the formats of patient records so they can be transferred easily among insurance companies and the use of unique identifiers for patients. (The Social Security number may not be used.) Most importantly for database administrators, the law requires that security measures be in place to protect the privacy of medical records.
- *Family Educational Rights and Privacy Act (FERPA):* FERPA is designed to safeguard the privacy of educational records. Although the U.S. federal government has no direct authority over private schools, it does wield considerable power over funds that are allocated to schools. Therefore, FERPA denies federal funds to those schools that don't meet the requirements of the law. It states that parents have a right to view the records of children under 18 and that the records

of older students (those 18 and over) cannot be released to anyone but the student without the written permission of the student. Schools therefore have the responsibility to ensure that student records are not disclosed to unauthorized people, increasing the need for secure information systems that store student information.

- *Children's Online Privacy Protection Act:* Provisions of this law govern which data can be requested from children (those under 13) and which of those data can be stored by a site operator. It applies to Web sites, "pen pal services," e-mail, message boards, and chat rooms. In general, the law aims to restrict the soliciting and disclosure of any information that can be used to identify a child—beyond information required for interacting with the Web site—without approval of a parent or guardian. Covered information includes first and last name, any part of a home address, e-mail address, telephone number, Social Security number, or any combination of the preceding. If covered information is necessary for interaction with a Web site—for example, registering a user—the Web site must collect only the minimally required amount of information, ensure the security of that information, and not disclose it unless required to do so by law.

Legacy Databases

Many businesses keep their data "forever." They never throw anything out, nor do they delete electronically stored data. For a business that has been using computing since the 1960s or 1970s, this typically means that old database applications are still in use. We refer to such databases that use pre-relational data models as *legacy databases*. The presence of legacy databases presents several challenges to an organization, depending on the need to access and integrate the older data.

If legacy data are needed primarily as an archive (either for occasional access or retention required by law), then a company may choose to leave the database and its applications as they stand. The challenge in this situation occurs when the hardware on which the DBMS and application programs run breaks down and cannot be repaired. The only alternative may be to recover as much of the data as possible and convert it to be compatible with newer software.

Businesses that need legacy data integrated with more recent data must answer the question "Should the data be converted for storage in the current database, or should intermediate software be used to move data between the old and the new as needed?" Because we are typically talking about large databases running on mainframes, neither solution is inexpensive.

The seemingly most logical alternative is to convert legacy data for storage in the current database. The data must be taken from the legacy database and reformatted for loading into the new database. An organization can hire one of a number of companies that specialize in data conversion, or it can perform the transfer itself. In both cases, a major component of the transfer process is a program that reads data from the legacy database, reformats them as necessary so that they match the requirements of the new database, and then loads them into the new database. Because the structure of legacy databases varies so much among organizations, the transfer program is usually custom-written for the business using it.

Just reading the procedure makes it seem fairly simple, but keep in mind that because legacy databases are old, they often contain "bad data" (data that are incorrect in some way). Once bad data get into a database, it is very difficult to get rid of them. Somehow, the problem data must be located and corrected. If there is a pattern to the bad data, that pattern must be identified to prevent any more bad data from getting into the database. The process of cleaning the data can therefore be the most time-consuming part of data conversion. Nonetheless, it is still far better to spend the time cleaning the data as they come out of the legacy database than attempting to find and correct the data once they get into the new database.

The bad data problem can be compounded by missing mandatory data. If the new database requires that data be present (for example, requiring a zip code for every order placed in the United States) and some of the legacy data are missing the required values, there must be some way to "fill in the blanks" and provide acceptable values. Supplying values for missing data can be handled by conversion software, but application programs that use the data must then be modified to identify and handle the instances of missing data.

Data migration projects also include the modification of application programs that ran solely using the legacy data. In particular, it is likely that the data manipulation language used by the legacy database is not the same as that used by the new database.

Some very large organizations have determined that it is not cost effective to convert data from a legacy database. Instead, they choose to use some type of middleware that moves data to and from the legacy database in real time as needed. An organization that has a widely used legacy database can usually find middleware. IBM markets software that translates and transfers data between IMS (the legacy product) and DB2 (the current, relational product). When such an application does not exist, it will need to be custom-written for the organization.

Note: One commonly used format for transferring data from one database to another is XML, which you will read more about in Chapter 18.

FOR FURTHER READING

Berson, Alex. *Client/Server Architecture*, 2nd ed. McGraw-Hill, 1996.

Chong, Raul F., Xiamei Wang, Michael Dang, and Dwaine R. Snow. *Understanding DB2: Learning Visually with Examples*, 2nd ed. IBM Press, 2008.

Erl, Thomas. *SOA Principles of Service Design*. Prentice Hall, 2007.

Feller, Jesse. *FileMaker Pro 10 in Depth*. Que, 2009.

Greenwald, Rick, Robert Stackowiak, and Jonathan Stern. *Oracle Essentials: Oracle Database 11g*. O'Reilly Media, 2007.

Kofler, Michael. *The Definitive Guide to MySQL 5*, 3rd ed. Apress, 2005.

McDonald, Matthew. *Access 2007: The Missing Manual*. Pogue Press, 2006.

McGrew, P. C., and W. D. McDaniel. *Wresting Legacy Data to the Web & Beyond: Practical Solutions for Managers & Technicians*. McGrew & Daniel Group, Inc., 2001.

Chapter 2

Systems Analysis and Database Requirements

As you will see when you read Parts Two and Three of this book, a large measure of what constitutes the "right" or "correct" database design for an organization depends on the needs of that organization. Unless you understand the meaning and uses of data in the database environment, you can't produce even an adequate database design.

The process of discovering the meaning of a database environment and the needs of the users of that data is known as *systems analysis*. It is part of a larger process that involves the creation of an information system from the initial conception all the way through the evaluation of the newly implemented system. Although a database designer may indeed be involved in the design of the overall system, for the most part the database designer is concerned with understanding how the database environment works and therefore in the result of the systems analysis.

Many database design books pay little heed to how the database requirements come to be. Sometimes they seem to appear out of thin air, although clearly that is not the case. A systems analysis is an important part of the database design process, and it benefits a database designer to be familiar with how an analysis is conducted and what it produces. In this chapter you will be introduced to a classic process for conducting a systems analysis. The final section of the chapter provides an overview of two alternative methods.

The intent of this chapter is not to turn you into a systems analyst—it would take a college course and some years of on-the-job experience to do that—but to give you a feeling of what happens *before* the database designer goes to work.

DEALING WITH RESISTANCE TO CHANGE

Before we look at systems analysis methodologies, we must first consider one very important factor: A new system, or modifications to an existing system, may represent a significant change in the work environment, something we humans usually do not accept easily. We tend to become comfortable in the way we operate, and change creates some level of discomfort (how uneasy, of course, depends on the individual).

Even the best-designed and -implemented information system will be useless if users don't accept it. This means that as well as determining the organization's data management needs, those in charge of system change must be very sensitive to how users react to modifications.

The simplest way to handle resistance to change is to understand that if people have a stake in the change, then they will be personally invested in seeing that the change succeeds. Many of the needs assessment techniques that you read about in this chapter can foster that type of involvement. Ask the users what they need, and then really listen to what they are saying. Show the users how you are implementing what they need. For those requests that you can't satisfy, explain why they aren't feasible. Users who feel that they matter, that their input is valued, are far more likely to support procedural changes that may accompany a new information system.

The are a number of theoretical models for managing change, including the following:[1]

ADKAR: ADKAR is a model created with international input. Its five components make up its acronym:

- *Awareness:* Make users aware of why there must be a change.
- *Desire:* Involve and educate users so they have a desire to be part of the change process.
- *Knowledge:* Educate users and system development personnel in the process of making the change.
- *Ability:* Ensure that users and system development personnel have the skills necessary to implement the change. This may include training IT staff in using new development tools and training users to use the new system.

---

[1]For a good overview of change management, see *http://home.att.net/~nickols/change.htm*.

- *Reinforcement:* Continued follow-up after the system is implemented to ensure that the new system continues to be used as intended.

Unfreeze–Change–Refreeze: This is a three-stage model with the following components:

- *Unfreezing:* Overcoming inertia by getting those who will be affected by the change to understand the need for change and to take steps to accept it.
- *Change:* Implementing the change, recognizing that users may be uneasy with new software and procedures.
- *Refreeze:* Taking actions to ensure that users are as comfortable with the new system as they were with the one it replaced.

THE STRUCTURED DESIGN LIFE CYCLE

The classic method for developing an information system is known as the *structured design life cycle*. It works best in environments where it is possible to specify the requirements before the system is developed because they are fairly well known. Typically, the process includes the following activities:

1. Conduct a needs assessment to determine what the new or modified system should do. (This is the portion of the process typically known as a *systems analysis*.)
2. Assess the feasibility of implementing the new/modified system.
3. Generate a set of alternative plans for the new/modified system. (At this point, the team involved with designing and developing the system usually prepares a *requirements document*, which contains specifications of the requirements of the system, the feasibility analysis, and system development alternatives.)
4. Evaluate the alternatives and choose one for implementation.
5. Design the system.
6. Develop and test the system.
7. Implement the system.
8. Evaluate the system.

The reason the preceding process is called a "cycle" is that when you finish Step 7, you go right back to Step 1 to modify the system to

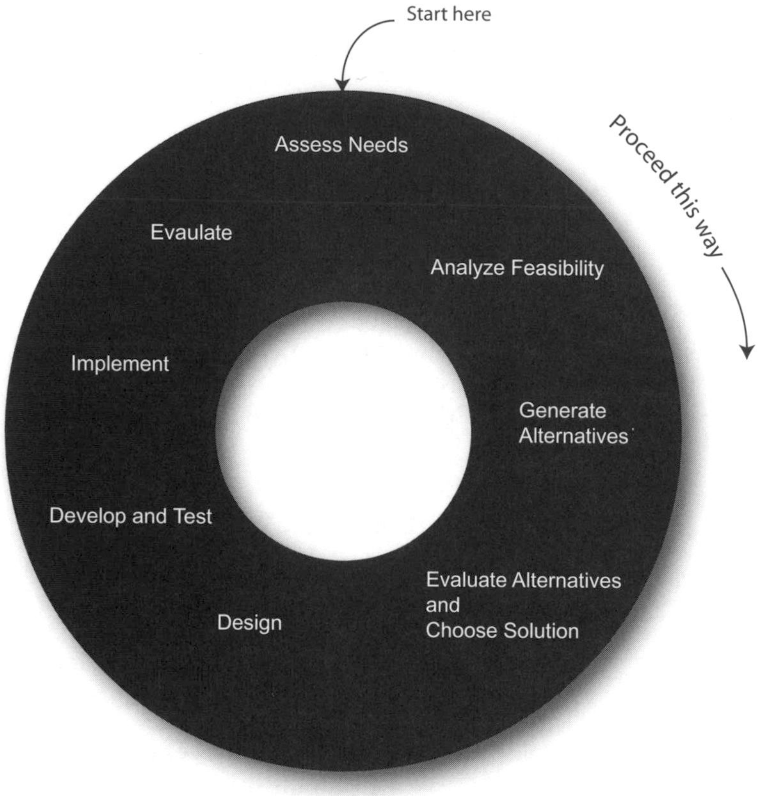

■ **FIGURE 2-1** The traditional systems development life cycle.

handle any problems identified in the evaluation (see Figure 2-1). If no problems were found during the evaluation, then you wait awhile and evaluate again. However, the process is also sometimes called the *waterfall method* because the project falls from one step to another, like the waterfall in Figure 2-2. Database designers are typically involved in Steps 1 through 5. The database design itself takes place during Step 5, but that process cannot occur until the preceding steps are completed.

CONDUCTING THE NEEDS ASSESSMENT

Many systems analysts believe that the needs assessment is the most important part of the systems development process. No matter how well developed, even the best information system is useless if it doesn't

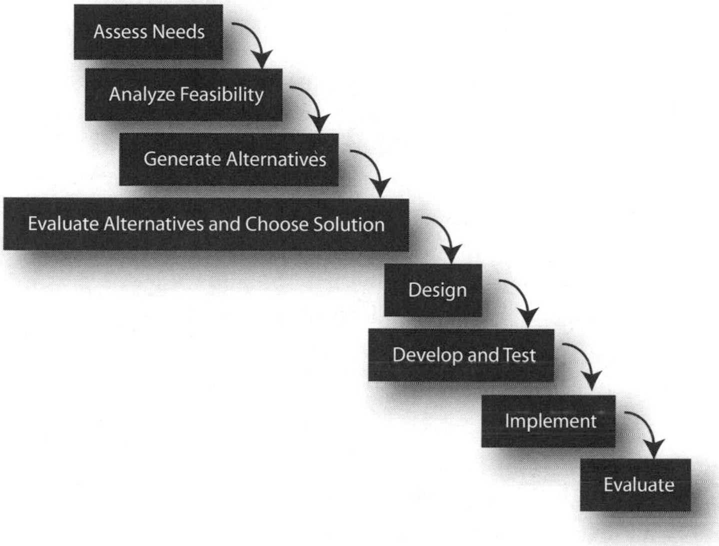

■ **FIGURE 2-2** The waterfall view of the traditional systems development life cycle.

meet the needs of its organization. A system that isn't used is just a waste of money.

A systems analyst has many tools and techniques available to help identify the needs of a new or modified information system, including:

- *Observation:* To conduct an observation, the systems analyst watches employees without interference. This allows users to demonstrate how they actually use the current system (be it automated or manual).
- *Interviewing:* The systems analyst interviews employees at various levels in the organizational hierarchy. This process allows employees to communicate what works well with the current system and what needs to be changed. During the interviews, the analyst attempts to identify the differences among the perceptions of managers and those who work for them.

Sometimes a systems analyst will discover that what actually occurs isn't what is supposed to be standard operating procedure. If there is a difference between what is occurring and the way in which things "should" happen, then either employee behavior will need to change or procedures will need to change to match employee behavior. It's not the systems analyst's job to make the choice but only to document what is occurring and to present alternative solutions.

Occasionally observations and interviews can expose informal processes that may or may not be relevant to a new system. Consider what happened to a systems analyst who was working on a team that was developing an automated system for a large metropolitan library system. (This story is based on an incident that actually occurred in the 1980s.) The analyst was assigned to interview staff of the mobile services branch, the group that provided bookmobiles as well as individualized service to housebound patrons. The process in question was book selection and ordering.

Here's how it was supposed to happen: Each week, the branch received a copy of a publication called *Publishers Weekly*. This magazine, which is still available, not only documents the publishing trade but also lists and reviews forthcoming media (primarily books). The librarians (four adult librarians and one children's librarian) were to go through the magazine and place a check mark next to each book the branch should order. Once a month, the branch librarian was to take the marked-up magazine to the central order meeting with all the other branch librarians in the system. All books with three or more checks were to be ordered, although the branch librarian was to exercise her own judgment and knowledge of the branch patrons to help make appropriate choices.

The preceding is what the systems analyst heard from the branch librarian. The five librarians, however, told a different story. At one point they concluded that the branch librarian wasn't exercising any judgment at all but was simply ordering all books with three checks. There was only one children's librarian, and therefore children's books almost never received three checks. Few children's books were being ordered.

To test their theory, the librarians placed four check marks next to a significantly inappropriate title—a coffee table book that was too heavy for many of their elderly patrons to handle and that exceeded the branch's price limit—and waited to see what happened. The coffee table book was ordered, so they thought that no professional judgment was being used at the order meeting.

The librarians therefore took the situation into their own hands. When the branch librarian returned from the order meeting, she gave the copy of the *Publishers Weekly* to one of the clerks, who created cards for each ordered book. The cards were to be matched to the new books when they arrived. However, the librarians arranged for the clerk to let them see the cards as soon as they were made. The librarians removed books that shouldn't be ordered and added those that had been omitted (primarily children's books). The clerk then phoned the changes to the order department.

What should the analyst have done? The process was clearly broken, and it appeared that the branch librarian wasn't doing her job. The librarians had arranged things so the branch functioned well, but they were circumventing SOP and were probably putting their jobs in jeopardy by doing so. This was a case of "the end justifies the means." No one was being harmed, and the branch patrons were being helped. How should the analyst have reported her findings? Should she have exposed what was really happening, or should she simply have documented how the procedure was *supposed* to work? What would happen when the ordering process was automated and there were no longer any centralized order meetings? There would be no order cards held at the branch and no opportunity for the librarians to correct the book order.

This was a very delicate situation because if it were exposed, either the branch librarian or the other librarians (or both) would face significant problems. A systems analyst's job is to observe, interview, and record, not to intervene in employee relations. The book-ordering process would be changing anyway with an automated system. If the librarians had to continue to work around the branch librarian, they would need to change their informal process as well. Therefore, the best strategy for the analyst probably was to remove herself from the personnel problems and report the process as it was supposed to work.

In cases where informal procedures do not violate SOP, an analyst can feel free to report what is actually occurring. This will help in tailoring the new information system to the way in which the business actually operates.

- *Questionnaires:* The systems analyst prepares questionnaires to be completed by employees. Like interviews, questionnaires give the systems analyst information about what is working currently and what needs to be fixed. The drawback to questionnaires, however, is that they are limited by the questions asked—even if they include open-ended questions—and may miss important elements of what a system needs to do.

- *Focus groups:* The systems analyst conducts a focus group to hear from employees who don't use the system directly and those who may not be employees but who use the system in some way. For example, accountants may not use the payroll system directly but may receive output from that system as input to the accounting system. A focus group can give them a forum to express how well the input meets their needs and how it might be changed to better suit them. A retail firm that sells through a Web site may conduct a focus group for customers to find out what changes should be made to the catalog and shopping cart interfaces.

  A focus group can be a double-edged sword. The members of the focus group are not privy to many of the constraints under which a business operates and the limitations of technology. Their suggestions may be impractical. The analyst conducting the focus session needs to be careful not to make promises to group members that can't be kept. Participants in a focus group can have their expectations raised so high that those expectations can never be met, creating disappointment and disaffection with the business.

- *Brainstorming sessions:* When employees know that something isn't right with the current system but are unable to articulate how it should be changed, a brainstorming session allows people to toss about ideas that may or may not be feasible. The intent is to stimulate everyone's thinking about the needs of a new or modified system without being critical.

The results of the needs assessment are collected into a *requirements document*. At this point in the process, the needs identified by the analyst are expressed in general terms. For example, the requirements document might include a call for a new Web site shopping cart that allowed users to check out on one page rather than three. The fact that the redesigned Web page needs to include the customer's area code as a separate piece of data isn't documented at this point.

ASSESSING FEASIBILITY

Once the operational requirements of a new system have been documented, the systems analyst turns to assessing the feasibility of the required system. There are three types of feasibility that systems analysts consider:

1. *Operational feasibility:* Is it possible to develop a system that will fit within the organization's way of doing business, or are any of the business process changes required unrealistic?

2. *Technical feasibility:* Does the technology exist to implement a system to meet the organization's needs?
3. *Financial feasibility:* Are the costs of implementing the system in a range that the organization is able and willing to pay?

Operational feasibility looks at whether it makes sense for the company to change any part of its operating procedures to accommodate a new system. If payroll employees currently enter data from time cards by hand, a change to a machine-readable system is operationally feasible. The procedure for entering hours worked changes slightly, but the employees will still use some sort of time card, and payroll employees will still be processing the data. In contrast, consider the situation where a new system would require all purchase requisitions to be placed using an online form. However, some offices in remote locations do not have Internet access, so it is not feasible to shut down paper-based requisitions entirely.

Operational feasibility also relies to a large extent on an organization's and its employees' willingness to change. Assume, for example, that insurance company representatives currently fill out paper forms when making a sale at a customer's home. The company would like to replace the paper with laptops that use wireless connections to exchange data with the home office. Certainly, this is a reasonable choice given the way in which the company operates, but if many of the salespeople are resistant to working with a laptop, then a project to introduce the laptops may fail. Sometimes the introduction of new technology, especially in a manufacturing environment, is crucial to maintaining a company's competitive position and therefore its ability to stay in business. Employees who are resistant to the new technology (either unwilling or unable to be retrained) may need to be laid off to ensure that the company survives.

Technological feasibility is relatively easy to assess. Can the necessary technology be purchased? If not, is it possible to develop that technology in a reasonable amount of time and at a reasonable cost? Consider, for example, the situation of a rural library cooperative in the mid-1980s. Most library information systems used minicomputers. However, the rural cooperative was interested in a client/server architecture with small servers at each library. Before proceeding, the cooperative needed to determine whether such a system actually existed or whether one was soon to become available.[2]

[2]The final decision was to become beta-testers for the first client/server hardware/software combination. Although the cooperative did have to deal with some bugs in the system, it cost less than it would have otherwise.

Financial feasibility means asking the question "Can we afford it?" Often the answer is "We can't afford *not* to do it." In such a situation, an organization will spend as much as it can to implement a new information system.

Because no specific system alternative has been selected at this point, financial feasibility assessment is often very general. It can be conducted in-house, or an outside firm can be hired to conduct the analysis. The analysis includes market research to describe the market, its size, and typical customers as well as competition in the marketplace. From those data the analyst can estimate demand for the company's product and generate an estimate of revenue. In addition to hardware and software costs, the cost estimates include facility expenses (rental, construction, and so on), financing (loan costs), and personnel expenses (hiring, training, salaries, and so on). The result is a projection of how a new information system will affect the bottom line of the company. As with the needs assessment, the results of the feasibility analysis are presented as part of the requirements document.

One thing to keep in mind during a feasibility analysis is that the systems analyst—whether an employee of the company contemplating a new system or an employee of an outside firm hired specifically to conduct the analysis—will not be making the decision as to whether an entire project will proceed. The decision is made by the organization's management.

GENERATING ALTERNATIVES

The third section in the system requirements document is a list of two or more system design alternatives for an organization to consider. Often they will be distinguished by cost (low cost, medium cost, and high cost). However, the first alternative is almost always "Do nothing; keep the current system."

A low-cost alternative generally takes advantage of as much existing facilities, hardware, and software as possible. It may rely more on changing employee behavior than installing new technology.

A moderate-cost alternative includes some new hardware and software purchases, some network modification, and some changes in employee behavior. It may not, however, include the top-of-the-line hardware or software. It may also use off-the-shelf software packages rather than custom-programmed applications. Employee training may include sending users to take classes offered by hardware and software vendors.

The high-cost solution usually includes the best of everything. Hardware and software are top-of-the-line and include a significant amount of excess capacity. Custom programming is included where appropriate. Employee training includes on-site seminars tailored specifically to the organization.

EVALUATING AND CHOOSING AN ALTERNATIVE

Evaluating alternatives involves assigning numeric values to the costs and the benefits of each alternative. Some costs are easy to quantify, especially the cost of hardware and prepackaged software. Labor can be estimated relatively accurately as well. However, assigning dollar values to the benefits of a systems development project can be difficult because they are often intangible. For example, when a system is being designed to generate an increase in sales volume, the amount of increase is by its very nature an estimate. Increased customer satisfaction and better employee attitudes are difficult to measure. The impacts on system maintenance costs and future system development costs are at best only estimates.

Note: Doing nothing may not be the cost-free alternative that it at first appears to be. When doing nothing means losing customers because they can't order online, then doing nothing has a negative cost.

The analyst completes the requirements document by adding the cost/benefit analyses of the proposed alternatives and then presents it to company management. Although the requirements document typically includes specific groups of hardware, software, and labor for each alternative, management may decide to use part of one alternative (for example, existing hardware) and part of another (for example, custom-written application programs).

Once company management agrees to the project and its specifications, the requirements document can become a contract between IT and management, defining what IT will provide and what management should expect. The more seriously all parties view the document as a contract, the more likely the system development project is to succeed.

CREATING DESIGN REQUIREMENTS

The alternative chosen by an organization is usually expressed as a general strategy such as "Implement a new Web site backed by an inventory database." Although many of the exact requirements of the database were collected during the systems analysis phase of the life cycle, company management doesn't really care about the details of which specific data will be in the database. The system that they chose has been specified as a series of outputs, the details of which may not have been designed yet.

Therefore, the first job in the design phase is to document exactly what data should be in the database and the details of application programs. This is the time when user interfaces are designed and an organization begins to build its data dictionary. Once the data specifications are in place, actual database design can begin.

ALTERNATIVE ANALYSIS METHODS

As mentioned at the beginning of this chapter, the structured design life cycle works best when the requirements of an information system can be specified before development of the system begins. However, that is not always possible. In some cases, users need the system developer to produce something to which they can react. They may not be able to articulate their needs in the abstract, but they can indicate whether an existing piece of software works for them, and if it does not, how the software should be changed to better meet their needs.

Prototyping

Prototyping is a form of systems development that is particularly appropriate in situations where the exact requirements of an information system aren't known in advance. Often the potential users know that help is needed, but can't articulate exactly what they want. The developer therefore begins by creating a shell for the system consisting of user interface components but not the programs or databases behind them—the prototype.

The developer shows the users the prototype and gets their feedback. Then, based on their comments, the developer refines the prototype. The next version shown to the users may include user interface changes and some of the background programming. The entire process can be summarized as follows:

1. Get a general idea of what the new information system should do.
2. Create a prototype.
3. Let the users react to the prototype.
4. Refine the prototype based on user input.
5. Return to step 3.
6. Repeat as many times as necessary until the users are satisfied.

A prototype may be missing some of the features of the final system. For example, initial programming may not include some of the security features or integrity controls that are likely to appear in the production product.

A prototype may be enhanced until it becomes the final system (*evolutionary prototyping*). In contrast, the prototype may be discarded once the system requirements have been determined and the final system has been developed from scratch (*throwaway prototyping*). The latter is particularly useful when the code underlying the prototype has become difficult to follow (and thus maintain) because of the many changes that have been made during the prototyping process. Throwaway prototyping is also a very fast form of system development because it doesn't have to be "clean."

Prototyping, however, can have several drawbacks. First, users may become confused between a prototype and a production system. They may expect the prototype to be a functioning whole and are therefore frustrated and disappointed when it isn't. Second, prototyping doesn't include an analysis phase and relies solely on interaction between the users and the system developers to identify system requirements. Requirements that management may want to add to the system may not be included; users may leave out necessary system functions. Finally, prototyping may be expensive if the costs for developing the prototype are not controlled.

Database designers are usually involved after the first prototype is developed and users have responded to it. The database design is created to provide whatever is needed to generate the outputs in the prototype and changes as the prototype is refined. The flexibility of relational database design is an enormous help to this methodology because of the ease in modifying the database structure.

Note: You will see an example of prototyping used in the case study in Chapter 13.

Spiral Methodology

The *spiral methodology* of systems analysis and design, which employs prototyping in a more formal way than the prototyping method, uses a gradual process in which each cycle further refines the system, bringing it closer to the desired end point. As you can see in Table 2-1, the methodology has four broad stages, each of which represents one trip around the spiral. The same type of activities is performed in each quadrant during each cycle. As you examine the table, also look at Figure 2-3. The activity numbers in the table correspond to the numbers on the spiral in the illustration.

Notice that there are no specific activities listed for Quadrant 2 in any of the cycles. Systems analysis occurs in this quadrant, using the same techniques that are used to gather information for needs assessment in the traditional systems life cycle.

The spiral model is intended to address a perceived failing in the traditional system design cycle: analysis of the risk of the project. Although the traditional systems life cycle includes a feasibility analysis, there is no specific provision for looking at the chances that the system development project will succeed.

Because there are prototype systems created during every cycle, database designers may be involved from throughout the entire process, depending on the characteristics of each prototype. The flexibility of a database design to change during the iterative development process becomes essential so that the database can be refined just as the other parts of the new system.

Object-Oriented Analysis

Object-oriented analysis is a method for viewing the interaction of data and manipulations of data that is based on the object-oriented programming paradigm. The traditional systems life cycle looks at the outputs the system requires and then assembles the database so that it contains the data needed to produce those outputs. Documentation reflects the "input-process-output" approach such that the inputs are identified to achieve a specified output; the process of translating the inputs into desired outputs is where the database and the programs that manipulate the database are found. Where the traditional systems analysis life cycle considers data and data manipulation two distinct parts of the system, object-oriented analysis focuses on units (*classes*) that combine data and procedures.

Table 2-1 The Steps in the Spiral Systems Analysis and Design Methodology

Cycle	Quadrant	Specific Activities
1	Quadrant 1: Plan Next Phases	1. Requirements Plan; Life Cycle Plan
	Quadrant 2: Determine Objectives, Abstractions, and Constraints	
	Quadrant 3: Evaluate Alternatives; Identify, Resolve Risks	2. Risk Analysis 3. Prototype #1
	Quadrant 4: Design, Verify Next-Level Product	4. Concept of Operation
2	Quadrant 1: Plan Next Phases	5. Development Plan
	Quadrant 2: Determine Objectives, Abstractions, and Constraints	
	Quadrant 3: Evaluate Alternatives; Identify, Resolve Risks	6. Risk Analysis 7. Prototype #2
	Quadrant 4: Design, Verify Next-Level Product	8. Simulations 9. System Requirements 10. Requirements Validation
3	Quadrant 1: Plan Next Phases	11. Integration and Test Plan
	Quadrant 2: Determine Objectives, Abstractions, and Constraints	
	Quadrant 3: Evaluate Alternatives; Identify, Resolve Risks	12. Risk Analysis 13. Prototype #3
	Quadrant 4: Design, Verify Next-Level Product	14. Models 15. System Design 16. Design Validation and Verification
4	Quadrant 1: Plan Next Phases	17. Determine Process Objectives, Alternatives, and Constraints. 18. Evaluate Process Alternatives, Modify, Resolve Product Risks 19. Design, Verify Next-Level Process Plans
	Quadrant 2: Determine Objectives, Abstractions, and Constraints	
	Quadrant 3: Evaluate Alternatives; Identify, Resolve Risks	20. Risk Analysis 21. Operational Prototype
	Quadrant 4: Design, Verify Next-Level Product	22. Benchmarks 23. Detailed Design 24. Code 25. Unit Test 26. Integration and Test 27. Acceptance Test 28. Implementation

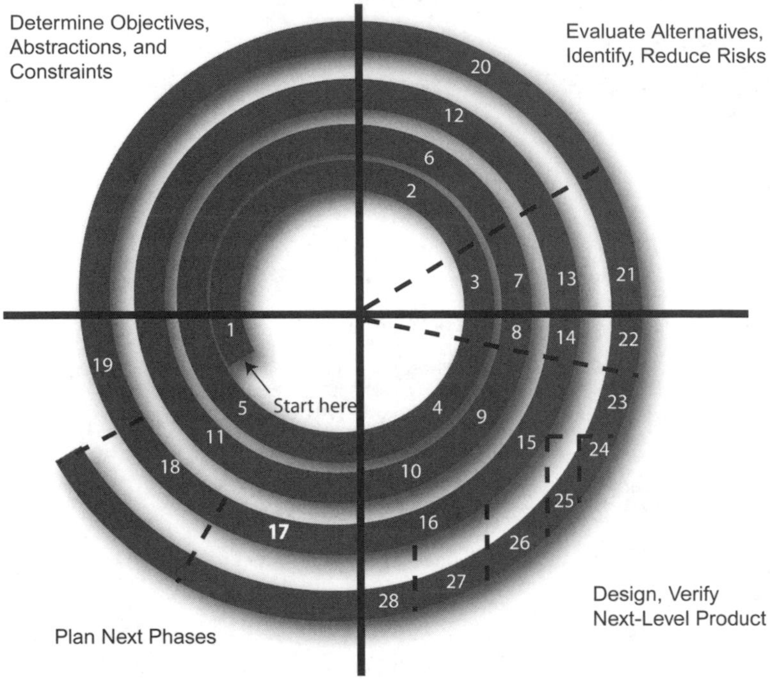

■ **FIGURE 2-3** The spiral systems analysis and design methodology (numbers refer to Table 2-1).

Although a complete discussion of object-oriented concepts is well beyond the scope of this book, a small example might help to make the distinction between the traditional and object-oriented analysis clearer. Assume that you are developing a system that will provide an employee directory of a company. Both forms of analysis begin with the requirements, such as the ability to search for employees in the directory and the ability to update employee information. Then the two approaches diverge.

Traditional analysis indicates the specifics of the application programs that will provide the updating and searching capabilities. The database specifications include the data needed to support those applications. The requirements document might contain something like Figure 2-4. The database itself won't have been designed, but when it is, an employee might be represented something like Figure 2-5.

In contrast, object-oriented analysis specifies both the data and the procedures together. Figure 2-6 contains a graphic representation of the employee directory environment. The rectangle labeled Employee

%NAME prepare_online_directory
%DEFINITION
Format and display an electronic version of the employee directory

%NAME prepare_print_directory
%DEFINITION
Format a directory for hard copy output

%NAME search_for_employee
%DEFINITION
Find an employee using the format "Last name, first name"

%NAME update_employee_information
%DEFINITION
Insert, modify, and delete employee information

■ **FIGURE 2-4** Requirements for the employee directory.

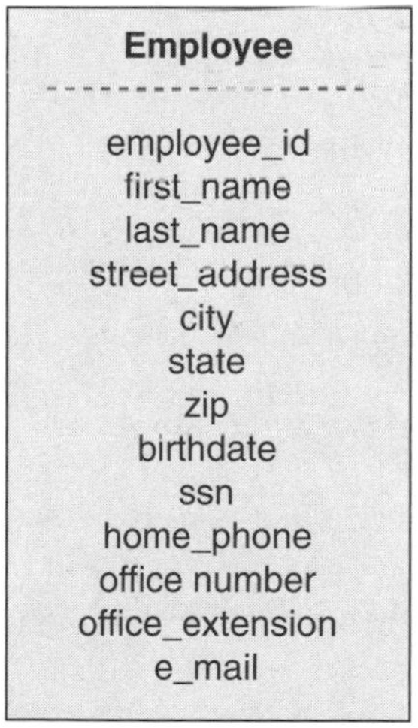

■ **FIGURE 2-5** A graphic representation of the data describing an employee for the employee directory.

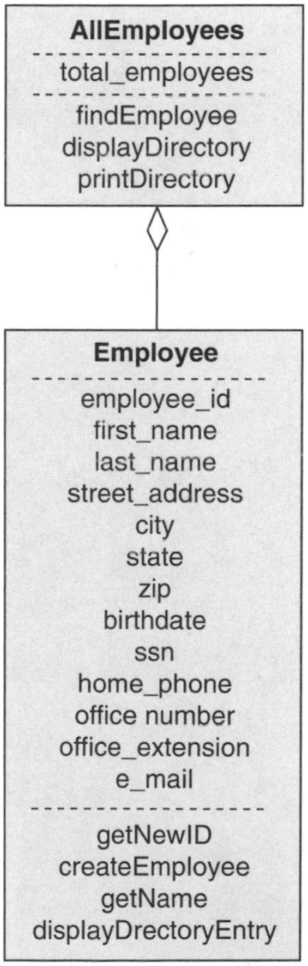

■ **FIGURE 2-6** A graphic representation of the object-oriented approach to the employee directory.

is a class representing a single employee. The middle section of the rectangle contains the data that describe an employee for the directory. The bottom portion lists the things that an employee *object* (an instance of the class containing actual data) knows how to do.

The rectangle labeled AllEmployees is a class that gathers together all of the employee objects (an *aggregation*). Procedures that are to be performed on all of the employees are part of this class. Diagrams of this type form the basis of an object-oriented requirements document and system design.

Object-oriented analysis is well suited for large projects, especially those where requirements are likely to change as the system is being designed and developed. As object-oriented software development has replaced structured programming, object-oriented systems analysis has become increasingly popular.

FOR FURTHER READING

Arnowitz, Jonathan, Michael Arent, and Nevin Berger. *Effective Prototyping for Software Makers*. Morgan Kaufmann, 2006.

Boehm, B. "A Spiral Model of Software Development and Enhancement." *IEEE Computer* 21(5), 61–72, 1988.

Clegg, Brian, and Paul Birch. *Instant Creativity: Techniques to Ignite Innovation & Problem Solving*. Kogan Page, 2007.

Kendall, Kenneth E., and Julie E. Kendall. *Systems Analysis and Design*, 7th ed. Prentice Hall, 2007.

Kock, Ned Florencio. *Systems Analysis & Design Fundamentals: A Business Process Redesign Approach*. Sage Publications, 2006.

Krueger, Richard A. *Focus Groups: A Practical Guide for Applied Research*, 4th ed. Sage Publications, 2008.

Luecke, Richard. *Managing Change and Transition*. Harvard Business School Press, 2003.

Shoval, Peretz. *Functional and Object Oriented Analysis and Design: An Integrated Methodology*. IGI Global, 2006.

Whitten, Jeffrey. *Systems Analysis and Design Methods*, 7th ed. McGraw-Hill/Irwin, 2005.

Part II

Database Design Theory

Part II of this book considers the theoretical aspects of relational database design. You will read about identifying data relationships in your database environment, the details of the relational data model, and how to translate data relationships into a well-designed relational database that avoids most of the problems associated with bad designs.

Chapter 3

Why Good Design Matters

Many of today's businesses rely on their database systems for accurate, up-to-date information. Without those repositories of mission-critical data, most businesses are unable to perform their normal daily transactions, much less create summary reports that help management make strategic corporate decisions. To be useful, the data in a database must be accurate, complete, and organized in such a way that data can be retrieved when needed and in the format desired.

Well-written database application programs—whether they execute locally, run over a local area network, or feed information to a Web site—are fundamental to timely and accurate data retrieval. However, without a good underlying database design, even the best program cannot avoid problems with inaccurate and inconsistent data.

EFFECTS OF POOR DATABASE DESIGN

To make it a bit clearer why the design of a database matters so much, let's take a look at a business that has a very bad design and the problems that the poor design brings. The business is named Antique Opticals and DVDs (called Antique Opticals for short by its regular customers).

Note: Remember the definition of a database that was presented in Chapter 1. As you will see, the data storage used by Antique Opticals and DVDs isn't precisely a database.

Back in the early 1980s, when most people were just discovering videotapes, Mark Watkins and Emily Stone stumbled across a fledgling technology known as the laser disc. There were several competing formats, but by 1986 the industry had standardized on a 12-inch silver platter on which either 30 or 60 minutes of video and audio could be recorded. Although the market was still small, it was at that time that Watkins and Stone opened the first incarnation of their business, originally named Lasers Only, to sell and rent laser discs. Some of its income came from sales and rentals directly from its single retail store, but the largest part of its revenue came from mail-order sales.

The appearance of DVDs in 1995 put a quick end to the release of new laser discs. The last new title was released in 2000, but the number of new titles had decreased significantly even before that time. Watkins and Stone saw their business dwindling rapidly in the late 1990s. They soon realized that if they were to stay in business, they had to change their merchandise focus. Laser discs were now the "antiques" of the optical media world, with DVDs—and most recently Blu-ray high-definition discs—the current technology.

Antique Opticals and DVDs now sells and rents DVDs and Blu-ray discs from the retail store. It also sells used laser discs that it purchases from individuals. The company has a primitive Web site for mail-order sales. The current catalog is updated weekly and uploaded to the site, where users place orders. However, the catalog is not integrated with any live data storage. An employee must take the order from the Web site and then shop for the customer. As a result, customers occasionally do not receive their entire order when ordered items have been sold at the retail store. This is particularly true in the case of used laser discs, where the quantity in stock is rarely more than one per title.

In 1990, when the store began its mail-order business, Watkins created a "database" to handle the orders and sales. Customers were (and still are) enticed to order titles before the official release date by offering a 15 to 20 percent discount on preorders. (All titles are always discounted 10 percent from the suggested retail price.) The mail-order database (which has evolved into today's Web order database) therefore needed to include a way to handle backorders so that preordered items could be shipped as soon as they came into the store.

At the time we visit Antique Opticals, it is still using the software that Watkins created. The primary data entry interface is a form like that in Figure 3-1. Customer numbers are created by combining the customer's zip code, the first three letters of his or her last name, and a three-digit sequence number. For example, if Stone lives in zip code 12345 and she is the second customer in that zip code with a last name beginning with STO, then her customer number is 12345STO002. The sequence numbers ensures that no two customer numbers will have the same number.

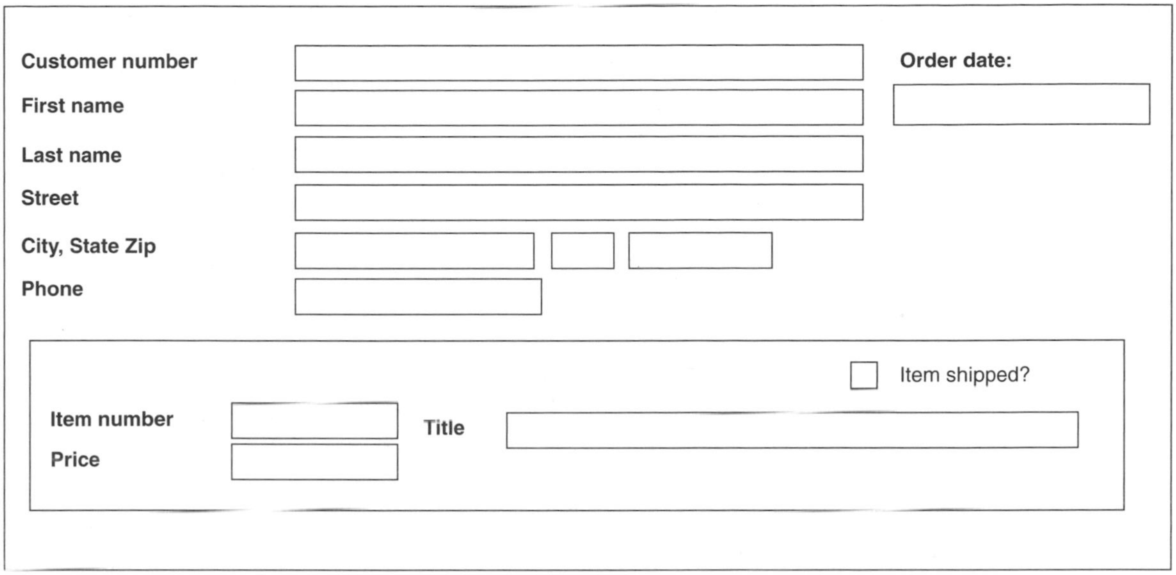
Customer number
Order date:
First name
Last name
Street
City, State Zip
Phone
Item shipped?
Item number
Title
Price

■ **FIGURE 3-1** The data entry form used by Antique Opticals and DVDs for their mail-order business.

When a new title comes into the store, an employee searches the database to find all those who have preordered that title. The employee prints a packing slip from the stored data and then places an X in the "item shipped" check box.

At first glance, Antique Opticals' software seems pretty simple and straightforward. So it should work just fine, right? (This is assuming we ignore the issue of integration with the Web site.) Well, it worked fine for a while, but as the business expanded, problems began to arise.

UNNECESSARY DUPLICATED DATA AND DATA CONSISTENCY

The Antique Opticals database has a considerable amount of unnecessary duplicated data. For example, a customer's name, address, and phone number are duplicated for every item the customer orders; a merchandise item's title is duplicated every time the item is ordered.

What is the problem with this duplication? When you have duplicated data in this way, the data should be the same throughout the database. In other words, every order for a given customer should have the same name, address, and phone number, typed exactly the same way. Every order for a single title should have the exact same title, typed exactly the same way. We want the duplicated data to be consistent throughout the database.

As the database grows larger, this type of consistency is very difficult to maintain. Most business-oriented database software is *case sensitive*, in that it considers upper- and lowercase letters to be different characters. In addition, no one is a perfect typist. A difference in capitalization or even a single mistyped letter will cause database software to consider two values to be distinct.

When an Antique Opticals employee performs a search to find all the people who have ordered a specific title, the database software will retrieve only those orders that match the title entered by the employee exactly. For example, assume that a movie named *Summer Days* is scheduled to be released soon. In some orders, the title is stored correctly as "Summer Days," but in others it is stored as "summer days" or even "sumer days." When an employee searches for all the people to whom the movie should be shipped, the orders for "summer days" and "sumer days" will not be retrieved. Those customers will not receive their orders, causing disgruntled customers and probably lost business.

The current Antique Opticals software has no way to ensure that duplicated data are entered consistently. There are, however, two solutions. The first is to eliminate as much of the duplicated data as possible. (As you will see, it is neither possible nor desirable to eliminate all of it.) The second is to provide some mechanism for verifying that when data must be duplicated, they are entered correctly. A well-designed database will do both.

Note: Unnecessary duplicated data also take up extra disk space, but given that disk space is relatively inexpensive today, that isn't a major reason for getting rid of redundant data.

DATA INSERTION PROBLEMS

When operations first began, the Lasers Only staff generated the catalog of forthcoming titles by hand. By 1995, however, Stone realized that this was a very cumbersome process and thought it would be much better if the catalog could be generated from the database.

"Why not get a list of forthcoming titles from the database and have a database program generate the entire catalog?" Stone discovered, however, that it could not be done from the existing database, for two reasons.

First, the database did not contain all of the information needed for the catalog, in particular a synopsis of all the content of the disc. This problem could be remedied by adding that information to the database, but doing so would only exacerbate the problem with unnecessary duplicated data if the company were to include the summary with every order. If the summary was included only once, how would the company know which order contained the summary?

Second, and by far more important, there is no way to enter data about a title unless someone has ordered it. This presents a very large Catch-22. The company couldn't insert data about a title unless it had been ordered at least once, but customers won't know that it is available to be ordered without seeing it in the catalog. But the catalog can't contain data about the new title until someone can get the data into the database, and that can't happen until the title has been ordered.

Note: This problem is more formally known as an "insertion anomaly," and you will learn about it more formally throughout this book.

Antique Opticals solved the problem by creating a second database for forthcoming titles from which the catalog can be generated. Unfortunately, the second database produced problems of its own, in particular because it introduced yet another source of duplicated data. The catalog database and the orders database do not communicate to verify that duplicated data are consistent, creating another potential source of errors in the orders database.

DATA DELETION PROBLEMS

Antique Opticals also has problems when it comes to deleting data. Assume, for example, that a customer orders only one item. After the order has been processed, the item is discontinued by the manufacturer. Antique Opticals therefore wants to delete all references to the item from its database because the item is no longer available.

When the orders containing the item are deleted, information about any customer who has ordered only that item is also deleted. No other orders remain in the database for that customer. Antique Opticals will be unable to e-mail that customer any more catalogs and must hope that the customer visits the Web site without being contacted by the company. A very real potential exists that Antique Opticals has lost that individual as a customer.

Note: This problem is more formally known as a "deletion anomaly." It, too, will be discussed in greater depth throughout this book.

MEANINGFUL IDENTIFIERS

The Antique Opticals orders database has another major problem: those customer numbers. It is very tempting to code meaning into identifiers, and it usually works well *until* the values on which the identifiers are based change.

Consider what happens when an Antique Opticals customer moves. The person's customer number must change. At that point, there will be orders for the same customer with two different customer numbers in the same database.

If a customer who has moved since first ordering from the store calls and asks for a list of all items he or she has on order, the first thing the employee who answers the telephone does is ask the customer for his or her customer number. The customer, of course, provides the current value, which means that anything ordered under the old customer number will be missed during a search. The customer may assume that titles ordered under the old customer number are not on order. As a result, the customer may place another order, causing two copies of the same item to be shipped. Antique Opticals is then faced with another disgruntled customer who has to go to the trouble of returning the duplicate and getting the second charge removed from his or her credit card.

Chapter 4

Entities and Relationships

In this chapter we look at the basis for all database systems: the relationships between elements in the database environment. The formal term for expressing data relationships to a DBMS is a *data model*. The relational data model, which you will learn about in this book, is just such a formal structure. However, the underlying relationships in a database are independent of the data model and therefore also independent of the DBMS you are using. Before you can design a database for any data model, you need to be able to identify data relationships.

> Note: Most DBMSs support only one data model. Therefore, when you choose a DBMS, you are also choosing your data model.

ENTITIES AND THEIR ATTRIBUTES

An *entity* is something about which we store data. A customer is an entity, as is a merchandise item stocked by Antique Opticals. Entities are not necessarily tangible. For example, a concert or a doctor's appointment is an entity.

Entities have data that describe them (their *attributes*). For example, a customer entity is usually described by a customer number, first name, last name, street, city, state, zip code, and phone number. A concert entity might be described by a title, date, location, and name of the performer.

When we represent entities in a database, we actually store only the attributes. Each group of attributes that describes a single real-world

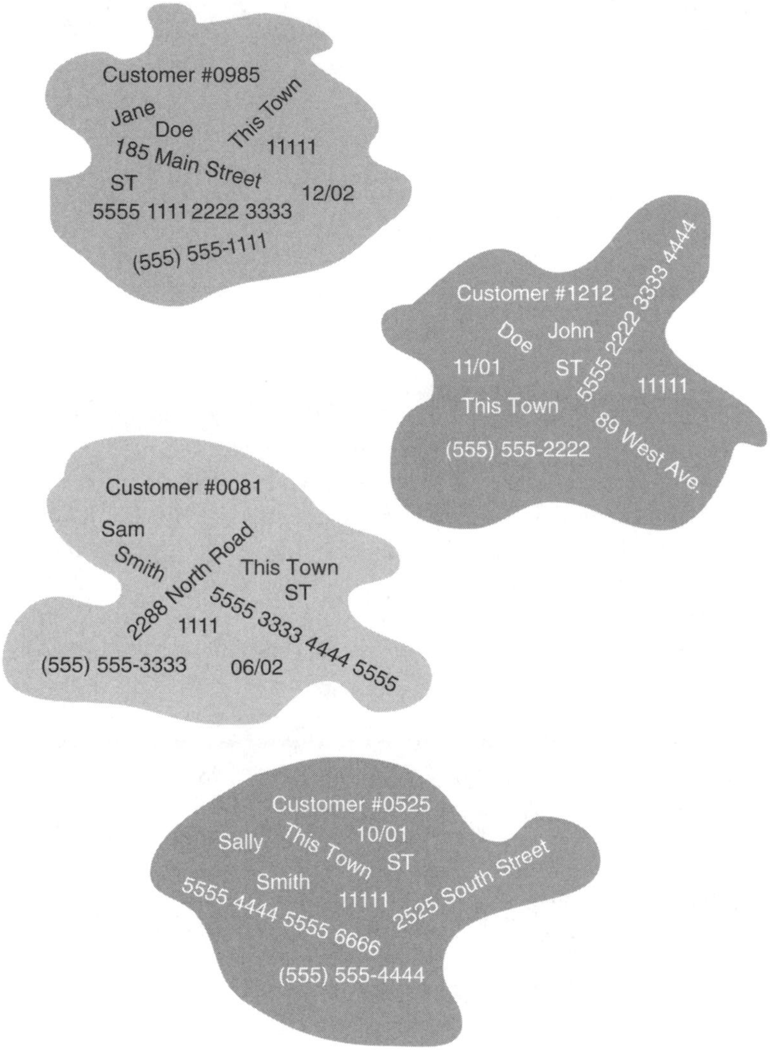

■ **FIGURE 4-1** Instances of a customer entity in a database.

occurrence of an entity acts to represent an *instance* of an entity. For example, in Figure 4-1, you can see four instances of a customer entity stored in a database. If we have 1000 customers in our database, there will be 1000 collections of customer attributes.

Note: Keep in mind that we are not making any statements about how the instances are physically stored. What you see in Figure 4-1 is purely a conceptual representation.

Entity Identifiers

The only purpose for putting the data that describe an entity into a database is to retrieve the data at some later date. This means that we must have some way of distinguishing one entity from another so that we can always be certain that we are retrieving the precise entity we want. We do this by ensuring that each entity has some attribute values that distinguish it from every other entity in the database (an *entity identifier*).

Assume, for example, that Antique Opticals has only two customers named John Smith. If an employee searches for the items John Smith has ordered, which John Smith will the DBMS retrieve? In this case, the answer is both of them. Because there is no way to distinguish between the two customers, the result of the query will be inaccurate. Antique Opticals solved the problem by creating customer numbers that were unique. That is indeed a common solution to identifying instances of entities where there is no simple unique identifier suggested by the data itself.

Another solution would be to pair the customer's first name and last name with his or her telephone number. This combination of data values (a *concatenated identifier)* would also uniquely identify each customer. There are, however, two drawbacks to doing so this. First, the identifier is long and clumsy; it would be easy to make mistakes when entering any of the parts. Second, if the customer's phone number changes, then the identifier must also change. As you read in Chapter 3, changes made in an entity identifier can cause serious problems in a database.

Some entities, such as invoices, come with *natural identifiers* (the invoice number). We assign unique, meaningless numbers to others, especially accounts, people, places and things. Still others require concatenated identifiers.

Note: We will examine the issue of what makes a good unique identifier more closely in Chapter 5 when we discuss "primary keys."

When we store an instance of an entity in a database, we want the DBMS to ensure that the new instance has a unique identifier. This is an example of a *constraint* on a database, a rule to which data must adhere. The enforcement of a variety of database constraints helps us to maintain data consistency and accuracy.

Single-Valued versus Multivalued Attributes

Because we are eventually going to create a relational database, the attributes in our data model must be *single-valued*. This means that for a given instance of an entity, each attribute can have only one value. For example, a customer entity allows only one telephone number for each customer. If a customer has more than one phone number and wants all of them in the database, then the customer entity cannot handle them. The existence of more than one phone number turns the phone number attribute into a *multivalued attribute*. Because an entity in a relational database cannot have multivalued attributes, you must handle those attributes by creating an entity to hold them.

Note: While it is true that the entity-relationship model of a database is independent of the formal data model used to express the structure of the data to a DBMS, we often make decisions on how to model the data based on the requirement of the formal data model we will be using. Removing multivalued attributes is one such case. You will also see an example of this when we deal with many-to-many relationships between entities.

In the case of the multiple phone numbers, we could create a phone number entity. Each instance of the entity would include the customer number of the person to whom the phone number belonged along with the telephone number. If a customer had three phone numbers, then there would be three instances of the phone number entity for the customer. The entity's identifier would be the concatenation of the customer number and the telephone number.

Note: There is no way to avoid using the telephone number as part of the entity identifier in the telephone number entity. As you will come to understand as you read this book, in this particular case there is no harm in using it in this way.

What is the problem with multivalued attributes? Multivalued attributes can cause problems with the meaning of data in the database, significantly slow down searching, and place unnecessary restrictions on the amount of data that can be stored.

Assume, for example, that you have an employee entity with attributes for the name and birth dates of dependents. Each attribute is allowed to store multiple values, as in Figure 4-2, where each gray blob represents a single instance of the employee entity. How will you associate the correct birth date with the name of the dependent to which it applies? Will it be by the position of a value stored in the attribute (i.e., the first name is related to the first birth date, and so on)? If so, how will you ensure that there is a birth date for each name and a name for each birth date? How will you ensure that the order of the values is never mixed up?

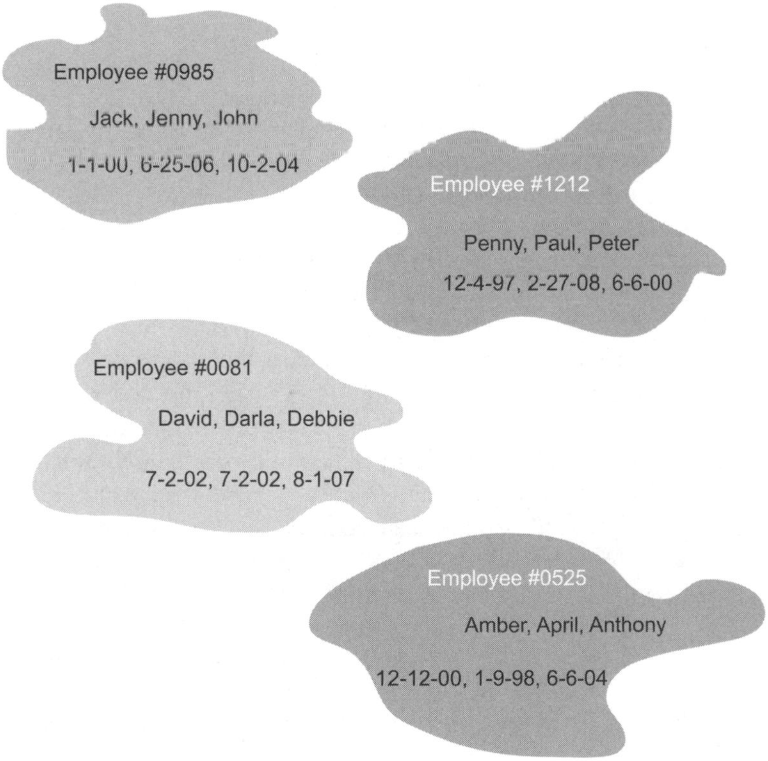

■ **FIGURE 4-2** Entity instances containing multivalued attributes.

When searching a multivalued attribute, a DBMS must search each value in the attribute, most likely scanning the contents of the attribute sequentially. A sequential search is the slowest type of search available.

In addition, how many values should a multivalued attribute be able to store? If you specify a maximum number, what will happen when you need to store more than the maximum number of values? For example, what if you allow room for 10 dependents in the employee entity just discussed and you encounter an employee with 11 dependents? Do you create another instance of the employee entity for that person? Consider all the problems that doing so would create, particularly in terms of the unnecessary duplicated data.

Note: Although it is theoretically possible to write a DBMS that will store an unlimited number of values in an attribute, the implementation would be difficult and searching much slower than if the maximum number of values were specified in the database design.

As a general rule, if you run across a multivalued attribute, this is a major hint that you need another entity. The only way to handle multiple values of the same attribute is to create an entity in which you can store multiple instances, one for each value of the attribute (for example, Figure 4-3). In the case of the employee entity, we would need a dependent entity that could be related to the employee entity. There would be one instance of the dependent entity related to an instance of the employee entity for each of an employee's dependents. In this way, there is no limit to the number of an employee's dependents. In addition, each instance of the dependent entity would contain the name and birth date of only one dependent, eliminating any confusion about which name was associated with which birth date. Searching would also be faster because the DBMS could use fast searching techniques on the individual dependent entity instances without resorting to the slow sequential search.

Avoiding Collections of Entities

When you first begin to work with entities, you may find the nature of an entity to be somewhat confusing. Consider, for example, the merchandise inventory handled by Antique Opticals. Is "inventory"

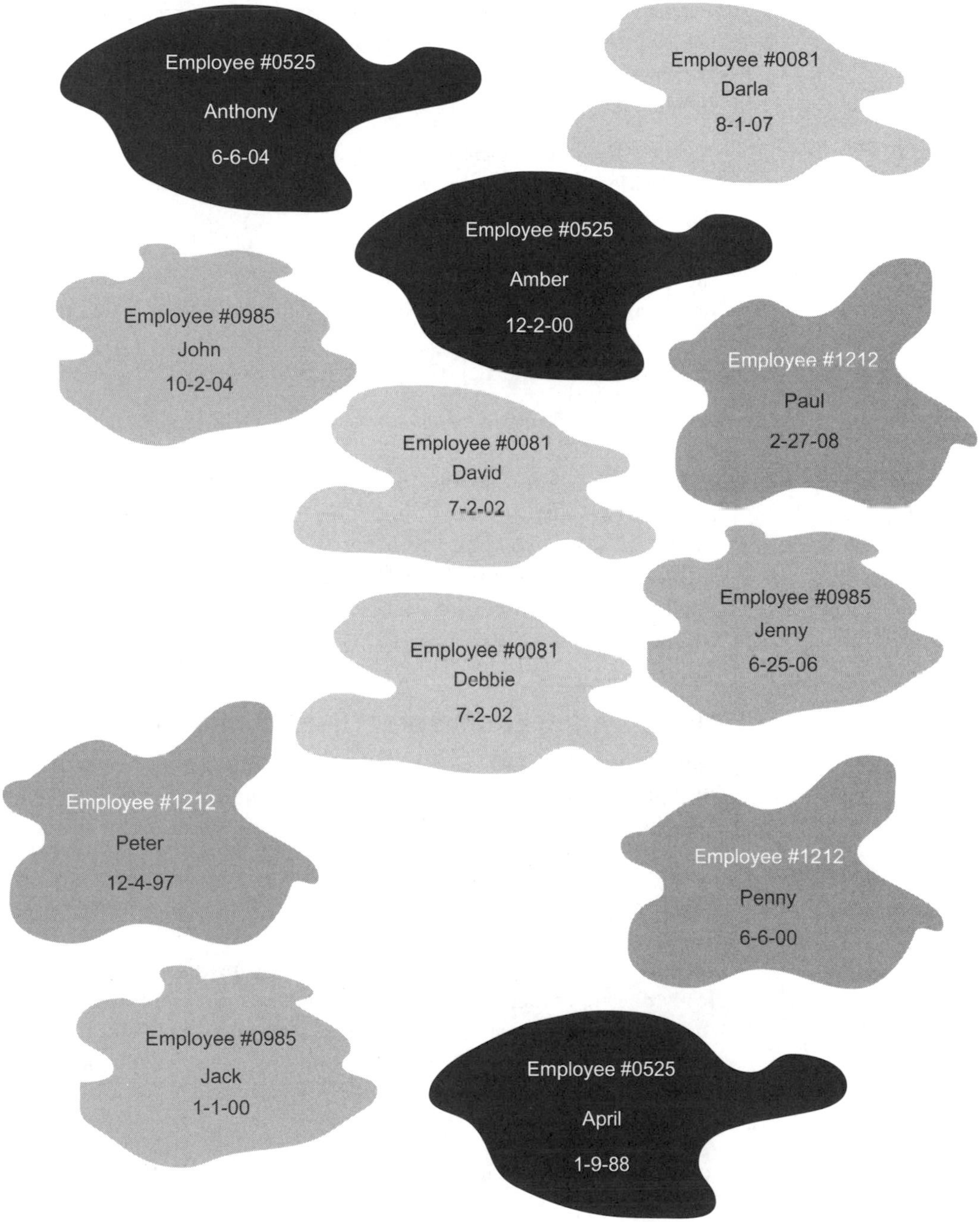

■ **FIGURE 4-3** Using multiple instances of an entity to handle a multivalued attribute.

an entity? No. Inventory is a collection of the merchandise items handled by the store. The entity is actually the merchandise item. Viewing all of the instances of the merchandise item entity as a whole provides the inventory.

To make this a bit clearer, consider the attributes you would need if you decided to include an inventory entity: merchandise item number, item title, number in stock, retail price, and so on. But because you are trying to describe an entire inventory with a single entity, you need multiple values for each of those attributes. As you read earlier, however, attributes cannot be multivalued. This tells you that inventory cannot stand as an entity. It must be represented as a collection of instances of a merchandise item entity.

As another example, consider a person's medical history maintained by a doctor. Like an inventory, a medical history is a collection of more than one entity. A medical history is made up of appointments and the events that occur during those appointments. Therefore, the history is really a collection of instances of appointment entities and medical treatment entities. The "history" is an output that a database application can obtain by gathering the data stored in the underlying instances.

Documenting Entities and Their Attributes

Entity-relationship (ER) *diagrams* (ERDs) provide a way to document the entities in a database along with the attributes that describe them. There are actually several styles of ER diagrams. Today there are three major methods: the Chen model (named after the originator of ER modeling, Dr. Peter P.S. Chen), Information Engineering (IE, or "crows feet"), and Unified Modeling Language (UML).

If you are not including object-oriented concepts in a data model, it really doesn't matter which you use, as long as everyone who is using the diagram understands the symbols. However, UML is specifically intended for the object-oriented environment and is usually the choice when objects are included.

All three diagramming styles use rectangles to represent entities. Each entity's name appears in the rectangle and is expressed in the singular, as in

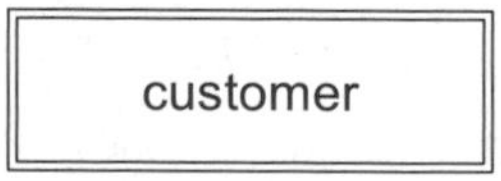

The original Chen model has no provision for showing attributes on the ER diagram itself. However, many people have extended the model to include the attributes in ovals:

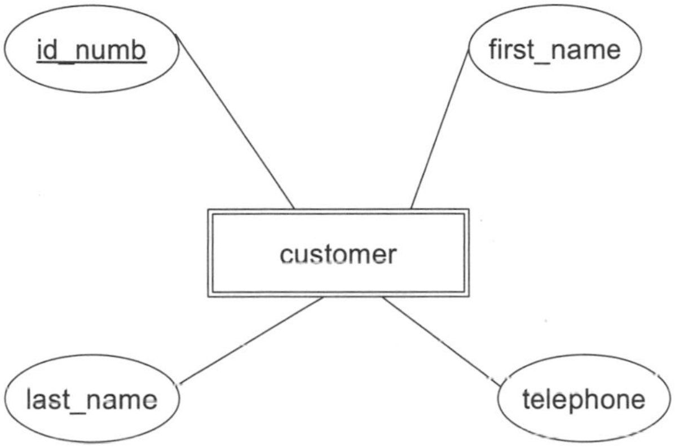

The entity's identifier is underlined (*id_numb*).

Note: An alternative to the Chen style of diagramming, which does include the attribute ovals, is the Information Engineering style, which grew out of the work of James Martin and Clive Finkelstein.

The IE and UML styles of ER diagramming include the attributes in the rectangle with the entity:

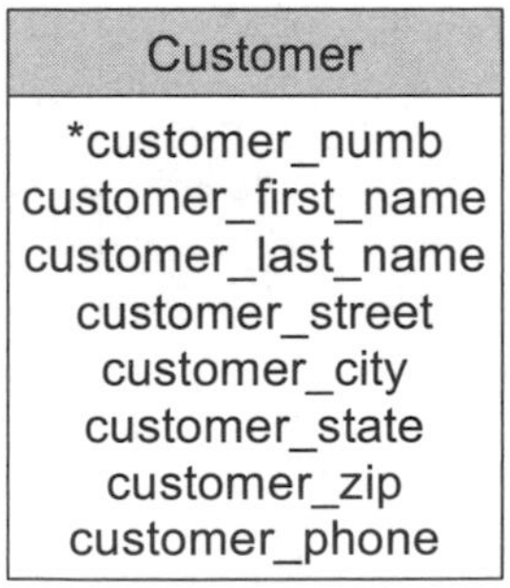

Because the IE and UML approaches tend to produce a less-cluttered diagram and because they are the more flexible styles, we will be using IE for most of the diagrams in this book, although you will be introduced to elements of the Chen style and the UML style throughout this chapter.

Entities and Attributes for Antique Opticals

The major entities and their attributes for the Antique Opticals database can be found in Figure 4-4. As you will see, the design will require additional entities as we work with the relationships between those already identified. In particular, there is no information in Figure 4-4 that indicates which items appear on which orders and no information about which used laser discs are purchased by the store during a single transaction. This occurs because the missing information is a part of the logical relationships between customers, orders, purchases, and items.

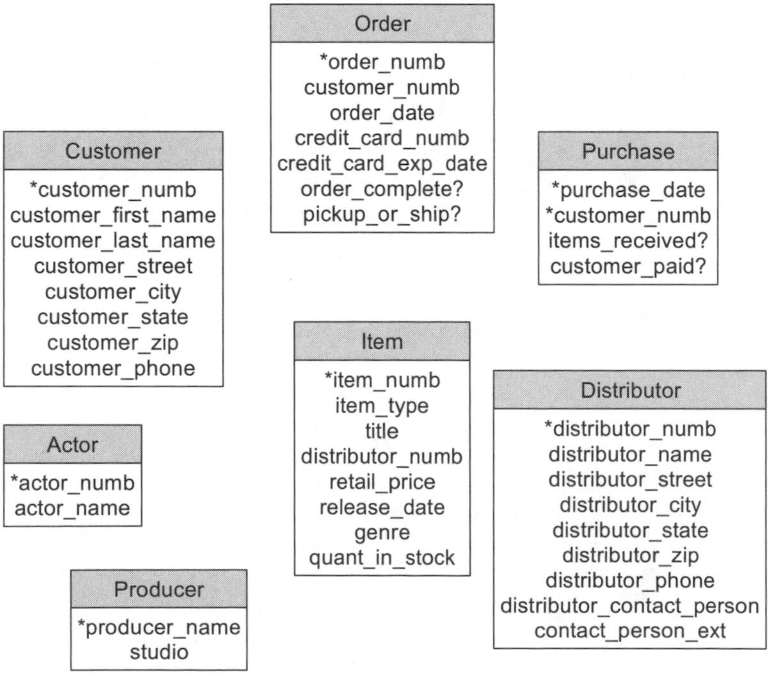

■ **FIGURE 4-4** Major entities and their attributes for the Antique Opticals database.

Note: The entities in Figure 4-4 and the remainder of the diagrams in this book were created with a special type of software known as a computer-aided software engineering (CASE) tool. CASE tools provide a wide range of data and systems modeling assistance. You will find more details on how CASE tools support the database design process in Chapter 11.

Figure 4-4 demonstrates some of the choices made for the Antique Opticals database. Notice, for example, that there is only one entity for merchandise items, yet the store carries new DVDs, new high-definition DVDs, and used laser discs. The *item_type* attribute distinguishes the three types of merchandise. Because all merchandise items are stored as the same type of entity, queries such as "Show me *Star Wars IV* in any format" will be easy to perform using just the item name, and queries such as "Do you have a used *Star Wars IV* laser disc?" will be easy to satisfy using both the title of the item and its type.

DOMAINS

Each attribute has a *domain*, an expression of the permissible values for that attribute. A domain can be very small. For example, a T-shirt store might have a size attribute for its merchandise items with the values L, XL, and XXL comprising the entire domain. In contrast, an attribute for a customer's first name, being very long might be specified only as "text" or "human names."

A DBMS enforces a domain through a *domain constraint*. Whenever a value is stored in the database, the DBMS verifies that it comes from the attribute's specified domain. Although in many cases we cannot specify small domains, at the very least the domain assures us that we are getting data of the right type. For example, a DBMS can prevent a user from storing 123 × 50 in an attribute whose domain is currency values. Most DBMSs also provide fairly tight domain checking on date and time attributes, which can help you avoid illegal dates such as February 30.

Documenting Domains

The common formats used for ER diagrams do not usually include domains on the diagrams themselves but store the domains in an associated document (usually a *data dictionary*, something you will learn more about later in this book). However, the version of the Chen

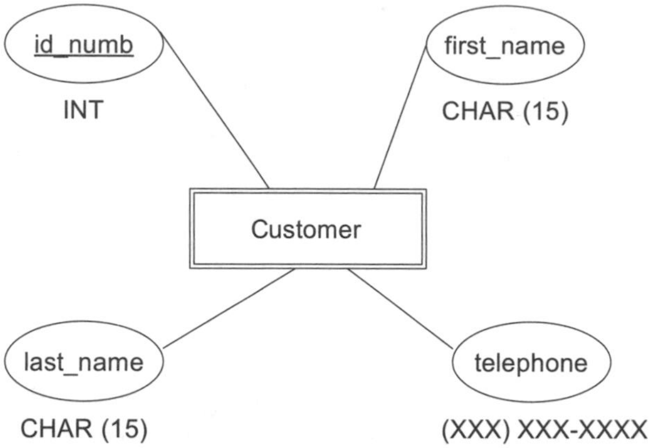

■ **FIGURE 4-5** Indicating domains on an ER diagram.

method that includes attributes can also include domains underneath each attribute. Notice in Figure 4-5 that three of the domains are fairly general (integer and character), while the domain for the telephone number attribute includes a very specific format. Whether a domain can be constrained in this way depends on the DBMS.

Note: There is no specific syntax for indicating domains. However, if you know which DBMS you will be using, consider using the column data types supported by that product as domains in an ERD to simplify the later conversion to the DBMS's representation.

Practical Domain Choices

The domains that Antique Opticals chooses for its attributes should theoretically be independent of the DBMS that the company will use. In practical terms, however, it makes little sense to assign domains that you cannot implement. Therefore, the database designer working for Antique Opticals takes a look at the DBMS to see what data types are supported.

Most relational DBMSs that use SQL as their query language provide the following among their data types, any of which can be assigned as a domain to an attribute:

- *CHAR:* A fixed-length string of text, usually up to 256 characters

- *VARCHAR:* A variable-length string of text, usually up to 256 characters
- *INT:* An integer, the size of which varies depending on the operating system
- *DECIMAL and NUMERIC:* Real numbers, with fractional portions assigned to the right of the decimal point. When you assign a real number domain, you must specify how many digits the number can contain (including the decimal point) and how many digits should be to the right of the decimal point (the value's *precision*). For example, currency values usually have a precision of two, so a number in the format XXX.XX might have a domain of DECIMAL (6,2).
- *DATE:* A date
- *TIME:* A time
- *DATETIME:* The combination of a date and a time
- *BOOLEAN:* A logical value (true or false)

Many current DBMSs also support a data type known as a BLOB (binary large object), which can store anything binary, such as a graphic.

Choosing the right domain can make a big difference in the accuracy of a database. For example, a U.S. zip code is made up of five or nine digits. Should an attribute for a zip code therefore be given a domain of INT? The answer is no, for two reasons. First, it would be nice to be able to include the hyphen in nine-digit zip codes. Second, and more important, zip codes in the Northeast begin with a zero. If they are stored as a number, the leading zero disappears. Therefore, we always choose a CHAR domain for zip codes. Since we never do arithmetic with zip codes, nothing is lost by using character rather than numeric storage.

By the same token, it is important to choose domains of DATE and TIME for chronological data. As an example, consider what would happen if the dates 01/12/2009 and 08/12/2008 were stored as characters. If you ask the DBMS to choose which date comes first, the DBMS will compare the character strings in alphabetical order and indicate that 01/12/2009 comes first, because 01 alphabetically precedes 08. The only way to get character dates to order correctly is to use the format YYYY/MM/DD, a format that is rarely used anywhere in the world. However, if the dates were given a domain of DATE, then the DBMS would order them properly. The DBMS would also be able to perform date arithmetic, finding the interval between two dates or adding constants (for example, 30 days) to dates.

BASIC DATA RELATIONSHIPS

Once you have a good idea of the basic entities in your database environment, your next task is to identify the relationships among those entities. There are three basic types of relationships that you may encounter: one-to-one (1 : 1), one-to-many (1 : M), and many-to-many (M : N or M : M).

Before examining each type, you should keep one thing in mind: The relationships that are stored in a database are between instances of entities. For example, an Antique Opticals customer is related to the items that he or she orders. Each instance of the customer entity is related to instances of the specific items ordered (see Figure 4-6).

When we document data relationships, such as when we draw an ER diagram, we show the types of relationships among entities. We are showing the possible relationships that are allowable in the database. Unless we specify that a relationship is mandatory, there is no requirement that every instance of every entity must be involved in every documented relationship. For example, Antique Opticals could store data about a customer without the customer having any orders to which it is related.

One-to-One Relationships

Consider, for a moment, an airport in a small town, where both the airport and the town are described in a database of small-town airports. Each of these might be represented by an instance of a different type of entity. The relationship between the two instances can be expressed as "The airport is located in one and only one town, and the town has one and only one airport."

This is a true *one-to-one relationship* because at no time can a single airport be related to more than one town, and no town can be related to more than one airport. (Although there are municipalities that have more than one airport, the towns in the database are too small for that to ever happen.)

If we have instances of two entities (A and B) called A_i and B_i, then a one-to-one relationship exists if at all times A_i is related to no instances

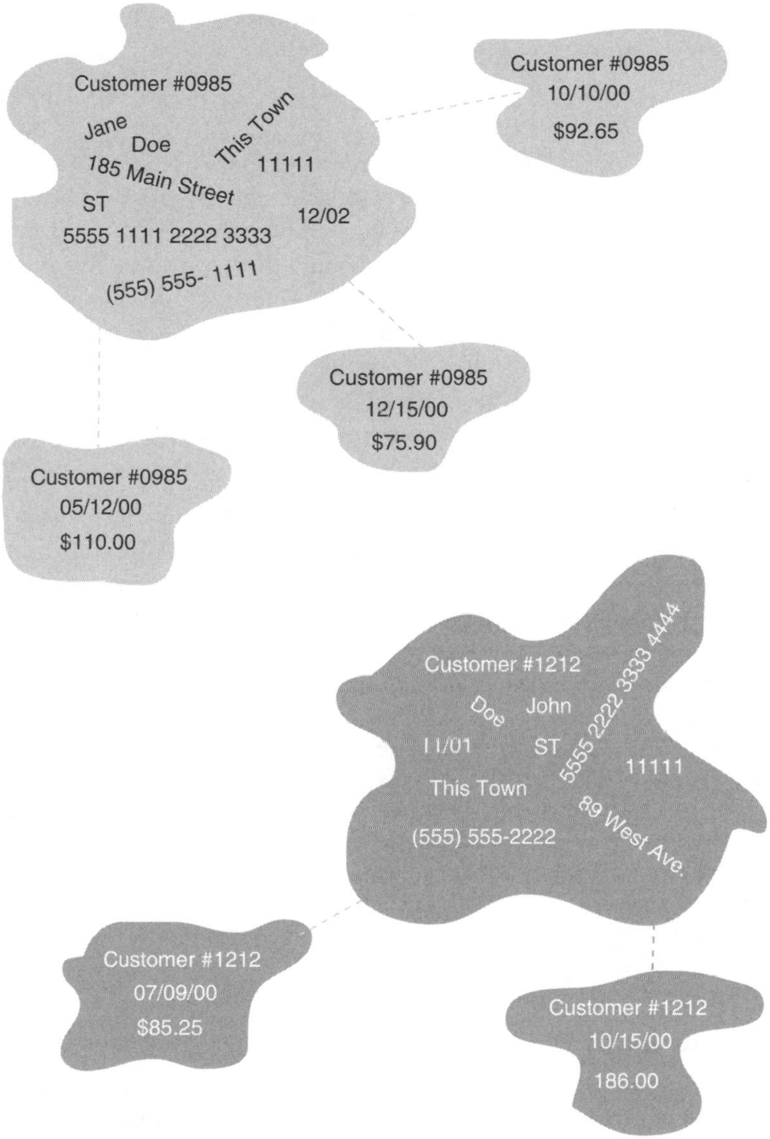

■ **FIGURE 4-6** Relationships between instances of entities in a database.

of entity B or one instance of entity B, and B_i is related to no instances of entity A or one instance of entity A.

True one-to-one relationships are very rare in business. For example, assume that Antique Opticals decides to start dealing with a new distributor of DVDs. At first, the company orders only one specialty title from the new distributor. If we peered inside the database, we would see that the instance of the distributor entity was related to just the one merchandise item instance. This would then appear to be a one-to-one relationship. However, over time, Antique Opticals may choose to order more titles from the new distributor, which would violate the rule that the distributor must be related to no more than one merchandise item. (This is an example of a one-to-many relationship, which is discussed in the next section of this chapter.)

By the same token, what if Antique Opticals created a special credit card entity to hold data about the credit cards that customers use to place orders? Each order can be charged to only one credit card. Thus, there would seem to be a one-to-one relationship between an instance of an order entity and an instance of a credit card entity. However, in this case we are really dealing with a single entity. The credit card number and the credit card's expiration date can become attributes of the order entity. Given that only one credit card is allowed per order, the attributes are not multivalued, and no separate entity is needed.

If you think you are dealing with a one-to-one relationship, look at it very carefully. Be sure that you are not really dealing with a special case of a one-to-many relationship or two entities that should really be one.

One-to-Many Relationships

The most common type of relationship is a *one-to-many relationship*. (In fact, most relational databases are constructed from the rare one-to-one relationship and numerous one-to-many relationships.) For example, Antique Opticals typically orders many titles from each distributor, and a given title comes from only one distributor. By the same token, a customer places many orders, but an order comes from only one customer. If we have instances of two entities (A and B), then a one-to-many relationship exists between two instances (A_i and B_i) if A_i is related to zero, one, or more instances of entity B and B_i is related to zero or one instance of entity A.

Other one-to-many relationships include that between a daughter and her biological mother. A woman may have zero, one, or more biological daughters; a daughter can have only one biological mother. As another example, consider a computer and its CPU. A CPU may not be installed in any computer, or it may be installed in at most one computer. A computer may have no CPU, one CPU, or more than one CPU.

Our previous example of Antique Opticals and the distributor from which it ordered only one title is actually a one-to-many relationship where the "many" is currently "one." Remember that when we are specifying data relationships, we are indicating possible relationships and not necessarily requiring that all instances of all entities participate in every documented relationship. There is absolutely no requirement that a distributor be related to any merchandise item, much less one or more merchandise items. (It might not make much sense to have a distributor in the database from which the company does not order, but there is nothing to prevent data about that distributor from being stored.)

Many-to-Many Relationships

Many-to-many relationships are also very common. There is, for example, a many-to-many relationship between an order placed by an Antique Opticals customer and the merchandise items carried by the store. An order can contain multiple items, and each item can appear on more than one order. The same is true of the orders placed with distributors. An order can contain multiple items and each item can appear on more than one order.

A many-to-many relationship exists between entities A and B if for two instances of those entities (A_i and B_i) A_i can be related to zero, one, or more instances of entity B and B_i can be related to zero, one, or more instances of entity A.

Many-to-many relationships present two major problems to a database's design. These issues and the way in which we solve them are discussed later in the next major section, of this chapter ("Dealing with Many-to-Many Relationships").

Weak Entities and Mandatory Relationships

In our discussion of types of data relationships, we have defined those relationships by starting each with "zero," indicating that the participation by a given instance of an entity in a relationship is optional. For example, Antique Opticals can store data about a customer in its database before the customer places an order. Therefore, an instance of the customer entity does not have to be related to any instances of the order entity.

However, the reverse is not true in this database. An order *must* be related to a customer. Without a customer, an order cannot exist. An order is therefore an example of a *weak entity*, one that cannot exist in the database unless a related instance of another entity is present and related to it. An instance of the customer entity can be related to zero, one, or more orders. However, an instance of the order entity must be related to one and only one customer. The "zero" option is not available to a weak entity. The relationship between an instance of the order entity and an instance of the customer entity is therefore a *mandatory* relationship.

Identifying weak entities and their associated mandatory relationships can be very important for maintaining the consistency and integrity of the database. Consider the effect, for example, of storing an order without knowing the customer to which it belongs. There would be no way to ship the item to the customer, and the company would lose business.

By the same token, we typically specify the relationship between an order and the order lines (the specific items on the order) as mandatory because we don't want to allow an order line to exist in the database without it being related to an order. (An order line is meaningless without knowing the order to which it belongs.)

In contrast, we can allow a merchandise item to exist in a database without indicating the supplier from which is comes (assuming that there is only one source per item). This lets us store data about new items before we have decided on a supplier. In this case, the relationship between a supplier and an item is not mandatory (often described as zero-to-many rather than one-to-many).

Documenting Relationships

The Chen and UML methods of drawing ER diagrams have very different ways of representing relationships, each of which has its advantages in terms of the amount of information it provides and its complexity.

The Chen Method

The Chen method uses diamonds for relationships and lines with arrows to indicate the relationships between entities. For example, in Figure 4-7 you can see the relationship between an Antique Opticals customer and an order. The single arrow pointing toward the customer entity indicates that an order belongs to at most one customer. The double arrow pointing toward the order entity indicates that a customer can place one or more orders. The word within the relationship diamond gives some indication of the meaning of the relationship.

There are two alternative styles within the Chen method. The first replaces the arrows with numbers and letters (see Figure 4-8). A "1" indicates that an order comes from one customer. The "M" (or an "N") indicates that a customer can place many orders. The second alternative addresses the problem of trying to read the relationship in both directions when the name of the relationship is within the diamond. "Customer places order" makes sense, but "order places customer" does not. To solve the problem, this alternative removes the relationship name from the diamond and adds both the relationship and its inverse to the diagram, as in Figure 4-9. This version of the diagram can be read easily in either direction: "A customer places many orders" and "An order is placed by one customer."

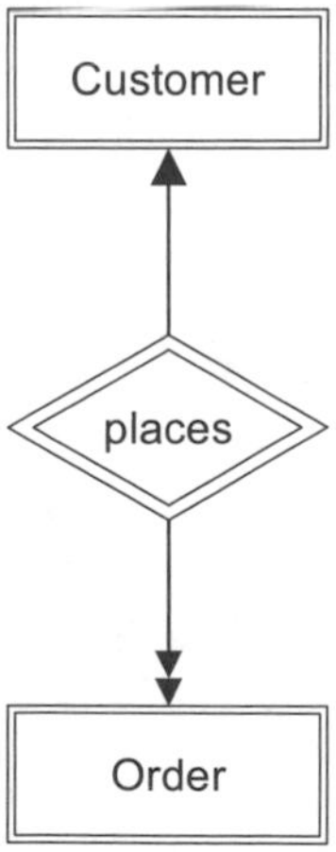

■ **FIGURE 4-7** Using the Chen method with relationship diamonds and arrows.

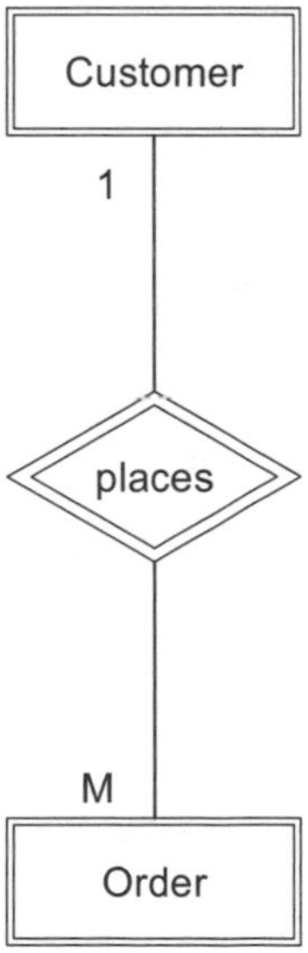

■ **FIGURE 4-8** A Chen ER diagram using letters and numbers rather than arrows to show relationships.

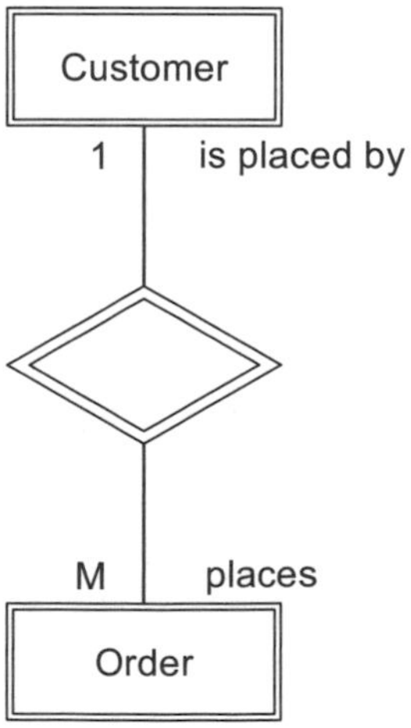

■ **FIGURE 4-9** Adding inverse relationships to a Chen method ER diagram.

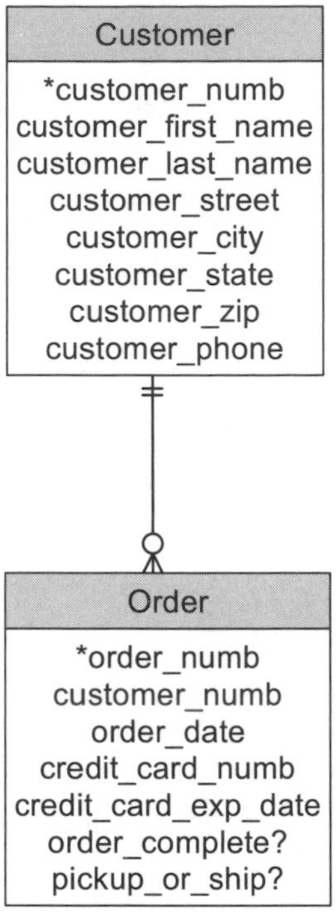

■ **FIGURE 4-10** A one-to-many relationship using the IE method.

There is one major limitation to the Chen method of drawing ER diagrams: There is no obvious way to indicate weak entities and mandatory relationships. For example, an order should not exist in the database without a customer. Therefore, order is a weak entity and its relationship with a customer is mandatory.

IE Style Diagrams

The IE diagramming style exchanges simplicity in line ends for added information. As a first example, consider Figure 4-10. This is the same one-to-many relationship we have been using to demonstrate the Chen method ER diagrams. However, in this case, the ends of the lines (which look a little like a bird's foot and are often called "crows feet") indicate which relationships are mandatory.

The double line below the customer entity means that each order is related to one and only one customer. Because zero is not an option, the relationship is mandatory. In contrast, the 0 and the crow's foot connected to the order entity mean that a customer may have zero, one, or more orders.

There are four symbols used at the ends of lines in an IE diagram:

||: One and one only (mandatory relationship)
0|: Zero or one
>1: One or more (mandatory relationship)
>0: Zero, one, or more

Although we often see the symbols turned 90 degrees, as they are in Figure 4-10, they are actually readable if viewed sideways as in the preceding list. An IE method ER diagram often includes attributes directly on the diagram. As you can see in Figure 4-10, entity identifiers are marked with an asterisk.

UML Style Diagrams

UML notation for entity relationships is very similar to IE notation. However, the symbols at the ends of lines are replaced by numeric representations of the type of relationship (see Figure 4-11). There are four possible relationships:

1: One and only one (mandatory)
1...:* One or more (mandatory)
0...1: Zero or one
0...:* Zero, one, or more

Basic Relationships for Antique Opticals

The major entities in the Antique Opticals database are diagrammed in Figure 4-12. You read the relationships in the following way:

- One customer can place zero, one, or more orders. An order comes from one and only one customer.
- The store may make many purchases of used discs from one customer. A purchase transaction comes from one and only one customer.

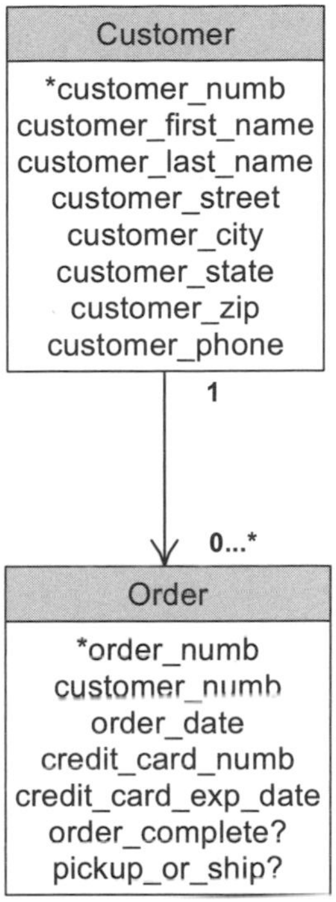

■ **FIGURE 4-11** A many-to-many relationship using UML notation.

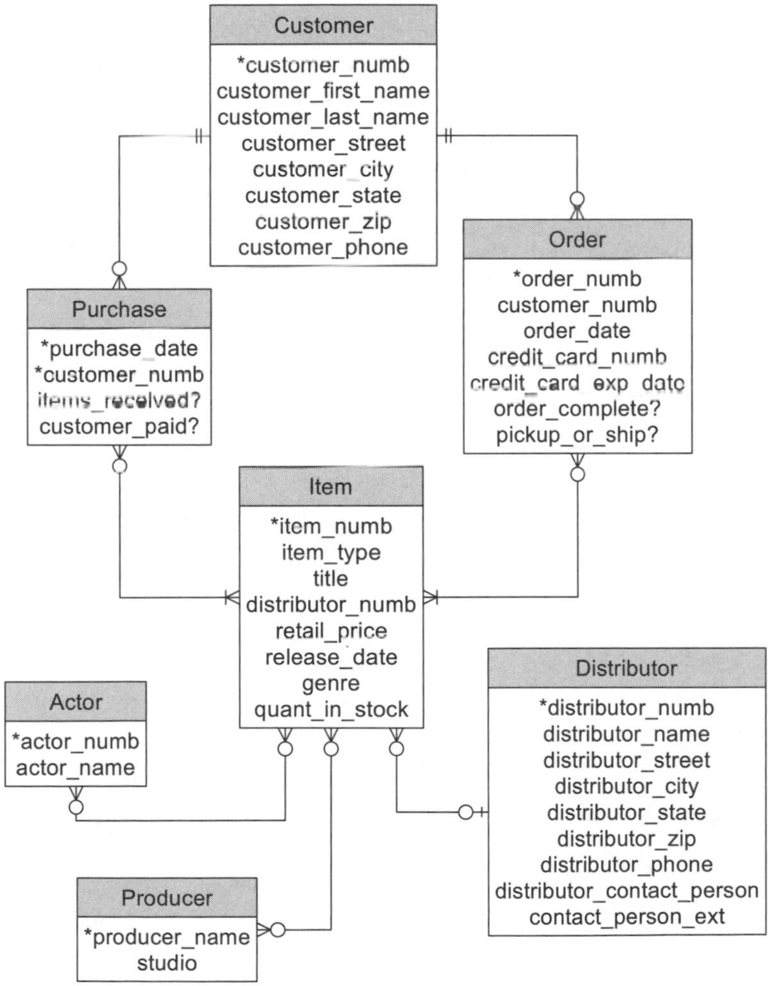

■ **FIGURE 4-12** The major entities and the relationships between them in the Antique Opticals database.

- An order has one or more items on it. An item can appear in zero, one, or more orders.
- A purchase is made up of one or more items. An item can be purchased zero, one, or more times.
- An actor appears in zero, one, or more items. An item has zero, one, or more actors in it. (There may occasionally be films that feature animals rather than human actors; therefore, it is probably unwise to require that every merchandise item be related to at least one actor.)
- Each item has zero, one, or more producers. Each producer is responsible for zero, one, or more items. (Although in practice you would not store data about a producer unless that producer was related to an item, leaving the relationship between a producer and an item as optional means that you can store producers without items if necessary.)
- Each item comes from zero or one distributor. Each distributor supplies zero, one, or more items.

The major thing to notice about this design is that there are four many-to-many relationships: order to item, purchase to item, actor to item, and producer to item. Before you can map this data model to a relational database, they must be handled in some way.

DEALING WITH MANY-TO-MANY RELATIONSHIPS

As you read earlier, there are problems with many-to-many relationships. The first is fairly straightforward: The relational data model cannot handle many-to-many relationships directly; it is limited to one-to-one and one-to-many relationships. This means that you must replace the many-to-many relationships that you have identified in your database environment with a collection of one-to-many relationships if you want to be able to use a relational DBMS.

The second, however, is a bit more subtle. To understand it, consider the relationship between an order a customer places with Antique Opticals and the merchandise items on the order. There is a many-to-many relationship between the order and the item because each order can be for many items and each item can appear on many orders (typically orders from different customers). Whenever a customer orders an item, the number of copies of the item varies, depending on how many copies the customer needs. (Yes, typically people order only one copy of a movie, but we need to allow them to order as many as they want.)

Now the question: Where should we store the quantity being ordered? It cannot be part of the order entity because the quantity depends on which item we are talking about. By the same token, the quantity cannot be part of the item entity because the quantity depends on the specific order.

This scenario is known as *relationship data*—data that apply to the relationship between two entities rather than to the entities themselves. Relationships, however, cannot have attributes. We therefore must have some entity to represent the relationship between the two, an entity to which the relationship data can belong.

Composite Entities

Entities that exist to represent the relationship between two or more other entities are known as *composite entities*. As an example of how composite entities work, consider once again the relationship between an order placed by an Antique Opticals customer and the items on that order.

What we need is an entity that tells us that a specific title appears on a specific order. If you look at Figure 4-13, you will see three order instances and three merchandise item instances. The first order for customer 0985 (Order #1) contains only one item (item 09244). The second order for customer 0985 (Order #2) contains a second copy of item 09244 as well as item 10101. Order #3, which belong to customer 1212, also has two items on it (item 10101 and item 00250).

There are five items ordered among the three orders. The middle of the diagram therefore contains five instances of a composite entity we will call a "line item" (think of it as a line item on a packing slip). The line item entity has been created solely to represent the relationship between an order and a merchandise item.

Each order is related to one line item instance for each item in the order. In turn, each item is related to one line item instance for each order on which it appears. Each line item instance is related to one and only one order, and it is also related to one and only one merchandise item. As a result, the relationship between an order and its line items is one-to-many (one order has many line items), and the relationship between an item and the orders on which it appears is

■ **FIGURE 4-13** Using instances of composite entities to change many-to-many relationships into one-to-many relationships.

one-to-many (one merchandise item appears in many line items). The presence of the composite entity has removed the original many-to-many relationship.

If necessary, the composite entity can be used to store relationship data. In the preceding example, we might include an attribute for the quantity ordered, a flag to indicate whether it has been shipped, and a shipping date.

Documenting Composite Entities

In some extensions of the Chen method for drawing ER diagrams, the symbol for a composite entity is the combination of the rectangle used for an entity and the diamond used for a relationship:

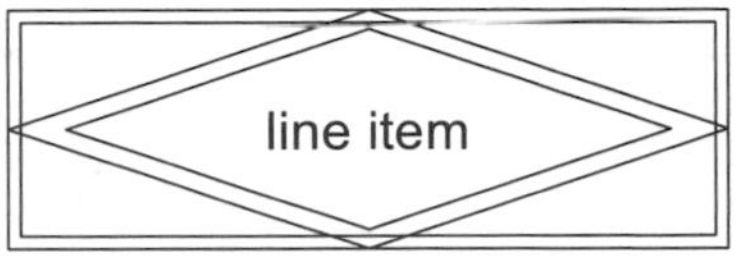

The IE and UML styles, however, have no special symbol for a composite entity.

Resolving Antique Opticals' Many-to-Many Relationships

To eliminate Antique Opticals' many-to-many relationships, the database designer must replace each many-to-many relationship with a composite entity and two one-to-many relationships. As you can see in Figure 4-14, the four new entities are as follows:

- *Order item:* An instance of the order item entity represents one item appearing on one order. Each order can have many "order items," but an ordered item must appear on one and only one order. By the same token, an ordered item contains one and only one item, but the same item can appear in many order item instances, each of which is related to a different order.
- *Purchase item:* An instance of the purchase item entity represents one used laser disc purchased from one customer as part of a purchase of one or more discs. Many items can be purchased during a single transaction, but each item purchased is purchased during only one transaction. The purpose of the purchase item entity is therefore the same as the order item entity: to represent specific items in a single transaction.
- *Performance:* The performance entity represents one actor appearing in one film. Each performance is for one and only one film, although a film can have many performances (one for each actor in the film). Conversely, an actor is related to one performance for each film in which he or she appears, although each performance is in one and only one film.
- *Production:* The production entity represents one producer working on one film. A producer may be involved in many productions, although each production relates to one and only one producer. The relationship with the item indicates that each film can be produced by many producers but that each production relates to only one item.

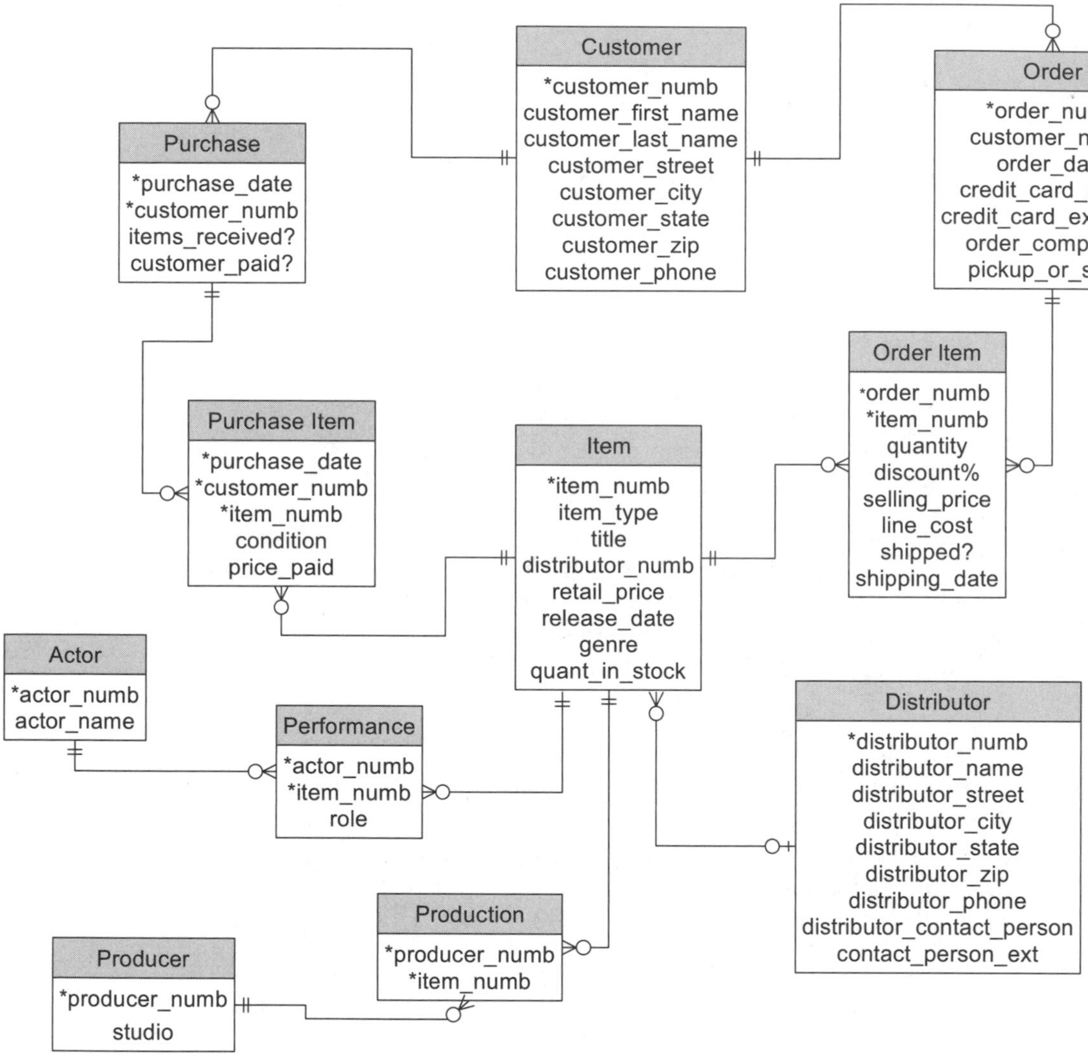

■ **FIGURE 4-14** The complete ER diagram for the Antique Opticals database.

Note: If you find sorting out the relationships in Figure 4-14 a bit difficult, keep in mind that if you rotate the up-and-down symbols 90 degrees, you will actually be able to read the relationships.

Because composite entities exist primarily to indicate a relationship between two other entities, they must be related to both of their parent entities. This is why the relationship between each composite entity in Figure 4-14 and its parents is mandatory.

RELATIONSHIPS AND BUSINESS RULES

In many ways, database design is as much an art as a science. Exactly what is the "correct" design for a specific business depends on the business rules; what is correct for one organization may not be correct for another. For example, assume that you are creating a database for a small establishment that has more than one store. One of the things you are being asked to model in the database is an employee's schedule. Before you can do that, you need to determine the relationship between an employee and a store. Is it one-to-many or many-to-many? Does an employee always work in one store—in which case the relationship is one-to-many—or can an employee divide his or her time among stores, which would mean a many-to-many relationship? This is not a matter of a correct or incorrect database design but an issue of how the business operates.

DATA MODELING VERSUS DATA FLOW

One of the most common mistakes people make when they begin data modeling is confusing data models with data flows. A *data flow* shows how data are handled within an organization, including who handles the data, where the data are stored, and what is done to the data. In contrast, a *data model* depicts the internal, logical relationships between the data, without regard to who is handling the data or what is being done with it.

Data flows are often documented in *data flow diagrams* (DFDs). For example, Figure 4-15 shows a top-level data flow diagram for Antique Opticals. The squares with drop shadows represent the people who are handling the data. Simple rectangles with numbers in them represent *processes*, or things that are done with the data. A place where data are stored (a *data store*) appears as two parallel lines—in this example containing the words "Main database." The arrows on the lines show the direction in which data pass from one place to another.

Data flow diagrams are often exploded to show more detail. For example, Figure 4-16 contains an explosion of the "Take order" process from Figure 4-15. You can now see that the process of taking an order involves two major steps: getting customer information and getting item information.

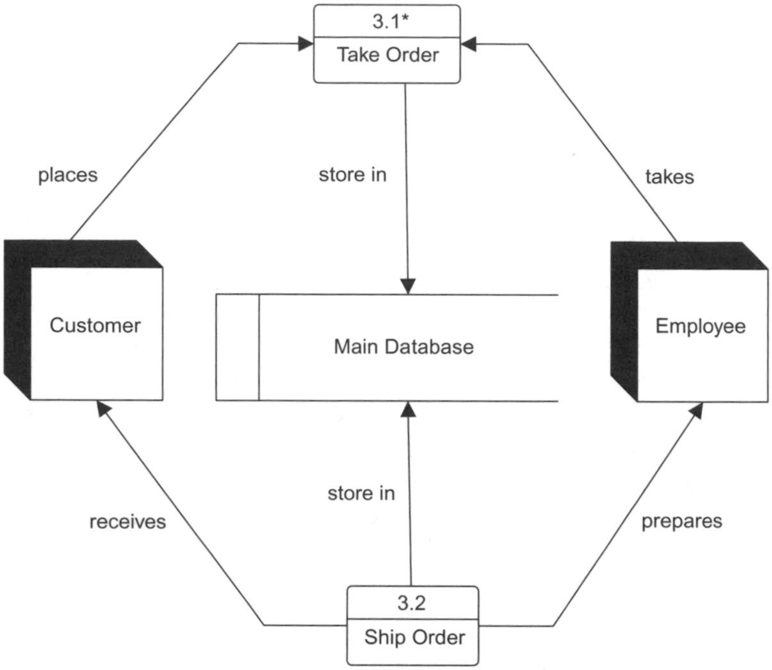

■ **FIGURE 4-15** A top-level data flow diagram for Antique Opticals.

Each of the processes in Figure 4-16 can be exploded even further to show additional detail (see Figures 4-17 and 4-18). At this point, the diagrams are almost detailed enough so that an application designer can plan an application program.

Where do the database and the ER diagram fit into all of this? The entire ER diagram is buried inside the "Main database." In fact, most CASE software allows you to link your ER diagram to a database's representation on a data flow diagram. Then, you can simply double-click on the database representation to the ER diagram into view.

There are a few guidelines for keeping data flows and data models separate:

- A data flow shows who uses or handles data. A data model does not.
- A data flow shows how data are gathered (the people or other sources from which they come). A data model does not.
- A data flow shows operations on data (the process through which data are transformed). A data model does not.

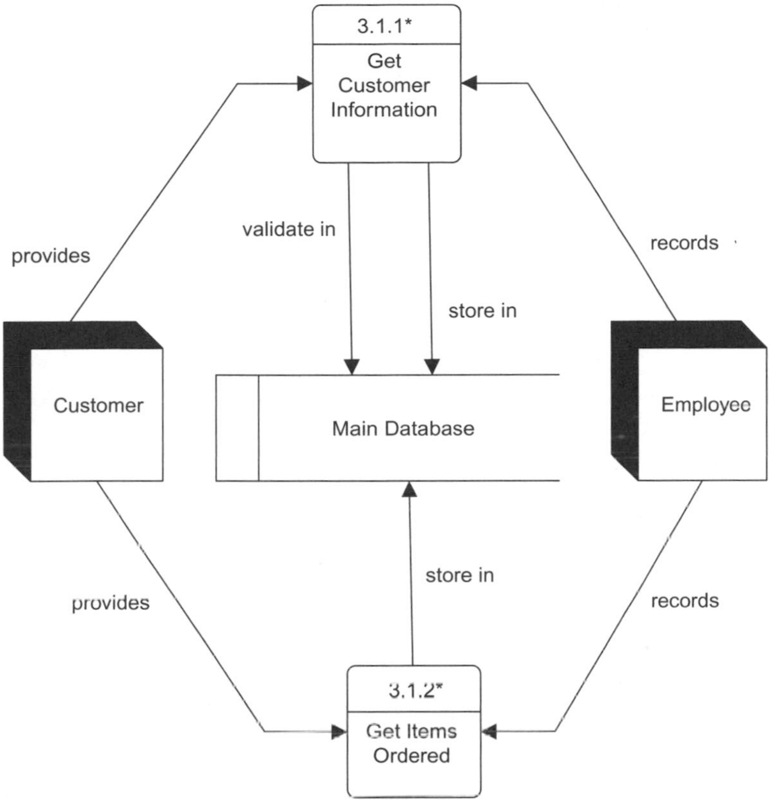

■ **FIGURE 4-16** An explosion of the "Take order" process from Figure 4-15.

- A data model shows how entities are interrelated. A data flow does not.
- A data model shows the attributes that describe data entities. A data flow does not.

The bottom line is this: A data model contains information about the data being stored in the database (entities, attributes, and entity relationships). If data about an entity are not going to be stored in the database, then that entity should not be part of the data model. For example, although the Antique Opticals data flow diagram shows the employee who handles most of the data, no data about employees are going to be stored in the database. Therefore, there is no employee entity in the ER diagram.

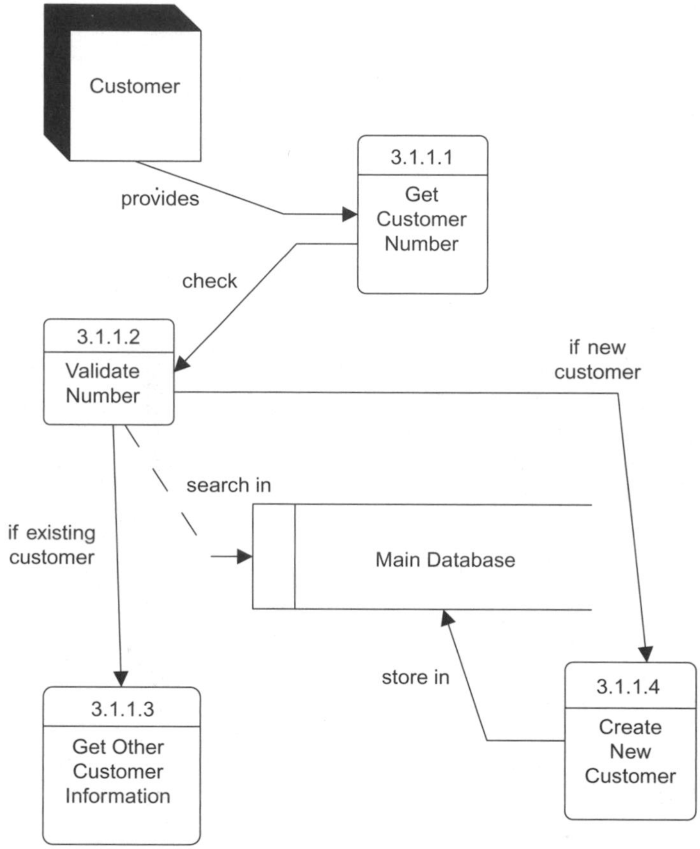

■ **FIGURE 4-17** An explosion of the "Get customer information" process from Figure 4-14.

SCHEMAS

A completed entity-relationship diagram represents the overall, logical plan of a database. In database terms, it is therefore known as a *schema*. This is how the people responsible for maintaining the database will see the design. However, users (both interactive users and application programs) may work with only a portion of the logical schema. And both the logical schema and the users' views of the data are at the same time distinct from the physical storage.

The underlying physical storage, which is managed by the DBMS, is known as the *physical schema*. It is for the most part determined by the DBMS. (Only very large DBMSs give you any control over physical storage.) The beauty of this arrangement is that both database design-

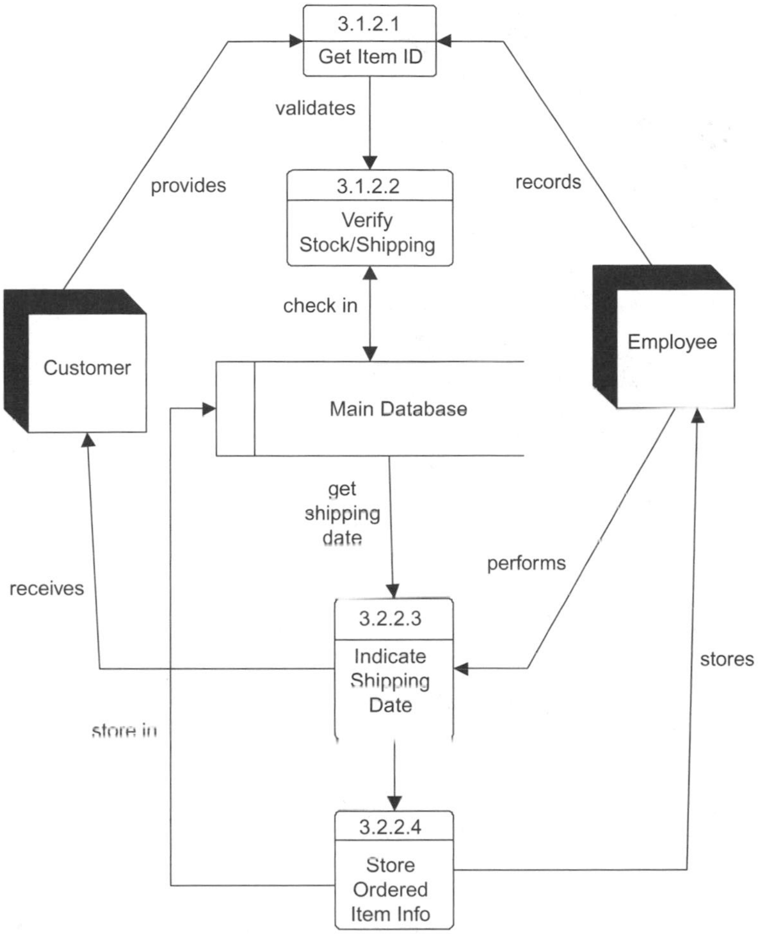

■ **FIGURE 4-18** An explosion of the "Get items ordered" process from Figure 4-16.

ers and users do not need to be concerned about physical storage, greatly simplifying access to the database and making it much easier to make changes to both the logical and physical schemas.

Because there are three ways to look at a database, some databases today are said to be based on a *three-schema architecture* (see Figure 4-19). Systems programmers and other people involved with managing physical storage deal with the physical schema. Most of today's relational DBMSs provide very little control over the file structure used to store database data. However, DBMSs designed to run on mainframes to handle extremely large datasets do allow some tailoring of the layout of internal file storage.

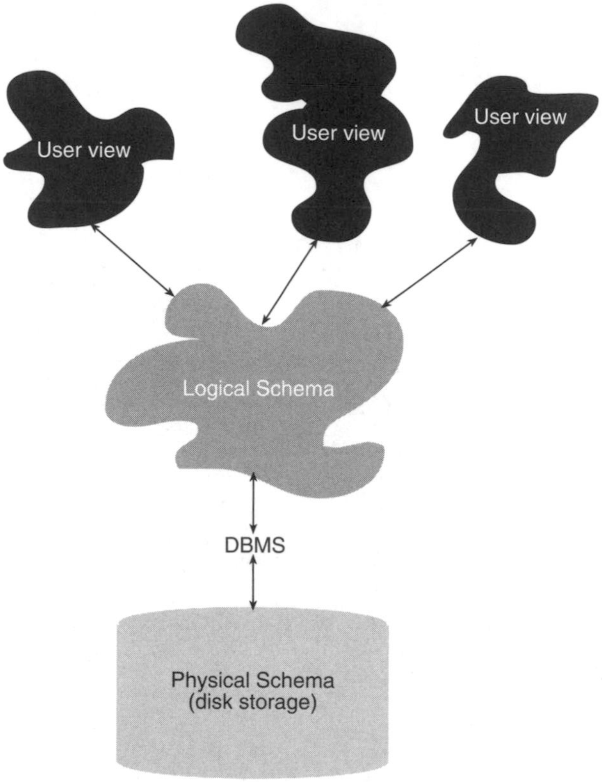

■ **FIGURE 4-19** Three-schema architecture.

Note: DBMSs based on earlier data models were more closed tied to their physical storage than relational DBMSs. Therefore, systems programmers were able to specify physical file structures to a much greater extent. An overview of the older database models can be found in Appendix A.

Data designers, database administrators, and some application programmers are aware of and use the logical schema. End users who work interactively and application programmers who are creating database applications for them work with the user view of the database.

Throughout most of this book we will focus on the design of the logical schema. You will also learn how to create and use database elements that provide users with limited portions of the database.

FOR FURTHER READING

The entity-relationship model was developed by Peter P. S. Chen. If you want to learn more about its early forms and how the model has changed, see the following:

Chen, P. "The Entity-Relationship Model: Toward a Unified View of Data." *ACM Transactions on Database Systems* 1(1), 1976.

Chen, P. *The Entity-Relationship Approach to Logical Database Design.* QED Information Sciences, Data Base Monograph Series, No. 6, 1977.

Chen, P. *Entity-Relationship Approach to Information Modeling.* E-R Institute, 1981.

The original work that described the Information Engineering approach can be found in the following:

Finkelstein, Clive. *An Introduction to Information Engineering.* Addison-Wesley, 1989.

Martin, James. *Information Engineering, Book I: Introduction; Book II: Planning and Analysis; Book III: Design and Construction.* Prentice Hall, 1989.

For information on the Unified Modeling Language, see the following:

Chonoles, Michael Jessie, and James A. Schardt. *UML 2 for Dummies.* For Dummies Press, 2003.

Fowler, Martin. *UML Distilled: A Brief Guide to the Standard Object Modeling Language,* 3rd ed. Addison-Wesley Professional, 2003.

Pilone, Dan, and Neil Pitman. *UML 2.0 in a Nutshell,* 2nd ed. O'Reilly Media, 2005.

For more in-depth coverage of ER modeling, see any of the following:

Baqui, Skiha, and Richard Earp. *Database Design Using Entity-Relationship Diagrams.* Auerbach, 2003.

Batini, Carlo, Stefano Ceri, and Shamkant B. Navathe. *Conceptual Database Design: An Entity-Relationship Approach.* Addison-Wesley, 1991.

Earp, Richard. *Database Design Using Entity-Relationship Diagrams.* Taylor & Frances, 2007.

Thalheim, Bernhard. *Entity-Relationship Modeling: Foundations of Database Technology.* Springer, 2000.

Chapter 5

The Relational Data Model

Once you have a completed ER diagram, you can translate that conceptual logical schema into the formal data model required by your DBMS. Today, most new database installations are based on the relational data model. We call databases that adhere to that model *relational databases*.

Note: The older data models that are described in Appendix A are still in use in many legacy database systems. However, it is extremely rare to find a business creating a new one. On the other hand, the object-oriented data model is still quite current, and although it has not replaced the relational data model and does not appear to be doing so, some new installations use either object-oriented or a combination of relational and object-oriented.

A *relational* database is one whose logical structure is made up of nothing but a collection of "relations." Although you may have read somewhere that a relational database has "relationships between files" nothing could be further from the truth. In this chapter, you will learn exactly what a relational database is and how relations provide representations of data relationships.

> *Note:* Remember from Chapter 4 that we said that a DBMS isolates database users from physical storage. A logical data model therefore has absolutely nothing to do with how the data are stored in files on disk.

The relational data model is the result of the work of one man: Edgar (E.F.) Codd. During the 1960s, Dr. Codd, although trained as a mathematician, worked with existing data models. His experience led him to believe that they were clumsy and unnatural ways of representing data relationships. He therefore went back to mathematical set theory and focused on the construct known as a relation. He extended that concept to produce the relational database model, which he introduced in a paper in 1970.

Note: You will find the citations for Codd's original paper and his other writings on the relational data model in the "For Further Reading" section at the end of this chapter.

Note: E.F. Codd was born in England in 1923 and later migrated to the United States, where he did most of his work on the relational data model at the IBM's Watson Research Center. He died in 2003.

UNDERSTANDING RELATIONS

In mathematical set theory, a *relation* is the definition of a table with columns (*attributes*) and rows (*tuples*). (The word *table* is used synonymously with *relation* in the relational data model.) The definition specifies what will be contained in each column of the table, but does not include data. When you include rows of data, you have an *instance* of a relation, such as the small Customer relation in Figure 5-1.

At first glance, a relation looks much like a flat file or a rectangular portion of a spreadsheet. However, because it has its underpinnings in mathematical set theory, a relation has some very specific characteristics that distinguish it from other rectangular ways of looking at data. Each of these characteristics forms the basis of a constraint that will be enforced by the DBMS.

Columns and Column Characteristics

A column in a relation has the following properties.

- *A name that is unique within the table:* Two or more tables within the same relational database schema may have columns with the same

Customer Number	First Name	Last Name	Phone
0001	Jane	Doe	(555) 555-1111
0002	John	Doe	(555) 555-2222
0003	Jane	Smith	(555) 555-3333
0004	John	Smith	(555) 555-4444

■ **FIGURE 5-1** A simple Customer relation.

names—in fact, as you will see shortly, in some circumstances this is highly desirable—but a single table must have unique column names. When the same column name appears in more than one table and tables that contain that column are used in the same manipulation operation, you qualify the name of the column by preceding it with the name of its table and a period:

```
customer.customer_number
```

- *A domain:* The values in a column are drawn from one and only one domain. As a result, relations are said to be *column homogeneous.* In addition, every column in a table is subject to a domain constraint. Depending on your DBMS the domain constraint may be as simple as a data type, such as integers or dates. Alternatively, your DBMS may allow you to create your own, very specific, domains that can be attached to columns.
- *There are no "positional concepts":* In other words, the columns can be viewed in any order without affecting the meaning of the data.

Rows and Row Characteristics

A row in a relation has the following properties.

- Only one value at the intersection of a column and row: A relation does not allow multivalued attributes.
- Uniqueness: There are no duplicate rows in a relation.
- A primary key: A primary key is a column or combination of columns with a value that uniquely identifies each row. As long as you have unique primary keys, you also have unique rows. We will look at the issue of what makes a good primary key in great depth in the next major section of this chapter.
- There are no positional concepts: The rows can be viewed in any order without affecting the meaning of the data.

> *Note:* For the most part, DBMSs do not enforce the unique row constraint automatically. However, as you will see shortly, there is another way to obtain the same effect.

Types of Tables

A relational database works with two types of tables. *Base tables* are relations that are actually stored in the database. These are the tables that make up your schema. However, relational operations on tables produce additional tables as their result. Such tables, which exist only in main memory, are known as *virtual tables*. Virtual tables may not be legal relations—in particular, they may have no primary key—but because virtual tables are never stored in the database, this presents no problem in terms of the overall design of the database.

The use of virtual tables benefits a DBMS in several ways. First, it allows the DBMS to keep intermediate query tables in main memory rather than storing them on disk, enhancing query performance. Second, it allows tables that violate the rules of the relational data model to exist in main memory without affecting the integrity of the database. Third, it helps avoid fragmentation of database files and disk surfaces by avoiding repeated write, read, and delete operations on temporary tables.

> *Note:* SQL, the language used to manage most relational databases, also supports "temporary base tables." Although called base tables, temporary tables are actually virtual tables in the sense that they exist only in main memory for a short time and are never stored in the physical database.

A Notation for Relations

You will see instances of relations throughout this book used as examples. However, we do not usually include data in a relation when documenting that relation. One common way to express a relation is as follows:

```
relation_name (primary_key, non_primary_key_column ...)
```

For example, the Customer relation that you saw in Figure 5-1 would be written as:

```
customers (customer_numb, first_name last_name, phone)
```

The preceding expression is a true relation, an expression of the structure of a relation. It correctly does not contain any data. (As mentioned earlier, when data are included, you have an instance of a relation.)

PRIMARY KEYS

As you have just read, a unique primary key makes it possible to uniquely identify every row in a table. Why is this so important? The issue is the same as with entity identifiers: You want to be able to retrieve every single piece of data you put into a database.

As far as a relational database is concerned, you should need only three pieces of information to retrieve any specific bit of data: the name of the table, the name of the column, and the primary key of the row. If primary keys are unique for every row, then we can be sure that we are retrieving exactly the row we want. If they are not unique, then we are retrieving only *some* row with the primary key value, which may not be the row that contains the data for which we are searching.

Along with being unique, a primary key must not contain the value *null*. Null is a special database value meaning "unknown." It is not the same as a zero or a blank. If you have one row with a null primary key, then you are actually all right. However, the minute you introduce a second one, you have lost the property of uniqueness. We therefore forbid the presence of nulls in any primary key columns. This constraint, known as *entity integrity*, will be enforced by a DBMS whenever data are entered or modified.

Selecting a good primary key can be a challenge. As you may remember from Chapter 4, some entities have natural primary keys, such as purchase order numbers. These are arbitrary, meaningless, unique identifiers that a company attaches to the orders it sends to vendors and are therefore ideal primary keys.

Primary Keys to Identify People

What about a primary key to identify people? The first thing that pops into your mind might be a Social Security number (or, for those outside the United States, a national identification number). Every person in the United States is supposed to have a Social Security number. Parents apply for them in the hospital where a baby is born, right? And because they are assigned by the U.S. government, they must be unique, right? Unfortunately, the answer to both questions is "no."

The Social Security Administration has been known to give everyone in an entire town the same Social Security number; over time, the numbers may be reused. However, these are minor problems compared to a Social Security number being null.

Consider what happens at a college that uses Social Security numbers as student numbers when international students enroll. Upon entry into the country, the international students do not have Social Security numbers. Because primary keys cannot be null, the international students cannot sign up for classes or even enroll in the college until they have a Social Security number.

The college's solution is to give them "fake" numbers in the format 999-99-XXXX, where XXXX is some number currently not in use. Then, when the student receives a "real" Social Security number from the government, the college supposedly replaces the fake value with the real one. Sometimes, however, the process does not work. A graduate student ended up with his first semester's grades being stored under the fake Social Security number but the rest of his grades under his real number. (Rather than changing the original data, someone created an entire new transcript for the student.) When the time came to audit his transcript to see if he had satisfied all of his graduation requirements, he was told that he was missing an entire semester's worth of courses.

This example leads us to two important desirable qualities of primary keys:

- A primary key should be some value that is highly unlikely ever to be null.
- A primary key value should never change.

In addition, there is significant concern about security problems that can arise from the use of Social Security numbers as identifiers in a database. The danger of identity theft has made it risky to share a national identifier. Many U.S. state governments, for example, have mandated that publicly supported organizations use something other than the Social Security number as a customer/client/student ID to help protect individual privacy.

Although Social Security numbers initially look like good natural identifiers, you will be much better off in the long run using arbitrary numbers for people—such as student numbers or account numbers—rather than relying on Social Security numbers.

Avoiding Meaningful Identifiers

It can be very tempting to code meaning into a primary key. For example, assume that Antique Opticals wants to assign codes to its distributors rather than giving them arbitrary distributor numbers. Someone might create codes such as TLC for The Laser Club and JS for Jones Services. At first, this might seem like a good idea. The codes are short, and by looking at them you can figure out which distributor they reference.

But what happens if one of the companies changes its name? Perhaps Jones Services is renamed Jones Distribution House. Do you change the primary key value in the distributor table? Do you change the code so that it reads JDH? If the distributor table were all that we cared about, that would be the easy solution.

However, consider that the table that describes merchandise items contains the code for the distributor so that Antique Opticals can know which distributor provides the item. (You'll read a great deal more about this concept in the next major section of this chapter.) If you change the distributor code value in the distributor table, you must change the value of the code for every merchandise item that comes from that distributor. Without the change, Antique Opticals will not be able to match the code to a distributor and get information about the distributor. It will appear that the item comes from a non-existent distributor!

Note: This is precisely the same problem you read about in Chapter 3 concerning Antique Opticals' identifiers for its customers.

Meaningful primary keys tend to change and therefore introduce the potential for major data inconsistencies between tables. Resist the temptation to use them at all costs. Here, then, is yet another property of a good primary key:

- *A primary key should avoid using meaningful data:* Use arbitrary identifiers or concatenations of arbitrary identifiers wherever possible.

It is not always possible to use completely meaningless primary keys. You may find, for example, that you need to include dates or times in primary keys to distinguish among events. The suggestion that you should not use meaningful primary keys is therefore not a hard and fast rule but a guideline you should follow whenever you can.

Concatenated Primary Keys

Some tables have no single column in which the values never duplicate. As an example, look at the sample order items table in

■ FIGURE 5-2 A sample order items table.

Order Number	Item Number	Quantity
10991	0022	1
10991	0209	2
10991	1001	1
10992	0022	1
10992	0486	1
10993	0209	1
10993	1001	2
10994	0621	1

Figure 5-2. Because there is more than one item on an order and because the same item can appear on more than one order, order numbers are repeated. Therefore, neither column by itself can serve as the table's primary key. The combination of an order number and an item number, however, *is* unique. We can therefore concatenate the two columns that form the table's primary key.

It is true that you could also concatenate all three columns in the table and still ensure a unique primary key. However, the quantity column is not necessary to ensure uniqueness and therefore should not be used. We now have some additional properties of a good primary key:

- A concatenated primary key should be made up of the smallest number of columns necessary to ensure the uniqueness of the primary key.
- Whenever possible, the columns used in a concatenated primary key should be meaningless identifiers.

All-Key Relations

It is possible to have a table in which every column is part of the primary key. As an example, consider a library book catalog. Each book title owned by a library has a natural unique primary key: the ISBN (International Standard Book Number). Each ISBN is assigned to one or more subject headings in the library's catalog, and each subject heading is also assigned to one or more books. We therefore have a many-to-many relationship between books and subject headings.

A relation to represent this relationship might be:

```
subject_catalog (isbn, subject_heading)
```

All we need to do is pair a subject heading with a book identifier. No additional data are needed. Therefore, all columns in the table become part of the primary key.

There is absolutely no problem with having all-key relations in a database. In fact, they occur whenever a database design contains a composite entity that has no relationship data. They are not necessarily errors, and you can use them wherever needed.

REPRESENTING DATA RELATIONSHIPS

In the preceding section we alluded to the use of identifiers in more than one relation. This is the one way in which relational databases represent relationships between entities. To make this concept clearer, take a look at the three tables in Figure 5-3.

Each table in the illustration is directly analogous to the entity by the same name in the Antique Opticals ER diagram. The Orders table (the order entity) is identified by an order number, an arbitrary unique

Items

Item Number	Title	Distributor Number	Price
1001	Gone with the Wind	002	39.95
1002	Star Wars: Special Edition	002	59.95
1003	Die Hard	004	29.95
1004	Bambi	006	29.95

Orders

Order Number	Customer Number	Order Date
11100	0012	12/18/09
11101	0186	12/18/09
11102	0056	12/18/09

Order Items

Order Number	Item Number	Quantity	Shipped?
11100	1001	1	Y
11100	1002	1	Y
11101	1002	2	Y
11102	1002	1	N
11102	1003	1	N
11102	1001	1	N

■ **FIGURE 5-3** Three relations from the Antique Opticals database.

primary key assigned by Antique Opticals. The Items table (the item entity) is identified by an item number, which could be another arbitrary unique identifier or a UPC.

The third table—Order Items (the order items entity)—tells the company which items are part of which order. As you saw earlier in this chapter, this table requires a concatenated primary key because multiple items can appear on multiple orders. The selection of the primary key, however, has more significance than simply uniquely identifying each row. It also represents a relationship between the order items, the orders on which they appear, and the items being ordered.

The item number column in the order items relation is the same as the primary key of the item table. This indicates a one-to-many relationship between the two tables. By the same token, there is a one-to-many relationship between the orders and order items tables because the order number column in the order items table is the same as the primary key of the orders table.

When a table contains a column (or concatenation of columns) that is the same as the primary key of a table, the column is called a *foreign key*. The matching of foreign key values to primary key values represents data relationships in a relational database. As far as the user of a relational database is concerned, there are no structures that show relationships other than the matching column's values.

Note: This is why the idea that relational databases have "relationships between files" is so absurd. The relationships in a relational database are between logical constructs—tables—and nothing else. Such structures make absolutely no assumptions about physical storage.

Foreign keys may be part of a concatenated primary key, or they may not be part of their table's primary key at all. Consider, for example, a pair of simple Antique Opticals customers and orders relations:

```
customers (customer_numb, first_name, last_name,
  phone)
orders (order_numb, customer_numb, order_date)
```

The customer number column in the orders table is a foreign key that matches the primary key of the customers table. It represents the one-to-many relationship between customers and the orders they place. However, the customer number is not part of the primary key of its table but is a non-key attribute that is nonetheless a foreign key.

Technically, foreign keys need not have values unless they are part of a concatenated primary key; they can be null. However, in this particular database, Antique Opticals would be in serious trouble if customer numbers were null: There would be no way to know which customer placed an order!

A relational DBMS uses the relationships indicated by matching data between primary and foreign keys. For example, assume that an Antique Opticals employee wanted to see what titles had been ordered on order number 11102. First, the DBMS identifies the rows in the order items table that contain an order number of 11102. Then, it takes the items number from those rows and matches them to the item numbers in the items table. In the rows where there are matches, the DBMS retrieves the associated data.

Referential Integrity

The procedure described in the preceding paragraph works very well—unless for some reason there is no order number in the orders table to match a row in the order items table. This is a very undesirable situation because you can't ship the ordered items if you don't know which customer placed the order.

This relational data model therefore enforces a constraint called *referential integrity*, which states that *every non-null foreign key value must match an existing primary key value*. Of all the constraints on a relational database, this is probably the most important because it ensures the consistency of the cross-references among tables.

Referential integrity constraints are stored in the database and enforced automatically by the DBMS. As with all other constraints, each time a user enters or modifies data, the DBMS checks the constraints and verifies that they are met. If the constraints are violated, the data modification will not be allowed.

Foreign Keys and Primary Keys in the Same Table

Foreign keys do not necessarily need to reference a primary key in a different table; they need only reference a primary key. As an example, consider the following employee relation:

```
employee (employee_ID, first_name, last_name,
  department, manager_ID)
```

A manager is also an employee. Therefore, the manager ID, although named differently from the employee ID, is actually a foreign key that references the primary key of its own table. The DBMS will therefore always ensure that whenever a user enters a manager ID, that manager already exists in the table as an employee.

VIEWS

The people responsible for developing a database schema and those who write application programs for use by technologically unsophisticated users typically have knowledge of and access to the entire schema, including direct access to the database's base tables. However, it is usually undesirable to have end users working directly with base tables, primarily for security reasons.

The relational data model therefore includes a way to provide end users with their own window into the database, one that hides the details of the overall database design and prohibits direct access to the base tables.

The View Mechanism

A view is not stored with data. Instead, it is stored under a name in the database itself along with a database query that will retrieve its data. A view can therefore contain data from more than one table, selected rows, and selected columns.

> *Note:* Although a view can be constructed in just about any way that you can query a relational database, many views can be used for data display. As you will learn in Chapter 10, only views that meet a strict set of rules can be used to modify data.

The real beauty of storing views in this way, however, is that whenever the user includes the name of the view in a data manipulation language statement, the DBMS executes the query associated with the view name and recreates the view's table. This means that the data in a view will always be current.

A view table remains in main memory only for the duration of the data manipulation statement in which it was used. As soon as the user issues another query, the view table is removed from main memory to be replaced by the result of the most recent query. A view table is therefore a virtual table.

Note: Some end user DBMSs give the user the ability to save the contents of a view as a base table. This is a particularly undesirable feature, as there are no provisions for automatically updating the data in the saved table whenever the tables on which it was based change. The view table therefore will quickly become out of date and inaccurate.

Why Use Views?

There are three good reasons to include views in the design of a database:

- As mentioned earlier, views provide a significant security mechanism by restricting users from viewing portions of a schema to which they should not have access.
- Views can simplify the design of a database for technologically unsophisticated users.
- Because views are stored as named queries, they can be used to store frequently used, complex queries. The queries can then be executed by using the name of the view in a simple query.

Like other structural elements in a relational database, views can be created and destroyed at any time. However, because views do not contain stored data but only specification of a query that will generate a virtual table, adding or removing view definitions has no impact on base tables or the data they contain. Removing a view will create problems only when that view is used in an application program and the program is not modified to work with a different view or base table.

THE DATA DICTIONARY

The structure of a relational database is stored in the database's *data dictionary* or *catalog*. The data dictionary is made up of a set of relations that are identical in properties to the relations used to hold data. They can be queried using the same tools used to query data-handling relations. No user can modify the data dictionary tables directly. However, data manipulation language commands that create, modify, and destroy database structural elements work by modifying rows in data dictionary tables.

You will typically find the following types of information in a data dictionary:

- Definitions of the columns that make up each table
- Integrity constraints placed on relations
- Security information (which user has the right to perform which operation on which table)
- Definitions of other database structure elements, such as views (discussed further in Chapter 8) and user-defined domains

When a user attempts to access data in any way, a relational DBMS first goes to the data dictionary to determine whether the database elements the user has requested are actually part of the schema. In addition, the DBMS verifies that the user has the access right to whatever he or she is requesting.

When a user attempts to modify data, the DBMS also goes to the data dictionary to look for integrity constraints that may have been placed on the relation. If the data meet the constraints, then the modification is permitted. Otherwise the DBMS returns an error message and does not make the change.

Because all access to a relational database is through the data dictionary, relational DBMSs are said to be *data dictionary driven*. The data in the data dictionary are known as *metadata*: data about data.

Sample Data Dictionary Tables

The precise tables that make up a data dictionary depend somewhat on the DBMS. In this section you will see one example of a typical way in which a DBMS might organize its data dictionary.

The linchpin of the data dictionary is actually a table that documents all the data dictionary tables (often named *syscatalog*, the first few rows of which can be found in Figure 5-4). From the names of the data dictionary tables, you can probably guess that there are tables to store data about base tables, their columns, their indexes, and their foreign keys.

The *syscolumn* table describes the columns in each table (including the data dictionary tables). In Figure 5-5, for example, you can see a portion of a *syscolumn* table that describes the Antique Opticals merchandise item table.

Keep in mind that these data dictionary tables have the same structure and must adhere to the same rules as base tables. They must have

creator	tname	dbspace	tabletype	ncols	Primary_key
SYS	SYSTABLE	SYSTEM	TABLE	12	Y
SYS	SYSCOLUMN	SYSTEM	TABLE	14	Y
SYS	SYSINDEX	SYSTEM	TABLE	8	Y
SYS	SYSIXCOL	SYSTEM	TABLE	5	Y
SYS	SYSFOREIGNKEY	SYSTEM	TABLE	8	Y
SYS	SYSKCOL	SYSTEM	TABLE	4	Y
SYS	SYSFILE	SYSTEM	TABLE	3	Y
SYS	SYSDOMAIN	SYSTEM	TABLE	4	Y
SYS	SYSUSERPERM	SYSTEM	TABLE	10	Y
SYS	SYTSTABLEPERM	SYSTEM	TABLE	11	Y
SYS	SYSCOLPERM	SYSTEM	TABLE	6	Y

■ **FIGURE 5-4** A portion of a *syscatalog* table.

creator	cname	tname	coltype	nulls	length	Inprimarykey	Colno
DBA	item_numb	items	integer	N	4	Y	1
DBA	title	items	varchar	Y	60	N	2
DBA	distributor_numb	items	integer	Y	4	N	3
DBA	release_date	items	date	Y	6	N	4
DBA	retail_price	items	numeric	Y	8	N	5

■ **FIGURE 5-5** Selected rows from a *syscolumn* table.

non-null unique primary keys, and they must enforce referential integrity among themselves.

A BIT OF HISTORY

When Codd published his paper describing the relational data model in 1970, software developers were bringing databases based on older data models to market. The software was becoming relatively mature and was being widely installed. Although many theorists recognized the benefits of the relational data model, it was some time before relational systems actually appeared.

IBM had a working prototype of its System R by 1976. This product, however, was never released. Instead, the first relational DBMS to feature SQL—an IBM development—was Oracle, released by the company of the same name in 1977. IBM didn't actually market a relational DBMS until 1981, when it released SQL/DS.

Oracle debuted on minicomputers running UNIX. SQL/DS ran under VM (often specifically using CMS on top of VM) on IBM mainframes.

There was also a crop of early products that were designed specifically for PCs, the first of which was dBase II, from a company named Ashton-Tate. Released in 1981, the product ran on IBM PCs and Apple II+s.

Note: It is seriously questionable whether dBase was ever truly a "relational" DBMS. However, most consumers saw it as such, and it is therefore considered the first relational product for PCs.

Oracle was joined by a large number of competing products in the UNIX market, including Informix and Ingres. Oracle has been the biggest winner in this group because it now runs on virtually every OS/hardware platform combination imaginable and has scaled well (down to PCs and up to mainframes). Prior to the widespread deployment of mySQL as a database server for Web sites, it was safe to say that there were more copies of Oracle running on computers than any other DBMS.

The PC market for relational DBMSs has been flooded with products. As often happens with software, the best has not necessarily become the most successful. In 1983, Microrim released its R:BASE product, the first truly relational product for a PC. With its support for standard SQL, a powerful integrity rule facility, and a capable programming language, R:BASE was a robust product. It succumbed, however, to the market penetration of dBASE. The same can be said for Paradox (originally a Borland product and later purchased by Corel) and FoxPro (a dBase-compatible product originally developed by Fox Software).

dBase faded from prominence after being purchased by Borland in 1991. FoxPro, dBase's major competitor, was purchased by Microsoft in 1992. It, too, has faded from the small computer DBMS market. Instead, the primary end user desktop DBMS for Windows today is Access, first released by Microsoft in 1993.

Note: You may be wondering why no newer products are mentioned in the preceding discussion. That is because, for the most part, there haven't been any major new relational DBMSs released in some time. A DBMS is a complex product for a software developer to create. Added to that, once an organization has invested time and money in purchasing, installing, and writing applications for a specific product, it is unlikely to want to change as long as the current product can be made to work. The barriers to entry into the DBMS software market are very high for a new product.

FOR FURTHER READING

If you want to follow the history of Codd's specifications for relational databases, consult the following:

Codd, E. F. "A Relational Model of Data for Large Shared Databanks." *Communications of the ACM* 13(6), 377–387, 1970.

Codd, E. F. "Extending the Relational Model to Capture More Meaning." *Transactions on Database Systems* 4(4), 397–434, 1979.

Codd, E. F. "Relational Database: A Practical Foundation for Productivity." *Communications of the ACM*. 25(2), 109–117, 1982.

Codd, E. F. "Is Your DBMS Really Relational?" *Computerworld*, October 14: ID/1-1D/9, 1983.

Codd, E. F. *The Relational Data Model, Version 2*. Addison-Wesley, 1990.

There are also literally hundreds of books that discuss the details of specific relational DBMSs. After you finish reading this book, you may want to consult one or more books that deal with your specific product to help you learn to develop applications using that product's tools.

Another title of interest is:

Lightstone, Sam S., Toby J. Teorey, and Tom Nadeau. *Physical Database Design: The Database Professional's Guide to Exploiting Views, Storage and More*. Morgan Kaufmann, 2007.

Chapter 6

Normalization

Given any pool of entities and attributes, you can group them into relations in many ways. In this chapter, you will be introduced to the process of *normalization*, through which you create relations that avoid most of the problems that arise from bad relational design.

There are at least two ways to approach normalization. The first is to work from an ER diagram. If the diagram is drawn correctly, then there are some simple rules you can use to translate it into relations that will avoid most relational design problems. The drawback to this approach is that it can be difficult to determine whether your design is correct. The second approach is to use the theoretical concepts behind good design to create your relations. This is a bit more difficult than working from an ER diagram, but it often results in a better design.

In practice, you may find it useful to use a combination of both approaches. First, create an ER diagram and use it to design your relations. Then, check those relations against the theoretical rules for good design and make any changes necessary to meet the rules.

TRANSLATING AN ER DIAGRAM INTO RELATIONS

An ER diagram in which all many-to-many relationships have been transformed into one-to-many relationships through the introduction of composite entities can be translated directly into a set of relations. To do so:

- Create one table for each entity.
- For each entity that is only at the "one" end of one or more relationships and not at the "many" end of any relationship, create a single-column primary key, using an arbitrary unique identifier if no natural primary key is available.

- For each entity that is at the "many" end of one or more relationships, include the primary key of each parent entity (those at the "one" end of the relationships) in the table as foreign keys.
- If an entity at the "many" end of one or more relationships has a natural primary key (for example, an order number or an invoice number), use that single column as the primary key. Otherwise, concatenate the primary key of its parent with any other column or columns needed for uniqueness to form the table's primary key.

Following these guidelines, we end up with the following tables for the Antique Opticals database:

```
Customer (customer_numb, customer_first_name,
   customer_last_name, customer_street,
   customer_city, customer_state, customer_zip,
   customer_phone)
Distributor (distributor_numb, distributor_name,
   distributor_street, distributor_city,
   distributor_state, distributor_zip,
   distributor_phone, distributor_contact_person,
   contact_person_ext)
Item (item_numb, item_type, title, distributor_numb,
   retail_price, release_date, genre, quant_in_stock)
Order (order_numb, customer_numb, order_date,
   credit_card_numb, credit_card_exp_date,
   order_complete?, pickup_or_ship?)
Order item (order_numb, item_numb, quantity,
   discount_percent, selling_price, line_cost,
   shipped?, shipping_date)
Purchase (purchase_date, customer_numb,
   items_received?, customer_paid?)
Purchase item (purchase_date, customer_numb,
   item_numb, condition, price_paid)
Actor (actor_numb, actor_name)
Performance (actor_numb, item_numb, role)
Producer (producer_name, studio)
Production (producer_name,item_numb)
```

Note: You will see these relations reworked a bit throughout the remainder of the first part of this book to help illustrate various aspects of database design. However, the preceding is the design that results from a direct translation of the ER diagram.

NORMAL FORMS

The theoretical rules that the design of a relation meet are known as *normal forms*. Each normal form represents an increasingly stringent set of rules. Theoretically, the higher the normal form, the better the design of the relation. As you can see in Figure 6-1, there are six nested normal forms, indicating that if a relation is in one of the higher, inner normal forms, it is also in all of the normal forms below it.

In most cases, if you can place your relations in third normal form (3NF), then you will have avoided most of the problems common to bad relational designs. The three higher normal forms—Boyce-Codd, fourth normal form (4NF), and fifth normal form (5NF)—handle special situations that arise only occasionally. However, the situations that these normal forms handle are conceptually easy to understand and can be used in practice if the need arises.

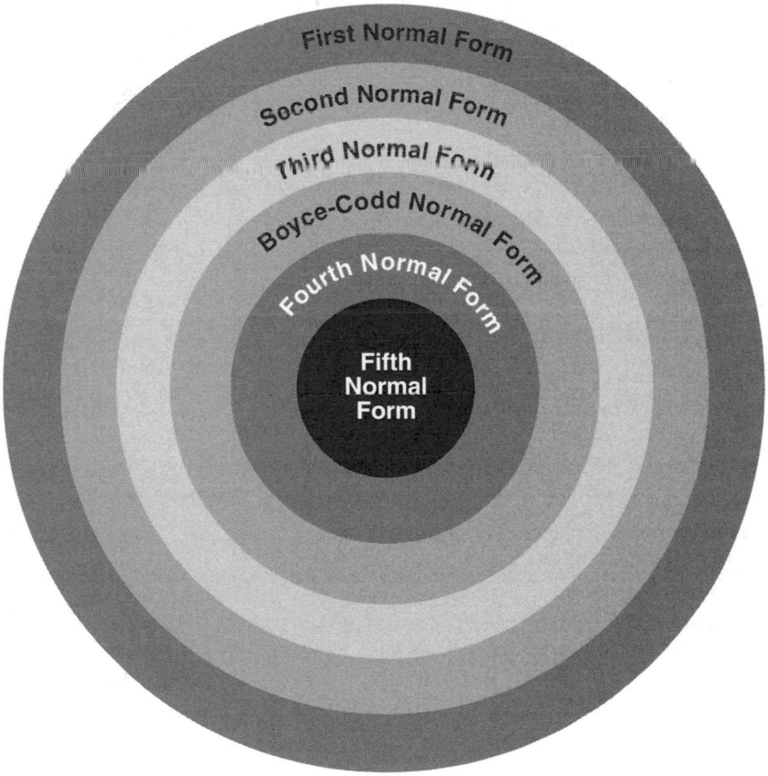

■ **FIGURE 6-1** Nested normal forms.

In recent years, sixth normal form has been added to relational database design theory. It is not precisely a more rigorous normal form than fifth normal form, although it uses the same principles to transform relations from one form to another. You will be introduced to it briefly at the end of this chapter.

> *Note:* In addition to the normal forms in Figure 6-1 and sixth normal form, another normal form—domain/key normal form—which is of purely theoretical importance, has not been used as a practical design objective.

FIRST NORMAL FORM

A table is in first normal form (1NF) if it meets the following criteria:

1. The data are stored in a two-dimensional table.
2. There are no repeating groups.

The key to understanding 1NF, therefore, is understanding the nature of a repeating group of data.

Understanding Repeating Groups

A *repeating group* is an attribute that has more than one value in each row of a table. For example, assume that you were working with an employee relation and needed to store the names and birth dates of the employees' children. Because each employee can have more than one child, the names of the children and their birth dates each form a repeating group.

> *Note:* A repeating group is directly analogous to a multivalued attribute in an ER diagram.

There is actually a very good reason why repeating groups are not permitted. To see what might happen if they were used, take a look at Figure 6-2, an instance of an employee table containing repeating groups. Notice that there are multiple values in a single row in both the children's names and the children's birth dates columns. This presents two major problems:

Emp#	First	Last	Children's Names	Children's Birthdates
1001	Jane	Doe	Mary, Sam	1/9/02, 5/15/04
1002	John	Doe	Lisa, David	1/9/00, 5/15/01
1003	Jane	Smith	John, Pat, Lee, Mary	10/5/04, 10/12/00, 6/6/2006, 8/21/04
1004	John	Smith	Michael	7/4/06
1005	Jane	Jones	Edward, Martha	10/21/05, 10/15/99

■ **FIGURE 6-2** A table with repeating groups.

- There is no way to know exactly which birth date belongs to which child. It is tempting to say that we can associate the birth dates with the children by their positions in the list, but there is nothing to ensure that the relative positions will always be maintained.
- Searching the table is very difficult. If, for example, we want to know which employees have children born before 2005, the DBMS will need to perform data manipulation to extract the individual dates themselves. Given that there is no way to know how many birth dates there are in the column for any specific row, the processing overhead for searching becomes even greater.

The solution to these problems, of course, is to get rid of the repeating groups altogether.

Note: The table in Figure 6-2 is not a legal relation because it contains those repeating groups. Therefore, we should not call it a relation.

Handling Repeating Groups

There are two ways to get rid of repeating groups to bring a table into conformance with the rules for first normal form: a right way and a wrong way. We will look first at the wrong way so you will know what *not* to do.

In Figure 6-3 you can see a relation that handles repeating groups by creating multiple columns for the multiple values. This particular example includes three pairs of columns for a child's name and birth date. The relation in Figure 6-3 does meet the criteria for first normal form. The repeating groups are gone, and there is no problem identifying which birth date belongs to which child. However, the design has introduced several problems of its own, as follows:

Emp#	First	Last	Child Name 1	Child Bdate 1	Child Name 2	Child Bdate 2	Child Name 3	Child Bdate 3
1001	Jane	Doe	Mary	1/1/02	Sam	5/15/04		
1002	John	Doe	Lisa	1/1/00	David	5/15/01		
1003	Jane	Smith	John	10/5/04	Pat	10/12/00	Lee	6/6/06
1004	John	Smith	Michael	7/4/06				
1005	Joe	Jones	Edward	10/21/05	Martha	10/15/99		

■ **FIGURE 6-3** A relation handling repeating groups in the wrong way

- The relation is limited to three children for any given employee. This means that there is no room to store Jane Smith's fourth child. Should you put another row for Jane Smith into the table? If so, then the primary key of this relation can no longer be just the employee number. The primary key must include one child's name as well.
- The relation wastes space for people who have less than three children. Given that disk space is one of the least expensive elements of a database system, this is probably the least of the problems with this relation.
- Searching for a specific child becomes very clumsy. To answer the question "Does anyone have a child named Lee?," the DBMS must construct a query that includes a search of all three child name columns because there is no way to know in which column the name might be found.

The right way to handle repeating groups is to create another table (another entity) to handle multiple instances of the repeating group. In the example we have been using, we would create a second table for the children, producing something like Figure 6-4.

Neither of the two new tables contains any repeating groups, and this form of the design avoids all the problems of the preceding solution:

- There is no limit to the number of children that can be stored for a given employee. To add another child, you simply add another row to the table.
- There is no wasted space. The children table uses space only for data that are present.
- Searching for a specific child is much easier because children's names are found in only one column.

Employee

Emp#	First	Last
1001	Jane	Doe
1002	John	Doe
1003	Jane	Smith
1004	John	Smith
1005	Joe	Jones

Children

1001	Mary	1/1/02
1001	Sam	5/15/04
1002	Lisa	1/1/00
1002	David	5/15/01
1003	John	10/5/04
1003	Pat	10/12/00
1003	Lee	6/6/06
1003	Mary	8/21/04
1004	Michael	7/4/06
1005	Edward	10/21/05
1005	Martha	1015/99

■ **FIGURE 6-4** The correct way to handle a repeating group.

Problems with First Normal Form

Although first normal form relations have no repeating groups, they usually have many other problems. To examine the most typical, we will look at the table underlying the data entry form in Chapter 3. (This table comes from Antique Opticals' original data management system rather than the new and improved design you saw earlier in this chapter.) Expressed in the notation for relations that we have been using, the relation is:

```
orders (customer_numb, first_name, last_name, street,
  city, state, zip, phone, order_numb, order_date,
  item_numb, title, price, has_shipped?)
```

The first thing we need to do is determine the primary key for this table. The customer number alone will not be sufficient because the customer number repeats for every item ordered by the customer. The item number will also not suffice because it is repeated for every order on which it appears. We cannot use the order number because it is repeated for every item on the order. The only solution is a concatenated key, in this example, the combination of the order number and the item number.

Given that the primary key is made up of the order number and the item number, there are two important things we *cannot* do with this relation:

1. We cannot add data about a customer until the customer places at least one order because without an order and an item on that order, we do not have a complete primary key.
2. We cannot add data about a merchandise item we are carrying without that item being ordered. There must be an order number to complete the primary key.

The preceding are *insertion anomalies*, situations that arise when you are prevented from inserting data into a relation because a complete primary key is not available. (Remember that *no* part of a primary key can be null.)

Note: To be strictly correct, there is a third insertion anomaly in the orders relation. You cannot insert an order until you know one item on the order. In a practical sense, however, no one would enter an order without there being an item ordered.

Insertion anomalies are common in first normal form relations that are not also in any of the higher normal forms. In practical terms, they occur because there are data about more than one entity in the relation. The anomaly forces you to insert data about an unrelated entity (for example, a merchandise item) when you want to insert data about another entity (such as a customer).

First normal form relations can also cause problems when data are deleted. Consider, for example, what happens if a customer cancels the order of a single item:

- In cases where the deleted item was the only item on the order, you lose all data about the order.
- In cases where the order was the only order on which the item appeared, you lose data about the item.
- In cases where the deleted item was the item ordered by a customer, you lose all data about the customer.

These *deletion anomalies* occur because part of the primary key of a row becomes null when the merchandise item data are deleted, forcing you to remove the entire row. The result of a deletion anomaly is the loss of data that you would like to keep. In practical terms, you are forced to remove data about an unrelated entity when you delete data about another entity in the same table.

> *Note:* Moral to the story: More than one entity in a table is a bad thing.

There is a final type of anomaly in the orders relation that is not related to the primary key: a *modification,* or *update, anomaly.* The order relation has a great deal of unnecessary duplicated data—in particular, information about customers. When a customer moves, then the customer's data must be changed in every row, for every item on every order ever placed by the customer. If every row is not changed, then data that should be the same are no longer the same. The potential for these inconsistent data is the modification anomaly.

SECOND NORMAL FORM

The solution to anomalies in a first normal form relation is to break down the relation so there is one relation for each entity in the 1NF relation. The orders relation, for example, will break down into four relations (customers, items, orders, and line items). Such relations are in at least second normal form (2NF).

In theoretical terms, second formal form relations are defined as follows:

1. The relation is in first normal form.
2. All non-key attributes are functionally dependent on the entire primary key.

The new term in the preceding is *functionally dependent,* a special relationship between attributes.

Understanding Functional Dependencies

A functional dependency is a one-way relationship between two attributes such that at any given time, for each unique value of attribute A, only one value of attribute B is associated with it through the relation. For example, assume that A is the customer number from the orders relation. Each customer number is associated with one customer first name, one last name, one street address, one city, one state, one zip code, and one phone number. Although the values for those attributes may change, at any moment, there is only one.

We can therefore say that first name, last name, street, city, state, zip, and phone are functionally dependent on the customer number. This relationship is often written:

```
Customer_numb -> first_name, last_name, street, city,
  state, zip, phone
```

and read "customer number determines first name, last name, street, city, state, zip, and phone." In this relationship, customer number is known as the *determinant* (an attribute that determines the value of other attributes).

Notice that the functional dependency does not necessarily hold in the reverse direction. For example, any given first or last name may be associated with more than one customer number. (It would be unusual to have a customer table of any size without some duplication of names.)

The functional dependencies in the orders table are:

```
Customer_numb -> first_name, last_name, street, city,
  state, zip, phone
Item_numb -> title, price
Order_numb -> customer_numb, order_date
Item_numb + order_numb -> has_shipped?
```

Notice that there is one determinant for each entity in the relation and the determinant is what we have chosen as the entity identifier. Notice also that when an entity has a concatenated identifier, the determinant is also concatenated. In this example, whether an item has shipped depends on the combination of the item and the order.

Using Functional Dependencies to Reach 2NF

If you have correctly identified the functional dependencies among the attributes in a database environment, then you can use them to create second normal form relations. Each determinant becomes the primary key of a relation. All the attributes that are functionally dependent on it become non-key attributes in the relation.

The original orders relation should be broken into the following four relations:

```
Customer (customer_numb, first_name, last_name,
  street, city, state, zip, phone)
Item (item_numb, title, price)
```

```
Order (order_numb, customer_numb, order_date)
Order items (order_numb, item_numb, has_shipped?)
```

Each of these should in turn correspond to a single entity in your ER diagram.

> *Note:* When it comes to deciding what is driving database design—functional dependencies or entities—it is really a "chicken and egg" situation. What is most important is that there is consistency between the ER diagram and the functional dependencies you identify in your relations. It makes no difference whether you design by looking for functional dependencies or for entities. In most cases, database design is an iterative process in which you create an initial design, check it, modify it, and check it again. You can look at either functional dependencies and/or entities at any stage in the process, checking one against the other for consistency.

The relations we have created from the original orders relation have eliminated the anomalies present in the original:

- It is now possible to insert data about a customer before the customer places an order.
- It is now possible to insert data about an order before we know an item on the order.
- It is now possible to store data about merchandise items before they are ordered.
- Line items can be deleted from an order without affecting data describing that item, the order itself, or the merchandise item.
- Data describing the customer are stored only once, and therefore any change to those data needs to be made only once. A modification anomaly cannot occur.

Problems with 2NF Relations

Although second normal form eliminates problems from many relations, you will occasionally run into relations that are in second normal form yet still exhibit anomalies. Assume, for example, that each new DVD title that Antique Opticals carries comes from one distributor and that each distributor has only one warehouse that has only one phone number. The following relation is therefore in second normal form:

```
Item (item_numb, title, distrib_numb,
  warehouse_phone_number)
```

For each item number, there is only one value for the item's title, distributor, and warehouse phone number. However, there is one insertion anomaly: You cannot insert data about a distributor until you have an item from that distributor. There is one deletion anomaly: If you delete the only item from a distributor, you lose data about the distributor. There is also a modification anomaly: The distributor's warehouse phone number is duplicated for every item the company gets from that distributor. The relation is in second normal form but not third.

THIRD NORMAL FORM

Third normal form is designed to handle situations like the one you just read about in the preceding section. In terms of entities, the item relation does contain two entities: the merchandise item and the distributor. That alone should convince you that the relation needs to be broken down into two smaller relations, both of which are now in third normal form:

```
Item (item_numb, distrib_numb)
Distributor (distrib_numb, warehouse_phone_number)
```

The theoretical definition of third normal form says:

1. The relation is in second normal form.
2. There are no transitive dependencies.

The functional dependencies found in the original relation are an example of a *transitive dependency*.

Transitive Dependencies

A transitive dependency exists when you have the following functional dependency pattern:

$$A \rightarrow B \text{ and } B \rightarrow C\text{; therefore } A \rightarrow C$$

This is precisely the case with the original items relation. The only reason that the warehouse phone number is functionally dependent on the item number is because the distributor is functionally dependent on the item number and the phone number is functionally dependent on the distributor. The functional dependencies are really:

```
Item_numb -> distrib_numb
Distrib_numb -> warehouse_phone_number
```

Note: Transitive dependencies take their name from the transitive property in mathematics, which states that if a > b and b > c, then a > c.

There are two determinants in the original items relation, each of which should be the primary key of its own relation. However, it is not merely the presence of the second determinant that creates the transitive dependency. What really matters is that the second determinant is not a candidate key for the relation.

Consider for example, this relation:

```
Item (item_numb, UPC, distrib_numb, price)
```

The item number is an arbitrary number that Antique Opticals assigns to each merchandise item. The UPC is an industry-wide code that is unique to each item as well. The functional dependencies in this relation are:

```
Item_numb -> UPC, distrib_numb, price
UPC -> item_numb, distrib_numb, price
```

Is there a transitive dependency here? No, because the second determinant is a candidate key. (Antique Opticals could have just as easily used the UPC as the primary key.) There are no insertion, deletion, or modification anomalies in this relation; it describes only one entity: the merchandise item.

A transitive dependency therefore exists only when the determinant that is not the primary key is not a candidate key for the relation. In the items table we have been using, for example, the distributor is a determinant but not a candidate key for the table. (There can be more than one item coming from a single distributor.)

When you have a transitive dependency in a 2NF relation, you should break the relation into two smaller relations, each of which has one of the determinants in the transitive dependency as its primary key. The attributes determined by the determinant become non-key attributes in each relation. This removes the transitive dependency—and its associated anomalies—and places the relation in third normal form.

Note: A second normal form relation that has no transitive dependencies is, of course, automatically in third normal form.

BOYCE-CODD NORMAL FORM

For most relations, third normal form is a good design objective. Relations in that state are free of most anomalies. However, occasionally you run into relations that exhibit special characteristics where anomalies still occur. Boyce-Codd normal form (BCNF), fourth normal form (4NF), and fifth normal form (5NF) were created to handle such special situations.

Note: If your relations are in third normal form and do not exhibit the special characteristics that BCNF, 4NF, and 5NF were designed to handle, then they are automatically in 5NF.

The easiest way to understand BCNF is to start with an example. Assume that Antique Opticals decides to add a relation to its database to handle employee work scheduling. Each employee works one or two 4-hour shifts a day at the store. During each shift, an employee is assigned to one station (a place in the store, such as the front desk or the stockroom). Only one employee works a station during the given shift.

A relation to handle the schedule might be designed as follows:

```
Schedule (employee_ID, date, shift, station,
  worked_shift?)
```

Given the rules for the scheduling (one person per station per shift), there are two possible primary keys for this relation:

```
employee_ID + date + shift or date + shift +
  station
```

The functional dependencies in the relation are:

```
employee_ID + date + shift -> station, worked_shift?
date + shift + stations -> employee_ID,
  worked_shift?
```

Keep in mind that this holds true only because there is only one person working each station during each shift.

Note: There is very little difference between the two candidate keys as far as the choice of a primary key is concerned. In cases like this, you can choose either one.

This schedule relation exhibits overlapping candidate keys. (Both candidate keys have date and shift in common.) Boyce-Codd normal form was designed to deal with relations that exhibit this characteristic. To be in Boyce-Codd normal form, a relation must meet the following rules:

1. The relation must be in third normal form.
2. All determinants must be candidate keys.

BCNF is considered to be a more general way of looking at 3NF because it includes those relations with the overlapping candidate keys. The sample schedule relation we have been considering does meet the criteria for BCNF because the two determinants are indeed candidate keys.

FOURTH NORMAL FORM

Like BCNF, fourth normal form was designed to handle relations that exhibit a special characteristic that does not arise too often. In this case, the special characteristic is something known as a *multivalued dependency*.

As an example, consider the following relation:

```
movie info (title, star, producer)
```

A given movie can have more than one star; it can also have more than one producer. The same star can appear in more than one movie; a producer can also work on more than one movie (for example, see the instance in Figure 6-5). The relation must therefore include all columns in its key.

Title	Star	Producer
Great Film	Lovely Lady	Money Bags
Great Film	Handsome Man	Money Bags
Great Film	Lovely Lady	Helen Pursestrings
Great Film	Handsome Man	Helen Pursestrings
Boring Movie	Lovely Lady	Helen Pursestrings
Boring Movie	Precocious Child	Helen Pursestrings

■ **FIGURE 6-5** A relation with a multivalued dependency.

Because there are no non-key attributes, this relation is in BCNF. Nonetheless, the relation exhibits anomalies:

- You cannot insert the stars of a movie without knowing at least one producer.
- You cannot insert the producer of a movie without knowing at least one star.
- If you delete the only producer from a movie, you lose information about the stars.
- If you delete the only star from a movie, you lose information about its producers.
- Each producer's name is duplicated for every star in the movie. By the same token, each star's name is duplicated for each producer of the movie. These unnecessary duplicated data form the basis of a modification anomaly.

There are at least two unrelated entities in this relation: one that handles the relationship between a movie and its stars and another that handles the relationship between a movie and its producers. In a practical sense, that is the cause of the anomalies. (Arguably, there are also movie, star, and producer entities involved.)

However, in a theoretical sense, the anomalies are caused by the presence of a multivalued dependency in the same relation, which must be eliminated to get to fourth normal form. The rules for fourth normal form are:

1. The relation is in Boyce-Codd normal form.
2. There are no multivalued dependencies.

Multivalued Dependencies

A multivalued dependency exists when for each value of attribute A, there exists a finite set of values of both attribute B and attribute C that are associated with it. Attributes B and C, however, are independent of each other. In the example that we have been using, there is just such a dependency. First, for each movie title, there is a group of actors (the stars) who are associated with the movie. For each title, there is also a group of producers who are associated with it. However, the actors and the producers are independent of one another.

Note: At this point, do not let semantics get in the way of database theory. Yes, it is true that producers fund the movies in which the actors are starring, but in terms of database relationships, there is no direct connection between the two.

The multivalued dependency can be written:

title —>> star

title —>> producer

and read "title multidetermines star and title multidetermines producer."

Note: To be strictly accurate, a functional dependency is a special case of a multivalued dependency, where what is being determined is one value rather than a group of values.

To eliminate the multivalued dependency and bring this relation into fourth normal form, you split the relation, placing each part of the dependency in its own relation:

```
movie_stars (title, star)
movie_producers (title, producer)
```

With this design, you can independently insert and remove stars and producers without affecting the other. Star and producer names also appear only once for each movie with which they are involved.

FIFTH NORMAL FORM

Fifth normal form—also known as projection-join normal form—is designed to handle a general case of a multivalued dependency, known as a *join dependency*. Before we can consider 5NF, we must therefore look at the *relational algebra* operations project and join.

Note: Relational algebra is a set of operations used to manipulate and extract data from relations. Each operation performs a single manipulation of one or two tables. To complete a query, a DBMS uses a sequence of relational algebra operations; relational algebra is therefore procedural. It is not used directly by people using a database but instead is a tool used by the DBMS.

Projections and Joins

When you split relations during the normalization process, you are actually creating a relational algebra projection. Join combines tables on matching attributes and is used extensively in queries to match data based on primary and foreign keys.

Projection

The project operation creates a subset of any relation by extracting specified columns. It makes no provision for choosing rows: You get all of them. The theoretical project operation removes duplicate rows so that the result is a legal relation.

As an example, consider the following relation that you saw earlier in this chapter:

```
Item (item_numb, UPC, distrib_numb, price)
```

We can make a number of projections, all of which are legal relations:

```
(item_numb, UPC)
(item_numb, distrib_numb)
(item_numb, price)
(UPC, distrib_numb)
(UPC, price)
(distrib_numb, price)
(item_numb, UPC, distrib_numb)
(item_numb, UPC, price)
(UPC, distrib_numb, price)
```

Equi-Join

In its most common form, a join forms new rows when data in the two source tables match. Because we are looking for rows with equal values, this type of join is known as an *equi-join* (or a *natural equi-join*). As an example, consider the two tables in Figure 6-6. Notice that the customer number column is the primary key of the Customers table and that the same column is a foreign key in the Orders table. The customer number column in orders therefore serves to relate orders to the customers to which they belong.

Assume that you wanted to see the names of the customers who placed each order. To do so, you must join the two tables, creating combined rows wherever there is a matching customer number. In database terminology, we are joining the two tables "over" the customer number. The result table can be found in Figure 6-7.

Customers

customer_numb	first_name	last_name
001	Jane	Doe
002	John	Doe
003	Jane	Smith
004	John	Smith
005	Jane	Jones
006	John	Jones

Orders

order_numb	customer_numb	order_date	order_total
1001	002	10/10/09	250.85
1002	002	2/21/10	125.89
1003	003	11/15/09	1567.99
1004	004	11/22/09	180.92
1005	004	12/15/09	565.00
1006	006	11/22/09	25.00
1007	006	10/8/09	85.00
1008	006	12/29/09	109.12

■ **FIGURE 6-6** Two tables with a primary key-foreign key relationship.

Result Table

customer_numb	first_name	last_name	order_numb	order_date	order_total
002	John	Doe	1001	10/10/09	250.65
002	John	Doe	1002	2/21/10	125.89
003	Jane	Smith	1003	11/15/09	1597.99
004	John	Smith	1004	11/22/09	180.92
004	John	Smith	1005	12/15/09	565.00
006	John	Jones	1006	11/22/09	25.00
006	John	Jones	1007	10/8/09	85.00
006	John	Jones	1008	12/29/09	109.12

■ **FIGURE 6-7** The joined table.

An equi-join can begin with either source table. (The result should be the same regardless of the direction in which the join is performed.) The join compares each row in one source table with the row in the second. For each row in the first source table that matches data in the second source table in the column or columns over which the join is being performed a new row is placed in the result table.

Assuming that we are using the customers table as the first source table, producing the result table in Figure 6-7 might therefore proceed conceptually as follows:

1. Search orders for rows with a customer number of 001. Because there are now matching rows in orders, do not place a row in the result table.
2. Search orders for rows with a customer number of 002. There are two matching rows in orders. Create two new rows in the result table, placing the same customer information at the end of each row in orders.
3. Search orders for rows with a customer number of 003. There is one matching row in orders. Place one new row in the result table.
4. Search orders for rows with a customer number of 004. There are two matching rows in orders. Place two rows in the result table.
5. Search orders for rows with a customer number of 005. There are no matching rows in orders. Therefore, do not place a row in the result table.
6. Search orders for rows with a customer number of 006. There are three matching rows in orders. Place three rows in the result table.

Notice that if a customer number does not appear in both tables, then no row is placed in the result table. This behavior categorizes this type of join as an *inner join*.

Understanding 5NF

Now that you know how the project and join operations work, we can take a look at fifth normal form. As an example, consider the following relation:

```
Selections (customer_numb, series, item_numb)
```

This relation represents various series of discs, such as Spider-Man or Rambo. Customers place orders for a series; when a customer orders a series, he or she must take all items in that series. Determining fifth normal form becomes relevant only when this type of rule is in place. If customers could request selected titles from a series, then the relation would be fine. Because it would be all-key, it would automatically fall through the normal form rules to 5NF.

Customer Number	Series	Item Number
1005	Star Wars	2090
1005	Star Wars	2091
1005	Star Wars	2092
1005	Star Wars	4689
1005	Star Wars	4690
1005	Star Wars	4691
1010	Harry Potter	3200
1010	Harry Potter	3201
1010	Harry Potter	3202
1010	Harry Potter	3203
1010	Harry Potter	3204
2180	Star Wars	2090
2180	Star Wars	2091
2180	Star Wars	2092
2180	Star Wars	4689
2180	Star Wars	4690
2180	Star Wars	4691

■ **FIGURE 6-8** A relation in 4NF but not 5NF.

To make the problems with this table under the preceding rule clearer, consider the instance of the relation in Figure 6-8. Because this table is all-key, it is automatically in fourth normal form. However, there is a great deal of unnecessary duplicated data in this relation. For example, the item numbers are repeated for every customer that orders a given series. The series name is also repeated for every item in the series and for every customer ordering that series. This relation is therefore prone to modification anomalies.

There is also a more subtle issue: Under the rules of this relation, if customer 2180 orders the first Harry Potter movie and indicates that he or she would like more movies in the series, then the only way to put that choice in the table is to add rows for all five Harry Potter movies. You may be forced to add rows that you don't want to add and introduce data that aren't accurate.

Note: There is no official term for the preceding anomaly. It is precisely the opposite of the insertion anomalies described earlier in this chapter, although it does involve a problem with inserting data.

By the same token, if a customer doesn't want one item in a series, then you must remove from the table all the rows for that customer for that series. If the customer still wants the remaining items in the series, then you have a deletion anomaly.

As you might guess, you can solve the problem by breaking the table into two smaller tables, eliminating the unnecessary duplicated data and the insertion and deletion anomalies:

```
series_subscription (customer_numb, series)
series_content (series, item_numb)
```

The official definition for 5NF is:

1. The relation is in fourth normal form.
2. All join dependencies are implied by the candidate keys.

A join dependency occurs when a table can be put together correctly by joining two or more tables, all of which contain only attributes from the original table. The original selections relation does have a join dependency because it can be created by joining the series subscription and series content relations. The join is valid only because of the rule that requires a customer to order all of the items in a series.

A join dependency is implied by candidate keys when all possible projections from the original relation that form a join dependency are candidate keys for the original relation. For example, the following projections can be made from the selections relation:

```
A: (customer_numb, series)
B: (customer_numb, item_numb)
C: (series, item_numb)
```

We can regenerate the selections relation by combining any two of the preceding relations. Therefore, the join dependencies are A + B, A + C, B + C, and A + B + C. Like other relational algebra operations, the join theoretically removes duplicate rows, so although the raw result of the join contains extra rows, they will be removed from the result, producing the original table.

> *Note:* One of the problems with 5NF is that as the number of columns in a table increases, the number of possible projections increases exponentially. It can therefore be very difficult to determine 5NF for a large relation.

However, each of the projections is not a candidate key for the selections relation. All three columns from the original relation are required for a candidate key. Therefore, the relation is not in 5NF. When we break down the selections relation into series_selections and series_content, we eliminate the join dependencies, ensuring that the relations are in 5NF.

SIXTH NORMAL FORM

Normalization theory has been very stable for nearly 40 years. However, in the late 1990s, C.J. Date, one of the foremost experts in database theory, proposed sixth normal form, particularly to handle situations in which there is temporal data. However, this is not technically a project-join normal form like the others we discussed earlier in this chapter.

Consider the following relation:

```
customers (ID, valid interval, street, city, state,
  zip, phone)
```

The intent of this relation is to maintain a history of a customer's location and when they were valid (starting date to ending date). Depending on the circumstances, there may be a great deal of duplicated data in this relation (for example, if only the phone number changed) or very little (for example, if there is a move to a new state with a new phone number). Nonetheless, there is only one functional dependency in the relation:

ID + valid_interval → street, city, state, zip, phone)

There are no transitive dependencies, no overlapping candidate keys, no multivalued dependencies, and all join dependencies are implied by the candidate key(s). The relation is therefore in fifth normal form.

Sixth normal form was created to handle the situation where temporal data vary independently to avoid unnecessary duplication. The result is tables that cannot be decomposed any further; in most cases, the tables include the primary key and a single non-key attribute. The sixth normal form tables for the sample customers relation would be as follows:

```
street_addresses (ID, valid interval, street)
cities (ID, valid interval, city)
states (ID, valid interval, state)
```

```
zip_codes (ID, valid interval, zip)
phone_numbers (ID, valid interval, phone)
```

The resulting tables eliminate the possibility of redundant data but introduce some time-consuming joins to find a customer's current address or to assemble a history for a customer.

Going to sixth normal form may also introduce the need for a *circular inclusion constraint*. There is little point in including a street address for a customer unless a city, state, and zip code exist for the same date interval. The circular inclusion constraint would therefore require that if a row for any given interval and any given customer ID exists in any of street_addresses, cities, states, or zip_codes, matching rows must exist in all of those tables. Today's relational DBMSs do not support circular inclusion constraints, nor are they included in the current SQL standard. If such a constraint is necessary, it will need to be enforced through application code.

FOR FURTHER READING

There are many books available that deal with the theory of relational databases. You can find useful supplementary information in the following:

Chapple, Mike. "Database Normalization Basics"; available at *http://databases.about.com/od/specificproducts/a/normalization.htm*

Date, C. J. "On DN/NF Normal Form"; available at *www.dbdebunk.com/page/page/621935.htm*

Date, C. J., Hugh Darwen, and Nikos Lorentzos. *Temporal Data and the Relational Model*. Morgan Kaufmann, 2002.

Earp, Richard. *Database Design Using Entity-Relationship Diagrams*. Taylor & Frances, 2007.

Halpin, Terry, and Tony Morgan. *Information Modeling and Relational Databases*, 2nd ed. Morgan Kaufmann, 2008.

Hillyer, Mike. "An Introduction to Database Normalization"; available at *http://dev.mysql.com/tech-resources/articles/intro-to-normalization.html*

Olivé, Antoni. *Conceptual Modeling of Information Systems*. Springer, 2007.

Pratt, Philip J., and Joseph J. Adamski. *Concepts of Database Management*, 6th ed. Course Technology, 2007.

Ritchie, Colin. *Database Principles and Design*, 3rd ed. Cengage Learning Business Press, 2008.

Wise, Barry. "Database Normalization and Design Techniques"; available at *www.barrywise.com/2008/01/database-normalization-and-design-techniques/*

Chapter 7

Database Structure and Performance Tuning

How long are you willing to wait for a computer to respond to your request for information? 30 seconds? 10 seconds? 5 seconds? In truth, we humans aren't very patient at all. Even five seconds can seem like an eternity when you're waiting for something to appear on the screen. A database that has a slow response time to user queries usually means that you will have dissatisfied users.

Slow response times can be the result of any number of problems. You might be dealing with a client workstation that isn't properly configured, a poorly written application program, a query involving multiple join operations, a query that requires reading amounts of data from disk, a congested network, or even a DBMS that isn't robust enough to handle the volume of queries submitted to it.

One of the duties of a *database administrator* (DBA) is to optimize database performance (also known as *performance tuning*). This includes modifying the design—where possible—to avoid performance bottlenecks, especially involving queries.

For the most part, a DBMS takes care of storing and retrieving data based on a user's commands without human intervention. The strategy used to process a data manipulation request is handled by the DBMS's *query optimizer*, a portion of the program that determines the most efficient sequence of relational algebra operations to perform a query.

Although most of the query optimizer's choices are out of the hands of a database designer or application developer, you can influence the behavior of the query optimizer and also optimize database performance to some extent with database design elements. In this chapter you will be introduced to several such techniques.

JOINS AND DATABASE PERFORMANCE

In Chapter 6 we discussed the use of joins as part of the theory of relational database design. Joins, however, can also have a major impact on query performance. The extent of the impact depends on your DBMS and how it implements a join.

From a relational algebra point of view, a join can be implemented using two other operations: product and restrict. As you will see, this sequence of operations requires the manipulation of a great deal of data and, if used by a DBMS, can result in very slow query performance.

The restrict operation retrieves rows from a table by matching each row against logical criteria (a *predicate*). Those rows that meet the criteria are placed in the result table, and those that do not meet the criteria are omitted. Restrict, which was originally called select, cannot choose columns; you get every column in the table.

> *Note:* The confusion with the term *select* arises because the SQL query command is also "select." The SQL select is a command that triggers many relational algebra operations, some of which are determined by the DBMS rather than the user.

The product operation (the mathematical Cartesian product) makes every possible pairing of rows from two source tables. In Figure 7-1, for example, the product of the customer and order tables that you saw in Chapter 6 produces a result table with 48 rows (6 customers times the 8 orders). The customer number column appears twice because it is part of both source tables.

> *Note:* Although 48 rows might not seem like a lot, consider the size of a product table created from tables with 1000 or even 10,000 rows! The manipulation of a table of this size can tie up a lot of disk I/O and CPU time.

In some rows, the customer number is the same. These are the rows that should be included in a join. We can therefore apply a restrict

customer_numb (customer)	first_name	last_name	Customer_numb (order)	order_numb	Order_date	Order_total
001	Jane	Doe	002	1001	10/10/09	250.65
001	Jane	Doe	002	1002	2/21/10	125.89
001	Jane	Doe	003	1003	11/15/09	1597.99
001	Jane	Doe	004	1004	11/22/09	180,92
001	Jane	Doe	004	1005	12/15/09	565.00
001	Jane	Doe	006	1006	10/8/09	25.00
001	Jane	Doe	006	1007	11/12/09	85.00
001	Jane	Doe	006	1008	12/29/09	125.90
002	John	Doe	002	1001	10/10/09	250.65
002	John	Doe	002	1002	2/21/10	125.89
002	John	Doe	003	1003	11/15/09	1597.99
002	John	Doe	004	1004	11/22/09	180,92
002	John	Doe	004	1005	12/15/09	565.00
002	John	Doe	006	1006	10/8/09	25.00
002	John	Doe	006	1007	11/12/09	85.00
002	John	Doe	006	1008	12/29/09	125.90
003	Jane	Smith	002	1001	10/10/09	250.65
003	Jane	Smith	002	1002	2/21/10	125.89
003	Jane	Smith	003	1003	11/15/09	1597.99
003	Jane	Smith	004	1004	11/22/09	180,92
003	Jane	Smith	004	1005	12/15/09	565.00
003	Jane	Smith	006	1006	10/8/09	25.00
003	Jane	Smith	006	1007	11/12/09	85.00
003	Jane	Smith	006	1008	12/29/09	125.90
004	John	Smith	002	1001	10/10/09	250.65
004	John	Smith	002	1002	2/21/10	125.89
004	John	Smith	003	1003	11/15/09	1597.99
004	John	Smith	004	1004	11/22/09	180,92
004	John	Smith	004	1005	12/15/09	565.00
004	John	Smith	006	1006	10/8/09	25.00
004	John	Smith	006	1007	11/12/09	85.00
004	John	Smith	006	1008	12/29/09	125.90
005	Jane	Jones	002	1001	10/10/09	250.65
005	Jane	Jones	002	1002	2/21/10	125.89
005	Jane	Jones	003	1003	11/15/09	1597.99
005	Jane	Jones	004	1004	11/22/09	180,92
005	Jane	Jones	004	1005	12/15/09	565.00
005	Jane	Jones	006	1006	10/8/09	25.00
005	Jane	Jones	006	1007	11/12/09	85.00
005	Jane	Jones	006	1008	12/29/09	125.90
006	John	Jones	002	1001	10/10/09	250.65
006	John	Jones	002	1002	2/21/10	125.89
006	John	Jones	003	1003	11/15/09	1597.99
006	John	Jones	004	1004	11/22/09	180,92
006	John	Jones	004	1005	12/15/09	565.00
006	John	Jones	006	1006	10/8/09	25.00
006	John	Jones	006	1007	11/12/09	85.00
006	John	Jones	006	1008	12/29/09	125.90

■ **FIGURE 7-1** The product of the customer and order tables.

predicate to the product table to end up with the same table provided by the join you saw in Chapter 6. The predicate's logical condition can be written:

```
customer.customer_numb = order.customer_numb
```

The rows that are chosen by this predicate appear in boldface in Figure 7-2; those eliminated by the predicate are in regular type. Notice that the boldface rows are exactly the same as those in the result table of the join from Chapter 6.

Note: Although this may seem like a highly inefficient way to implement a join, it is actually quite flexible, in particular because the relationship between the columns over which the join is being performed doesn't have to be equal. A user could just as easily request a join where the value in table A is greater than the value in table B.

Because of the processing overhead created when performing joins in this way, some database designers make a conscious decision to leave tables unnormalized. For example, if Antique Opticals always accessed the line items at the same time it accessed order information, then a designer might choose to combine the order item and order data into one table, knowing full well that the unnormalized relation exhibits anomalies. The benefit is that the retrieval of order information will be faster than if it were split into two tables.

Should you leave unnormalized relations in your database to achieve better retrieval performance? In this author's opinion, there is rarely any need to do so. First, not all DBMSs implement a join in this way. Before you decide not to normalize tables, investigate how your DBMS performs a join. In addition, there are ways to prepare SQL queries (in particular, using uncorrelated subqueries) that can produce the same result as a join but without actually performing the join. That being the case, it does not seem worth the problems that unnormalized relations present to leave them in the database. Careful writing of retrieval queries can provide performance that is nearly as good as that of retrieval from unnormalized relations.

Note: For a complete discussion of writing SQL queries to avoid joins, see the author's book *SQL Clearly Explained*, also published by Morgan Kaufmann.

customer_numb (customer)	first_name	last_name	Customer_numb (order)	order_numb	Order_date	Order_total
001	Jane	Doe	002	1001	10/10/09	250.65
001	Jane	Doe	002	1002	2/21/10	125.89
001	Jane	Doe	003	1003	11/15/09	1597.99
001	Jane	Doe	004	1004	11/22/09	180,92
001	Jane	Doe	004	1005	12/15/09	565.00
001	Jane	Doe	006	1006	10/8/09	25.00
001	Jane	Doe	006	1007	11/12/09	85.00
001	Jane	Doe	006	1008	12/29/09	125.90
002	**John**	**Doe**	**002**	**1001**	**10/10/09**	**250.65**
002	**John**	**Doe**	**002**	**1002**	**2/21/10**	**125.89**
002	John	Doe	003	1003	11/15/09	1597.99
002	John	Doe	004	1004	11/22/09	180,92
002	John	Doe	004	1005	12/15/09	565.00
002	John	Doe	006	1006	10/8/09	25.00
002	John	Doe	006	1007	11/12/09	85.00
002	John	Doe	006	1008	12/29/09	125.90
003	Jane	Smith	002	1001	10/10/09	250.65
003	Jane	Smith	002	1002	2/21/10	125.89
003	**Jane**	**Smith**	**003**	**1003**	**11/15/09**	**1597.99**
003	Jane	Smith	004	1004	11/22/09	180,92
003	Jane	Smith	004	1005	12/15/09	565.00
003	Jane	Smith	006	1006	10/8/09	25.00
003	Jane	Smith	006	1007	11/12/09	85.00
003	Jane	Smith	006	1008	12/29/09	125.90
004	John	Smith	002	1001	10/10/09	250.65
004	John	Smith	002	1002	2/21/10	125.89
004	John	Smith	003	1003	11/15/09	1597.99
004	**John**	**Smith**	**004**	**1004**	**11/22/09**	**180,92**
004	**John**	**Smith**	**004**	**1005**	**12/15/09**	**565.00**
004	John	Smith	006	1006	10/8/09	25.00
004	John	Smith	006	1007	11/12/09	85.00
004	John	Smith	006	1008	12/29/09	125.90
005	Jane	Jones	002	1001	10/10/09	250.65
005	Jane	Jones	002	1002	2/21/10	125.89
005	Jane	Jones	003	1003	11/15/09	1597.99
005	Jane	Jones	004	1004	11/22/09	180,92
005	Jane	Jones	004	1005	12/15/09	565.00
005	Jane	Jones	006	1006	10/8/09	25.00
005	Jane	Jones	006	1007	11/12/09	85.00
005	Jane	Jones	006	1008	12/29/09	125.90
006	John	Jones	002	1001	10/10/09	250.65
006	John	Jones	002	1002	2/21/10	125.89
006	John	Jones	003	1003	11/15/09	1597.99
006	John	Jones	004	1004	11/22/09	180,92
006	John	Jones	004	1005	12/15/09	565.00
006	**John**	**Jones**	**006**	**1006**	**10/8/09**	**25.00**
006	**John**	**Jones**	**006**	**1007**	**11/12/09**	**85.00**
006	**John**	**Jones**	**006**	**1008**	**12/29/09**	**125.90**

■ **FIGURE 7-2** The product of the customer and orders tables after applying a restrict predicate.

INDEXING

Indexing is a way of providing a fast access path to the values of a column or a concatenation of columns. New rows are typically added to the bottom of a table, resulting in a relatively random order of the values in any given column. Without some way of ordering the data, the only way the DBMS can search a column is by sequentially scanning each row from top to bottom. The larger a table becomes, the slower a sequential search will be.

Note: On average, in a table of N rows, a sequential search will need to examine N/2 rows to find a row that matches a query predicate. However, the only way for the DBMS to determine that no rows match the predicate is to examine all N rows. A table with 1000 rows requires on average looking at 500 rows; an unsuccessful search requires consulting all 1000 rows. However, the fast searching techniques provided by indexes require looking at about six rows to find a matching row; an unsuccessful search requires consulting about ten rows.

The alternative to indexing for ordering the rows in a table is sorting. A *sort* physically alters the position of rows in a table, placing the rows in order starting with the first row in the table. Most SQL implementations do sort the virtual tables that are created as the result of queries when directed to do so by the SQL query. However, SQL provides no way to sort base tables, and there is good reason for this. Regardless of the sorting method used, as a table grows large (hundreds of thousands to millions of rows), sorting takes a very long time.

Keeping a table in sorted order also means that on average half of the rows in the table will need to be moved to make room for a new row. In addition, searching a sorted base table takes longer than searching an index, primarily because the index search requires less disk access. The overhead in maintaining indexes is far less than that required to sort base tables whenever a specific data order is needed.

The conceptual operation of an index is diagrammed in Figure 7-3. (The different weights of the lines have no significance other than to make it easier for you to follow the crossed lines.) This illustration shows Antique Opticals' item relation and an index that provides fast access to rows in the table based on the item's title. The index itself contains an ordered list of keys (the titles) along with the locations of the associated rows in the item table. The rows in the item table are

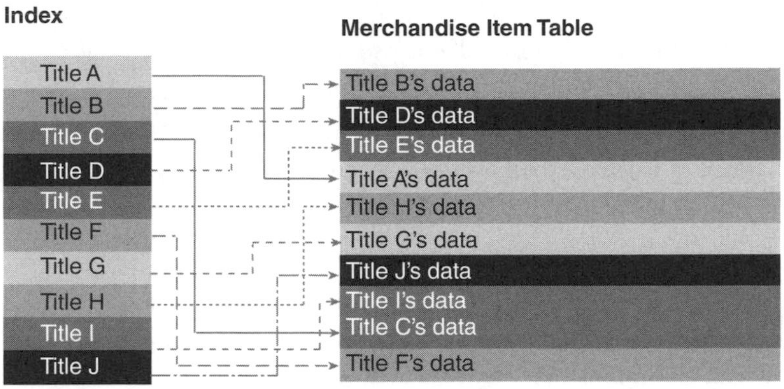

■ **FIGURE 7-3** Indexing.

in relatively random order. However, because the index is in alphabetical order by title, it can be searched quickly to locate a specific title. Then the DBMS can use the information in the index to go directly to the correct row or rows in the item table, thus avoiding a slow sequential search of the base table's rows.

Once you have created an index, the DBMS's query optimizer will use the index whenever it determines that using the index will speed up data retrieval. You never need to access the index again yourself unless you want to delete it.

When you create a primary key for a table, the DBMS automatically creates an index for that table, using the primary key column or columns in the primary key as the index key. The first step in inserting a new row into a table is therefore verification that the index key (the primary key of the table) is unique in the index. In fact, uniqueness is enforced by requiring the index entries to be unique, rather than by actually searching the base table. This is much faster than attempting to verify uniqueness directly on the base table because the ordered index can be searched much more rapidly than the unordered base table.

Deciding Which Indexes to Create

You have no choice as to whether the DBMS creates indexes for your primary keys; you get them whether you want them or not. In addition, you can create indexes on any column or combination of columns you want. However, before you jump headfirst into creating indexes on every column in every table, you must consider some trade-offs:

- Indexes take up space in the database. Given that disk space is relatively inexpensive today, this is usually not a major drawback.
- When you insert, modify, or delete data in indexed columns, the DBMS must update the index as well as the base table. This may slow down data modification operations, especially if the tables have a lot of rows.
- Indexes definitely speed up access to data.

The trade-off is therefore generally between update speed and retrieval speed. A good rule of thumb is to create indexes for foreign keys and for other columns that are used frequently for queries that apply criteria to data. If you find that update speed is severely affected, you may choose at a later time to delete some of the indexes you created.

Also avoid indexes on columns that contain *nondiscriminatory* data. Nondiscriminatory columns have only a few values throughout the entire table, such as Boolean columns that contain only true and false. Gender (male or female) is also nondiscriminatory. Although you may search on a column containing nondiscriminatory data—for example, a search for all open orders—an index will not provide much performance enhancement because the DBMS must examine so many keys to complete the query.

CLUSTERING

The slowest part of a DBMS's actions is retrieving data from or writing data to a disk. If you can cut down on the number of times the DBMS must read from or write to a disk, you can speed up overall database performance. The trick to doing this is understanding that a database must retrieve an entire disk page of data at one time.

The size of a page varies from one computing platform to another; it can be anywhere from 512 bytes to 4 K, with 1 K being typical on a PC. Data always travel to and from disk in page-sized units. Therefore, if you store data that are often accessed together on the same disk page (or pages that are physically close together), you can speed up data access. This process is known as *clustering* and is available with many large DBMSs (for example, Oracle).

> *Note:* The term *clustering* has another meaning in the SQL standard. It refers to groups of catalogs (which in turn are groups of schemas) manipulated by the same DBMS. The use of the term in this section, however, is totally distinct from the SQL meaning.

In practice, a cluster is designed to keep together rows related by matching primary and foreign keys. To define the cluster, you specify a column or columns on which the DBMS should form the cluster and the tables that should be included. Then, all of the rows that share the same value of the column or columns on which the cluster is based are stored as physically close together as possible. As a result, the rows in a table may be scattered across several disk pages, but matching primary and foreign keys are usually on the same disk page.

Clustering can significantly speed up join performance. However, just as with indexes, there are some trade-offs to consider when contemplating creating clusters:

- Because clustering involves physical placement of data in a file, a table can be clustered on only one column or combination of columns.
- Clustering can slow down performance of operations that require a scan of the entire table because clustering may mean that the rows of any given table are scattered throughout many disk pages.
- Clustering can slow down insertion of data
- Clustering can slow down modifying data in the columns on which the clustering is based.

PARTITIONING

Partitioning is the opposite of clustering. It involves the splitting of large tables into smaller ones so that the DBMS does not need to retrieve as much data at any one time. Consider, for example, what happens to Antique Opticals' order and order items tables over time. Assuming that the business is reasonably successful, those tables (especially order items) will become very large. Retrieval of data from those tables will therefore begin to slow down. It would speed up retrieval of open orders if filled orders and their items could be separated from open orders and their items.

There are two ways to partition a table: horizontally and vertically. *Horizontal partitioning* involves splitting the rows of a table between two or more tables with identical structures. *Vertical partitioning* involves dividing the columns of a table and placing them in two or more tables linked by the original table's primary key. As you might expect, there are advantages and disadvantages to both.

Horizontal Partitioning

Horizontal partitioning involves creating two or more tables with exactly the same structure and splitting rows between those tables. Antique Opticals might use this technique to solve the problem with the order and order items tables becoming increasingly large. The database design might be modified as follows:

```
open_order (order_numb, customer_numb, order_date)
open_order_items (order_numb, item_numb, quantity,
  shipped?)
filled_order (order_numb, customer_numb, order_date)
filled_order_items (order_numb, item_numb, quantity,
  shipped?)
```

Whenever all items in an open order have shipped, an application program deletes rows from the open order and open order items table and inserts them into the filled order and filled order items table. The open order and open order items tables remain relatively small, speeding up both retrieval and modification performance. Although retrieval from filled order and filled order lines will be slower, Antique Opticals uses those tables much less frequently.

The drawback to this solution occurs when Antique Opticals needs to access all of the orders and/or order items at the same time. A query whose result table includes data from both sets of open and filled tables must actually be two queries connected by the union operator. (The union operation creates one table by merging the rows of two tables with the same structure.) Performance of such a query will be worse than that of a query of either set of tables individually. Nonetheless, if an analysis of Antique Opticals' data access patterns reveals that such queries occur rarely and that most retrieval involves the open set of tables, then the horizontal partitioning is worth doing.

The only way you can determine whether horizontal partitioning will increase performance is to examine the ways in which your database applications access data. If there is a group of rows that are accessed together significantly more frequently than the rest of the rows in a table, then horizontal partitioning may make sense.

Vertical Partitioning

Vertical partitioning involves creating two or more tables with selected columns and all rows of a table. For example, if Antique Opticals accesses the titles and prices of their merchandise items more frequently than the other columns in the item table, the item table might be partitioned as follows:

```
item_titles (item_numb, title, price)
item_details (item_numb, distributor, release_date,
  . . .)
```

The benefit of this design is that the rows in the smaller item titles table will be physically closer together; the smaller table will take up fewer disk pages and thus support faster retrieval.

Queries that require data from both tables must join the tables over the item number. Like most joins, this will be a relatively slow operation. Therefore, vertical partitioning makes sense only when there is a highly skewed access pattern from the columns of a table. The more often a small, specific group of columns is accessed together, the more vertical partitioning will help.

FOR FURTHER READING

Atonini, Christian. *Troubleshooting Oracle Performance*. Apress, 2008.

Delaney, Kalen, Sunil Agarwal, Craig Freedman, Ron Talmage, and Adam Machanic. *Inside Microsoft SQL Server 2005: Query Tuning and Optimization*. Microsoft Press, 2007.

Harrison, Guy. *Oracle SQL High-Performance Tuning*. Prentice Hall PTR, 2000.

IBM Redbooks. *A Deep Blue View of DB2 Performance*. IBM.com/Redbooks, 2006.

Mittra, Sitansu S. *Database Performance Tuning and Optimization*. Springer, 2002.

Schwartz, Baron, Peter Zaitsev, Vadim Tkachenko, Jeremy Zawony, Arien Lentz, and Derek Balling. *High Performance MySQL: Optimization, Backups, Replication, and More*. O'Reilly, 2008.

Tow, Dan. *SQL Tuning*. O'Reilly, 2003.

Chapter 8

Codd's Rules for Relational Database Design

In October 1985, E.F. Codd published a series of two articles in the computer industry weekly *Computerworld*. The first article laid out 12 criteria to which a "fully relational" database should adhere. The second article compared current mainframe products to those 12 rules, producing a flurry of controversy over whether it was important that database management systems (DBMSs) be theoretically rigorous or that they simply work effectively.

Note: If you have read Appendix A, you will be aware of a product based on the simple network data model called IDMS/R. When Codd rated IDMS/R which at the time was being marketed as a relational DBMS—it met none (0) of his 12 rules. DB/2, IBM's flagship relational product, met 10 of the rules.

To help you understand the issues raised and why Codd's rules for relational databases for the most part make sense, in this chapter we will look at those criteria along with the implications of their implementation. Should you then choose not to adhere to one or more of the rules, you will be doing so with full understanding of the consequences. In some cases, the consequences are minimal; in others they may significantly affect the integrity of the data that is in a database.

RULE 1: THE INFORMATION RULE

The first criterion for databases deals with the data structures that are used to store data and represent data relationships:

> *All information in a relational database is represented explicitly at the logical level in exactly one way—by values in tables.*

The purpose of this rule is to require that relations (two-dimensional tables) be the *only* data structure used in a relational database. Therefore, products that require hard-coded links between tables are not relational.

At the time Codd's article was published, one of the most widely used mainframe products was IDMS/R, a version of IDMS that placed a relational-style query language on top of a simple network database. The simple network data model requires data structures, such as pointers or indexes, to represent data relationships. Therefore, IDBMS/R, although being marketed as relational, was not relational according to the very first rule of a relational database. It was this product that was at the heart of the "who cares about rules if my product works" controversy.

Regardless of which side you take in this particular argument, there are two very good reasons why creating a database from nothing but tables is a good idea:

- *Logical relationships are very flexible.* In a simple network or hierarchical database, the only relationships that can be used for retrieval are those that have been predetermined by the database designer who wrote the schema. However, because a relational database represents its relationships through matching data values, the join operation can be used to implement relationships on the fly—even those that a database designer may not have anticipated.
- *Relational database schemas are very flexible.* You can add, modify, and remove individual relations without disturbing the rest of the schema. In fact, as long as you are not changing the structure of tables currently being used, you can modify the schema of a live database. However, to modify the schema of a simple network or hierarchical database, you must stop all processing of data and regenerate the entire schema. In many cases, modifying the database design also means recreating all the physical files (using a dump and load process) to correspond to the new design.

Note: DBMSs that require you to specify "relationships between files" when you design a database fail this first rule. If you have read Appendix A, you know that a number of PC-only products work in this way and that although they are marketed as relational, they really use the simple network data model. Keep in mind that the ER diagrams for simple networks and 3NF relational databases are identical. The differences come in how the relationships between the entities are represented. In a simple network, it is with hard-coded relationships; in a relational database, it is with primary key–foreign key pairs.

When Codd originally wrote his rules, databases couldn't store images. Today, many DBMSs store images in a variety of formats or store the path names (or URL) to images in external files. Technically, path names or URLs to external files are pointers to something other than tables and therefore would seem to cause a DBMS to violate this rule. However, the spirit of the rule is that relationships between entities—the logical relationships in the database—are represented by matching data values, without the use of pointers of any kind to indicate entity connections.

Note: This is not the only rule that needs to be stretched a bit to accommodate graphics in a database environment. See also Rule 5 later in this chapter.

RULE 2: THE GUARANTEED ACCESS RULE

Given that the entire reason we put data into a database is to get the data out again, we must be certain that we can retrieve every single piece of data:

> *Each and every datum (atomic value) in a relational database is guaranteed to be logically accessible by resorting to a combination of table name, primary key value, and column name.*

This rule states that you need to know only three things to locate a specific piece of data: the name of the table, the name of the column, and the primary key of the row containing the data.

Note: With today's DBMSs, the definition of a table name can mean many things. For example, if you are working with IBM's DB/2, a table name is the table creator's loginName.tableName. If you are working with Oracle, then a complete table name may include a catalog name, a schema name, and an Oracle owner name, as well as the name of the individual table.

There is no rule in this set of 12 rules that specifically states that each row in a relation must have a unique primary key. However, a relation cannot adhere to the guaranteed access rule unless it does have unique primary keys. Without unique primary keys, you will be able to retrieve *some* row with the primary key value used in a search but not necessarily the exact row you want. Some data may therefore be inaccessible without the ability to uniquely identify rows.

Early relational databases did not require primary keys at all. You could create and use tables without primary key constraints. Today, however, SQL will allow you to create a table without a primary key specification, but most DBMSs will not permit you to enter data into that table.

Note: A DBMS that requires "relationships between files" cannot adhere to this rule because you must specify the file in which the data reside to locate the data.

RULE 3: SYSTEMATIC TREATMENT OF NULL VALUES

As you know, null is a special database value that means "unknown." Its presence in a database brings special problems during data retrieval. Consider, for example, what happens if you have an employees' relation that contains a column for salary. Assume that the salary is null for some portion of the rows. What, then, should happen if someone queries the table for all people who make more than $60,000 a year? Should the rows with null be retrieved, or should they be left out?

When the DBMS evaluates a null against the logical criterion of salary value greater than 60,000, it cannot determine whether the row containing the null meets the criteria. Maybe it does, and maybe it doesn't. For this relation, we say that relational databases use *three-valued logic*. The result of the evaluation of a logical expression is true, false, or maybe. Codd's third rule therefore deals with the issue of nulls:

> *Null values (distinct from the empty character string or a string of blank characters or any other number) are supported in the fully relational DBMS for representing missing information in a systematic way, independent of data type.*

First, a relational DBMS must store the same value for null in all columns and rows where the user does not explicitly enter data values. The value used for null must be the same, regardless of the data type of the column. Note that null is not the same as a space character or zero; it has its own distinct ASCII or UNICODE value. However, in most cases when you see a query's result table on the screen, nulls do appear as blank.

Second, the DBMS must have some consistent, known way of handling those nulls when performing queries. Typically, you will find that rows with nulls are not retrieved by a query, such as the salary greater than 60,000 example, unless the user explicitly asks for rows with a value of null. Most relational DBMSs today adhere to a three-valued logic truth table to determine retrieval behavior when they encounter nulls.

The inclusion of nulls in a relation can be extremely important. They provide a consistent way to distinguish between valid data such as a 0 and missing data. For example, there is a big difference between the balance in an account payable being 0 and being unknown. The account with 0 is something we like to see; the account with an unknown balance could be a significant problem.

Note: The concept of unknown values is not unique to relational databases. Regardless of the data model it uses, a DBMS must contend with the problem of how to behave when querying against a null.

RULE 4: DYNAMIC ONLINE CATALOG BASED ON THE RELATIONAL MODEL

In Chapter 5, you read about relational database data dictionaries. Codd very clearly specifies that those dictionaries (which he calls *catalogs*) should be made up of nothing but relations:

> *The database description is represented at the logical level in the same way as ordinary data so that authorized users can apply the same relational language to the interrogation as they apply to regular data.*

One advantage of using the same data structures for the data dictionary as for data tables is that you have a consistent way to access all elements of the database. You need to learn only one query language. This also simplifies the DBMS itself, since it can use the same mechanism for handling data about the database (*metadata*) as it can data about the organization.

When you purchase a DBMS, it comes with its own way of handling a data dictionary There is rarely anything you can do to change it Therefore, the major implication of this particular rule comes in selecting relational software: You want to look for something that has a data dictionary that is made up of nothing but tables.

> *Note:* Because of the way in which their schemas were implemented, it was rare for a pre-relational DBMS to have an online data dictionary.

RULE 5: THE COMPREHENSIVE DATA SUBLANGUAGE RULE

A relational database must have some language that can maintain database structural elements, modify data, and retrieve data. Codd included the following rule that describes his ideas about what such a language should do:

> *A relational system may support several languages and various modes of terminal use (for example, fill-in-the-blank mode). However, there must be at least one language whose statements are expressible, per some well-defined syntax, as character strings and that is comprehensive in supporting all of the following items:*
>
> - *Data definition*
> - *View definition*
> - *Data manipulation (interactive and by program)*
> - *Integrity constraints*
> - *Transaction boundaries (begin, commit, and roll back)*

The current SQL language does meet all of these rules. (Versions earlier than SQL-92 did not include complete support for primary keys and referential integrity.) Given that most of today's relational DBMSs use SQL as their primary data manipulation language, there would seem to be no issue here.

However, a DBMS that does not support SQL but uses a graphic language would technically not meet this rule. Nonetheless, there are several products today whose graphic language can perform all the tasks that Codd has listed without a command-line syntax. Such DBMSs might not be theoretically "fully relational," but since they can perform all the necessary relational tasks, you lose nothing by not having the command-line language.

> *Note:* Keep in mind the time frame in which Codd was writing. In 1985, the Macintosh—whose operating system legitimized the graphic user interface—was barely a year old. Most people still considered the GUI-equipped computers to be little more than toys.

RULE 6: THE VIEW UPDATING RULE

As you will read more about in Chapter 10, some views can be used to update data. Others—those created from more than one base table or view, those that do not contain the primary keys of their base tables, and so on—cannot be used for updating. Codd's sixth rule speaks only about those that meet the criteria for updatability:

> *All views that are theoretically updatable are also updatable by the system.*

This rule simply means that if a view meets the criteria for updatability, a DBMS must be able to handle that update and propagate the updates back to the base tables.

> *Note:* DBMSs that used pre-relational data models included constructs similar in concept to views. For example, CODASYL DBMSs included "subschemas," which allowed an application programmer to construct a subset of a schema to be used by a specific end user or by an application program.

RULE 7: HIGH-LEVEL INSERT, UPDATE, DELETE

Codd wanted to ensure that a DBMS could handle multiple rows of data at a time, especially when data were modified. Therefore, his seventh rule requires that a DBMS's data manipulation be able to insert, update, and delete more than one row with a single command:

> *The capability of handling a base relation or a derived relation as a single operand applies not only to the retrieval of data but also to the insertion, update, and deletion of data.*

SQL provides this capability for today's relational DBMSs. What does it bring you? Being able to modify more than one row with a single command simplifies data manipulation logic. Rather than having to scan a relation row by row to locate rows for modification, for example, you can specify logical criteria that identify rows to be affected and then let the DBMS find the rows for you.

RULE 8: PHYSICAL DATA INDEPENDENCE

One of the benefits of using a database system rather than a file processing system is that a DBMS isolates the user from physical storage details. The physical data independence rule speaks to this issue:

> *Applications and terminal activities remain logically unimpaired whenever any changes are made in either storage representation or access methods.*

This means that you should be able to move the database from one disk volume to another, change the physical layout of the files, and so on, without any impact on the way in which application programs and end users interact with the tables in the database.

Most of today's DBMSs give you little control over the file structures used to store data on a disk. (Only the very largest mainframe systems allow systems programmers to determine physical storage structures.) Therefore, in a practical sense, physical data independence means that you should be able to move the database from one disk volume or directory to another without affecting the logical design of the database, and therefore the application programs and interactive users remain unaffected. With a few exceptions, most of today's DBMSs do provide physical data independence.

> *Note:* Pre-relational DBMSs generally fail this rule to a greater or lesser degree. The older the data model, the closer it was tied to its physical data storage. The trade-off, however, is performance. Hierarchical systems are much faster than relational systems when processing data in tree traversal order. The same can be said for a CODASYL database. When traversing in set order, access will be faster than row-by-row access within a relational database. The trade-off is flexibility to perform ad hoc queries, something at which relational systems excel.

RULE 9: LOGICAL DATA INDEPENDENCE

Logical data independence is a bit more subtle than physical data independence. In essence, it means that if you change the schema—perhaps adding or removing a table or adding a column to a table—then other parts of the schema that should not be affected by the change remain unaffected:

> *Application programs and terminal activities remain logically unimpaired when information-preserving changes of any kind that theoretically permit unimpairment are made to the base tables.*

As an example, consider what happens when you add a table to a database. Since relations are logically independent of one another, adding a table should have absolutely no impact on any other table. To adhere to the logical data independence rule, a DBMS must ensure that there is indeed no impact on other tables.

On the other hand, if you delete a table from the database, such a modification is not "information preserving." Data will almost certainly be lost when the table is removed. Therefore, it is not necessary that application programs and interactive users be unaffected by the change.

RULE 10: INTEGRITY INDEPENDENCE

Although the requirement for unique primary keys is a corollary to an earlier rule, the requirement for non-null primary keys and for referential integrity is very explicit:

> *Integrity constraints specific to a particular relational database must be definable in the relational data sublanguage and storable in the catalog, not in the application programs.*
>
> *A minimum of the following two integrity constraints must be supported:*
>
> 1. *Entity integrity: No component of a primary key is allowed to have a null value.*
> 2. *Relational integrity: For each distinct non-null foreign key value in a relational database, there must exist a matching primary key value from the same domain.*

Notice that the rule requires that the declaration of integrity constraints must be a part of whatever language is used to define database structure. In addition, integrity constraints of any kind must be stored in a data dictionary that can be accessed while the database is being used.

When IBM released its flagship relational database DB/2, one of the two things users complained about was the lack of referential integrity support. IBM, and other DBMS vendors for that matter, omitted referential integrity because it slows down performance. Each time you modify a row of data, the DBMS must go to the data dictionary, search for an integrity rule, and perform the test indicated by the rule, all before performing an update. A referential integrity check of a single column can involve two or more disk accesses, all of which take more time than simply making the modification directly to the base table.

However, without referential integrity, the relationships in a relational database very quickly become inconsistent. Retrieval operations therefore do not necessarily retrieve all data because the missing cross-references cause joins to omit data. In that case, the database is unreliable and virtually unusable. (Yes, IBM added referential integrity to DB/2 fairly quickly!)

Note: One solution to the problem of a DBMS not supporting referential integrity was to have application programmers code the referential integrity checks into application programs. This certainly works, but it puts the burden of integrity checking in the wrong place. It should be an integral part of the database rather than left up to an application programmer.

Note: Most DBMSs that used pre-relational data models provided some types of integrity constraints, including domain constraints, unique entity identifiers, and required values (non-null). CODASYL could also enforce mandatory relationships, something akin to referential integrity.

RULE 11: DISTRIBUTION INDEPENDENCE

As you will remember from Chapter 1, a distributed database is a database where the data are stored on more than one computer. The database is therefore the union of all its parts. In practice, the parts are not unique but contain a great deal of duplicated data. Nonetheless, according to Rule 11:

> *A relational DBMS has distribution independence.*

In other words, a distributed database must look like a centralized database to the user. Application programs and interactive users should not be required to know where data are stored, including the location of multiple copies of the same data.

DBMS vendors have been working on distributed DBMS software since the late 1970s. However, current relational DBMS truly meet this rule. Even the most sophisticated distributed DBMS software requires that the user indicate some location information when retrieving data.

RULE 12: NONSUBVERSION RULE

The final rule could also be called the "no cheating" rule:

> *If a relational system has a low-level (single-record-at-a-time) language, that low-level language cannot be used to subvert or bypass the integrity rules or constraints expressed in the higher level relational language (multiple-records-at-a-time).*

Many DBMS products during the 1980s had languages that could directly access rows in tables separate from SQL, which operates on multiples rows at a time. This rule states that there must be no way to use that direct-access language to get around the constraints stored in the data dictionary. The integrity rules must be observed without exception.

Chapter 9

Using SQL to Implement a Relational Design

As a complete data manipulation language, SQL contains statements that allow you to insert, modify, delete, and retrieve data. However, to a database designer, the portions of SQL that support the creation of database structural elements are of utmost importance. In this chapter you will be introduced to the SQL commands that you will use to create and maintain the tables, views, indexes, and other structure that make up a relational database.

The actual file structure of a database is implementation dependent, as is the procedure needed to create a database file. Therefore, the discussion in this chapter assumes that the necessary database files are already in place.

> *Note:* You will see extensive examples of the use of the syntax presented in this chapter at the end of each of the three case studies that follow in this book.

DATABASE STRUCTURE HIERARCHY

The elements that describe the structure of an SQL:2006-compliant database are arranged in a hierarchy, which appears in Figure 9-1. The smallest units with which the DBMS works—columns and rows—appear in the center. These in turn are grouped into tables and views.

The tables and views that comprise a single logical database are collected into a schema. Multiple schemas are grouped into catalogs, which can then be grouped into clusters. A catalog usually contains

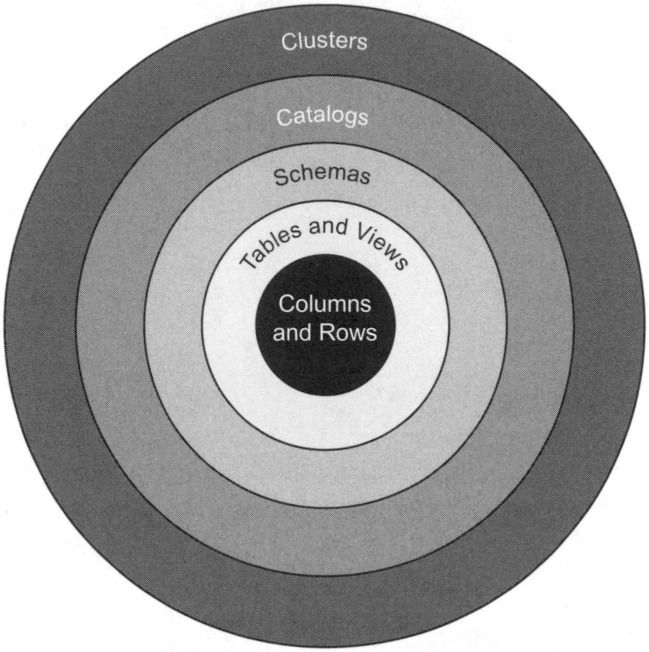

■ **FIGURE 9-1** The SQL:2006 database structure hierarchy.

information describing all the schemas handled by one DBMS. Catalog creation is implementation dependent and therefore not part of the SQL standard.

Prior to SQL-92, clusters often represented database files, and the clustering of database elements into files was a way to increase database performance by placing data accessed together in the same physical file. The SQL-92 and beyond concept of a cluster, however, is a group of catalogs that are accessible using the same connection to a database server.

Note: SQL is a dynamic language. The standard was updated in 1999, 2003, and 2006.

In current versions of SQL, none of the groupings of database elements are related to physical storage structures. If you are working with a centralized mainframe DBMS, you may find multiple catalogs stored in the same database file. However, on smaller or distributed systems, you are likely to find one catalog or schema per database file or to find a catalog or schema divided among multiple files.

Clusters, catalogs, and schemas are not required elements of a database environment. In a small installation where there is one collection of tables serving a single purpose, for example, it may not even be necessary to create a schema to hold them.

Naming and Identifying Structural Elements

The way in which you name and identify database structural elements is in some measure dictated by the structure hierarchy:

- Column names must be unique within the table.
- Table names must be unique within the schema.
- Schema names must be unique within their catalog.
- Catalog names must be unique within their cluster.

When a column name appears in more than one table in a query, the user must specify the table from which a column should be taken (even if it makes no difference which table is used). The general form for qualifying duplicate column names is:

```
table_name.column_name
```

If an installation has more than one schema, then a user must also indicate the schema in which a table resides:

```
schema_name.table_name.column_name
```

This naming convention means that two different schemas can include tables with the same name.

By the same token, if an installation has multiple catalogs, a user will need to indicate the catalog from which a database element comes:

```
catalog_name.schema_name.table_name.column_name
```

The names that you assign to database elements can include the following:

- Letters
- Numbers
- Underscores (_)

SQL names can be up to 128 characters long. They are not case sensitive. (In fact, many SQL command processors convert names to all upper- or lowercase before submitting a SQL statement to a DBMS for processing.)

> *Note:* Some DBMSs also allow pound signs (#) and dollar signs ($) in element names, but neither is recognized by SQL queries, so their use should be avoided.

SCHEMAS

To a database designer, a schema represents the overall, logical design of a complete database. As far as SQL is concerned, however, a schema is nothing more than a container for tables, views, and other structural elements. It is up to the database designer to place a meaningful group of elements within each schema.

A schema is not required to create tables and views. In fact, if you are installing a database for an environment in which there is likely to be only one logical database, then you can just as easily do without one. However, if more than one database will be sharing the same DBMS and the same server, then organizing database elements into schemas can greatly simplify the maintenance of the individual databases.

Creating a Schema

To create a schema, you use the CREATE SCHEMA statement. In its simplest form it has the syntax:

```
CREATE SCHEMA schema_name
```

as in:

```
CREATE SCHEMA antiqueOpticals
```

> *Note:* Some SQL command processors require a semicolon at the end of each statement. However, that end-of-statement marker is not a part of the SQL standard and you may encounter DBMSs that do not use it. The examples in this chapter do not include the trailing semicolon, but be aware that your specific DBMS may need it.

By default, a schema belongs to the user who created it (the user ID under which the schema was created). The owner of the schema is the only user ID that can modify the schema unless the owner grants that ability to other users.

To assign a different owner to a schema, you add an AUTHORIZATION clause:

```
CREATE SCHEMA schema_name AUTHORIZATION
  owner_user_ID
```

For example, to assign the Antique Opticals' schema to the user ID DBA, someone could use:

```
CREATE SCHEMA antiqueOpticals AUTHORIZATION dba
```

When creating a schema, you can also create additional elements at the same time. To do so, you use braces to group the CREATE statements for the other elements, as in:

```
CREATE SCHEMA schema_name AUTHORIZATION
  owner_user_id { // other CREATE statements go
  here }
```

This automatically assigns the elements with the braces to the schema.

Identifying the Schema You Want to Use

One of the nicest things about a relational database is that you can add or delete database structural elements at any time. There must therefore be a way to specify a current schema for new database elements after the schema has been created initially with the CREATE SCHEMA statement.

One way to do this is with the SET SCHEMA statement:

```
SET SCHEMA schema_name
```

To use SET SCHEMA, the user ID under which you are working must have authorization to work with that schema.

Alternatively, you can qualify the name of a database element with the name of the schema. For example, if you are creating a table, then you would use something like:

```
CREATE TABLE schema_name.table_name
```

For those DBMSs that do not support SET SCHEMA, this is the only way to attach new database elements to a schema after the schema has been created.

DOMAINS

As you know, a domain is an expression of the permitted values for a column in a relation. When you define a table, you assign each column a data type (example, character or integer) that provides a broad domain. A DBMS will not store data that violate that constraint.

The SQL-92 standard introduced the concept of user-defined domains, which can be viewed as user-defined data types that can be applied to columns in tables. (This means you have to create a domain before you can assign it to a column!)

Domains can be created as part of a CREATE SCHEMA statement, which has the following syntax:

```
CREATE DOMAIN domain_name data_type CHECK
  (expression_to_validate_values)
```

The CHECK clause is actually a generic way of expressing a condition that the data must meet. It can include a SELECT to validate data against other data stored in the database, or it can include a simple logical expression. In that expression, the keyword VALUE represents the data being checked.

For example, if Antique Opticals wanted to validate the price of a disc, someone might create the following domain:

```
CREATE DOMAIN price numeric (6,2) CHECK (VALUE >=
  19.95)
```

After creating this domain, a column in a table can be given the data type of price. The DBMS will then check to be certain that the value in that column is always greater than or equal to 19.95. (We will leave a discussion of the data type used in the preceding SQL statement until we cover creating tables in the next section of this chapter.)

The domain mechanism is very flexible. Assume, for example, that you want to ensure that telephone numbers are always stored in the format XXX-XXX-XXXX. A domain to validate that format might be created as:

```
CREATE DOMAIN telephone char (12) CHECK (SUBSTRING
  (VALUE FROM 4 FOR 1 = '-') AND SUBSTRING (VALUE
  FROM 8 FOR 1 = '-'))
```

You can use the CREATE DOMAIN statement to give a column a default value. For example, the following statement sets up a domain that holds either Y or N and defaults to Y:

```
CREATE DOMAIN boolean char (1) DEFAULT = 'Y' CHECK
  (UPPER(VALUE) = 'Y' OR UPPER(VALUE) = 'N')
```

TABLES

The most important structure within a relational database is the table. As you know, tables contain just about everything, including business data and the data dictionary. SQL divides tables into three categories:

- *Permanent base tables:* Permanent base tables are tables whose contents are stored in the database and remain permanently in the database unless they are explicitly deleted.
- *Global temporary tables:* Global temporary tables are tables for working storage that are destroyed at the end of an SQL session. The definitions of the tables are stored in the data dictionary, but their data are not. The tables must be loaded with data each time they are going to be used. Global temporary tables can be used only by the current user, but they are visible to an entire SQL session (either an application program or a user working with an interactive query facility).
- *Local temporary tables:* Local temporary tables are similar to global temporary tables. However, they are visible only to the specific program module in which they are created.

Temporary base tables are subtly different from views, which assemble their data by executing an SQL query. You will read more about this difference and how temporary tables are created and used later in this chapter.

Most of the tables in a relational database are permanent base tables. You create them with the CREATE TABLE statement:

```
CREATE TABLE table_name ( column1_name
  column1_data_type column1_constraints, column2_name
  column2_data_type column2_constraints,
  … table_constraints)
```

The constraints on a table include declarations of primary and foreign keys. The constraints on a column include whether values in the column are mandatory, as well as other constraints you may decide to include in a CHECK clause.

Column Data Types

Each column in a table must be given a data type. Although data types are somewhat implementation dependent, most DBMSs that support SQL include the following predefined data types:

- *INTEGER (abbreviated INT):* A positive or negative whole number. The number of bits occupied by the value is implementation dependent. In most cases, integers are either 32 or 64 bits.
- *SMALLINT:* A positive or negative whole number. A small integer is usually half the size of a standard integer. Using small integers when you know you will need to store only small values can save space in the database.
- *NUMBER:* A fixed-point positive or negative number. A numeric value has a whole number portion and a fractional portion. When you create it, you must specify the total length of the number (including the decimal point) and how many of those digits will be to the right of the decimal point (its *precision*). For example:

  ```
  NUMERIC (6,2)
  ```

  creates a number in the format XXX.XX. The DBMS will store exactly two digits to the right of the decimal point.
- *DECIMAL:* A fixed-point positive or negative number. A decimal number is similar to a numeric value. However, the DBMS may store more digits to the right of the decimal point than you specify. Although there is no guarantee that you will get the extra precision, its use can provide more accurate results in computations.
- *REAL:* A "single-precision" floating point value. A floating point number is expressed in the format:

  ```
  XX.XXXXX * 10YY
  ```

  where YY is the power to which 10 is raised. Because of the way computers store floating point numbers, a real number may not be an exact representation of a value but only a close approximation. The range of values that can be stored is implementation dependent, as is the precision. You therefore cannot specify a size for a real number column.
- *DOUBLE PRECISION (abbreviated DOUBLE):* A "double-precision" floating point number. The range and precision of double-precision values are implementation dependent, but generally both will be greater than single-precision real numbers.

- *FLOAT:* A floating point number for which you can specify the precision. The DBMS will maintain at least the precision that you specify. (It may be more.)
- *BIT:* Storage for a fixed number of individual bits. You must indicate the number of bits, as in:

  ```
  BIT (n)
  ```

  where *n* is the number of bits. (If you do not, you will have room for only one bit.)
- *BIT VARYING:* Storage for a varying number of bits up to a specified maximum, as in:

  ```
  BIT VARYING (n)
  ```

  where *n* is the maximum number of bits. In some DBMSs, columns of this type can be used to store graphic images.
- *DATE:* A date.
- *TIME:* A time.
- *TIMESTAMP:* The combination of a date and a time.
- *CHARACTER (abbreviated CHAR):* A fixed-length space to hold a string of characters. When declaring a CHAR column, you need to indicate the width of the column:

  ```
  CHAR (n)
  ```

  where *n* is the amount of space that will be allocated for the column in every row. Even if you store less than n characters, the column will always take up n bytes—or *n* * 2 bytes if you are storing UNICODE characters—and the column will be padded with blanks to fill up empty space. The maximum number of characters allowed is implementation dependent.
- *CHARACTER VARYING (abbreviated VARCHAR):* A variable-length space to hold a string of characters. You must indicate the maximum width of the column:

  ```
  VARCHAR (n)
  ```

  but the DBMS stores only as many characters as you insert, up to the maximum *n*. The overall maximum number of characters allowed is implementation dependent.

- *INTERVAL:* A date or time interval. An interval data type is followed by a qualifier that specifies the size of the interval and optionally the number of digits. For example:

  ```
  INTERVAL YEAR INTERVAL YEAR (n) INTERVAL MONTH
     INTERVAL MONTH (n) INTERVAL YEAR TO MONTH
     INTERVAL YEAR (n) TO MONTH INTERVAL DAY INTERVAL
     DAY (n) INTERVAL DAY TO HOUR INTERVAL DAY (n) TO
     HOUR INTERVAL DAY TO MINUTE INTERVAL DAY (n) TO
     MINUTE INTERVAL MINUTE INTERVAL MINUTE (n)
  ```

  In the preceding example, *n* specifies the number of digits. When the interval covers more than one date-time unit, such as YEAR TO MONTH, you can specify a size for only the first unit. Year-month intervals can include days, hours, minutes, and/or seconds.

- *BOOLEAN:* A true/false value.

- *BLOB (Binary Large Object):* A block of binary code (often a graphic) stored as a unit and retrievable only as a unit. In many cases, the DBMS cannot interpret the contents of a BLOB (although the application that created the BLOB can do so). Because BLOB data are stored as undifferentiated binary, BLOB columns cannot be searched directly. Identifying information about the contents of a BLOB must be contained in other columns of the table using data types that can be searched.

In Figure 9-2 you will find bare-bones CREATE TABLE statements for the Antique Opticals database. These statements include only column names and data types. SQL will create tables from statements in this format, but because the tables have no primary keys, many DBMSs will not allow you to enter data.

Default Values

As you are defining columns, you can designate a default value for individual columns. To indicate a default value, you add a DEFAULT keyword to the column definition, followed by the default value. For example, in the orders relation, the order date column defaults to the current system date. The column declaration is therefore written:

```
order_date date DEFAULT CURRENT_DATE
```

Notice that this particular declaration is using the SQL value CURRENT_DATE. However, you can place any value after DEFAULT that is a valid instance of the column's data type.

NOT NULL CONSTRAINTS

The values in primary key columns must be unique and not null. In addition, there may be columns for which you want to require a value. You can specify such columns by adding NOT NULL after the column declaration.

Since the Antique Opticals database wants to ensure that an order date is always entered, the complete declaration for that column in the orders table is:

```
order_date date NOT NULL DEFAULT CURRENT_DATE
```

Primary Keys

There are two ways to specify a primary key:

- Add a PRIMARY KEY clause to a CREATE TABLE statement. The keywords PRIMARY KEY are followed by the names of the primary key column or columns, surrounded by parentheses.
- Add the keywords PRIMARY KEY to the declaration of each column that is part of the primary key. Use a CONSTRAINT clause if you want to name the primary key constraint.

In Figure 9-3 you will find the CREATE TABLE statement for the Antique Opticals database including both PRIMARY KEY and CONSTRAINT clauses. Notice that in those tables that have concatenated primary keys, all the primary key columns have been included in a PRIMARY KEY clause.

Foreign Keys

As you know, a foreign key is a column (or combination of columns) that is exactly the same as the primary of some table. When a foreign key value matches a primary key value, we know that there is a logical relationship between the database objects represented by the matching rows.

One of the major constraints on a relation is referential integrity, which states that every non-null foreign key must reference an existing primary key value. To maintain the integrity of the database, it is vital that foreign key constraints be stored within the database's data dictionary so that the DBMS can be responsible for enforcing those constraints.

```
CREATE TABLE customer
    (customer_numb int,
    customer_first_name varchar (15),
    customer_last_name varchar (15),
    customer_street varchar (30),
    customer_city varchar (15),
    customer_state char (2),
    customer_zip char (10),
    customer_phone char (12))

CREATE TABLE distributor
    (distributor_numb int,
    distributor_name varchar (15),
    distributor_street varchar (30),
    distributor_city varchar (15),
    distributor_state char (2),
    distributor_zip char (10),
    distributor_phone char (12),
    distributor_contact_person varchar (30),
    contact_person_ext char (5))

CREATE TABLE item
    (item_numb int,
    item_type varchar (15),
    title varchar (60),
    distributor_numb int,
    retail_price numeric (6,2),
    release_date date,
    genre varchar (20),
    quant_in_stock int)

CREATE TABLE order
    order_numb int ,
    customer_numb int,
    order_date date,
    credit_card_numb char (16),
    credit_card_exp_date char (5),
    order_complete char (1),
    pickup_or_ship char (1))
```

■ **FIGURE 9-2** Initial CREATE TABLE statements for the Antique Opticals database.

```
CREATE TABLE order_line
    (order_numb int,
    item_numb int,
    quantity int,
    discount_percent int,
    selling_price numeric (6,2),
    line_cost numeric (7,2),
    shipped char (1),
    shipping_date date)

CREATE TABLE purchase
    (purchase_date date,
    customer_numb int,
    items_received char (1),
    customer_paid char (1))

CREATE TABLE purchase_item
    (purchase_date date,
    customer_numb int,
    item_numb int,
    condition char (15),
    price_paid numeric (6,2))

CREATE TABLE actor
    (actor_numb int,
    actor_name varchar (60))

CREATE TABLE performance
    (actor_numb int,
    item_numb int,
    role varchar (60))

CREATE TABLE producer
    (producer_name varchar (60),
    studio varchar (40))

CREATE TABLE production
    (producer_name varchar (60),
    item_numb int)
```

■ **FIGURE 9-2** Cont'd

```
CREATE TABLE customer
    (customer_numb int PRIMARY KEY,
    customer_first_name varchar (15),
    customer_last_name varchar (15),
    customer_street varchar (30),
    customer_city varchar (15),
    customer_state char (2),
    customer_zip char (10),
    customer_phone char (12))

CREATE TABLE distributor
    (distributor_numb int PRIMARY KEY,
    distributor_name varchar (15),
    distributor_street varchar (30),
    distributor_city varchar (15),
    distributor_state char (2),
    distributor_zip char (10),
    distributor_phone char (12),
    distributor_contact_person varchar (30),
    contact_person_ext char (5))

CREATE TABLE item
    (item_numb int CONSTRAINT item_pk PRIMARY KEY,
    item_type varchar (15),
    title varchar (60),
    distributor_numb int,
    retail_price numeric (6,2),
    release_date date,
    genre varchar (20),
    quant_in_stock int)

CREATE TABLE order
    (order_numb int,
    customer_numb int,
    order_date date,
    credit_card_numb char (16),
    credit_card_exp_date char (5),
    order_complete char (1),
    pickup_or_ship char (1)
    PRIMARY KEY (order_numb))

CREATE TABLE order_line
    (order_numb int,
```

■ **FIGURE 9-3** CREATE TABLE statements for the Antique Opticals database including primary key declarations.

```
    item_numb int,
    quantity int,
    discount_percent int,
    selling_price numeric (6,2),
    line_cost numeric (7,2),
    shipped char (1),
    shipping_date date
    PRIMARY KEY (order_numb, item_numb))

CREATE TABLE purchase
    (purchase_date date,
    customer_numb int,
    items_received char (1),
    customer_paid char (1)
    PRIMARY KEY (purchase_date, customer_numb))

CREATE TABLE purchase_item
    (purchase_date date,
    customer_numb int,
    item_numb int,
    condition char (15),
    price_paid numeric (6,2)
    PRIMARY KEY (purchase_date, customer_numb, item_numb))

CREATE TABLE actor
    (actor_numb int PRIMARY KEY,
     actor_name varchar (60))

CREATE TABLE performance
    (actor_numb int,
    item_numb int,
    role varchar (60)
    PRIMARY KEY (actor_numb, item_numb))

CREATE TABLE producer
    (producer_name varchar (60) CONSTRAINT producer_pk PRIMARY KEY,
    studio varchar (40))

CREATE TABLE production
    (producer_name varchar (60),
    item_numb int
    PRIMARY KEY (producer_name, item_numb))
```

■ **FIGURE 9-3** Cont'd

To specify a foreign key for a table, you add a FOREIGN KEY clause:

```
FOREIGN KEY foreign_key_name (foreign_key_columns)
  REFERENCES primary_key_table
  (primary_key_columns) ON UPDATE update_option ON
  DELETE delete_option
```

Each foreign key–primary key reference is given a name. This makes it possible to identify the reference at a later time—in particular, so you can remove the reference if necessary.

Note: Some DBMSs, such as Oracle, do not support the naming of foreign keys, in which case you would use preceding syntax without the name.

The names of the foreign key columns follow the name of the foreign key. The REFERENCES clause contains the name of the primary key table being referenced. If the primary key columns are named in the PRIMARY KEY clause of their table, then you don't need to list the primary key columns. However, if the columns are not part of a PRIMARY KEY clause, you must list the primary key columns in the REFERENCES clause.

The final part of the FOREIGN KEY specification indicates what should happen with a primary key value being referenced by a foreign key value that is updated or deleted. Three options apply to both updates and deletions and there is one additional option for each:

- *SET NULL:* Replace the foreign key value with null. This isn't possible when the foreign key is part of the table's primary key.
- *SET DEFAULT:* Replace the foreign key value with the column's default value.
- *CASCADE:* Delete or update all foreign key rows.
- *NO ACTION:* On update, make no modifications of foreign key values.
- *RESTRICT:* Do not allow deletions of primary key rows.

The complete declarations for the Antique Opticals database tables, which include foreign key constraints, can be found in Figure 9-4. Notice that although there are no restrictions on how to name foreign keys, the foreign keys in this database have been named to indicate the tables involved. This makes them easier to identify if you need to delete or modify a foreign key at a later date.

```
CREATE TABLE customer
    (customer_numb int PRIMARY KEY,
    customer_first_name varchar (15),
    customer_last_name varchar (15),
    customer_street varchar (30),
    customer_city varchar (15),
    customer_state char (2),
    customer_zip char (10),
    customer_phone char (12))

CREATE TABLE distributor
    (distributor_numb int PRIMARY KEY,
    distributor_name varchar (15),
    distributor_street varchar (30),
    distributor_city varchar (15),
    distributor_state char (2),
    distributor_zip char (10),
    distributor_phone char (12),
    distributor_contact_person varchar (30),
    contact_person_ext char (5))

CREATE TABLE item
    (item_numb int CONSTRAINT item_pk PRIMARY KEY,
    item_type varchar (15),
    title varchar (60),
    distributor_numb int,
    retail_price numeric (6,2),
    release_ date date,
    genre varchar (20),
    quant_in_stock int)

CREATE TABLE order
    (order_numb int,
    customer_numb int,
    order_date date,
    credit_card_numb char (16),
    credit_card_exp_date char (5),
    order_complete char (1),
    pickup_or_ship char (1)
    PRIMARY KEY (order_numb)
    FOREIGN KEY order2customer (customer_numb)
    REFERENCES customer
        ON UPDATE CASCADE
        ON DELETE RESTRICT)
```

■ **FIGURE 9-4** The complete CREATE TABLE statements for the Antique Opticals database.

```
CREATE TABLE order_line
    (order_numb int,
    item_numb int,
    quantity int,
    discount_percent int,
    selling_price numeric (6,2),
    line_cost numeric (7,2),
    shipped char (1),
    shipping_date date
    PRIMARY KEY (order_numb, item_numb)
    FOREIGN KEY order_line2item (item_numb)
    REFERENCES item
        ON UPDATE CASCADE
        ON DELETE RESTRICT
    FOREIGN KEY order_line2order (order_numb)
    REFERENCES order
        ON UPDATE CASCADE
        ON DELETE CASCADE)

CREATE TABLE purchase
    (purchase_date date,
    customer_numb int,
    items_received char (1),
    customer_paid char (1)
    PRIMARY KEY (purchase_date, customer_numb)
    FOREIGN KEY purchase2customer (customer_numb)
    REFERENCES customer
        ON UPDATE CASCADE)
        ON DELETE RESTRICT)

CREATE TABLE purchase_item
    (purchase_date date,
    customer_numb int,
    item_numb int,
    condition char (15),
    price_paid numeric (6,2)
    PRIMARY KEY (purchase_date, customer_numb, item_numb)
    FOREIGN KEY purchase_item2purchase (purchase_date, customer_numb
        ON UPDATE CASCADE
        ON DELETE CASCADE
    FOREIGN KEY purchase_item2item (item_numb)
```

■ **FIGURE 9-4** The complete CREATE TABLE statements for the Antique Opticals database—Cont'd

```
    REFERENCES item
        ON UPDATE CASCADE
        ON DELETE RESTRICT)

CREATE TABLE actor
    (actor_numb int PRIMARY KEY,
    actor_name varchar (60))

CREATE TABLE performance
    (actor_numb int,
    item_numb int,
    role varchar (60)
    PRIMARY KEY (actor_numb, item_numb)
    FOREIGN KEY performance2actor (actor_numb)
    REFERENCES actor
        ON UPDATE CASCADE
        ON DELETE CASCADE
    FOREIGN KEY performance2item (item_numb)
    REFERENCES item
        ON UPDATE CASCADE
        ON DELETE CASCADE)

CREATE TABLE producer
    (producer_name varchar (60) CONSTRAINT producer_pk PRIMARY KEY,
    studio varchar (40))

CREATE TABLE production
    (producer_name varchar (60),
    item_numb int
    PRIMARY KEY (producer_name, item_numb)
    FOREIGN KEY production2producer (producer_name)
    REFERENCES producer
        ON UPDATE CASCADE
        ON DELETE CASCADE
    FOREIGN KEY production2item
    REFERENCES item
        ON UPDATE CASCADE
        ON DELETE CASCADE)
```

■ **FIGURE 9-4** Cont'd

Additional Column Constraints

There are additional constraints that you can place on columns in a table beyond primary and foreign key constraints. These include requiring unique values and predicates in CHECK clauses.

Requiring Unique Values

If you want to ensure that the values in a non-primary key column are unique, then you can use the UNIQUE keyword. UNIQUE verifies that all non-null values are unique. For example, if you were storing Social Security numbers in an employees table that used an employee ID as the primary key, you could also enforce unique Social Security numbers with:

```
ssn char (11) UNIQUE
```

The UNIQUE clause can also be placed at the end of the CREATE TABLE statement, along with the primary key and foreign key specifications. In that case, it takes the form:

```
UNIQUE (column_names)
```

Check Clauses

The CHECK clause to which you were introduced earlier in the chapter in the "Domains" section can also be used with individual columns to declare column-specific constraints. To add a constraint, you place a CHECK clause after the column declaration, using the keyword VALUE in a predicate to indicate the value being checked.

For example, to verify that a column used to hold true-false values is limited to T and F, you could write a CHECK clause as:

```
CHECK (UPPER(VALUE) = 'T' OR UPPER(VALUE) = 'F')
```

VIEWS

As you saw in Chapter 5, views provide a way to give users a specific portion of a larger schema with which they can work. Before you actually can create views, there are two things you should consider: which views you really need and whether the views can be used for updating data.

Deciding Which Views to Create

Views take up very little space in a database, occupying only a few rows in a data dictionary table. That being the case, you can feel free to create views as needed.

A typical database might include the following views:

- One view for every base that is exactly the same as the base table but with a different name. Then you prevent end users from seeing the base tables and do not tell the end users the table names; you give end users access to only the views. This makes it harder for end users to gain access to the stored tables because they do not know their names. However, as you will see in the next section, it is essential for updating that there be views that do not match the base tables.
- One view for each primary key–foreign key relationship over which you join frequently. If the tables are large, the actual syntax of the statement may include methods for avoiding the join operation but still combining the tables.
- One view for each complex query that you issue frequently.
- Views as needed to restrict user access to specific columns and rows. For example, you might recreate a view for a receptionist that shows employee office numbers and telephone extensions but leaves out home address, telephone number, and salary.

View Updatability Issues

A database query can apply any operations supported by its DBMS's query language to a view, just as it can to base tables. However, using views for updates is a much more complicated issue. Given that views exist only in main memory, any updates made to a view must be stored in the underlying base tables if the updates are to have any effect on the database.

Not every view is updatable, however. Although the rules for view updatability vary from one DBMS to another, you will find that most DBMSs share the following restrictions:

- A view must be created from no more than one base table or view.
- If the source of the view is another view, then the source view must also adhere to the rules for updatability.
- A view must be created from only one query. Two or more queries cannot be assembled into a single view table using operations such as union.
- The view must include the primary key columns of the base table.
- The view must include all columns specified as not null (columns requiring mandatory values).

- The view must not include any groups of data. It must include the original rows of data from the base table rather than rows based on values common to groups of data.
- The view must not remove duplicate rows.

Creating Views

To create a view whose columns have the same name as the columns in the base tables from which it is derived, you give the view a name and include the SQL query that defines its contents:

```
CREATE VIEW view_name AS SELECT . . .
```

For example, if Antique Opticals wanted to create a view that included action films, the SQL is written:

```
CREATE VIEW action_films AS SELECT item_numb,
  title FROM item WHERE genre = 'action'
```

If you want to rename the columns in the view, you include the view's column names in the CREATE VIEW statement:

```
CREATE VIEW action_films (identifier, name) AS SELECT
  item_numb, title FROM item WHERE genre =
  'action'
```

The preceding statement will produce a view with two columns named *identifier* and *name*. Note that if you want to change even one column name, you must include *all* the column names in the parentheses following the view name. The DBMS will match the columns following SELECT with the view column names by their position in the list.

Views can be created from any SQL query, including those that perform joins, unions, and grouping. For example, to simplify looking at customers and their order totals, Antique Opticals might create a view like the following:

```
CREATE VIEW sales_summary AS SELECT customer_numb,
  order. order_numb, order.order_date, SUM
  (selling_price) FROM order_line JOIN order GROUP
  BY customer_number, orders.order_date, orders.
  order_numb
```

The view table will then contain grouped data along with a computed column.

TEMPORARY TABLES

A temporary table is a base table that is not stored in the database but instead exists only while the database session in which it was created is active. At first glance, this may sound like a view, but views and temporary tables are rather different:

- A view exists only for a single query. Each time you use the name of a view, its table is recreated from existing data.
- A temporary table exists for the entire database session in which it was created.
- A view is automatically populated with the data retrieved by the query that defines it.
- You must add data to a temporary table with SQL INSERT commands.
- Only views that meet the criteria for view updatability can be used for data modifications.
- Because temporary tables are base tables, all of them can be updated.
- Because the contents of a view are generated each time the view's name is used, a view's data are always current.
- The data in a temporary table reflect the state of the database at the time the table was loaded with data. If the data from which the temporary table was loaded are modified after the temporary table has received its data, then the contents of the temporary table may be out of sync with other parts of the database.

If the contents of a temporary table become outdated when source data change, why use a temporary table at all? Wouldn't it be better simply to use a view whose contents are continually regenerated? The answer lies in performance. It takes processing time to create a view table. If you are going to use data only once during a database session, then a view will actually perform better than a temporary table because you don't need to create a structure for it. However, if you are going to be using the data repeatedly during a session, then a temporary table provides better performance because it needs to be created only once. The decision therefore results in a trade-off: Using a view repeatedly takes more time but provides continuously updated data; using a temporary table repeatedly saves time, but you run the risk that the table's contents may be out of date.

Creating Temporary Tables

Creating a temporary table is very similar to creating a permanent base table. You do, however, need to decide on the *scope* of the table. A temporary table may be *global,* in which case it is accessible to the entire application program that created it. Alternatively, it can be *local,* in which case it is accessible only to the program module in which it was created.

To create a global temporary table, you add the keywords GLOBAL TEMPORARY to the CREATE TABLE statement:

```
CREATE GLOBAL TEMPORARY TABLE (remainder of CREATE
  statement)
```

By the same token, you create a local temporary table with:

```
CREATE LOCAL TEMPORARY TABLE (remainder of CREATE
  statement)
```

For example, if Antique Opticals was going to use the order summary information repeatedly, it might create the following temporary table instead of using a view:

```
CREATE GLOBAL TEMPORARY TABLE
  order_summary (customer_numb int, order_numb
  int, order_date date, order_total numeric
  (6,2), PRIMARY KEY (customer_numb, order_numb)
```

Loading Temporary Tables with Data

To place data in a temporary table, you use one or more SQL INSERT statements. For example, to load the order summary table created in the preceding section, you could type:

```
INSERT INTO order_summary SELECT customer_numb,
  order.order_numb, order.order_date, SUM
  (selling_price) FROM order_line JOIN order GROUP
  BY customer_number, orders.order_date, orders.
  order_numb
```

You can now query and manipulate the order_summary table just as you would a permanent base table.

Disposition of Temporary Table Rows

When you write embedded SQL (SQL statements coded as part of a program written in a high-level language such as C++ or Java), you have control over the amount of work that the DBMS considers to be a unit (a *transaction*). Although we will cover transactions in depth in Chapter 15, at this point you need to know that a transaction can end in one of two ways: It can be *committed* (its changes made permanent), or it can be *rolled back* (its changes undone).

By default, the rows in a temporary table are purged whenever a transaction is committed. You can, however, instruct the DBMS to retain the rows by including ON COMMIT PRESERVE ROWS to the end of the table creation statement:

```
CREATE GLOBAL TEMPORARY TABLE order_summary
  (customer_numb int, order_numb int, order_date
  date, order_total numeric (6,2), PRIMARY KEY
  (customer_numb, order_numb ON COMMIT PRESERVE
  ROWS))
```

Because a rollback returns the database to the state it was in before the transaction begins, a temporary table will also be restored to its previous state (with or without rows).

CREATING INDEXES

As you read in Chapter 7, an index is a data structure that provides a fast access path to rows in a table based on the value in one or more columns (the index key). Because an index stores key values in order, the DBMS can use a fast search technique to find the values rather than being forced to search each row in an unordered table sequentially.

You create indexes with the CREATE INDEX statement:

```
CREATE INDEX index_name ON table_name
  (index_key_columns)
```

For example, to create an index on the title column in Antique Opticals' item table, you could use:

```
CREATE INDEX item_title_index ON item (title)
```

By default, the index will allow duplicate entries and keeps the entries in ascending order (alphabetical, numeric, or chronological, whichever is appropriate). To require unique indexes, add the keyword UNIQUE after CREATE:

```
CREATE UNIQUE INDEX item_title_index ON item
  (title)
```

To sort in descending order, insert DESC after the column whose sort order you want to change. For example, Antique Opticals might want to create an index on the order date in the order relation in descending order so that the most recent orders are first:

```
CREATE INDEX order_order_date_index ON order
  (order_date DESC)
```

If you want to create an index on a concatenated key, include all the columns that should be part of the index key in the column list. For example, the following creates an index organized by actor and item number:

```
CREATE INDEX actor_actor_item_index ON actor
  (actor_numb, item_numb)
```

Although you do not need to access an index directly unless you want to delete it from the database, it helps to give indexes names that will tell you something about their tables and key columns. This makes it easier to remember them should you need to get rid of the indexes.

MODIFYING DATABASE ELEMENTS

With the exception of tables, database elements are largely unchangeable. When you want to modify them, you must delete them from the database and create them from scratch. In contrast, just about every characteristic of a table can be modified without deleting the table using the ALTER TABLE statement.

Adding Columns

To add a new column to a table, use the ALTER TABLE statement with the following syntax:

```
ALTER TABLE table_name ADD column_name
  column_data_type column_constraints
```

For example, if Antique Opticals wanted to add a telephone number column to the producer table, they would use:

```
ALTER TABLE producer ADD producer_phone char (12)
```

To add more than one column at the same time, simply separate the clauses with commas:

```
ALTER TABLE producer ADD producer_phone char (12),
  ADD studio_street char (30), ADD studio_city char
  (15), ADD studio_state char (2), ADD studio_zip
  char (10)
```

Adding Table Constraints

You can add table constraints such as foreign keys at any time. To do so, include the new constraint in an ALTER TABLE statement:

```
ALTER TABLE table_name ADD table_constraint
```

Assume, for example, that Antique Opticals created a new table named "states" and included in it all the two-character U.S. state abbreviations. The company would then need to add references to that table from the customer, distributor, and producer tables:

```
ALTER TABLE customer ADD FOREIGN KEY customer2states
  (customer_state) REFERENCES states (state_name)
ALTER TABLE distributor ADD FOREIGN KEY
  distributor2states (distributor_state) REFERENCES
  states (state_name)
ALTER TABLE producer ADD FOREIGN KEY producer2states
  (studio_state) REFERENCES states (state_name)
```

When you add a foreign key constraint to a table, the DBMS verifies that all existing data in the table must meet that constraint. If the data do not, the ALTER TABLE statement will fail.

Modifying Columns

You can modify columns by changing any characteristic of the column, including the data type, size, and constraints.

Changing Column Definitions

To replace a complete column definition, use the MODIFY command with the current column name and the new column characteristics. For example, to change the customer number in Antique Opticals' customer table from an integer to a character column, use:

```
ALTER TABLE customer MODIFY customer_numb char (4)
```

When you change the data type of a column, the DBMS will attempt to convert any existing values to the new data type. If the current values cannot be converted, then the table modification will not be performed. In general, most columns can be converted to characters. However, conversions from a character data type to numbers, dates, and/or times require that existing data represent legal values in the new data type.

Given that the DBMS converts values whenever it can, changing a column data type may seem like a simple change, but it isn't. In this particular example, the customer number is referenced by foreign keys, and therefore the foreign key columns must be modified as well. You need to remove the foreign key constraints, change the foreign key columns, change the primary key column, and then add the foreign key constraints back to the tables that contain the foreign keys. Omitting the changes to the foreign keys will make it impossible to add any rows to those foreign key tables because integer customer numbers will never match character customer numbers. Moral to the story: Before changing column characteristics, consider the effect of those changes on other tables in the database.

Changing Default Values

To add or change a default value only (without changing the data type or size of the column), include the DEFAULT keyword:

```
ALTER TABLE order_line MODIFY discount_percent
  DEFAULT 0
```

Changing Null Status

To switch between allowing nulls and not allowing nulls without changing any other characteristics, add NULL or NOT NULL as appropriate:

```
ALTER TABLE customer MODIFY customer_zip NOT NULL
```

or

```
ALTER TABLE customer MODIFY customer_zip NULL
```

Changing Column Constraints

To modify a column constraint without changing any other column characteristics, include a CHECK clause:

```
ALTER TABLE item MODIFY retail_price CHECK (VALUE >=
  12.95)
```

Deleting Table Elements

You can also delete structural elements from a table as needed, without deleting the entire table.

- To delete a column:

```
ALTER TABLE order_line DELETE line_cost
```

- To delete a CHECK table constraint (a CHECK that has been applied to an entire table rather than to a specific column):

```
ALTER TABLE customer DELETE CHECK
```

- To remove the UNIQUE constraint from one or more columns:

```
ALTER TABLE item DELETE UNIQUE (title)
```

- To remove a table's primary key:

```
ALTER TABLE customer DELETE PRIMARY KEY
```

Although you can delete a table's primary key, keep in mind that if you do not add a new one, you will not be able to modify any data in that table.

- To delete a foreign key:

```
ALTER TABLE item DELETE FOREIGN KEY item2distributor
```

Renaming Table Elements

You can rename both tables and columns.

- To rename a table, place the new table name after the RENAME keyword:

```
ALTER TABLE order_line RENAME line_item
```

- To rename a column, include both the old and new column names, separated by the keyword TO:

```
ALTER TABLE item RENAME title TO item_title
```

DELETING DATABASE ELEMENTS

To delete a structural element from a database, you "drop" the element. For example, to delete a table you would type:

```
DROP TABLE table_name
```

Dropping a table (or any database structural element, for that matter) is irrevocable. In most cases, the DBMS will not bother to ask you, "Are you sure?" but will immediately delete the structure of the table and all of its data if it can. A table deletion will fail, for example, if it has foreign keys referencing it and one or more of the foreign key constraints contain ON DELETE RESTRICT. Dropping a table or view will also fail if the element being dropped is currently in use by another user.

Note: There is one exception to the irrevocability of a delete. If an element is deleted during a program-controlled transaction and the transaction is rolled back, the deletion will be undone. Undoing transactions is covered in Chapter 15.

You can remove the following elements from a database with the DROP statement:

- Tables
- Views

```
DROP VIEW view_name
```

- Indexes

```
DROP INDEX index_name
```

- Domains

```
DROP DOMAIN domain_name
```

Chapter 10

Using CASE Tools for Database Design

A *CASE* (computer-aided software engineering) tool is a software package that provides support for the design and implementation of information systems. By integrating many of the techniques used to document a system design—including the data dictionary, data flows, and entity relationships—CASE software can increase the consistency and accuracy of a database design. They can also ease the task of creating the diagrams that accompany a system design.

Many CASE tools are on the market. The actual "look" of the diagrams is specific to each particular package. However, the examples presented in this chapter are typical of the capabilities of most CASE tools.

> *Note:* The specific CASE software used in Chapters 11 through 13 is Mac A&D by Excel Software (*www.excelsoftware.com*). (There's also a Windows version.) Other such packages that are well suited to database design include Visio (*www.microsoft.com*) and Visible Analyst (*www.visible.com*).

A word of warning is in order about CASE tools before we proceed any further: A CASE tool is exactly that—a tool. It can document a database design, and it can provide invaluable help in maintaining the consistency of a design. Although some current CASE tools can verify the integrity of a data model, they cannot design the database for you. There is no software in the world that can examine a database environment and identify the entities, attributes, and relationships that should be represented in a database. The model created with CASE software is therefore only as good as the analysis of the database environment provided by the people using the tool.

Relational Database Design and Implementation

CASE CAPABILITIES

Most CASE tools organize the documents pertaining to a single system into a "project." As you can see in Figure 10-1, by default a typical project supports the following types of documents:

- *Data dictionary:* In most CASE tools, the data dictionary forms the backbone of the project, providing a single repository for all processes, entities, attributes, and domains used anywhere throughout the project.
- *Requirements:* CASE tool requirements documents store the text descriptions of product specifications. They also make it possible to arrange requirements in a hierarchy, typically from general to specific.
- *Data flow diagrams:* As you read in Chapter 4, data flow diagrams document the way in which data travel throughout an organization, indicating who handles the data. Although it isn't necessary to create a data flow diagram if your only goal with the project is to document a database design, data flow diagrams can often be useful in documenting the relationships among multiple organization units and the data they handle. Data flow diagrams can, for example, help you determine whether an organization needs a single database or a combination of databases.

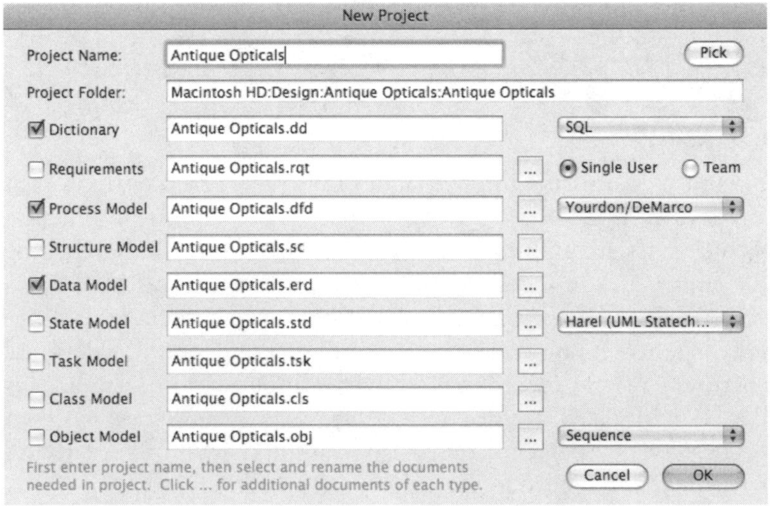

■ **FIGURE 10-1** CASE software project documents.

- *Structure charts:* Structure charts are used to model the structure of application programs that will be developed using structured programming techniques. The charts show the relationship between program modules.
- *Data models:* Data models are the ER diagrams about which you have been reading. The ER diagram on which the examples in this chapter are based can be found in Figure 10-2.
- *Screen prototypes:* Drawings of sample screen layouts are typically most useful for documenting the user interface of application programs. However, they can also act as a crosscheck to ensure that a database design is complete by allowing you to verify that everything needed to generate the sample screen designs is present in the database.
- *State models:* State models, documented in state transition diagrams, indicate the ways in which data change as they move through the information system.
- *Task diagrams:* Task diagrams are used to help plan application programs in which multiple operations (tasks) occur at the same time. They are therefore not particularly relevant to the database design process.
- *Class diagrams:* Class diagrams are used when performing object-oriented rather than structured analysis and design.
- *Object diagrams:* Object diagrams are used during object-oriented analysis to indicate how objects communicate with one another by passing messages.

Many of the diagrams and reports that a CASE tool can provide are designed to follow a single theoretical model. For example, the ER diagrams that you have seen earlier in this book might be based on the Chen model or the Information Engineering model. Any given CASE tool will support some selection of diagramming models. You must therefore examine what a particular product supports before you purchase it to ensure that it provides exactly what you need.

ER DIAGRAM REPORTS

In addition to providing tools for simplifying the creation of ER diagrams, many CASE tools can generate reports that document the contents of an ERD. For example, in Figure 10-3 you can see a portion of

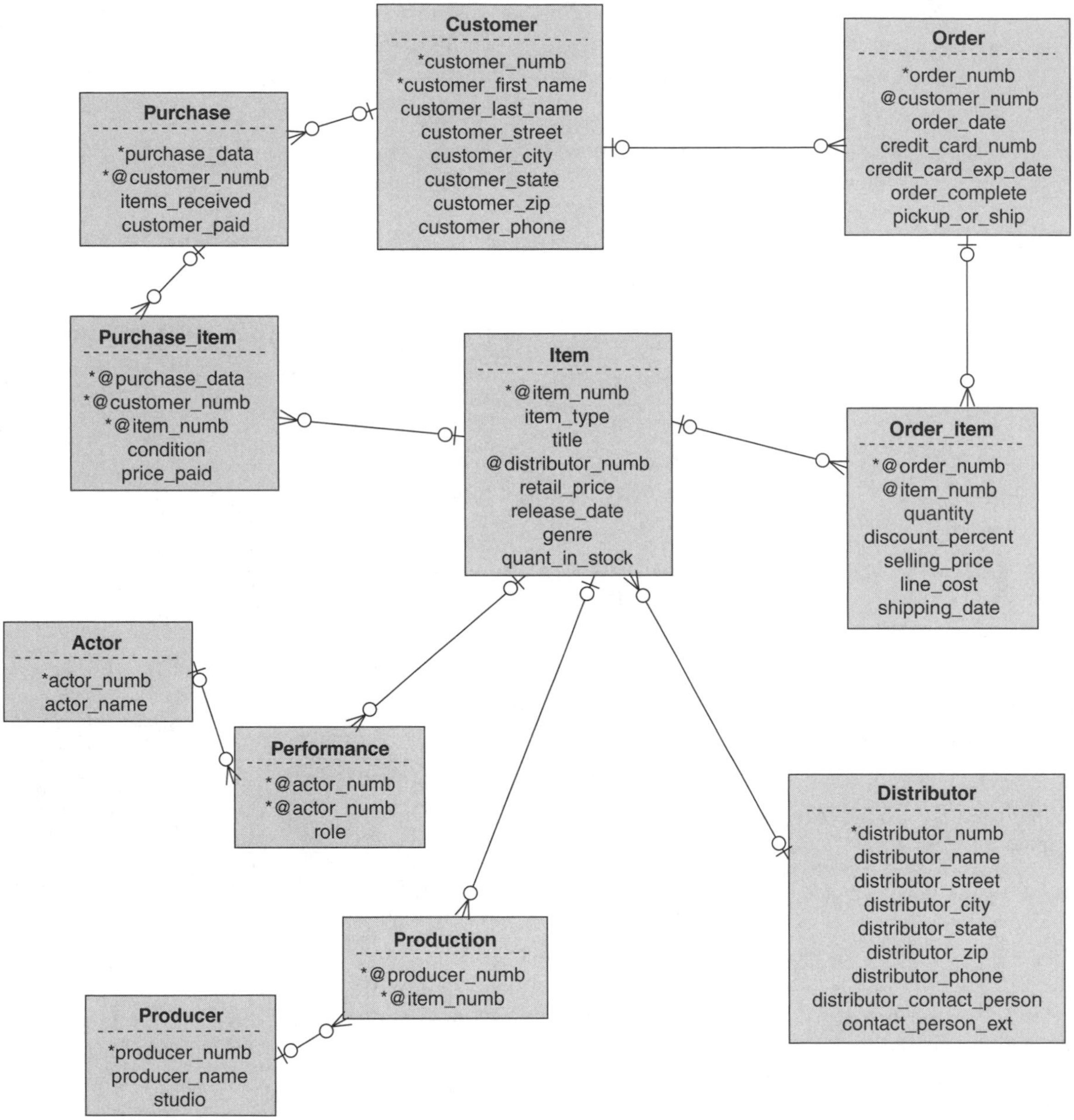

■ **FIGURE 10-2** ER diagram created with the sample CASE tool for Antique Opticals.

```
**************************************************

Entity: actor

Language: SQL
Physical: actor##

Attributes:

...*actor_numb
Language: SQL
DataType: INTEGER
Physical: actor_numb##

...actor_name
Language: SQL
DataType: long_name
Physical: actor_name##

**************************************************
```

■ **FIGURE 10-3** Part of an entity specification report.

a report that provides a description of each entity and its attributes, including the attribute's data type.

The "physical" line contains the name that the database element will have in SQL CREATE TABLE statements; it can be different from the element's data dictionary entry name. For many designers, this type of report actually constitutes a paper-based data dictionary.

A CASE tool can also translate the relationships in an ER diagram into a report such as that in Figure 10-4. The text in the report describes the *cardinality* of each relationship in the ERD (whether the relationship is one-to-one, one-to-many, or many-to-many) and can therefore be very useful for pinpointing errors that may have crept into the graphic version of the diagram.

actor is associated with zero or more instances of performance.
performance is associated with zero or one instance of actor.

customer is associated with zero or more instances of order.
order is associated with zero or one instance of customer.

customer is associated with zero or more instances of purchase.
purchase is associated with zero or one instance of customer.

distributor is associated with zero or more instances of item.
item is associated with zero or one instance of distributor.

item is associated with zero or more instances of order_item.
order_item is associated with zero or one instance of item.

item is associated with zero or more instances of performance.
performance is associated with zero or one instance of item.

item is associated with zero or more instances of production.
production is associated with zero or one instance of item.

item is associated with zero or more instances of purchase_item.
purchase_item is associated with zero or one instance of item.

order is associated with zero or more instances of order_item.
order_item is associated with zero or one instance of order.

producer is associated with zero or more instances of production.
production is associated with zero or one instance of producer.

purchase is associated with zero or more instances of purchase_item.
purchase_item is associated with zero or one instance of purchase.

■ **FIGURE 10-4** A relation specification report.

DATA FLOW DIAGRAMS

There are two widely used styles for data flow diagrams (DFDs): Yourdon/DeMarco, which has been used throughout this book, and Gene & Sarson.

The Yourdon/DeMarco style, which you can see in Figure 10-5, uses circles for processes. (This particular example is for a small taxi company that rents its cabs to drivers.) Data stores are represented by

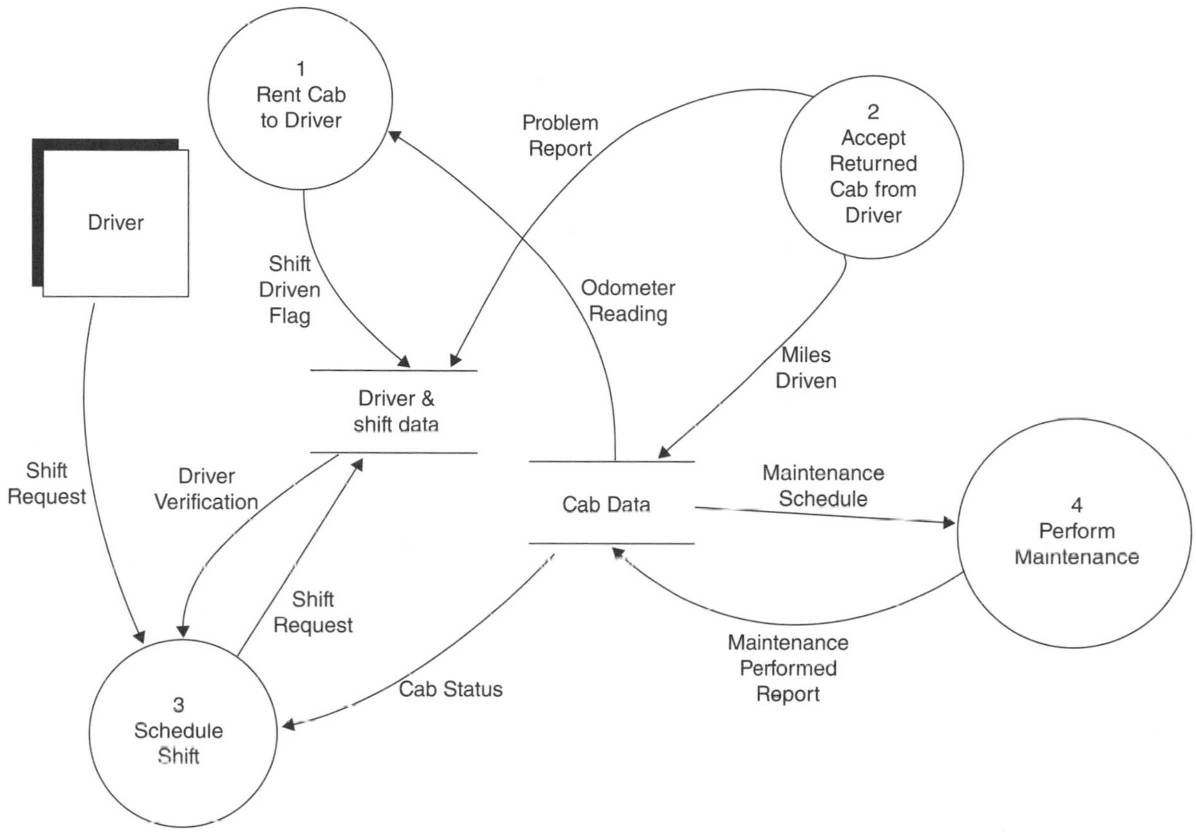

■ **FIGURE 10-5** Yourdon/DeMarco style DFD.

parallel lines. Data flows are curved or straight lines with labels that indicate the data that are moving along that pathway. External sources of data are represented by rectangles.

In concept, the Gene & Sarson style is very similar: It varies primarily in style. As you can see in Figure 10-6, the processes are round-cornered rectangles as opposed to circles. Data stores are open-ended rectangles rather than parallel lines. External sources of data remain as rectangles, and data flows use only straight lines. However, the concepts of numbering the processing and exploding each process with a child diagram that shows further detail is the same, regardless of which diagramming style you use.

As mentioned earlier, DFDs are very useful in the database design process for helping a designer to determine whether an organization

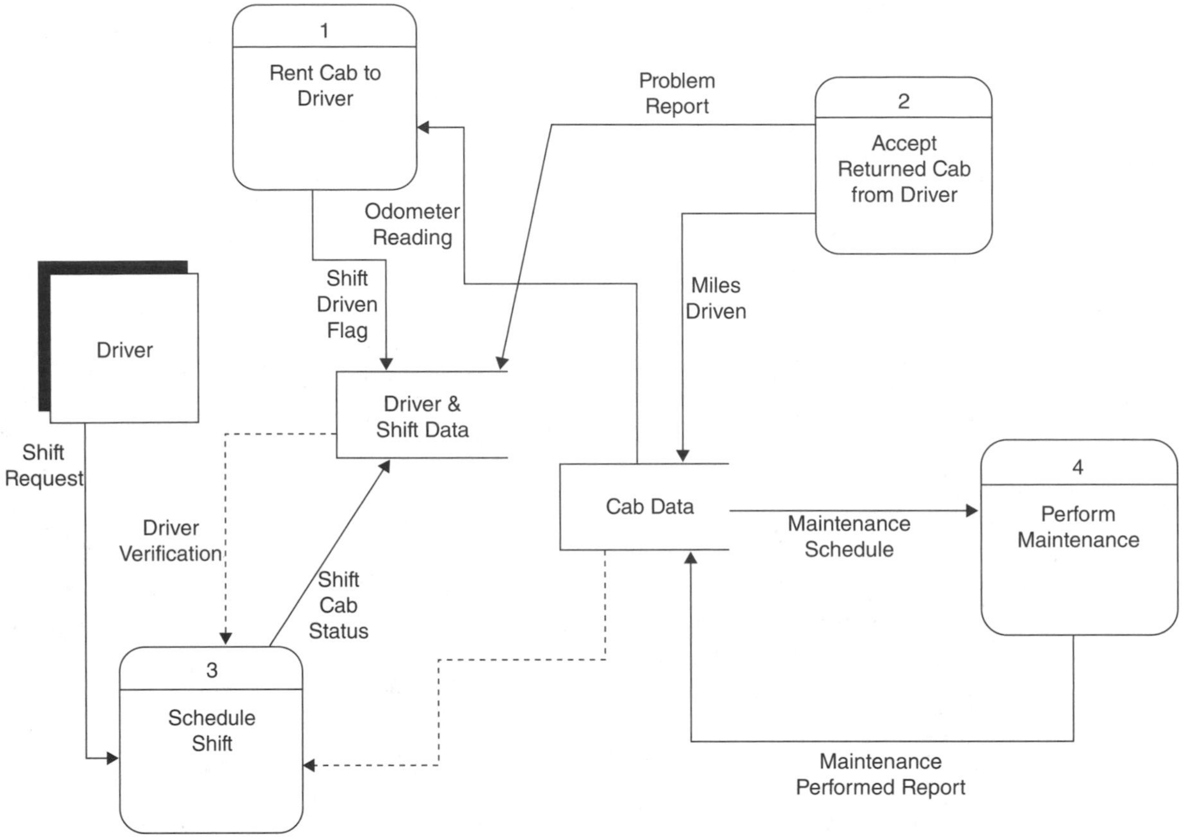

■ **FIGURE 10-6** Gene & Sarson style DFD.

needs a single, integrated database or a collection of independent databases. For example, it is clear from the taxi company's DFDs that an integrated database is required. Of the four processes shown in the diagram, three use data from both the cab data store and the drive and shift data store. (Only the maintenance process uses just one data store.) You will see examples of using DFDs in this way in the case studies in the following three chapters.

THE DATA DICTIONARY

From a database designer's point of view, the ER diagram and its associated data dictionary are the two most important parts of CASE software. Since you were introduced to several types of ER diagrams in Chapter 4, we will not repeat them here but instead focus on the interaction of the diagrams and the data dictionary.

A data dictionary provides a central repository for documenting entities, attributes, and domains. In addition, by linking entries in the ER diagram to the data dictionary you can provide enough information for the CASE tool to generate the SQL CREATE statements needed to define the structure of the database.

The layout of a data dictionary varies with the specific CASE tool, as does the way in which entries are configured. Entities are organized alphabetically, with the attributes following the entity name. Entity names are red, and attributes are blue. (Of course, you can't see the colors in this black-and-white book, so you'll have to take my word for it.) Domain names appear alphabetically among the entities. Each relationship in the related ERD also has an entry. Because each item name begins with "Relation," all relationship entries sort together in the data dictionary.

When you select an entity name, the display shows the entity's name, composition (the attributes in the entity), definition (details needed to generate SQL and so on), and type of database element (in the References section). Figure 10-7, for example, shows the information stored in the data dictionary for Antique Opticals' customer relations. All of the information about the entity (and all other entries, for that matter) is editable, but because the format is specific to the CASE tool, be careful when making changes unless you know exactly how entries should appear.

Attribute entries (Figure 10-8) are similar to entity entries, but they have no data in the composition section. Attribute definitions can include the attribute's data type, a default value, and any constraints that have been placed on that attribute. In most cases, these details are entered through a dialog box, relieving the designer of worrying about specific SQL syntax.

Relationships (Figure 10-9) are named by the CASE tool. Notice that the definition indicates which entities the relationship relates, as well as which is at the "many" end of the relationship (the child) and which is at the "one" end (the parent).

Many relational DBMSs now support the definition of custom domains. Such domains are stored in the data dictionary

■ **FIGURE 10-7** Definition of an entity in a data dictionary window.

(Figure 10-10) along with their definitions. Once a domain has been created and is part of the data dictionary, it can be assigned to attributes. If a database administrator needs to change a domain, it can be changed once in the data dictionary and propagated automatically to all attributes entries that use it.

The linking of data dictionary entries to an ER diagram has another major benefit: The data dictionary can examine its entries and automatically identify foreign keys. This is yet another way in which the consistency of attribute definitions enforced by a CASE tool's data dictionary can support the database design process.

Note: Mac A&D is good enough at identifying foreign keys to pick up concatenated foreign keys.

■ **FIGURE 10-8** Definition of an attribute in a data dictionary window.

Keep in mind that a CASE tool is not linked dynamically with a DBMS. Although data definitions in the data dictionary are linked to diagrams, changes made to the CASE tool's project will not affect the DBMS. It is up to the database administrator to make the actual changes to the database.

CODE GENERATION

The end product of most database design efforts is a set of SQL CREATE TABLE commands. If you are using CASE software and the software contains a complete data dictionary, then the software can generate the SQL for you. You will typically find that a given CASE tool can tailor the SQL syntax to a range of specific DBMSs. In most cases, the code will be saved in a text file, which you can then use as input to a DBMS.

■ **FIGURE 10-9** Data dictionary entry for a relationship between two entities in an ERD.

Note: Most of today's CASE tools will also generate XML for you. XML provides a template for interpreting the contents of files containing data and therefore is particularly useful when you need to transfer schemas and data between DBMSs with different SQL implementations or between DBMSs that do not use SQL at all. XML has become so important for data exchange that it is covered in Chapter 17.

The effectiveness of the SQL that a CASE tool can produce, as you might expect, depends on the completeness of the data dictionary entries. To get truly usable SQL, the data dictionary must contain the following:

- Domains for every attribute
- Primary key definitions (created as attributes are added to entities in the ER diagram)

■ **FIGURE 10-10** Data dictionary entry for a custom domain.

- Foreign key definitions (created as attributes are added to entities in the ER diagram or by the CASE tool after the ER diagram is complete)
- Any additional constraints that are to be placed on individual attributes or on the entity as a whole

SAMPLE INPUT AND OUTPUT DESIGNS

Sample input and output designs form part of the system documentation, especially in that they help document requirements. They can also support the database designer by providing a way to double-check that the database can provide all the data needed by application programs. Many CASE tools therefore provide a way to draw and label sample screen and report layouts.

Most of today's CASE tools allow multiple users to interaction with the same project. This means that interface designers can work with

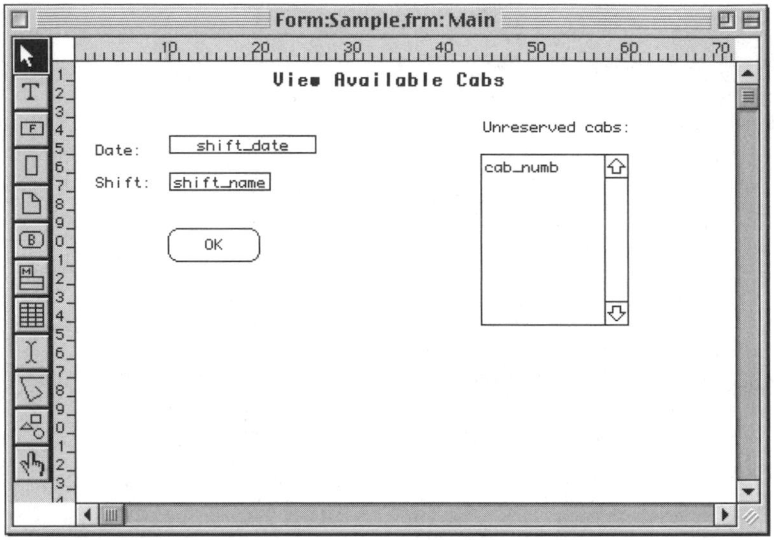

■ **FIGURE 10-11** Sample screen design.

the same data dictionary that the systems analysts and database designers are building, ensuring that all the necessary data elements have been handled.

For example, one of the most important things that the person scheduling cab reservations for the taxi company needs to know is which cabs are not reserved for a given date and shift. A sample screen such as that in Figure 10-11 will do the trick.[1] The diagram shows what data the user needs to enter (the shift date and the shift name). It also shows the output (cab numbers). The names of the fields on the sample screen design can be linked to the data dictionary.

A CASE tool can be used to model an entire application program. The "browse" tool at the very bottom of the tool bar in Figure 10-12 switches into browse mode, in which buttons and menus become active. Users can make choices from pull-down menus that can be

[1] In the interest of complete disclosure, you should know that when Mac A&D was ported from Mac OS 9 to Mac OS X, the screen and report design module wasn't included. (It will probably show up in a future release.) Therefore, the sample screen designs that you will see in this chapter and in Chapter 12 are from an older version of the product. The Windows version, however, does include the interface design module.

linked to other forms. Buttons can also trigger the opening of other forms. Users can click into data entry fields and tab between fields. Users can therefore not only see the layout and output screen and documents but also navigate through an application.

THE DRAWING ENVIRONMENT

Up to this point, you've been reading about the way in which the functions provided by CASE software can support the database design effort. In this last section we will briefly examine the tools you can expect to find as part of CASE software, tools with which you can create the types of documents you need.

Because many of the documents you create with CASE software are diagrams, the working environment of a CASE tool includes a specialized drawing environment. For example, in Figure 10-12 you can see the drawing tools provided by the sample CASE tool for creating ER diagrams. (Keep in mind that each CASE tool will differ somewhat in the precise layout of its drawing tool bars, but the basic capabilities will be similar.)

The important thing to note is that the major shapes needed for the diagrams—for ER diagrams, typically just the entity and relationship

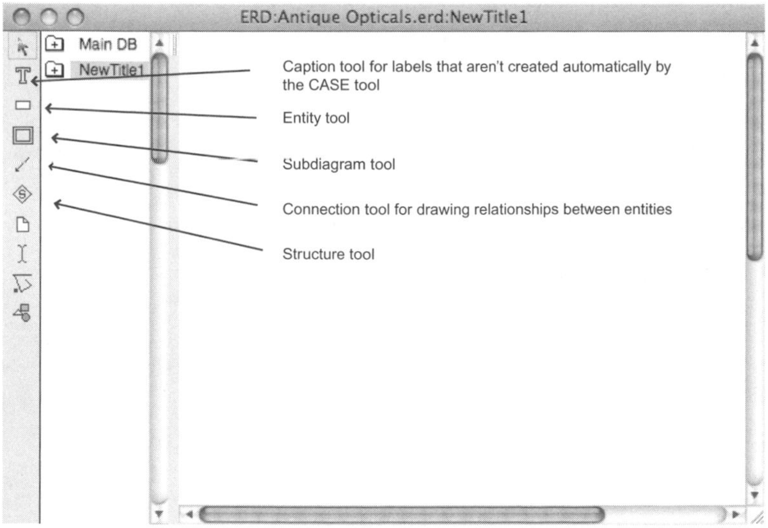

■ **FIGURE 10-12** Example CASE tool drawing environment for ER diagrams.

line—are provided as individual tools. You therefore simply click the tool you want to use in the tool bar and draw the shape in the diagram, much like you would if you were working with a general-purpose graphics program.

FOR FURTHER READING

To learn more about the Yourdon/DeMarco method of structure analysis using data flow diagrams, see either of the following:

DeMarco, Tom, and P. J. Flauger. *Structured Analysis and System Specification*. Prentice Hall, 1985.

Yourdon, Edward. *Modern Structured Analysis*. Prentice Hall PTR, 2000.

Chapter 11

Database Design Case Study 1: Mighty-Mite Motors

It is not unusual for a database designer to be employed to reengineer the information systems of an established corporation. As you will see from the company described in this chapter, information systems in older companies have often grown haphazardly, with almost no planning and integration. The result is a hodgepodge of data repositories that cannot provide the information needed for the corporation to function because they are isolated from one another. In such a situation, it is the job of the database designer to examine the environment as a whole and to focus on the integration of data access across the corporation, as well as the design of one or more databases that will meet individual department needs.

On the bright side, an organization such as Mighty-Mite Motors, which has a history of data processing of some kind, knows quite well what it needs in information systems, even if the employees are unable to articulate those needs immediately. There will almost certainly be a collection of paper forms and reports that the organization uses regularly to provide significant input to the systems design process.

CORPORATE OVERVIEW

Might-Mite Motors, Inc. (MMM) is a closely held corporation, established in 1980, that manufactures and markets miniature ridable motor vehicles for children. Products include several models of cars,

■ **FIGURE 11-1** Might-Mite Motors' product catalog.

trucks, all-terrain vehicles, and trains (see Figure 11-1). Vehicles are powered by car batteries and can achieve speeds of up to 5 mph.

At this time, MMM is organized into three divisions: Product Development, Manufacturing, and Marketing and Sales. Each division is headed by a vice president, who reports directly to the CEO. (An organization chart appears in Figure 11-2.) All of these divisions are housed in a single location that the corporation owns outright.

Model #001

All Terrain Vehicle: Accelerator in the handebar lets young riders reach speeds of up to 5 mph. Vehicle stops immediately when child removes his or her hand from the handbars. Can carry one up to 65-lb passenger.
Suggested retail price: $124.95

001

Model #002

4-Wheel Drive Cruiser: Two-pedal drive system lets vehicle move forward at 2 1/2 mph on hard surfaces, plus reverse. Electronic speed reduction for beginners. Includes one 6V battery and one recharger. Ages 3–7 (can carry two passengers up to 40 lbs each).
Suggested retail price: $249.99

002

■ **FIGURE 11-1** Cont'd

Product Development Division

The Product Development division is responsible for designing and testing both new and redesigned products. The division employs design engineers who use computer-aided design (CAD) software to prepare initial designs for new or redesigned vehicles. Once a design is complete, between one and ten prototypes are built. The prototypes are first tested in-house using robotic drivers/passengers. After refinement, the prototypes are test by children in a variety of settings. Feedback from the testers is used to refine product designs and to make

Model #003

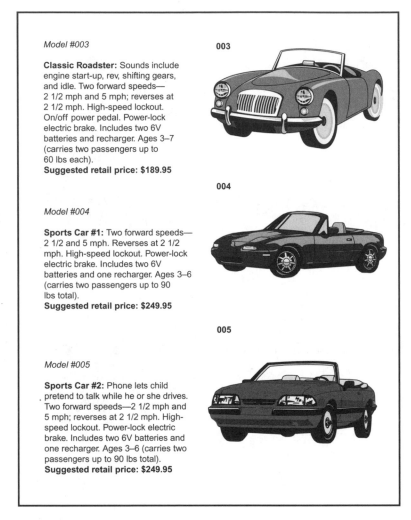

Classic Roadster: Sounds include engine start-up, rev, shifting gears, and idle. Two forward speeds—2 1/2 mph and 5 mph; reverses at 2 1/2 mph. High-speed lockout. On/off power pedal. Power-lock electric brake. Includes two 6V batteries and recharger. Ages 3–7 (carries two passengers up to 60 lbs each).
Suggested retail price: $189.95

003

004

Model #004

Sports Car #1: Two forward speeds—2 1/2 and 5 mph. Reverses at 2 1/2 mph. High-speed lockout. Power-lock electric brake. Includes two 6V batteries and one recharger. Ages 3–6 (carries two passengers up to 90 lbs total).
Suggested retail price: $249.95

005

Model #005

Sports Car #2: Phone lets child pretend to talk while he or she drives. Two forward speeds—2 1/2 mph and 5 mph; reverses at 2 1/2 mph. High-speed lockout. Power-lock electric brake. Includes two 6V batteries and one recharger. Ages 3–6 (carries two passengers up to 90 lbs total).
Suggested retail price: $249.95

■ **FIGURE 11-1** Might-Mite Motors' product catalog—Cont'd

decisions about which designs should actually be manufactured for mass marketing.

Manufacturing Division

The Manufacturing division is responsible for producing product for mass-market sales. Manufacturing procures its own raw materials and manages it own operations, including personnel (hiring, firing, scheduling) and assembly line management. Manufacturing maintains the

Model #008

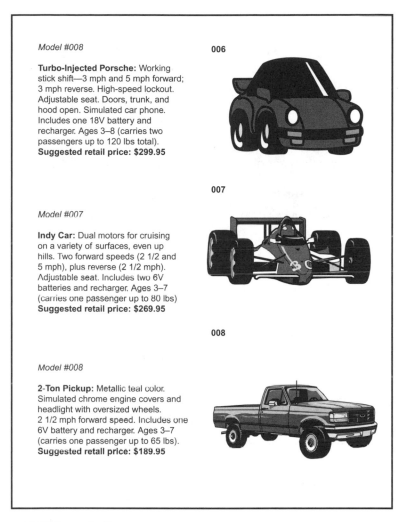

Turbo-Injected Porsche: Working stick shift—3 mph and 5 mph forward; 3 mph reverse. High-speed lockout. Adjustable seat. Doors, trunk, and hood open. Simulated car phone. Includes one 18V battery and recharger. Ages 3–8 (carries two passengers up to 120 lbs total).
Suggested retail price: $299.95

006

007

Model #007

Indy Car: Dual motors for cruising on a variety of surfaces, even up hills. Two forward speeds (2 1/2 and 5 mph), plus reverse (2 1/2 mph). Adjustable seat. Includes two 6V batteries and recharger. Ages 3–7 (carries one passenger up to 80 lbs)
Suggested retail price: $269.95

008

Model #008

2-Ton Pickup: Metallic teal color. Simulated chrome engine covers and headlight with oversized wheels. 2 1/2 mph forward speed. Includes one 6V battery and recharger. Ages 3–7 (carries one passenger up to 65 lbs).
Suggested retail price: $189.95

■ **FIGURE 11-1** Cont'd

inventory of products that are ready to go on sale. It also handles shipping of products to resellers, based on sales information received from Marketing and Sales.

Marketing and Sales Division

MMM sells directly to toy stores and catalog houses; the corporation has never used distributors. Marketing and Sales employs a staff of 25 salespeople who make personal contacts with resellers. Salespeople

Model #008

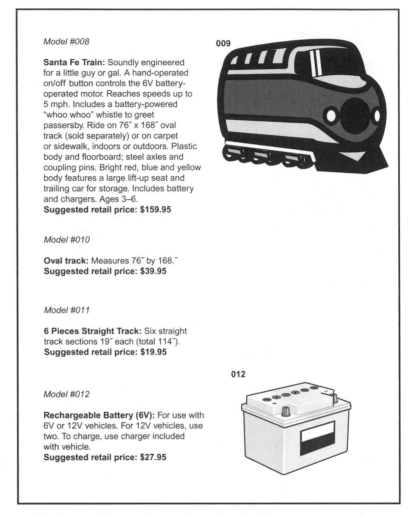

Santa Fe Train: Soundly engineered for a little guy or gal. A hand-operated on/off button controls the 6V battery-operated motor. Reaches speeds up to 5 mph. Includes a battery-powered "whoo whoo" whistle to greet passersby. Ride on 76″ x 168″ oval track (sold separately) or on carpet or sidewalk, indoors or outdoors. Plastic body and floorboard; steel axles and coupling pins. Bright red, blue and yellow body features a large lift-up seat and trailing car for storage. Includes battery and chargers. Ages 3–6.
Suggested retail price: $159.95

009

Model #010

Oval track: Measures 76″ by 168.″
Suggested retail price: $39.95

Model #011

6 Pieces Straight Track: Six straight track sections 19″ each (total 114″).
Suggested retail price: $19.95

Model #012

Rechargeable Battery (6V): For use with 6V or 12V vehicles. For 12V vehicles, use two. To charge, use charger included with vehicle.
Suggested retail price: $27.95

012

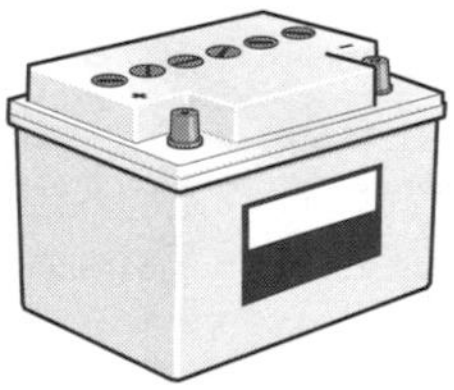

■ **FIGURE 11-1** Might-Mite Motors' product catalog—Cont'd

are also responsible for distributing catalogs in their territories, visiting and/or calling potential resellers, and taking reseller orders. Order accounting is handled by Marketing and Sales. As noted earlier, Marketing and Sales transmits shipping information to Manufacturing, which takes care of actual product delivery.

Current Information Systems

MMM's information systems are a hodgepodge of computers and applications that have grown up with little corporate planning. The

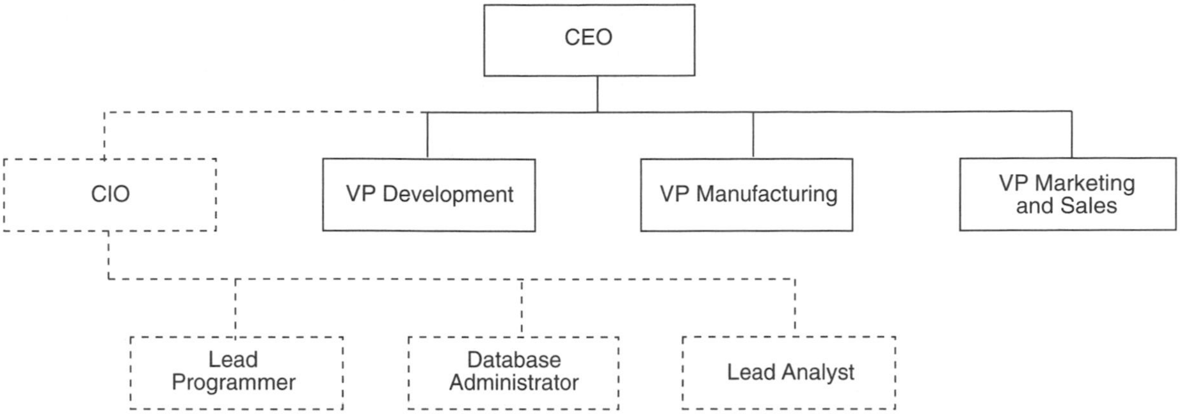

■ **FIGURE 11-2** Might-Mite Motors' organization chart.

Product Development division relies primarily on stand-alone CAD workstations. In contrast to the sophistication of the CAD machines, testing records are kept and analyzed manually. Product Development employs product designers (some of whom function as project leaders) and clerical support staff but no information systems personnel. Attempts to have clerical staff develop simple database applications to store data about children who test new and redesigned products and the results of those tests have proven futile. It has become evident that Product Development needs information systems professionals, and although the division is willing to hire information technology (IT) staff, corporate management has decided to centralize the IS staff rather than add to a decentralized model.

Manufacturing uses a stand-alone server to track purchases and inventory levels of raw materials, personnel scheduling, manufacturing line scheduling, and finished-product inventory. Each of the applications running on the server were custom-written by outside consultants in COBOL many years ago; the most significant maintenance they have had was when they were ported from the department's original minicomputer to the server about 15 years ago. The data used by a Manufacturing application are contained in files that do not share information with any of the other applications. Manufacturing employs one COBOL programmer and a system administrator. Although the programmer is talented, the most he can do is fix superficial user interface issues and repair corrupted data files; he was not part of the original program development, and does not understand the functioning of much of the application code, which was poorly written and even more poorly documented. The applications no longer meet the needs of the Manufacturing division, and management has determined that it isn't cost effective to write new applications to access the existing data files.

Marketing and Sales, which wasn't computerized until 1987, has a local area network consisting of one server and 15 workstations. The server provides shared applications such as word processing and spreadsheets. It also maintains a marketing and sales database that has been developed using a PC-based product. The database suffers from several problems, including a limit of ten users at a time and concurrency control problems that lead to severe data inconsistencies. The marketing and sales database was developed by the division's two IS employees at the time, both of whom have since left the company. None of the current staff understands the software. Regardless of the amount of time spent trying to maintain the database, inaccurate data continue to be introduced.

The Marketing and Sales network is not connected to the Internet. Salespeople must therefore transmit hard copies of their orders to the central office, where the orders are manually keyed into the existing database. Some of the salespeople do have laptop computers, but because the network has no Internet connection, the salespeople cannot connect to it when they are out of the office.

Reengineering Project

Because MMM seems to have lost its strategic advantage in the marketplace, the CEO has decided to undertake a major systems reengineering project. The overall thrust of the project is to provide an information system that will support better evaluation of product testing, better analysis of sales patterns, better control of the manufacturing process, and enhanced communications options throughout the corporation. New information systems will be based on a client/server model and include one or more databases running on an Internet-connected network of servers, workstations, and PCs.

New Information Systems Division

The first step in the reengineering project is to establish an information systems division. This new division will also be housed in the corporate headquarters, along with the three existing divisions. To accommodate the new division, MMM will be construction a 10,000-square-foot addition to its building.

MMM is in the process of searching for a chief information officer (CIO). This individual, who will report directly to the CEO, will manage the new division and be responsible for overseeing the reengineering of information systems that will handle all of the corporation's operations.

All current IS personnel (those who work for the Manufacturing and Marketing and Sales divisions) will be transferred to the new IS division. The division will hire (either internally or externally) three management-level professionals, a Lead Programmer (responsible for overseeing application development), a Database Administrator (responsible for database design and management), and a Lead Analyst (responsible for overseeing systems analysis and design efforts). Retraining in the client/server model and client/server development tools will be provided for all current employees who are willing to make the transition. Those who are unwilling to move to the new development environment will be laid off.

Basic System Goals

The CEO has defined the following goals for the reengineering project:

- Develop a corporation-wide data administration plan that includes a requirements document detailing organizational functions that require technology support and the functions that the reengineered system will provide.
- Provide an application road map that documents all application programs that will be needed to support corporate operations.
- Document all databases to be developed for the corporation. This documentation will include ER diagrams and data dictionaries.
- Create a timeline for the development of applications and their supporting databases.
- Specify hardware changes and/or acquisitions that will be necessary to support the reengineered information systems.
- Plan and execute a security strategy for an expanded corporate network that will include both internal and external users.
- Implement the planned systems.

Current Business Processes

To aid the systems analysts in their assessment of MMM's information systems needs, the CEO of MMM asked all existing division heads to document the way information is currently processed. This documentation, which also includes some information about what an improved system should do, provides a starting point for the redesign of both business and IS processes.

Sales and Ordering Processes

MMM receives orders at its plant in two ways: by telephone directly from customers or from members of the sales staff who have visited customers in person. Orders from the remote sales staff usually arrive by fax or overnight courier.

Each order is written on a standard order form (Figure 11-3). If the order arrives by fax, it will already be on the correct form, but telephone orders must be written on the form by in-house order takers. Several times a day, a clerk enters the orders into the existing database. Unfortunately, if the sales office is particularly busy, order entry may be delayed. This backup has a major impact on production line scheduling and thus on the company's ability to fill orders. The new information system must streamline the order entry process, including the electronic transmission of order data from the field and the direct entry of in-house orders.

The in-house sales staff has no access to the files that show the current finished-goods inventory. They are therefore unable to tell customers when their orders will be shipped. They can, however, tell customers how many orders are ahead of theirs to be filled and, based on general manufacturing timetables, come up with an approximation of how long it will take to ship a given order. One of the goals of the information systems reengineering project is to provide improved companywide knowledge of how long it will take to fill customer orders.

Manufacturing, Inventory, and Shipping Processes

The MMM Manufacturing division occupies a large portion of the MMM facility. The division controls the actual manufacturing lines (three assembly lines), a storage area for finished goods, a storage area for raw materials, and several offices for supervisory and clerical staff.

The manufacturing process is triggered when a batch of order forms is received each morning by the manufacturing office. The batch consists of all orders that were entered into the sales database the previous

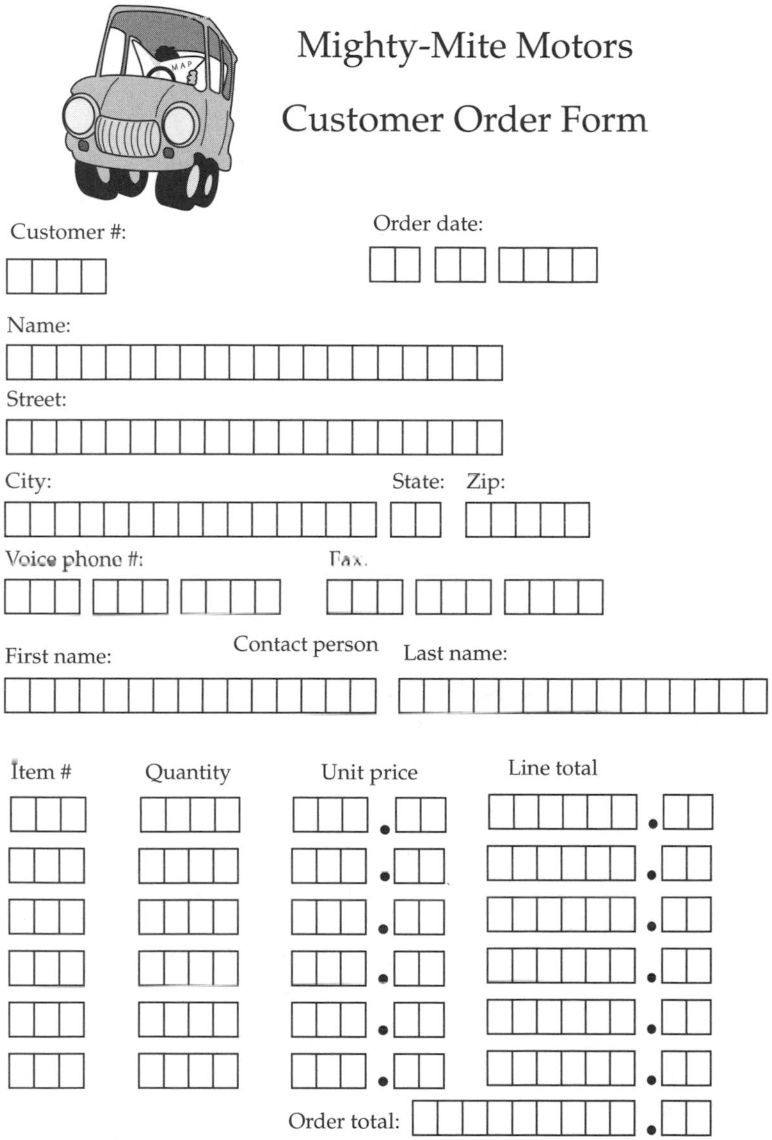
Mighty-Mite Motors
Customer Order Form
MAP
Customer #:
Order date:
Name:
Street:
City:
State:
Zip:
Voice phone #:
Fax:
First name:
Contact person
Last name:
Item #
Quantity
Unit price
Line total
Order total:

■ **FIGURE 11-3** Mighty-Mite Motors' order form.

working day. A secretary takes the individual order forms and completes a report summarizing the number ordered by model (Figure 11-4). This report is then given to the Manufacturing Supervisor, whose responsibility it is to schedule which model will be produced on each manufacturing line each day.

Mighty-Mite Motors
Order Summary

MM/DD/YYYY

Model #	Quantity Ordered
001	75
002	150
004	80
005	35
008	115
009	25
010	25
011	15

■ **FIGURE 11-4** Mighty-Mite Motors' order summary report format.

The scheduling process is somewhat complex because the Manufacturing Supervisor must take into account previously placed orders, which have determined the current manufacturing schedule and current inventory levels, as well as the new orders, when adjusting the schedule. The availability of raw materials and the time it takes to modify a manufacturing line to produce a different model are also entered into the scheduling decision. This is one function that MMM's management understands will be almost impossible to automate; there is just too much human expertise involved to translate into an automatic process. However, it is vital that the Manufacturing Supervisor have access to accurate, up-to-date information about orders, inventory, and the current time schedule so that judgments can be made based on as much hard data as possible.

As finished vehicles come off the assembly line, they are packed for shipping, labeled, and sent to finished-goods storage. Each shipping carton contains one vehicle, which is marked with its model number, serial number, and date of manufacture. The Shipping Manager, who oversees finished-goods storage and shipping, ensures that newly manufactured items are entered into the shipping inventory files.

The Shipping Manager receives the customer order forms after the order report has been completed. (Photocopies of the order forms are kept in the Marketing and Sales office as backups.) The orders are placed in a box in reverse chronological order so that the oldest orders can be filled first. The Shipping Manager checks orders against inven-

Current Finished Goods Inventory Levels MM/DD/YYYY	
Model #	Number on Hand
001	215
002	35
003	180
004	312
005	82
006	5
007	212
008	189
009	37
010	111
011	195
012	22

FIGURE 11-5 Mite-Mite Motors' inventory screen layout.

tory levels by looking at the inventory level output screen (Figure 11-5). If the manager sees that enough inventory is available to fill an order, the order is given to a shipping clerk for processing. If there isn't enough inventory, then the order is put back in the box, where it will be checked again the following day. Under this system, no partial orders are filled because they would be extremely difficult to track. (The reengineered information system should allow handling of partial shipments.)

Shipping clerks are given orders to fill. They create shipping labels for all vehicles that are part of a shipment. The cartons are labeled and set aside to be picked up by delivery services. The shipping clerks prepare the package labels (which also serve as packing slips), to ensure that the items being shipped are removed from the inventory file, and return the list of filled orders to the Shipping Manager. The orders are then marked as filled and returned to Marketing and Sales. The reengineered information system should automate the generation of pick-lists, packing slips, and updating of finished-goods inventory.

MMM's raw materials inventory is maintained on a just-in-time basis. The Manufacturing Supervisor checks the line schedule (Figure 11-6) and the current raw materials inventory (Figure 11-7) daily to determine what raw materials need to be ordered. This process relies heavily

	Line Schedule MM/DD/YYYY	
MM/DD/YYYY		
	Line #1: Model 008	300 units
	Line #2: Model 002	150 units
	Line #3: Model 010	200 units
MM/DD/YYYY		
	Line #1: Model 008	200 units
	Line #2: Model 003	400 units
	Line #3: Model 005	300 units
MM/DD/YYYY		
	Line #1: Model 008	250 units
	Line #2: Model 006	100 units
	Line #3: Model 002	300 units
	: : :	
Total production scheduled:		
	Model 002	450 units
	Model 003	400 units
	Model 005	300 units
	Model 006	100 units
	Model 008	750 units
	Model 010	200 units

■ **FIGURE 11-6** Mighty-Mite Motors' line schedule report format.

on the Manufacturing Supervisor's knowledge of which materials are needed for which model vehicle. MMM's CEO is very concerned about this process because the Manufacturing Supervisor, while accurate in scheduling the manufacturing line, is nowhere near as accurate in judging raw materials needs. The result is that occasionally manufacturing must stop because raw materials have run out. The CEO would therefore like to see ordering of raw materials triggered automatically. The new information system should keep track of the raw materials needed to produce each model and, based on the line schedule and a reorder point established for each item, generate orders for items when needed.

Raw materials are taken from inventory each morning as each manufacturing line is set up for the day's production run. The inventory files are modified immediately after all raw materials have been removed

Current Raw Materials Inventory Levels
MM/DD/YYYY

Item #	Item	QOH
001	Plastic #3	95 lbs.
002	Red dye 109	25 gals.
003	Wheel 12″	120 each
004	Plastic #4	300 lbs.
005	Yellow dye 110	5 gals.
006	Yellow dye 65	30 gals.
007	Strut 15″	99 each
008	Axle 24″	250 each
009	Blue dye 25	18 gals.
010	Plastic #8	350 lbs.
011	Cotter pin: small	515 each
012	Cotter pin: medium	109 each

Next screen

■ **FIGURE 11-7** Mighty-Mite Motors' raw materials inventory screen layout.

from storage for a given manufacturing line. There is no way to automate the reduction of inventory, but the new information system should make it very easy for nontechnical users to update inventory levels.

Product Testing and Support Function

MMM's top management make decisions about which model vehicles to produce based on data from three sources: product testing, customer registrations, and problem reports.

Customer registrations are received on cards packaged with sold vehicles (Figure 11-8). Currently, the registration cards are filed by customer name. However, MMM would also like access to these data by model and serial number to make it easier to notify customers if a recall occurs. Management would also like summaries of the data by model purchased, age of primary user, gender of primary user, and who purchased the vehicle for the child.

Problem reports (Figure 11-9) are taken by customer support representatives who work within the product testing division. These reports include the serial number and model that is having problems, along with the date and type of problem. Currently, the problem descriptions are nonstandard, made up of whatever terms the customer support representative happens to use. It is therefore difficult to sum-

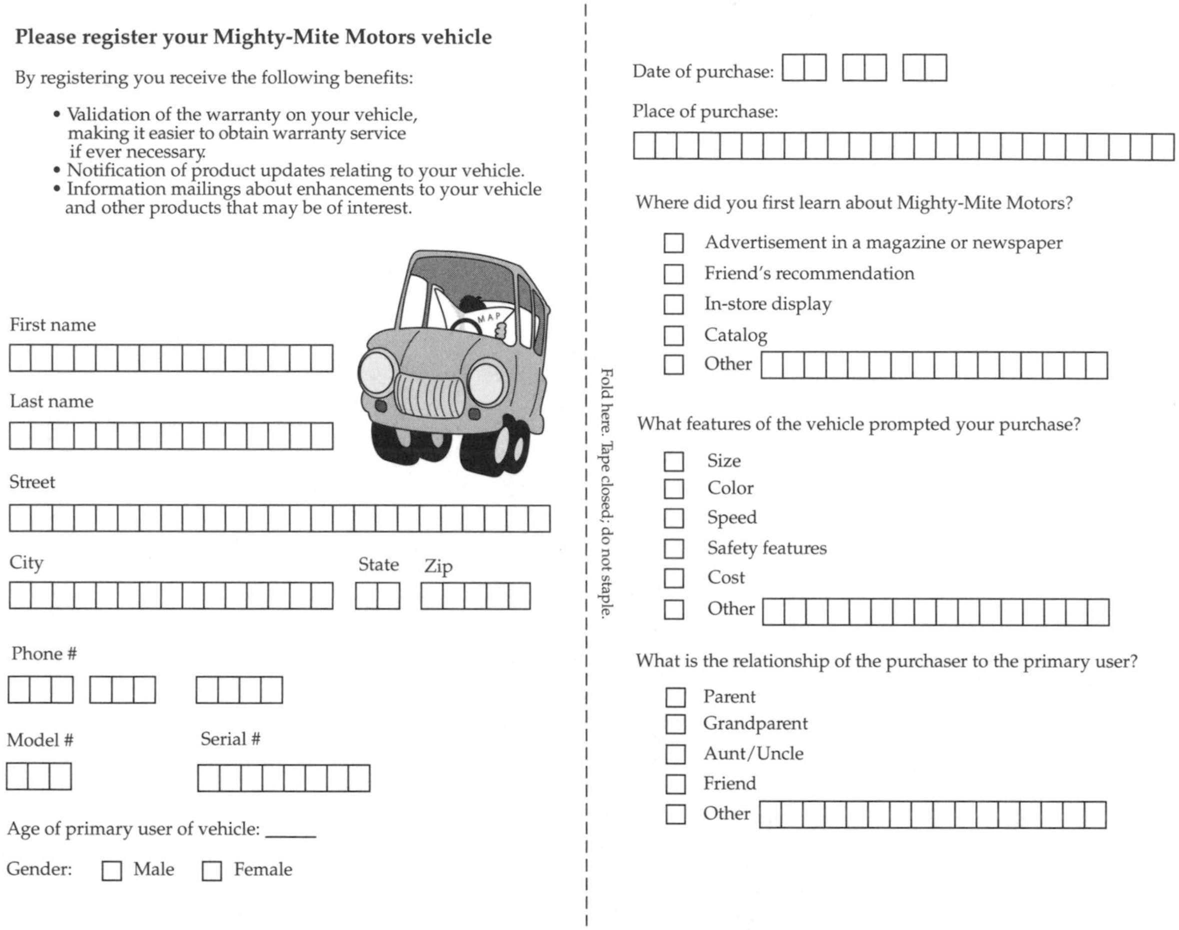

Please register your Mighty-Mite Motors vehicle

By registering you receive the following benefits:

- Validation of the warranty on your vehicle, making it easier to obtain warranty service if ever necessary.
- Notification of product updates relating to your vehicle.
- Information mailings about enhancements to your vehicle and other products that may be of interest.

First name

Last name

Street

City State Zip

Phone #

Model # Serial #

Age of primary user of vehicle: _____

Gender: ☐ Male ☐ Female

Fold here. Tape closed; do not staple.

Date of purchase:

Place of purchase:

Where did you first learn about Mighty-Mite Motors?

- ☐ Advertisement in a magazine or newspaper
- ☐ Friend's recommendation
- ☐ In-store display
- ☐ Catalog
- ☐ Other

What features of the vehicle prompted your purchase?

- ☐ Size
- ☐ Color
- ☐ Speed
- ☐ Safety features
- ☐ Cost
- ☐ Other

What is the relationship of the purchaser to the primary user?

- ☐ Parent
- ☐ Grandparent
- ☐ Aunt/Uncle
- ☐ Friend
- ☐ Other

■ **FIGURE 11-8** Mighty-Mite Motors' purchase registration form.

marize problem reports to get an accurate picture of which models are experiencing design problems that should be corrected. MMM would therefore like to introduce a standardized method for describing problems, probably through a set of problem codes. The result should be regular reports on the problems reported for each model that can be used to help make decisions about which models to continue, which to discontinue, which to redesign, and which to recall.

MMM does not repair its own products. When a problem report is received, the customer is either directed to return the product to the store were it was purchased for an exchange (during the first 30 days after purchase) or to an authorized repair center in the customer's area.

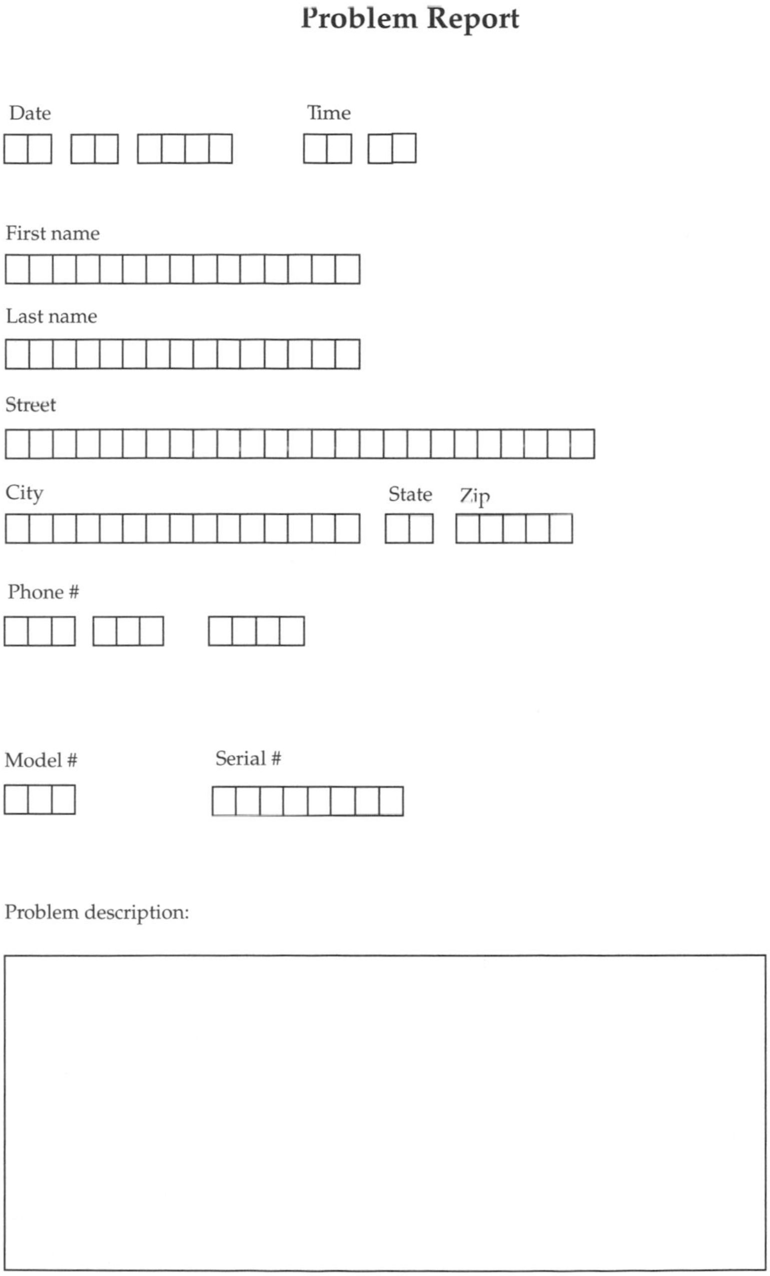

■ **FIGURE 11-9** Mighty-Mite Motors' problem report.

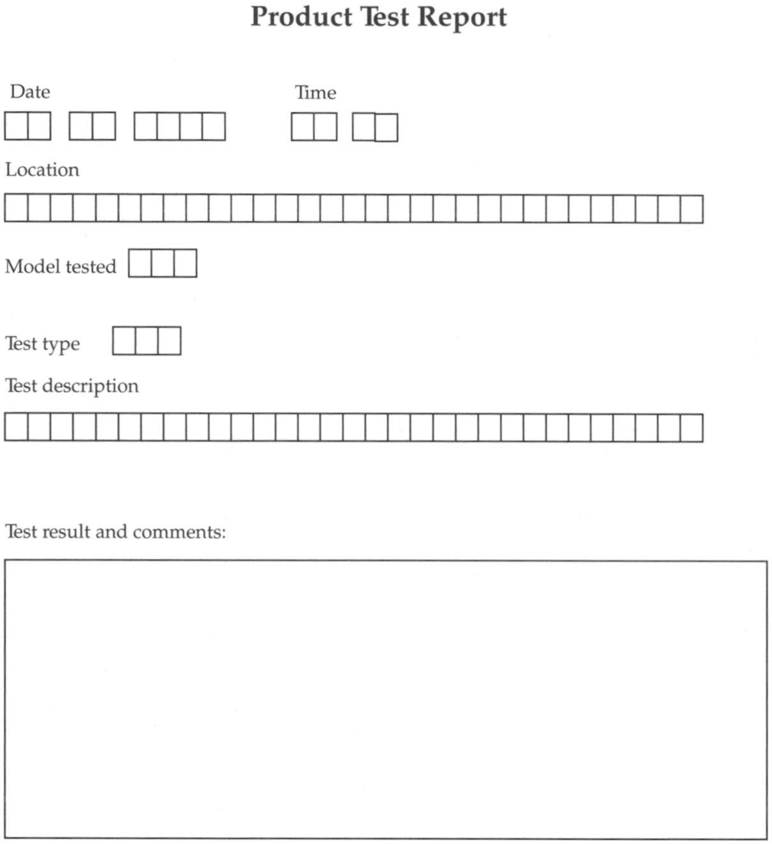

Product Test Report

Date

□□ □□ □□□□

Time

□□ □□

Location

□□□□□□□□□□□□□□□□□□□□□□□□□□□□□□□□□□□□□□

Model tested □□□

Test type □□□

Test description

□□□□□□□□□□□□□□□□□□□□□□□□□□□□□□□□□□□□□□

Test result and comments:

■ **FIGURE 11-10** Mighty-Mite Motors' product test report.

In the latter case, the problem report is faxed to the repair center so that it is already there when the customer arrives. MMM does not plan to change this procedure because it currently provides quick, excellent service to customers and alleviates the need for MMM to stock replacement parts. (Replacement parts are stocked by the authorized repair centers.)

Product test results are recorded on paper forms (Figure 11-10). After a testing period is completed, the forms are collated manually to produce a summary of how well a new product performed. MMM would like the test results stored within an information system so that the testing report can be produced automatically, saving time and effort. Such a report will be used to help decide which new models should be placed in production.

DESIGNING THE DATABASE

The most effective approach to the design of a database (or collection of databases) for an environment as diverse as that presented by Mighty-Mite Motors usually involves breaking the design into components indicated by the organization of the company. As the design evolves, the designer can examine the entities and the relationships to determine where parts of the organization will need to share data. Working on one portion of the design at a time also simplifies dealing with what might at first seem to be an overwhelmingly large database environment. Paying special attention to the need to share data helps ensure that shared data are consistent and suitable for all required uses.

A systems analysis indicates that the MMM database environment falls into the following areas:

- Manufacturing (including finished-goods inventory and raw materials ordering)
- Sales to toy stores and shipping of products ordered
- Purchase registrations
- Testing
- Problem handling

Examining the Data Flows

During the systems analysis, a data flow diagram can be a great help in identifying where data are shared by various parts of an organization. The top-level DFD (the *context diagram* in Figure 11-11) actually tells us very little. It indicates that three sources outside the company provide data: customers (the stores to which the company sells), purchasers (the individuals who purchase products from the stores), and raw materials suppliers. Somewhere, all those data are used by a general process called Manufacture and Sell Products to keep the company in business.

However, the level 1 DFD (Figure 11-12) is much more telling. As the data handling processes are broken down, five data stores emerge:

- *Raw materials:* This data store holds both the raw materials inventory and the orders for raw materials.
- *Product data:* The product data store contains data about the products being manufactured, product testing results, and the finished-goods inventory.
- *Customer orders:* This data store contains customer information as well as order data.

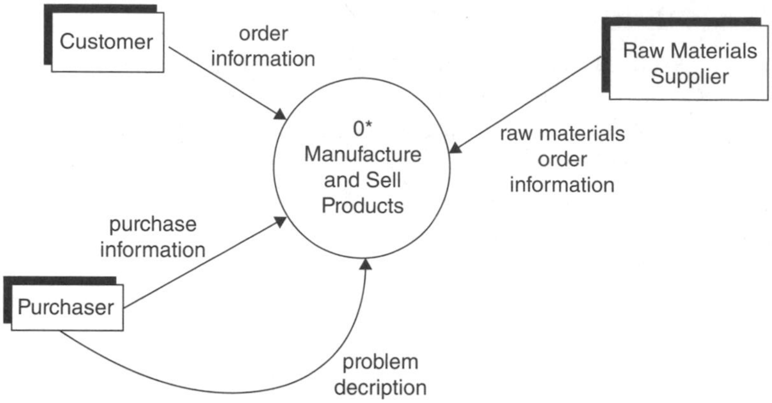

■ **FIGURE 11-11** Context DFD for Mighty-Mite Motors.

- *Purchaser data:* The purchaser data store contains information about the individuals who purchase products and the products they have purchased.
- *Problem data:* This final data store contains problem reports.

As you examine the processes that interact with these five data stores, you will find a number of processes that manipulate data in more than one data store, as well as data stores that are used by more than one process:

- The raw materials data store is used by the raw materials ordering and the manufacturing processes.
- Product data are used by manufacturing, sales, shipping, and product registration.
- Customer order data are used by sales and shipping.
- The purchases data store is used by purchaser registration and problem handling.
- The problem data store, used only by problem handling, is the only data store that is not shared by multiple processes.

The raw materials ordering process is the only process that uses only a single data store. Nonetheless, the level 1 DFD makes it very clear that there is no instance in which a single process uses a single data store without interaction with other data stores and processes. Given that each process in the DFD probably represents all or part of an application program, this suggests that the database designer should consider either a single database or a set of small databases along with software to facilitate the interchange of data.

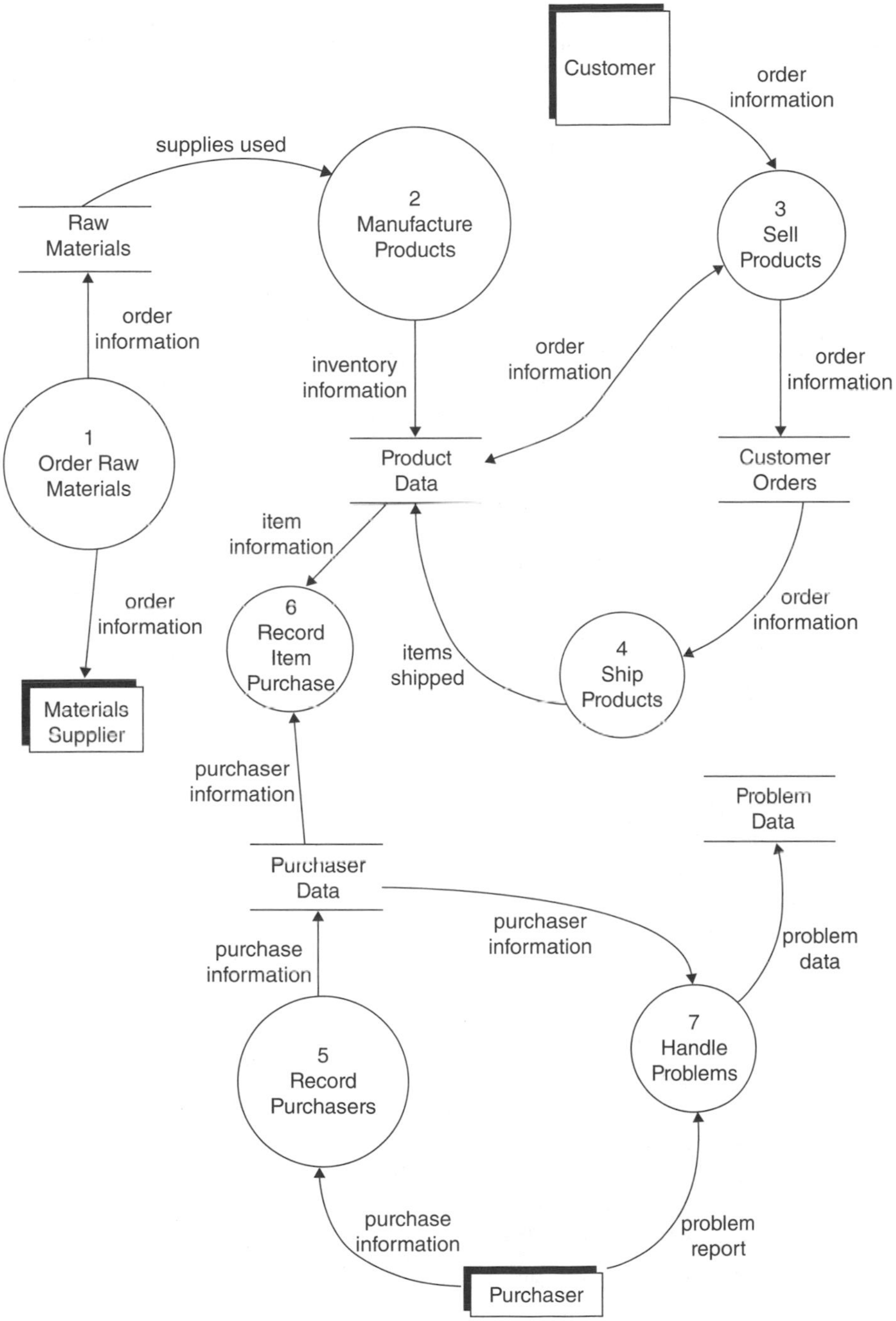

■ **FIGURE 11-12** Level 1 DFD for Mighty-Mite Motors.

The DFD makes it very clear that the need for the integration of the various data stores is very strong. In addition, Mighty-Mite Motors is a relatively small business, and therefore a single database that manages all needed aspects of the company will not grow unreasonably large. It will also be more cost effective and perform better than multiple databases that use some type of middleware to exchange data. Ultimately, the database designer may decide to distribute the database onto multiple servers, placing portions of it that are used most frequently in the division where that use occurs. The database design, however, will be the same regardless of whether the final implementation is centralized or distributed. The essential decision is to create a single database rather than several smaller, interrelated databases that must exchange data.

The ER Diagram

The systems analyst preparing the requirements document for the Mighty-Mite Motors reengineering project has had two very good sources of information about exactly what needs to be stored in the database: the employees of the company and the paper documents that the company has been using. The document that is given to the database design is therefore quite complete.

The design needs to capture all the information on the paper documents. Some documents are used only for input (for example, the product registration form or the order form). Others represent reports that an application program must be able to generate (for example, the line schedule report).

Although the current documents do not necessarily represent all of the outputs that the application programs running against the database will eventually prepare, they do provide a good starting place for the design. Whenever the designer has questions, he or she can then turn to Might-Mite's employees for clarification.

Working from the requirements document prepared by the systems analyst, along with the paper input and output documents, the database designer puts together the ER diagram. Because there are so many entities, all of which interconnect, the diagram is very wide and has been split into three pieces to make it easier to understand. As you look at each of the pieces, keep in mind that entities that appear on more than one piece represent the connection between the three illustrations.

The first part (Figure 11-13) contains the entities for raw materials and manufacturing. This portion of the data model is dealing with three many-to-many relationships:

- material_order to raw_material (resolved by the composite entity material_order_line)
- raw_material to model (resolved by the composite entity material needed)
- manufacturing_line to model (resolved by the composite entity line_schedule)

The second portion of the ERD (Figure 11-14) contains entities for product testing and sales. (Remember that in this instance, the customers are toy stores rather than individual purchasers.) There are two many-to-many relationships:

- test_type to model (resolved by the test entity)
- order to model (resolved by the order_line composite entity)

The test entity is somewhat unusual for a composite entity. It is an activity that someone performs and as such has an existence outside the database. It is not an entity created just to resolve a many-to-many relationship.

At this point, the diagrams become a bit unusual because of the need to keep track of individual products rather than simply groups of products of the same model. The model entity in Figure 11-13 represents a type of vehicle manufactured by Mighty-Mite Motors. However, the product entity in Figure 11-14 represents a single vehicle that is uniquely identified by a serial number. This means that the relationships among an order, the line items on an order, and the models and products are more complex than for most other sales database designs.

The order and line item entities are fairly typical. They indicate how many of a given model are required to fill a given order. The shipment entity then indicates how many of a specific model are shipped on a specific date. However, the database must also track the order in which individual products are shipped. As a result, there is a direct relationship between the product entity and the order entity, in addition to the relationship between order_line and model. In this way, Mighty-Mite Motors will know exactly where each product has gone. At the same time, the company will be able to track the status of orders (in particular, how many units of each model have yet to ship).

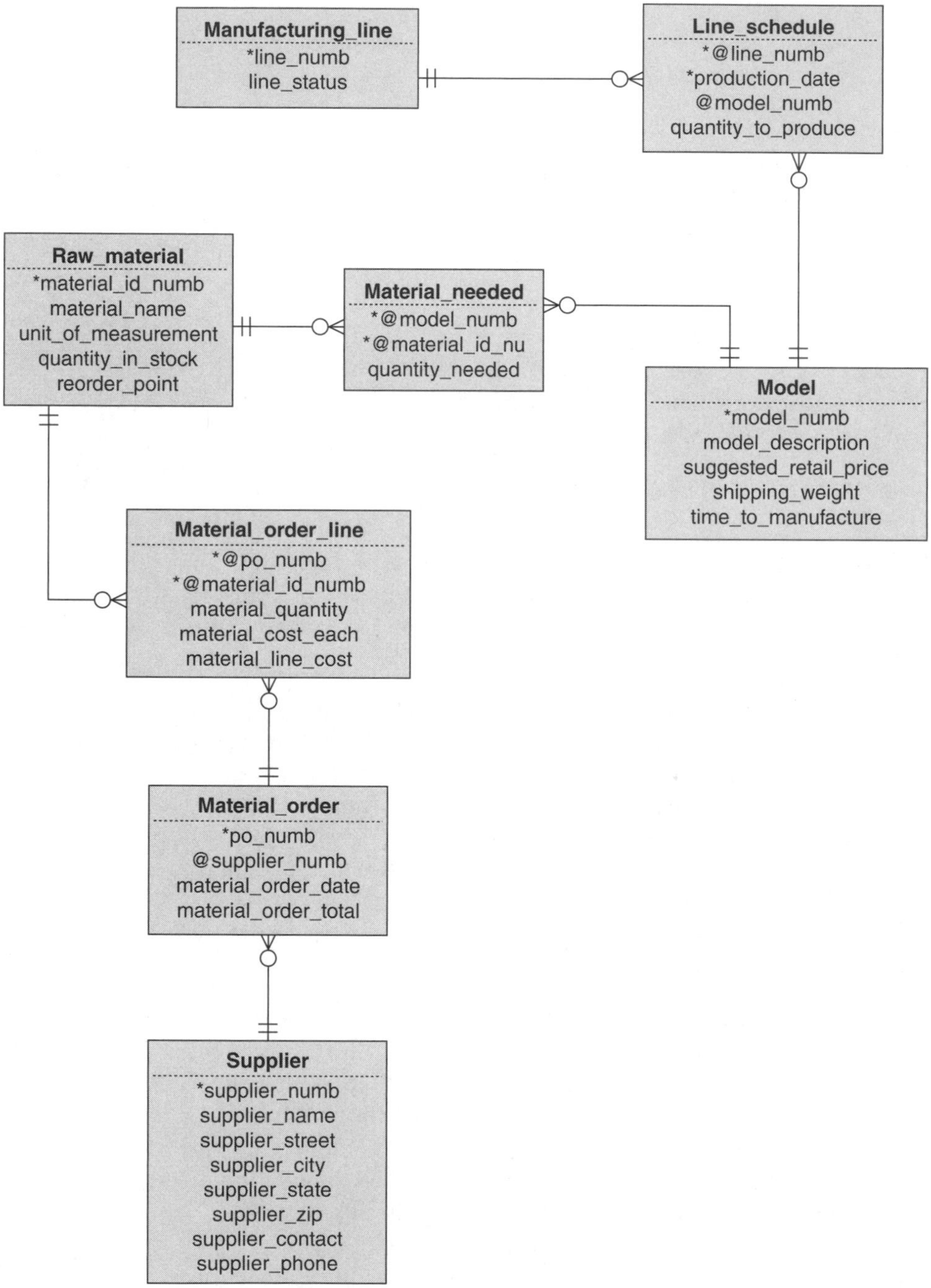

■ **FIGURE 11-13** Part 1 of ERD for Mighty-Mite Motors.

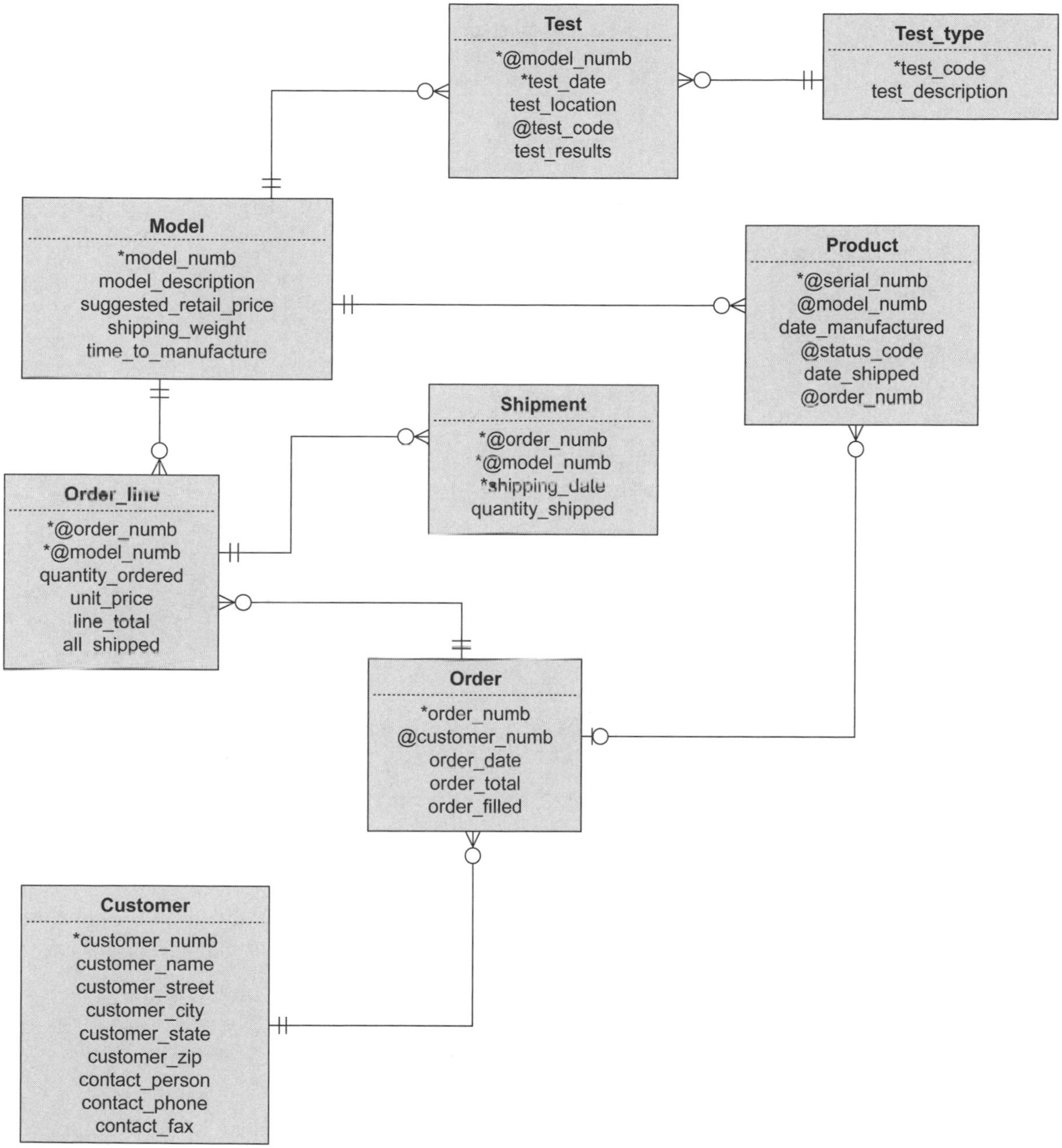

■ **FIGURE 11-14** Part 2 of ERD for Mighty-Mite Motors.

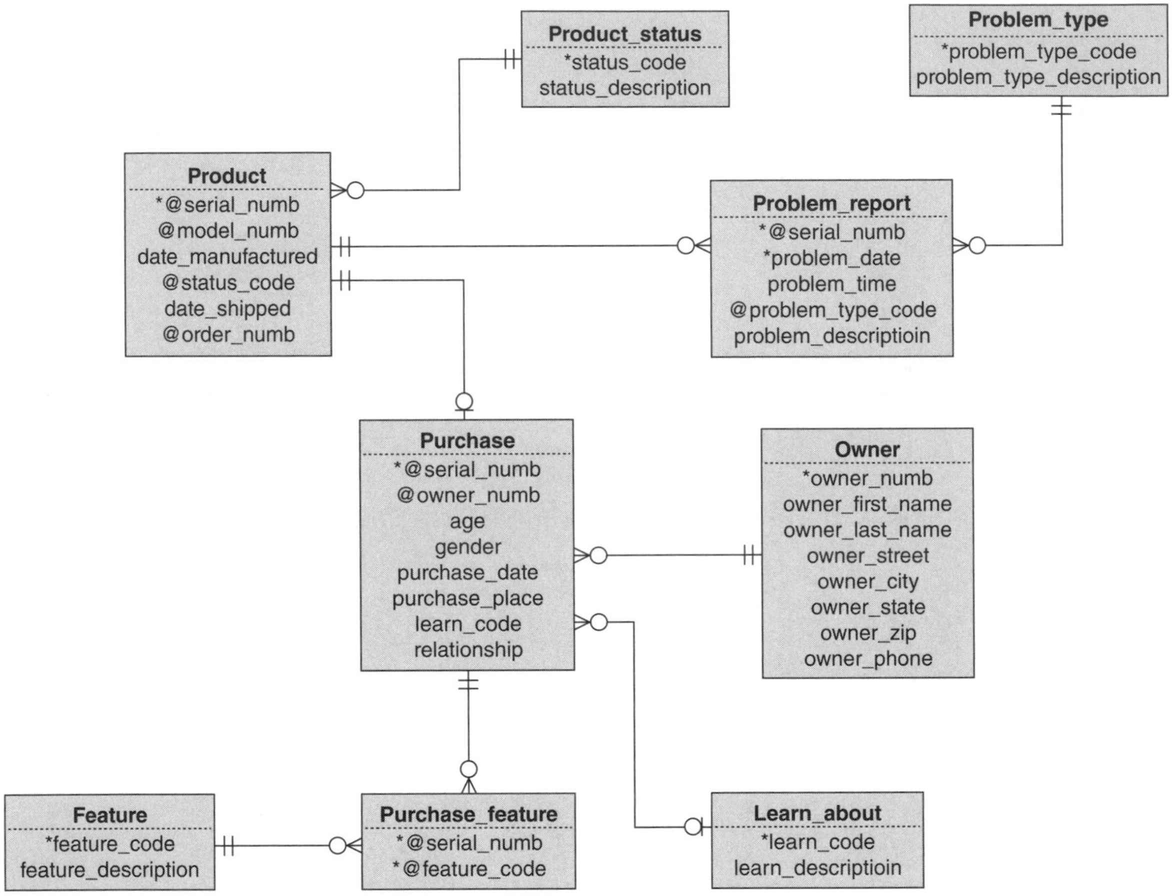

■ **FIGURE 11-15** Part 3 of ERD for Mighty-Mite Motors.

The final portion of the ERD (Figure 11-15) deals with the purchasers and problem reports. There are two many-to-many relationships:

- problem_type to product (resolved with the entity problem_report)
- purchase to feature (resolved with the composite entity purchase_feature)

Like the test entity you saw earlier, the problem_report entity acts like a composite entity to resolve many-to-many relationships, but it is really a simple entity. It is an entity that has an existence outside of the database and that was not created simply to take care of the M:N relationship.

Note: Calling an entity a "problem_report" can be a bit misleading. In this case, the word "report" does not refer to a piece of paper but to the action of reporting a problem. A "problem_report" is therefore an activity rather than a document. In fact, the printed documentation of a problem report will probably include data from several entities, including the product, problem_report, purchase, and owner entities.

If you look closely at Figure 11-15, you'll notice that there is a one-to-one relationship between the product and purchase entities. The handling of the data supplied by a purchaser on the product registration card presents an interesting dilemma for a database designer. Each product will be registered by only one purchaser. (Even if the product is later sold or given to someone else, the new owner will not have a registration card to send in.) There will be only one set of registration data for each product, which first suggests that all of the registration data should be part of the product entity.

However, there is a lot of registration data—including one repeating group (the features for which the purchaser chose the product, represented by the feature and purchase_feature entities)—and the product is involved in a number of relationships that have nothing to do with product registration. If the DBMS has to retrieve the registration data along with the rest of the product data, database performance will suffer. It therefore makes sense in this case to keep the purchase data separate and to retrieve it only when absolutely necessary.

Note: One common mistake made by novice database designers is to create an entity called "registration card." It is important to remember that the card itself is merely an input document. What is crucial is the data the card contains and the entity that the data describe, rather than the medium on which the data are supplied.

Creating the Tables

The tables for the Mighty-Mite Motors's database can come directly from the ER diagram:

```
model (model_numb, model_description,
   suggested_retail_price, shipping_weight,
   time_to_manufacture)
```

```
test (model_numb, test_date, test_location,
  test_code, test_results)
test_types (test_code, test_description)
customers (customer_numb, customer_name,
  customer_street, customer_city, customer_state,
  customer_zip, contact_person, contact_phone,
  contact_fax)
orders (order_numb, customer_numb, order_date,
  order_total, order_filled)
order_line (order_numbzu, model_numb,
  quantity_ordered, unit_price, line_total,
  all_shipped)
shipments (order_numb, model_numb, quantity_shipped)
product (serial_numb, model_numb, date_manufactured,
  status_code, order_numb, date_shipped)
raw_material (material_id_numb, material_name,
  unit_of_measurement, quantity_in_stock,
  reorder_point)
supplier (supplier_numb, supplier_name,
  supplier_street, supplier_city, supplier_state,
  supplier_zip, supplier_contact, supplier_phone)
material_order (po_numb, supplier_numb,
  material_order_date, material_oreder_total)
material_order_line (po_numb, material_id_numb,
  material_quantity, material_cost_each,
  material_line_cost)
manufacturing_line (line_numb, line_status)
line_schedule (line_numb, production_date,
  model_numb, quantity_to_produce)
owner (owner_numb, owner_first_name, owner_last_name,
  owner_street, owner_city, owner_state, owner_zip,
  owner_phone)
purchase (serial_numb, owner_numb, age, gender,
  purchase_date, purchase_price, learn_code,
  relationship)
purchase_feature (serial_numb, feature_code)
learn_about (learn_code, learn_description)
feature (feature_code, feature_description)
problem_report (serial_numb, problem_date,
  problem_time, problem_type_code, problem_details)
problem_type (problem_type_code, problem_type_
  description)
```

Generating the SQL

Assuming that the designers of the Mighty-Mite Motors database are working with a CASE tool, then generating SQL statements to create the database can be automated. For example, in Figure 11-16 you will find the SQL generated by Mac A&D from the ER diagram you saw earlier in this chapter.

```
CREATE TABLE model
(
    model_numb INTEGER,
    model_description VARCHAR (40),
    suggested_retail_price NUMBER (6,2),
    shipping_weight NUMBER(6,2),
    time_to_manufacture TIME,
    PRIMARY KEY (model_numb)
)

CREATE TABLE test_type
(
    test_code INTEGER,
    test_description VARCHAR (40),
    PRIMARY KEY (test_code)
)

CREATE TABLE test
(
    test_date DATE,
    test_location VARCHAR (40),
    test_code INTEGER,
    test_results VARCHAR (256),
    PRIMARY KEY (model_numb, test_date),
    FOREIGN KEY (model_numb) REFERENCES model,
    FOREIGN KEY (test_code) REFERENCES test_type
)

CREATE TABLE customer
{
    customer_numb INTEGER,
    customer_name VARCHAR (40),
    customer_street VARCHAR (50),
    customer_city VARCHAR (50),
```

■ **FIGURE 11-16** SQL statements needed to create Mighty-Mite Motors' database.

```
    customer_state CHAR (2),
    customer_zip CHAR (10),
    contact_person VARCHAR (30),
    contact_phone CHAR (12),
    contact_fax CHAR (12),
    PRIMARY KEY (customer_numb)
)

CREATE TABLE order
(
    order_numb INTEGER,
    customer_numb INTEGER,
    order_date DATE,
    order_total NUMBER (8,2),
    order_filled BOOLEAN,
    PRIMARY KEY (order_numb),
    FOREIGN KEY (customer_numb) REFERENCES customer
)

CREATE TABLE order_line
(
    order_numb INTEGER,
    model_numb INTEGER,
    quantity_ordered INTEGER,
    unit_price NUMBER (6,2),
    line_total NUMBER (8,2),
    all_shipped BOOLEAN,
    PRIMARY KEY (order_numb, model_numb),
    FOREIGN KEY (order_numb) REFERENCES order,
    FOREIGN KEY (model_numb) REFERENCES model
)

CREATE TABLE shipment
(
    order_numb INTEGER,
    model_numb INTEGER,
    shipping_date DATE,
    quantity_shipped INTEGER,
    PRIMARY KEY (order_numb, model_numb, shipping_date),
    FOREIGN KEY (order_numb, model_numb) REFERENCES order_line
)
```

■ **FIGURE 11-16** SQL statements needed to create Mighty-Mite Motors' database—Cont'd

```
CREATE TABLE product
{
    serial_numb INTEGER,
    model_numb INTEGER,
    date_manufactured DATE,
    status_code INTEGER,
    date_shipped DATE,
    order_numb INTEGER,
    PRIMARY KEY (serial_numb),
    FOREIGN KEY (model_numb) REFERENCES model,
    FOREIGN KEY (status_code) REFERENCES product_status,
    FOREIGN KEY (order_numb) REFERENCES order
)

CREATE TABLE product_status
{
    status_code INTEGER,
    status_description VARCHAR (40),
    PRIMARY KEY (status_code)
)

CREATE TABLE raw_material
{
    material_id_numb INTEGER,
    material_name VARCHAR (40),
    unit_of_measurement CHAR (12),
    quantity_in_stock INTEGER,
    reorder_point INTEGER,
    PRIMARY KEY (material_id_numb)
)

CREATE TABLE material_needed
{
    model_numb INTEGER,
    material_id_numb INTEGER,
    quantity_needed INTEGER,
    PRIMARY KEY (model_numb, material_id_numb),
    FOREIGN KEY (model_numb) REFERENCES model,
    FOREIGN KEY (material_id_numb) REFERENCES raw_material
}
```

■ **FIGURE 11-16** Cont'd

```
CREATE TABLE supplier
{
    supplier_numb INTEGER,
    supplier_name VARCHAR (40),
    supplier_street VARCHAR (50),
    supplier_city VARCHAR (50),
    supplier_state CHAR (2),
    supplier_zip CHAR (10),
    supplier_phone CHAR (12),
    PRIMARY KEY (supplier_numb)
}

CREATE TABLE material_order
{
    po_numb INTEGER,
    supplier_numb INTEGER,
    material_order_date DATE,
    material_order_total NUMBER (8,2),
    PRIMARY KEY (po_numb),
    FOREIGN KEY (supplier_numb) REFERENCES supplier
)

CREATE TABLE material_order_line
{
    po_numb INTEGER,
    material_id_numb INTEGER,
    material_quantity INTEGER,
    material_cost_each NUMBER (6,2),
    material_line_cost NUMBER (8,2),
    PRIMARY KEY (po_numb, material_id_numb),
    FOREIGN KEY (po_numb) REFERENCES material_order,
    FOREIGN KEY (material_id_numb) REFERENCES raw_material
}

CREATE TABLE manufacturing_line
{
    line_numb INTEGER,
    line_status CHAR (12),
    PRIMARY KEY (line_numb)
)
```

■ **FIGURE 11-16** SQL statements needed to create Mighty-Mite Motors' database—Cont'd

```
CREATE TABLE line_schedule
{
    line_numb INTEGER,
    production_date DATE,
    model_numb INTEGER,
    quantity_to_product INTEGER
    PRIMARY KEY (line_numb, production_date),
    FOREIGN KEY (lne_numb) REFERENCES manufacturing_line,
    FOREIGN KEY (model_numb) REFERENCES model
)

CREATE TABLE owner
{
    owner_numb INTEGER,
    owner_street VARCHAR (50),
    owner_city VARCHAR (50),
    owner_state CHAR (2),
    owner_zip CHAR (10),
    owner_phone CHAR (10),
    PRIMARY KEY (owner_numb)
}

CREATE TABLE purchase
{
    serial_numb INTEGER,
    owner_numb INTEGER,
    age INTEGER,
    gender CHAR (1),
    purchase_date DATE,
    purchase_place VARCHAR (50),
    learn_code INTEGER,
    relationship CHAR (10),
    PRIMARY KEY (serial_numb),
    FOREIGN KEY (serial_numb) REFERENCES product,
    FOREIGN KEY (owner_numb) REFERENCES owner
    FOREIGN KEY (learn_code) REFERENCES learn_about
)
```

■ **FIGURE 11-16** Cont'd

```
CREATE TABLE feature
{
    feature_code INTEGER,
    feature_description VARCHAR (40),
    PRIMARY KEY (feature_code)
)

CREATE TABLE purchase_feature
{
    serial_numb INTEGER,
    feature_code INTEGER,
    PRIMARY KEY (serial_numb, feature_code),
    FOREIGN KEY (serial_numb) REFERENCES product,
    FOREIGN KEY (feature_code) REFERENCES feature
}

CREATE TABLE learn_about
{
    learn_code INTEGER,
    learn_description VARCHAR (50),
    PRIMARY KEY (learn_code)
}

CREATE TABLE problem_type
{
    problem_type_code INTEGER,
    problem_type_description VARCHAR (50),
    PRIMARY KEY (problem_type_code)
)

CREATE TABLE problem_report
{
    serial_numb INTEGER,
    problem_date DATE,
    problem_time TIME,
    problem_type_code INTEGER,
    problem_details VARCHAR (50),
    PRIMARY KEY (serial_numb, problem_date),
    FOREIGN KEY (serial_numb) REFERENCES product,
    FOREIGN KEY (product_type_code) REFERENCES problem_type
}
```

■ **FIGURE 11-16** SQL statements needed to create Mighty-Mite Motors' database—Cont'd

Chapter 12

Database Design Case Study 2: East Coast Aquarium

Many-to-many relationships are often the bane of the relational database designer. Sometimes it is not completely clear that you are dealing with that type of relationship. However, failure to recognize the many-to-many relationship can result in serious data integrity problems.

The organization described in this chapter actually needs two databases, the larger of which is replete with many-to-many relationships. In some cases it will be necessary to create additional entities for composite entities to reference merely to ensure data integrity.

Perhaps the biggest challenge with a database design that works for East Coast Aquarium is the lack of complete specifications. As you will see, the people who will be using the application programs to manipulate the aquarium's two new databases have only a general idea of what the programs must do. Unlike Mighty-Mite Motors—which had the history of working from a large collection of existing forms, documents, and procedures—East Coast Aquarium has nothing of that sort.

ORGANIZATIONAL OVERVIEW

The East Coast Aquarium is a nonprofit organization dedicated to the study and preservation of marine life. Located on the Atlantic Coast in the heart of a major northeastern U.S. city, it provides a wide variety of educational services to the surrounding area. The aquarium is supported by donations, memberships, fees for private functions, gift shop revenues, class fees, and the small admission fee it charges to the public. Research activities are funded by federal and private grants. To help keep costs down, many of the public service jobs (leading tours, staffing the admissions counter, running the gift shop) are handled by volunteers.

The aquarium grounds consist of three buildings: the main facility, a dolphin house, and a marina where the aquarium's research barge is docked. The centerpiece of the main building is a three-story center tank that is surrounded by a spiral walkway. The sides of the tank are transparent, so that visitors can walk around the tank and observe its residents at various depths.

Note: If you happen to recognize the layout of this aquarium, please keep in mind that only the physical structure of the environment is modeled after anything that really exists. The way the organization functions is purely a product of my imagination, and no comment, either positive or negative, is intended with regard to the real-world aquarium.

The height of the tank makes it possible to simulate the way habitats vary at different ocean depths. Species that dwell on the ocean floor, coral reef fish, and sandbar dwellers therefore are all housed in the same tank, interacting in much the same way as they would in the ocean.

The remaining space on the first floor of the main building (Figure 12-1) includes the gift shop and a quarantine area for newly arrived animals. The latter area is not accessible to visitors. The second floor (Figure 12-2) contains a classroom and the volunteers' office. Small tanks containing single-habitat exhibits are installed in the outside walls. These provide places to house species that have special habitat requirements or that don't coexist well with other species. The third floor (Figure 12-3) provides wall space for additional small exhibits. It also houses the aquarium's administrative offices.

East Coast Aquarium has two very different areas where it needs data management. The first is in the handling of its animals: where they are housed in the aquarium, where they came from, what they are to be fed, problems that occur in the tanks, and so on. The second area concerns the volunteers, including who they are, what they have been trained to do, and when they are scheduled to work. For this particular organization, the two data environments are completely separate; that is, they share no data. A database designer who volunteers to work with the aquarium staff will therefore prepare two database designs, one to be used by the volunteer staff in the volunteers' office and the other to be used by the administrative and animal-care staff through the aquarium grounds.

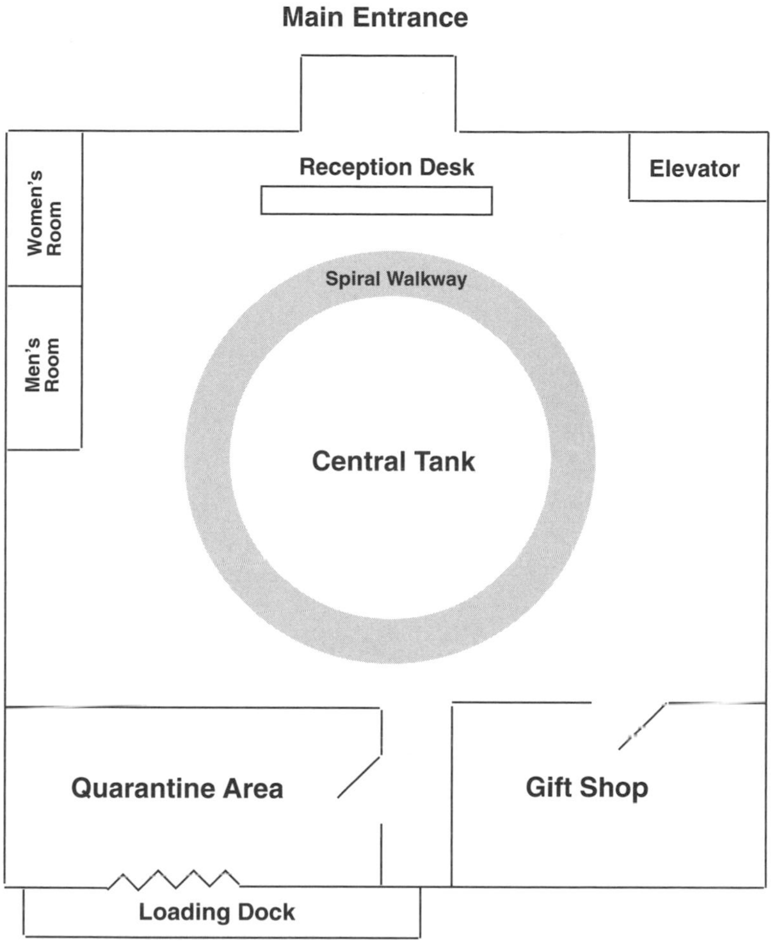

■ **FIGURE 12-1** First floor of East Coast Aquarium's main building.

Animal Tracking Needs

Currently, East Coast Aquarium uses a general-purpose PC accounting package to handle its data-processing needs. The software takes care of payroll as well as purchasing, accounts payable, and accounts receivable. Grant funds are managed by special-purpose software that is designed to monitor grant awards and how they are spent.

Although the accounting and grant management packages adequately handle the aquarium's finances, there is no data processing that tracks the actual animals housed in the aquarium. The three people in charge of the animals have expressed a need for the following:

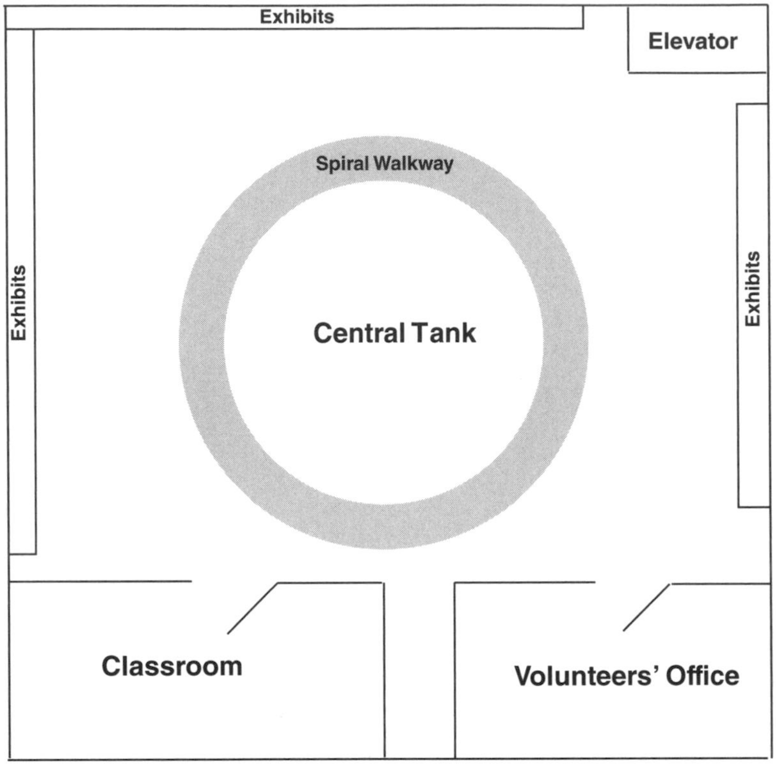

■ **FIGURE 12-2** Second floor of East Coast Aquarium's main building.

- *An "inventory" of which species are living in which locations in the aquarium.* Some species can be found in more than one tank, and several tanks in addition to the central tank contain more than one species. For larger animals, such as sharks and dolphins, the head animal keeper would like a precise count. However, for small fish that are often eaten by large fish and that breed in large numbers, only an estimate is possible. The animal handling staff would like to be able to search for information about animals using either the animal's English name or its Latin name.
- *Data about the foods each species eats, including how much should be fed at which interval.* The head animal keeper would like to be able to print out a feeding instruction list every morning to distribute to the staff. In addition, the animal-feeding staff would like to store information about their food inventory. Although purchasing of food is handled by the administrative office, the head animal keeper

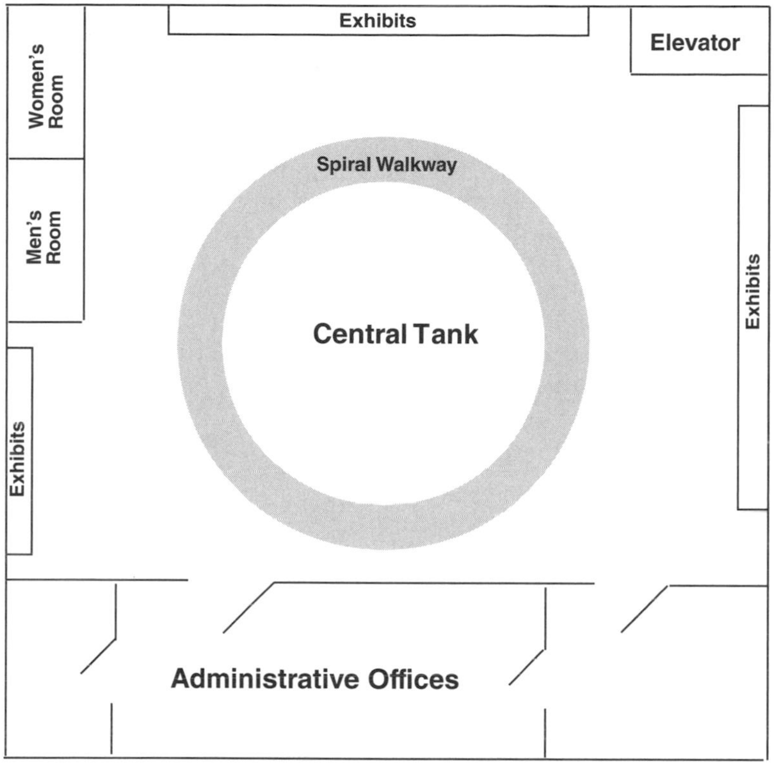

■ **FIGURE 12-3** Third floor of East Coast Aquarium's main building.

would like an application program to decrement the food inventory automatically by the amount fed each day and to generate a tickle request whenever the stock level of a type of food drops below the reorder point. This will make it much easier to ensure that the aquarium does not run short of animal food.

- *Data about the sizes, locations, and habitats of the tanks on the aquarium grounds.* Some tanks, such as the main tank, contain more than one habitat, and the same habitat can be found in more than one tank.
- *Data about tank maintenance.* Although the main tank is fed directly from the ocean, the smaller tanks around the walls of the main building are closed environments, much like a saltwater aquarium might be at home. This means that the pH and salinity of the tanks must be monitored closely. The head animal keeper therefore would like to print out a maintenance schedule each day, as well as be able to keep track of what maintenance is actually performed.

- *Data about the habitats in which a given species can live.* When a new species arrives at the aquarium, the staff can use this information to determine which locations could possibly house that species.
- *Data about where species can be obtained.* If the aquarium wants to increase the population of a particular species, and the increase cannot be generated through in-house breeding, then the staff would like to know which external supplier can be contacted. Some of the suppliers sell animals; others, such as zoos or other aquariums, will trade or donate animals.
- *Problems that arise in the tanks.* When animals become ill, the veterinarian wants to be able to view a history of both the animal and the tank in which it is currently living.
- *Data about the orders placed for animals, in particular the shipments in which animals arrive.* Since any financial arrangements involved in securing animals are handled by the administrative office, these data indicate only how many individuals of each species are included on a given order or shipment.

The shipment and problem data are particularly important to the aquarium. When animals first arrive, they are not placed immediately into the general population. Instead, they are held in special tanks in the quarantine area at the rear of the aquarium's first floor. The length of the quarantine period depends on the species.

After the quarantine period has passed and the animals are declared disease-free, they can be placed on exhibit in the main portion of the aquarium. Nonetheless, animals do become ill after they have been released from quarantine. It is therefore essential that records are kept of the sources of animals so that patterns of illness can be tracked back to specific suppliers, if such patterns appear. By the same token, patterns of illnesses in various species housed in the same tank can be an indication of serious problems with the environment in the tank.

The Volunteer Organization

The volunteer organization (Friends of the Aquarium) is totally separate from the financial and animal-handling areas of the aquarium. Volunteers perform tasks that do not involve direct contact with animals, such as leading tours, manning the admissions desk, and running the gift shop. The aquarium has provided office space and a telephone line for the volunteer coordinator and her staff. Beyond that, the Friends of the Aquarium organization has been on its own as far as securing office furniture and equipment.

The recent donation of a PC now makes it possible for the volunteers to input some of the volunteer data online, although the scheduling is still largely manual. Currently, the scheduling process works in the following way:

- The person on duty in the volunteers' office receives requests for volunteer services from the aquarium's administrative office. Some of the jobs are regularly scheduled (for example, staffing the gift shop and the admissions desk). Others are ad hoc, such as a request from a teacher to bring her class for a tour.
- The volunteer doing the scheduling checks the list of volunteers to see who is trained to do the job requested. Each volunteer's information is recorded in a data file that contains the volunteer's contact data along with the volunteer's skills. A skill is a general expression of something the volunteer knows how to do, such as lead a tour for elementary school children. The volunteer's information also includes an indication of when that person is available to work.
- The volunteer doing the scheduling searches the file for those people who have the required skills and have indicated that they are available at the required time. Most volunteers work on a regularly scheduled basis either at the admissions desk or in the gift shop. However, for ad hoc jobs, the person doing the scheduling must start making telephone calls until someone who is willing and able to do the job is found.
- The volunteer is scheduled for the job by writing in the master scheduling notebook. As far as the volunteer coordinator is concerned, a job is an application of a skill. Therefore, a skill is knowing how to lead a tour for elementary school students, while a job that applies that skill is leading a tour of Mrs. Brown's third-graders at 10 AM on Thursday.

One of the things that is very difficult to do with the current scheduling process is keeping track of the work record of each individual volunteer. The aquarium holds a volunteer recognition luncheon once a year, and the volunteer organization would like to find an easy way to identify volunteers who have put in an extra effort so they can be recognized at that event. In contrast, the volunteer organization would also like to be able to identify volunteers who rarely participate—the people who stay on the volunteer rolls only to get free admission to the aquarium—as well as people who make commitments to work but do not show up. (The latter are actually far more of a problem than the former.)

THE VOLUNTEERS DATABASE

In terms of scope, the volunteers database is considerably smaller than the animal-tracking database. It therefore makes sense to tackle the smaller project first. The database designer will create an application prototype and review it with the users. When the users are satisfied and the designers feel they have detailed information to actually design a database, they will move on to the more traditional steps of creating an ER diagram, tables, and SQL statements.

> *Note:* As you will see, there is a lot involved in creating a prototype. It requires very detailed, intensive work and produces a number of diagrams and/or application program shells. We will therefore look at the volunteers' prototype in full, but in the interest of length, we will look at only selected aspects of the animal tracking prototype.

Creating the Application Prototype

Given that the specifications of the database are rather general, the first step is to create a prototype of an application program interface. It begins with the opening screen and its main menu board (Figure 12-4). As you can see, when in browse mode, the CASE tool allows users and designers to pull down the menus in the menu bar.

The complete menu tree (with the exception of the Help menu, whose contents are determined by the user interface guidelines of the operating system on which the application is running) can be found in Figure 12-5. Looking at the menu options, users can see that their basic requirements have been fulfilled. The details, however, must be specified by providing users with specific input and output designs.

Each menu option in the prototype's main menu has therefore been linked to a screen form. For example, to modify or delete a volunteer, a user must first find the volunteer's data. Therefore the Modify or Delete a Volunteer menu option leads to a dialog box that lets the user either enter a volunteer number or select a volunteer by name

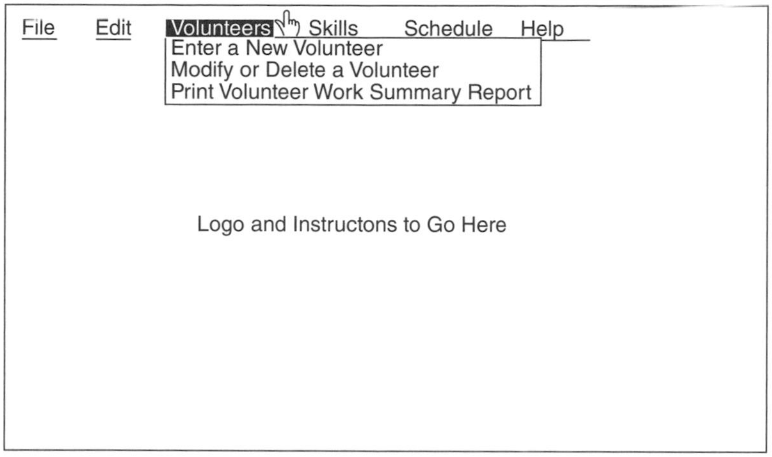

■ **FIGURE 12-4** Main menu prototype for the volunteers' application.

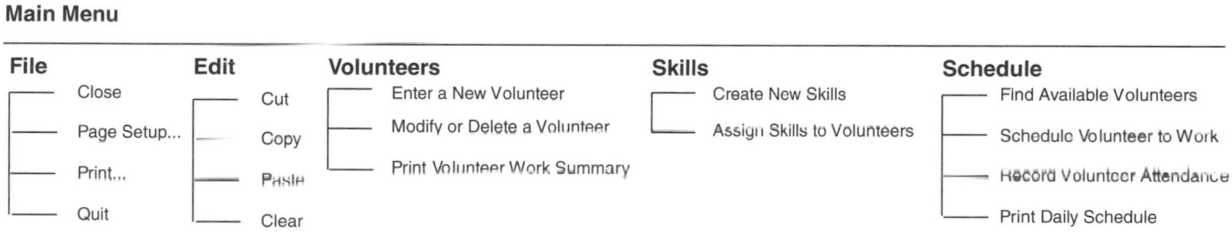

■ **FIGURE 12-5** Menu tree of the volunteers database prototype application.

and phone number from a list (Figure 12-6). With the prototype, clicking the Find button opens the modify/delete form (Figure 12-7). Users can click in the data entry fields and tab between them, but the buttons at the right of the window are not functional.

While in browse mode, the CASE tool presents a form as it would appear to the user. However, in design mode, a database designer can see the names of the fields on the form (for example, Figure 12-8). These field names suggest attributes that will be needed in the database.

In the case of the volunteer data, it is apparent to the designers that there are at least two entities (and perhaps three) involved with the data that describe a volunteer. The first entity is represented by the single-valued fields occupying the top half of the form (volunteer number, first name, last name, city, state, zip, and phone). However, the availability data—day of the week, starting time, and ending

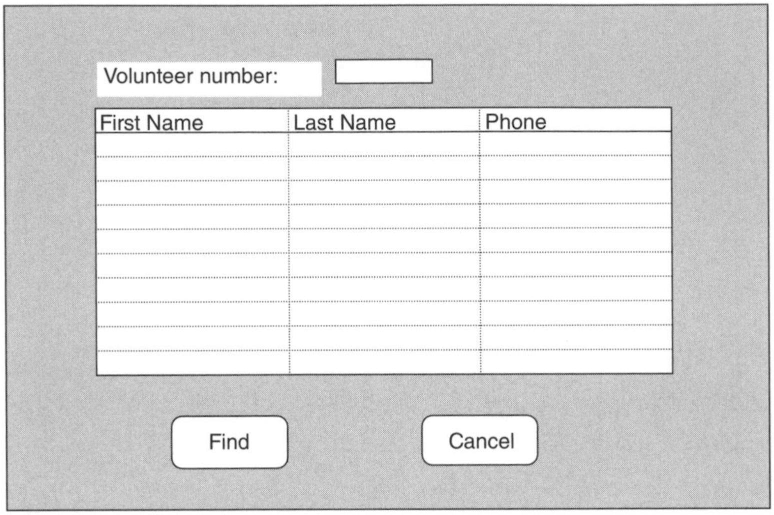

■ **FIGURE 12-6** Prototype of a dialog box for finding a volunteer for modifications.

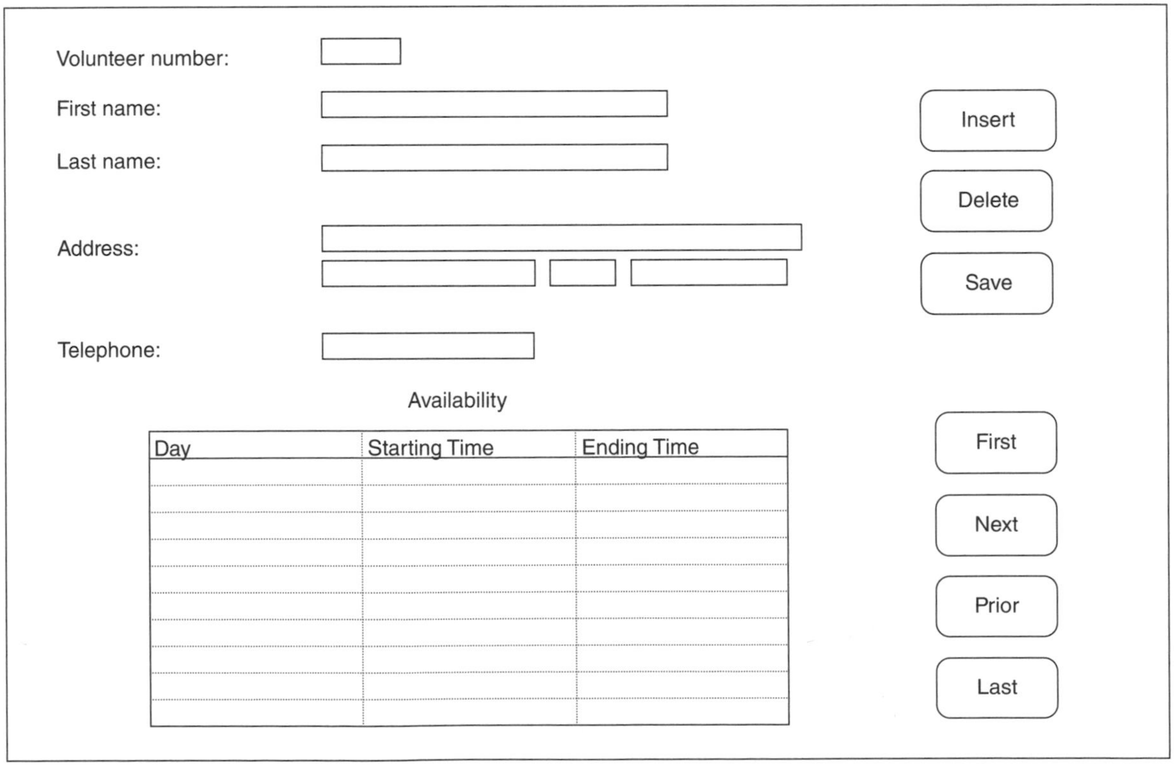

■ **FIGURE 12-7** Prototype of form for modifying and deleting a volunteer.

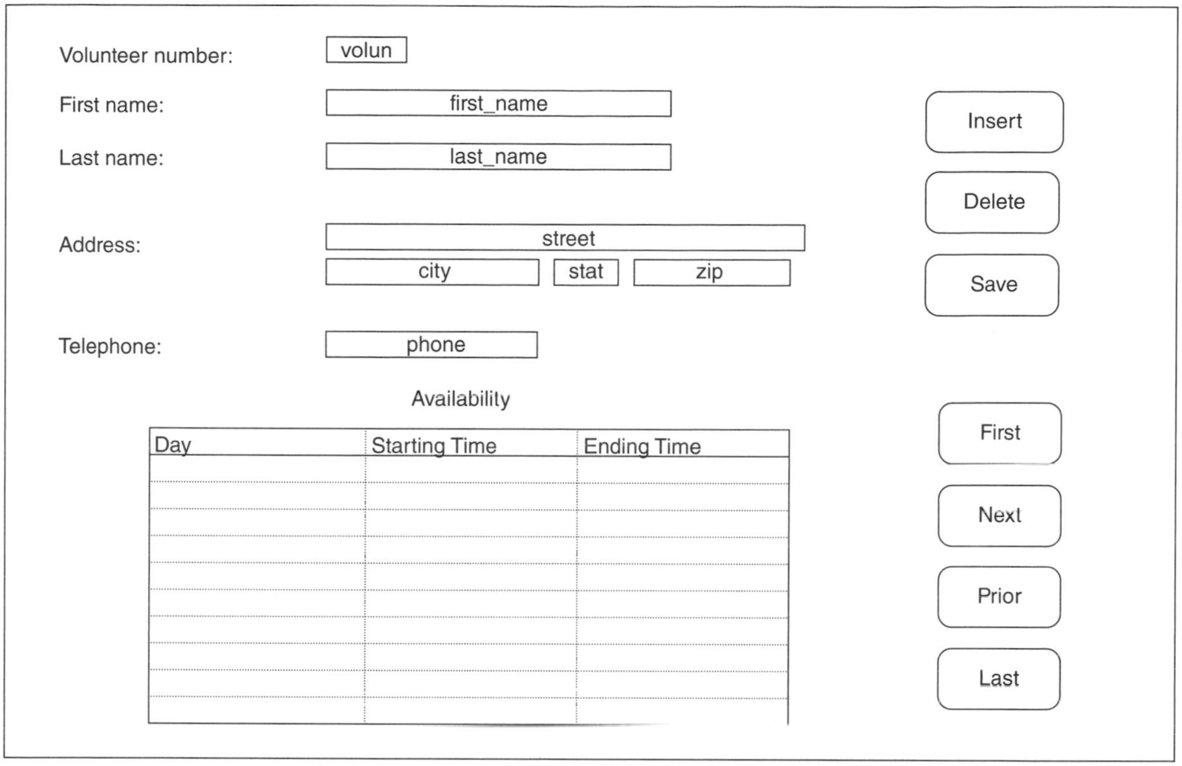

■ **FIGURE 12-8** Prototype data modification form showing field names.

time—are multivalued and therefore must be given an entity of their own. This also implies that there will be a one-to-many relationship between a volunteer and a period of time during which he or she is available.

> *Note:* Should you choose, the field names of a screen prototype can become part of the data dictionary. However, if the field names do not ultimately correspond to column names, their inclusion may add unnecessary complexity to the data dictionary.

The remainder of the prototype application and its forms are designed and analyzed in a similar way:

- The volunteer work summary report has been designed to let the user enter a range of dates that the report will cover (see Figure 12-9). The report itself (Figure 12-10) is a control-break report that

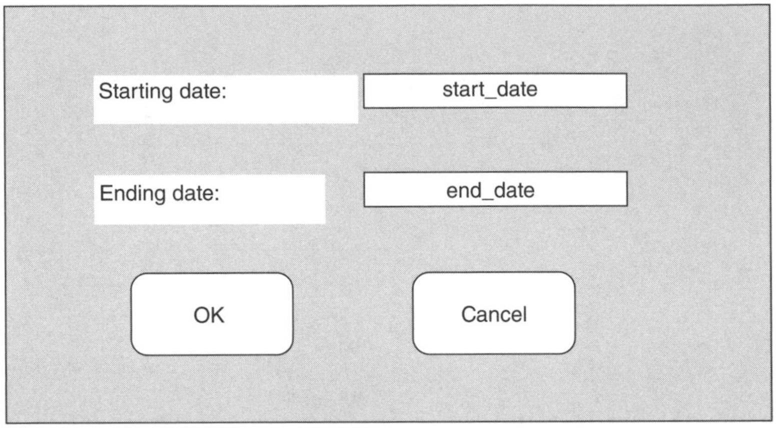

■ **FIGURE 12-9** A dialog box layout for entering dates for the work summary report.

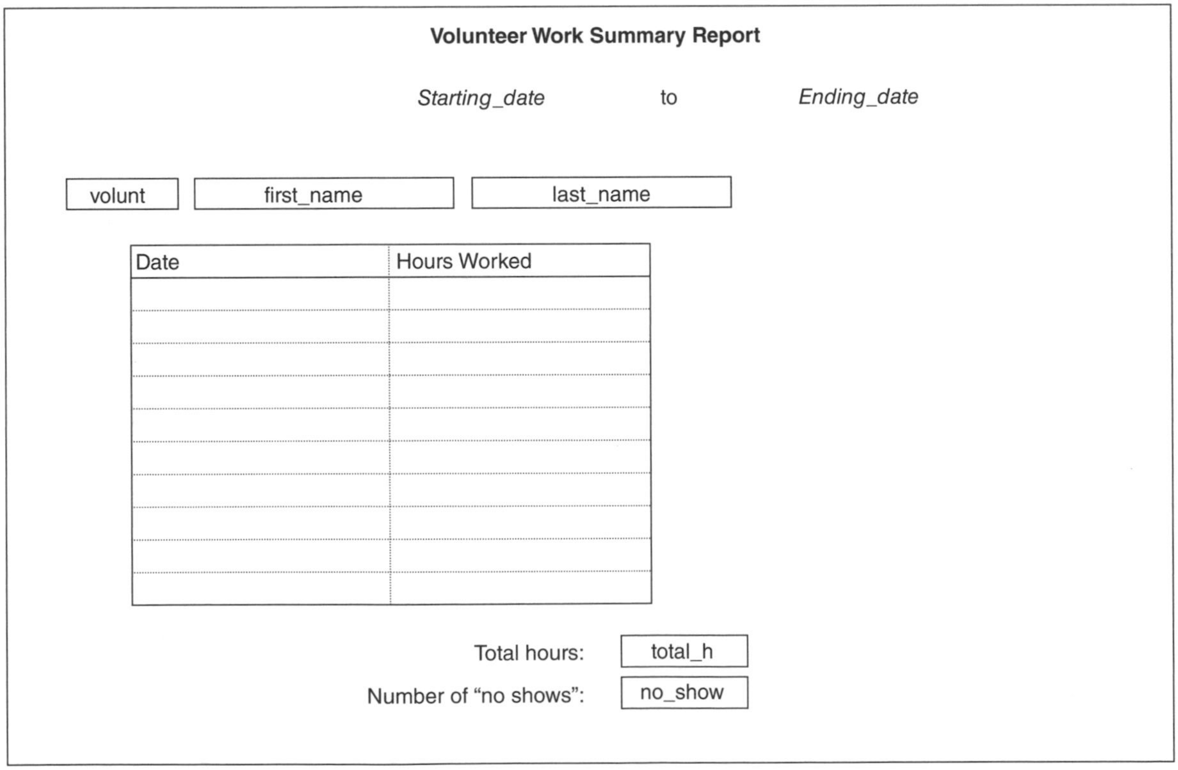

■ **FIGURE 12-10** Prototype layout for the work summary report.

displays the work performed by each volunteer along with the total hours worked and the number of times the volunteer was a "no show." The latter number was included because the volunteer coordinator had indicated that it was extremely important to know which volunteers consistently signed up to work and then didn't report when scheduled.

The need to report the "no shows" tells the designers that the schedule table needs to include a Boolean column that indicates whether a person showed up for a scheduled shift. The report layout also includes some computed fields (total hours worked and number of no shows) that contain data that do not need to be stored but can be generated when the report is displayed.

- Entering a new skill into the master list requires only a simple form (Figure 12-11). The end user sees only the description of a skill. However, the database designers know that the best way to handle an unstructured block of text is to assign each description a skill number, which can then be used as a foreign key throughout the database. Users, however, do not necessarily need to know that a skill number is being used; they will see just the text descriptions.
- To assign skills to a volunteer, the end user must first find the volunteer. The application can therefore use a copy of the dialog box in Figure 12-6. In this case, however, the Find button leads to the form in Figure 12-12.

A database designer will recognize quickly that there is a many-to-many relationship between a skill and a volunteer. There are actually

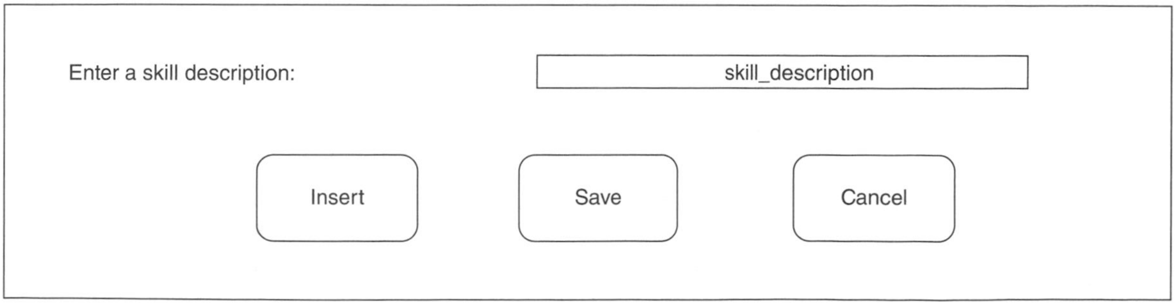

■ **FIGURE 12-11** Entering a new skill.

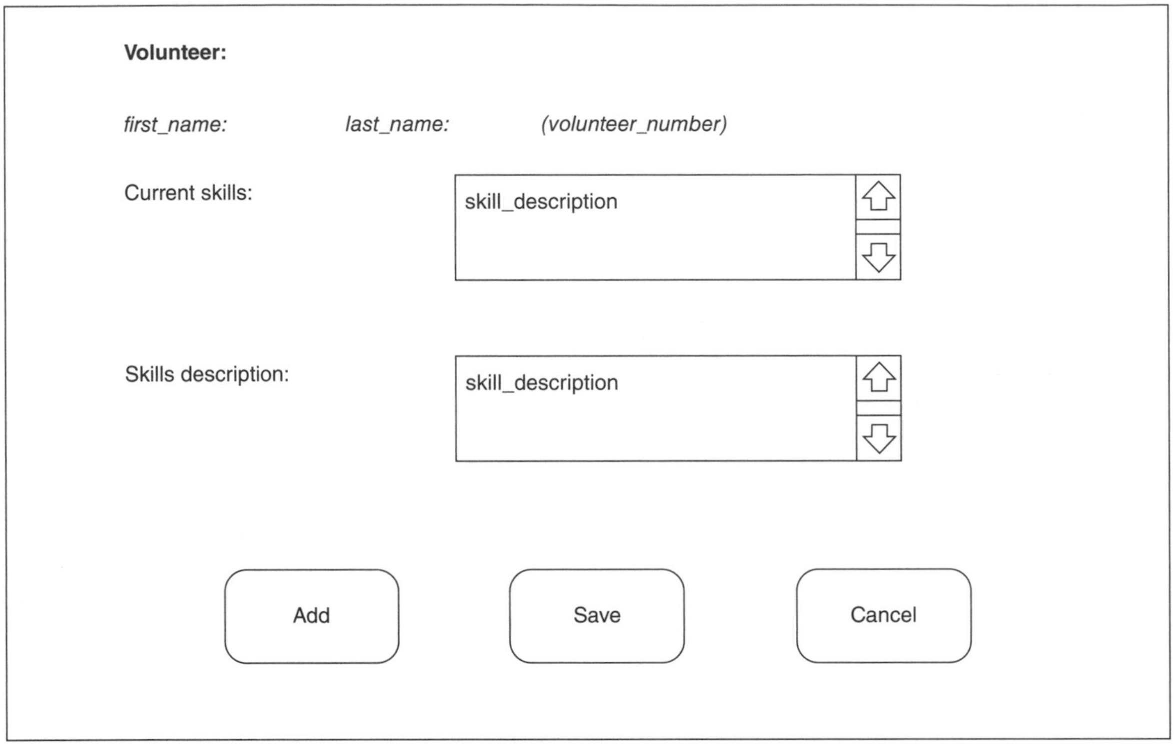

■ **FIGURE 12-12** Assigning skills to a volunteer.

three entities behind Figure 12-12: the skill, the volunteer, and the composite entity that represents the relationship between the two. The skill entry form displays data from the volunteer entity at the top, data from the composite entity in the current skills list, and all skills not assigned from the skills table in the skill description list. Of course, the foreign key used in the composite entity is a skill number, but the user sees only the result of a join back to the skills table that retrieves the skill description.

Note: Database integrity constraints will certainly prevent anyone from assigning the same skill twice to the same volunteer. However, it is easier if the user can see currently assigned skills. Then the application can restrict what appears in the skill description list to all skills not assigned to that volunteer. In this case, it is a matter of user interface design rather than database design.

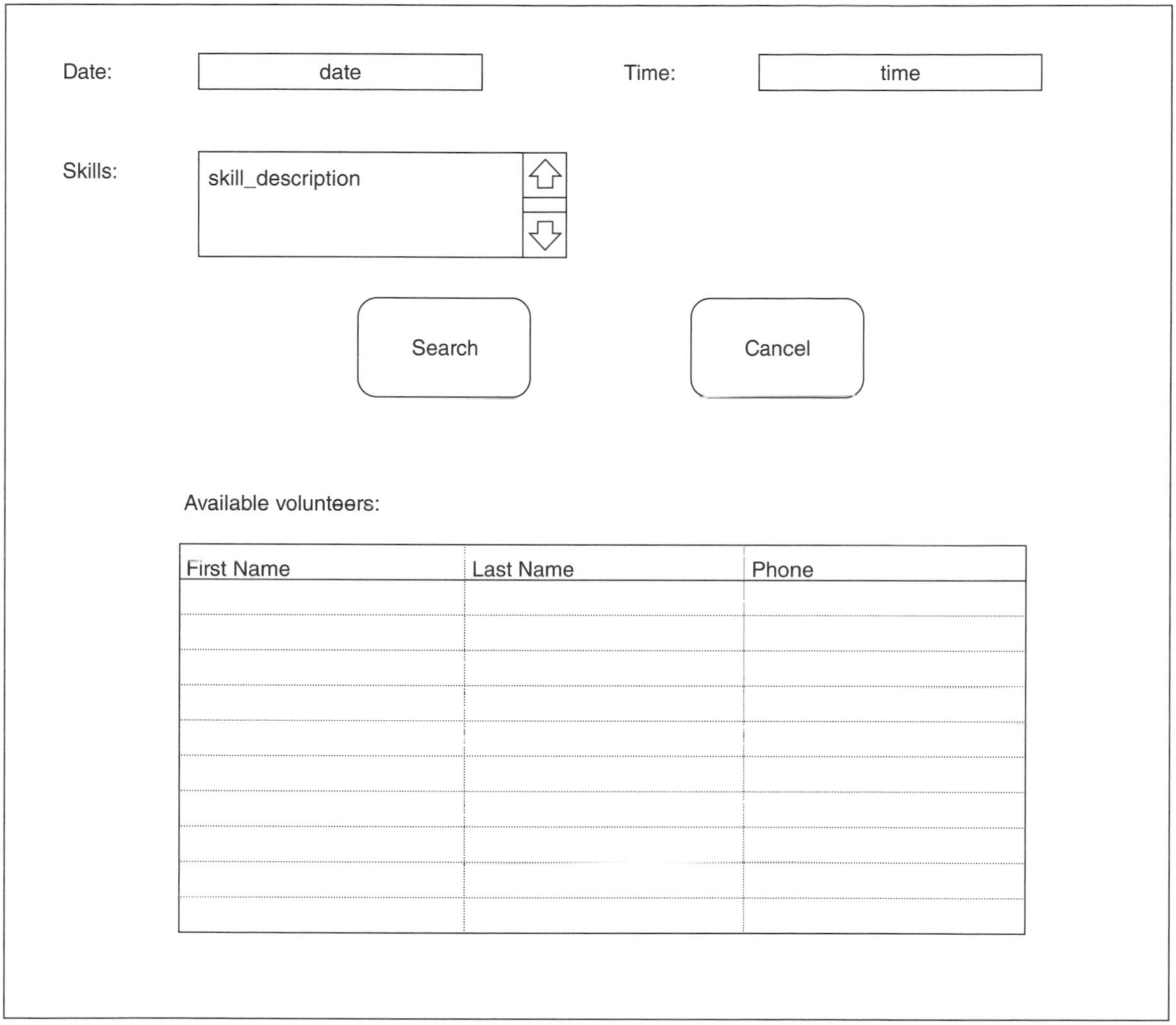

■ **FIGURE 12-13** Finding available volunteers.

- To find the volunteers available to perform a specific job, the volunteers' application needs a form like the one in Figure 12-13. The end user enters the date and time of the job and chooses the skill required by the job. Clicking the Search button fills in the table at the bottom of the form with the names and phone numbers of volunteers who are theoretically available.

Of all the outputs produced by this application, finding available volunteers is probably the most difficult to implement. The application program must not only work with overlapping intervals of time but also consider both when a volunteer indicates he or she will be available and when a volunteer is already scheduled to work. In most cases, however, a database designer does not have to write the application program code. The designer needs only to ensure that the data necessary to produce the output are present in the database.

- Once the person doing the volunteer scheduling has located a volunteer to fill a specific job, then the volunteer's commitment to work needs to become a part of the database. The process begins by presenting the user with a Find Volunteer dialog box like that in Figure 12-6. In this case, the Find button is linked to the Schedule Volunteer window (Figure 12-14). A database designer will recognize that this is not all the data that must be stored about a job,

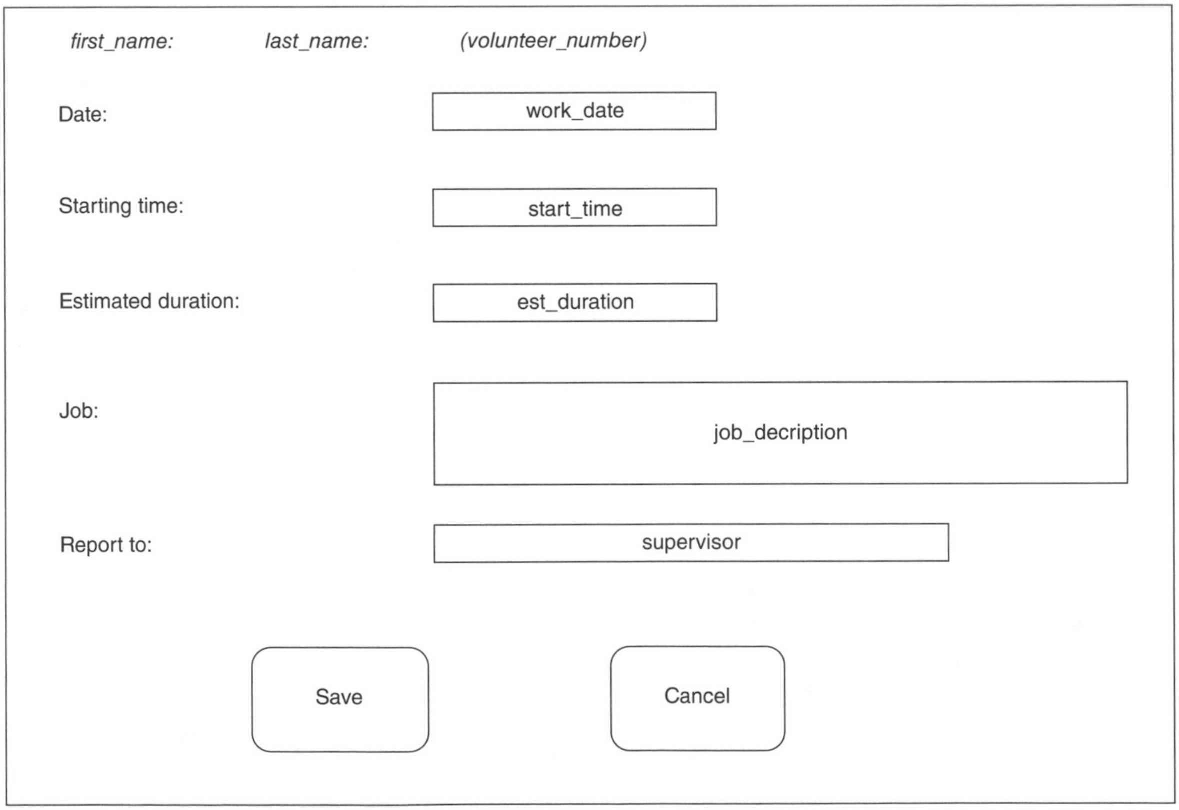

■ **FIGURE 12-14** Scheduling a volunteer to perform a job.

however. In particular someone will need to record whether the volunteer actually appeared to do the scheduled job on the day of the job; this cannot be done when the job is scheduled initially.

- To record attendance, an end user first locates the volunteer using a Find Volunteer dialog box (Figure 12-6), which then leads to a display of the jobs the volunteer has been scheduled to do in reverse chronological order (see Figure 12-15). For those jobs that have not been performed, the End Time and Worked? Columns will be empty. The user can then scroll the list to find the job to be modified and enter values for the two empty columns. The fields on this

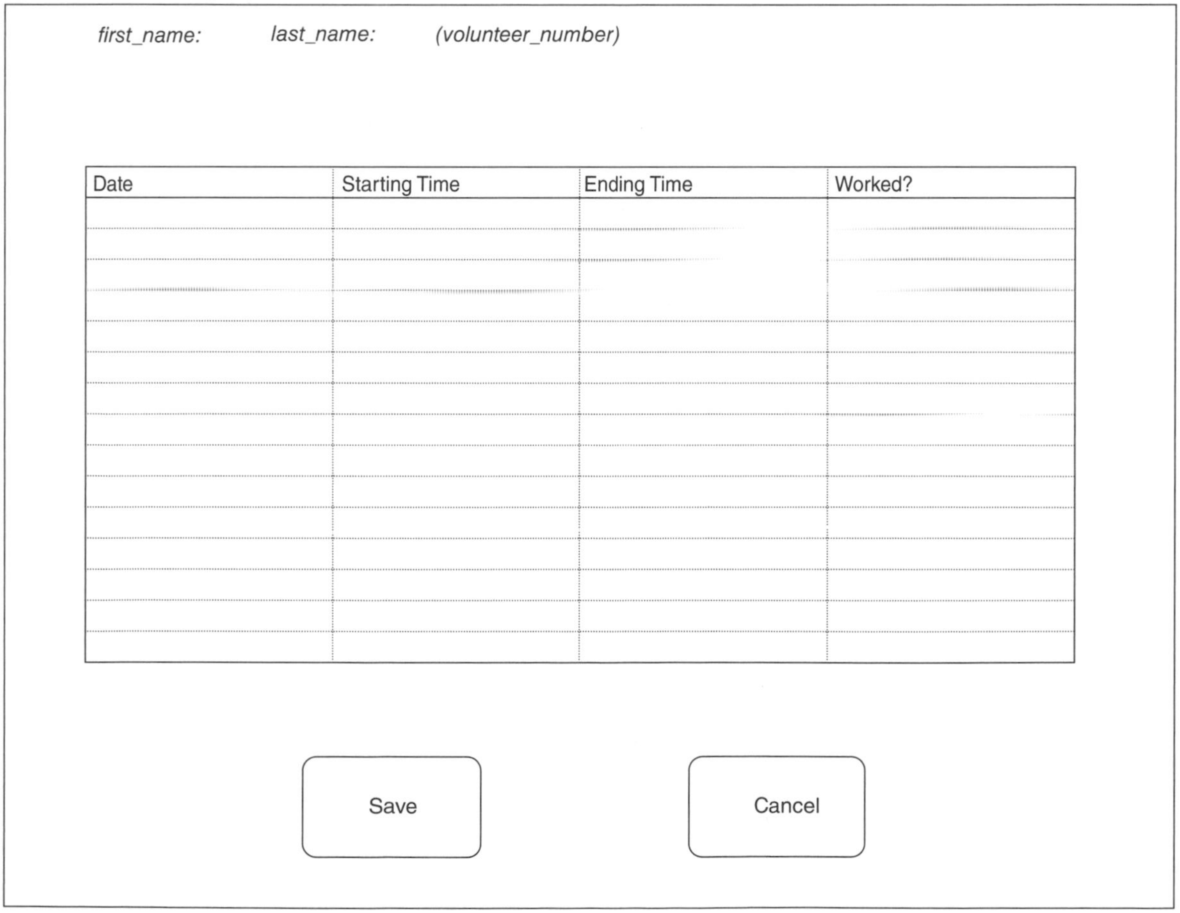

■ **FIGURE 12-15** Recording jobs worked.

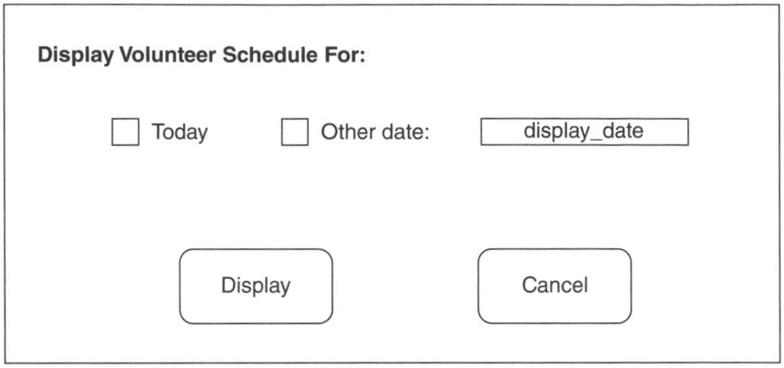

■ **FIGURE 12-16** Choosing a date for schedule display.

form, plus those on the job scheduling form, represent the attributes that will describe the job entity.

- To print a daily schedule, an end user first uses a dialog box to indicate the date for which a schedule should be displayed (Figure 12-16). The application program then assembles the report (Figure 12-17). To simplify working with the program, the application developers should probably allows users to double-click on any line in the listing to open the form in Figure 12-15 for the scheduled volunteer. However, this capability will have no impact on the database design.

Note: A smart database designer, however, would discuss any output that involves something as difficult as evaluating overlapping time intervals with application programmers to ensure that the output is feasible, not only in terms of data manipulation but of performance as well. There is no point in specifying infeasible output.

Creating the ER Diagram

From the approved prototype of the application design and conversations with the volunteers who do volunteer scheduling, the database designers can gather enough information to create a basic ER diagram for the volunteers' organization. The designers examine each screen form carefully to ensure that the database design provides the attributes and relationships necessary to generate the output.

Volunteer Work Schedule For: *selected_date*

Starting Time	First Name	Last Name	Phone	Job

■ **FIGURE 12-17** Volunteer work schedule.

At first, the ER diagram (Figure 12-18) may seem overly complex. However, two of the entities—state and day—are present for referential integrity purposes, ensuring that abbreviations for state and day names are entered consistently. The relationships among volunteers, jobs, and skills also aren't quite as simple as they might seem at first, in part because there are several many-to-many relationships:

- There is a many-to-many relationship between volunteers and skills, which is handled by the skills_known entity.
- Because a job may require more than one volunteer, there is a many-to-many relationship between volunteers and jobs that is handled by the volunteer_scheduled entity.
- A job may require more than one skill and a skill is used on many jobs. The many-to-many relationship between a job and a skill is therefore handled by the job_skill_required entity.

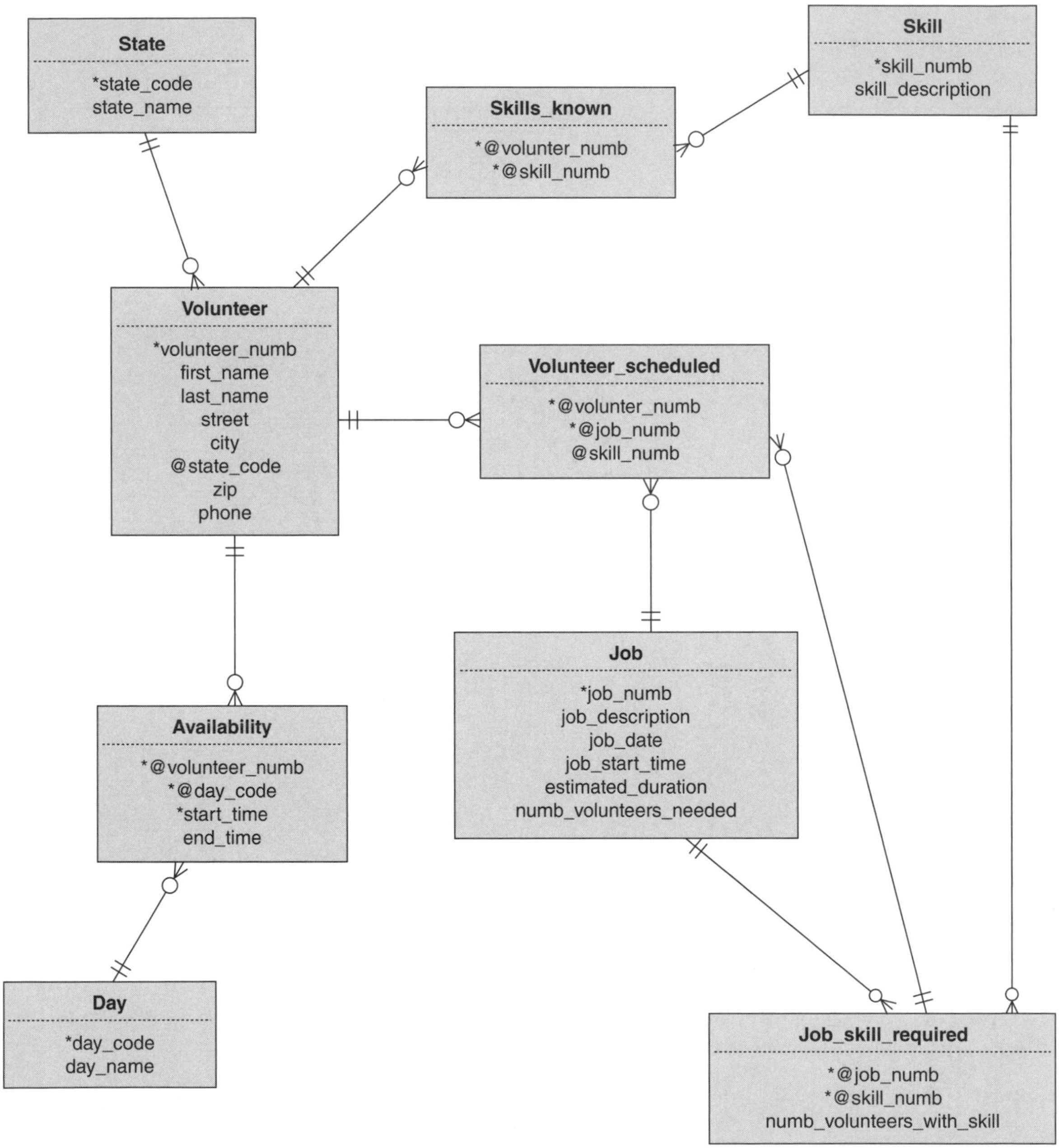

■ **FIGURE 12-18** ER diagram for the volunteers database.

What makes the situation a bit more complex is that the meaning of the M:M relationship between job and skill (through job_skill_required) is used differently than the relationship between volunteer_scheduled and job_skill_required. A row is added to job_skill_required for each skill required by a job; these data are available when the job is requested. As volunteers are scheduled for the job, rows are added to volunteer_scheduled, creating the relationship between that entity and job_skill_required. (This is essential for determining the correct volunteers still needed to be scheduled for specific skills for a specific job.) The foreign key in volunteer_scheduled uses one column from the table's primary key (job_numb) and one non-key attribute (skill_numb). Nonetheless, that concatenation is exactly the same as the primary key of the job_skill_required table (same columns with the same meaning).

Designing the Tables

The ER diagram in Figure 12-18 produces the following tables:

```
volunteer (volunteer_numb, first_name, last_name,
  street, city, state_code, zip, phone)
state (state_code, state_name)
availability (volunteer_numb, day_code, start_time,
  end_time)
day (day_code, day_name)
skill (skill_numb, skill_description)
skills_known (volunteer_numb, skill_numb)
job (job_numb, job_description, job_date,
  job_start_time, estimated_duration,
  numb_volunteers_needed)
job_skill_required (job_numb, skill_numb,
  numb_volunteers_with_skill)
volunteer_scheduled (volunteer_numb, job_numb,
  skill_numb)
```

Generating the SQL

The nine tables that make up the volunteers database can be created with the SQL in Figure 12-19. Notice that some of the attributes in the volunteers table have been specified as NOT NULL. This constraint ensures that at least a name and phone number are available for each volunteer.

```
CREATE TABLE skill
(
    skill_numb integer,
    skill_description char (50),
    CONSTRAINT PK_skill PRIMARY KEY (skill_numb)
);

CREATE TABLE job
(
    job_numb integer,
    job_description varchar (256),
    job_date date,
    job_start_time time,
    estimated_duration interval,
    numb_volunteers_needed integer,
    CONSTRAINT PK_job PRIMARY KEY (job_numb)
);

CREATE TABLE job_skill_required
(
    job_numb integer,
    skill_numb integer,
    numb_volunteers_with_skill integer,
    CONSTRAINT PK_job_skill_required PRIMARY KEY (job_numb,skill_numb),
    CONSTRAINT Relationjobjob_skill_required1 FOREIGN KEY ()
        REFERENCES job,
    CONSTRAINT Relationskilljob_skill_required1 FOREIGN KEY ()
        REFERENCES skill
);

CREATE TABLE state
(
    state_code char (2),
    state_name char (15),
    CONSTRAINT PK_state PRIMARY KEY (state_code)
);

CREATE TABLE volunteer
(
    volunteer_numb integer,
    first_name char (15) NOT NULL,
```

■ **FIGURE 12-19** SQL statements needed to create the tables for the volunteers database.

```
    last_name char (15) NOT NULL,
    street char (50),
    city char (30),
    state_code char (2),
    zip char (10),
    phone char (10) NOT NULL,
    CONSTRAINT PK_volunteer PRIMARY KEY (volunteer_numb),
    CONSTRAINT Relationstatevolunteer1 FOREIGN KEY (state_code)
        REFERENCES state
);

CREATE TABLE volunteer_scheduled
(
    volunteer_numb integer,
    job_numb integer,
    skill_numb integer,
    CONSTRAINT PK_volunteer_scheduled PRIMARY KEY
        (volunteer_numb,job_numb),
    CONSTRAINT Relationvolunteervolunteer_scheduled1 FOREIGN KEY ()
        REFERENCES volunteer,
    CONSTRAINT Relationjobvolunteer_scheduled1 FOREIGN KEY ()
        REFERENCES job,
    CONSTRAINT Relationjob_skill_requiredvolunteer_scheduled1
        FOREIGN KEY () REFERENCES job_skill_required
);

CREATE TABLE skills_known
(
    volunteer_numb integer,
    skill_numb integer,
    CONSTRAINT PK_skills_known PRIMARY KEY (volunteer_numb,skill_numb),
    CONSTRAINT Relationvolunteerskills_known1 FOREIGN KEY
        (VOLUNTEER_NUMB) REFERENCES volunteer,
    CONSTRAINT Relationskillskills_known1 FOREIGN KEY (skill_numb)
        REFERENCES skill
);

CREATE TABLE day
(
    day_code char (3),
    day_name char (10),
```

■ **FIGURE 12-19** Cont'd

```
    CONSTRAINT PK_day PRIMARY KEY (day_code)
);

CREATE TABLE availability
(
    volunteer_numb integer,
    day_code char (3),
    start_time time,
    end_time time,
    CONSTRAINT PK_availability PRIMARY KEY
        (volunteer_numb,day_code,start_time),
    CONSTRAINT Relationvolunteeravailability1 FOREIGN KEY
        (volunteer_numb) REFERENCES volunteer,
    CONSTRAINT Relationdayavailability1 FOREIGN KEY (day_code)
        REFERENCES day
);
```

■ **FIGURE 12-19** SQL statements needed to create the tables for the volunteers database—Cont'd

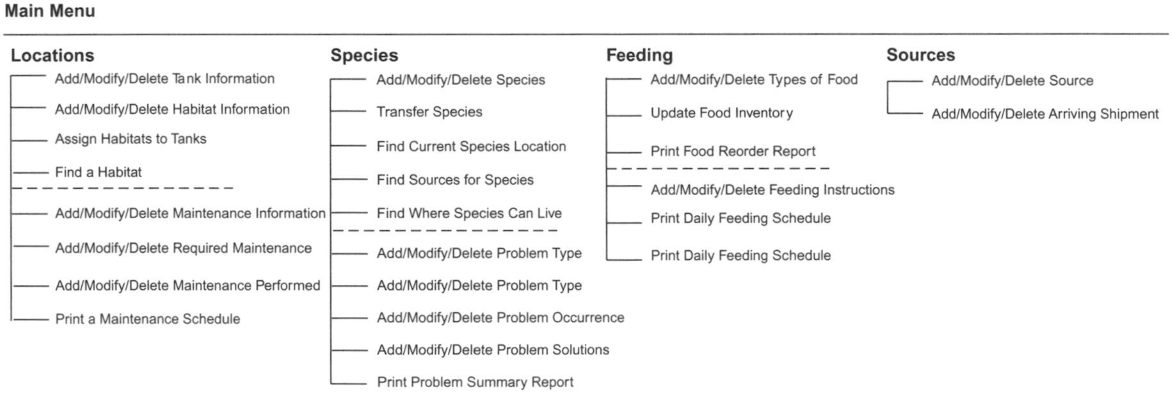

■ **FIGURE 12-20** Menu tree for the animal tracking application.

THE ANIMAL TRACKING DATABASE

The animal tracking database is considerably bigger than the volunteers database. The application that will manipulate that database therefore is concomitantly larger, as demonstrated by the menu tree in Figure 12-20. (The File and Edit menus have been left off so the diagram will fit across the width of the page. However, they are intended to be the first and second menus from the left, respectively. A Help menu can also be added along the right stage.)

The functionality requested by the animal handlers falls generally into four categories: the locations (the tanks) and their habitats, the species, the food, and the sources of animals. The organization of the application interface therefore was guided by those groups.

Highlights of the Application Prototype

The screen and report layouts designed for the animal tracking application provide a good starting place for the database designers to identify the entities and attributes needed in the database. As with the volunteers' application, there is not necessarily a one-to-one correspondence between an entity and an output.

Note: One common mistake made when designing the interface of database application programs is using one data entry form per table. Users do not look at their environments in the same way as a database designer, however, and often the organization imposed by tables does not make sense to the users. Another benefit of prototyping is therefore that it forces database and application designers to adapt to what the users really need, rather than the other way around.

Food Management

One of the important functions mentioned by the aquarium's animal handlers was management of the aquarium feeding schedule (including what *should* be fed and what *was* fed) and the food inventory. First, they wanted a daily feeding schedule that could be printed and carried with them as they worked (for example, Figure 12-21). They also wanted to be able to record when animals had been fed so that an updated feeding schedule could take prior feedings into account. Knowing that each species may eat more than one type of food and that each type of food can be eaten by many species, a database designer realizes that there are a number of entities required to implement what the users need:

- An entity that describes each species.
- An entity that describes each tank in the aquarium.
- An entity that describes a type of food.
- A composite entity between the species and location entities to record where a specific species can be found.

Feeding Schedule For: *date*

Tank number: tank_n | place_in_building

Species	Food	Quantity	How Often Today

■ **FIGURE 12-21** Daily feeding schedule.

- A composite entity between a species and a type of food recording which food a species eats, how much it eats, and how often it is fed.
- A composite entity between a species and a type of food recording which food was fed to an animal, when it was fed, and how much of it was fed.

Although it sounds like a separate application to the animal handlers, food inventory management actually requires nothing more than the food entity. The food entity needs to store data about how much food is currently in stock (modified by data from the entity that describes what was fed and by manual entries made when shipments of food arrive) and a reorder point.

Handling Arriving Animals

When a shipment of animals arrives at the aquarium, animal handlers first check the contents of the shipment against the shipment's paperwork. They then take the animals and place them in the aquarium's quarantine area. The data entry form that the animal handlers will use to store data about arrivals therefore includes a place for entering an identifier for the tank in which the new animals have been placed (Figure 12-22). Given that the aquarium staff needs to be able to locate animals at any time, this suggests that the quarantine tanks should be handled no differently from the exhibit tanks and that there is only one entity for a tank.

After the quarantine period has expired and the animals are certified as healthy, they can be transferred to another location in the building. This means an application program must delete the species from their current tank (regardless of whether it is a quarantine tank or an exhibit tank) and insert data for the new tank. The screen form

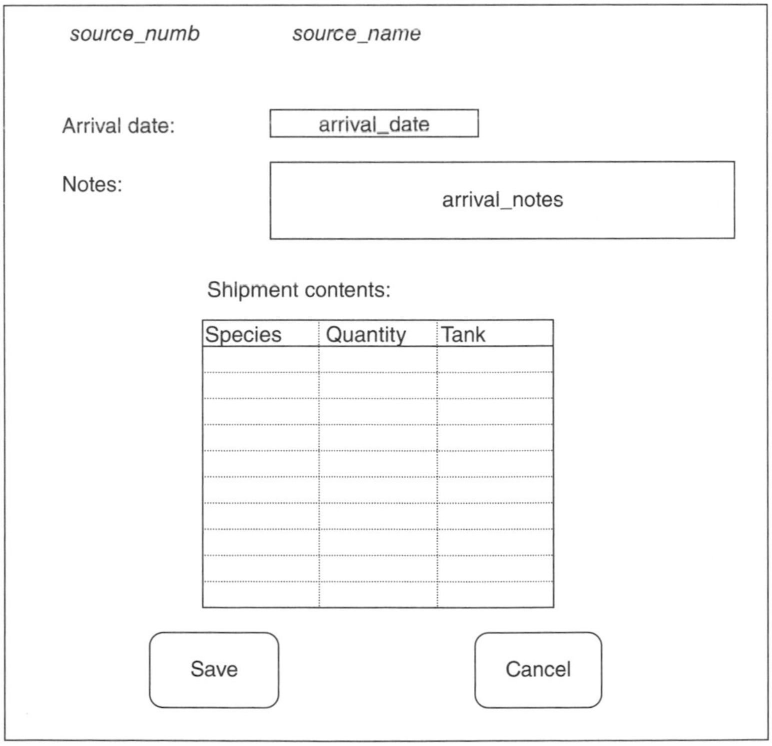

■ **FIGURE 12-22** Recording the arrival of a shipment of animals.

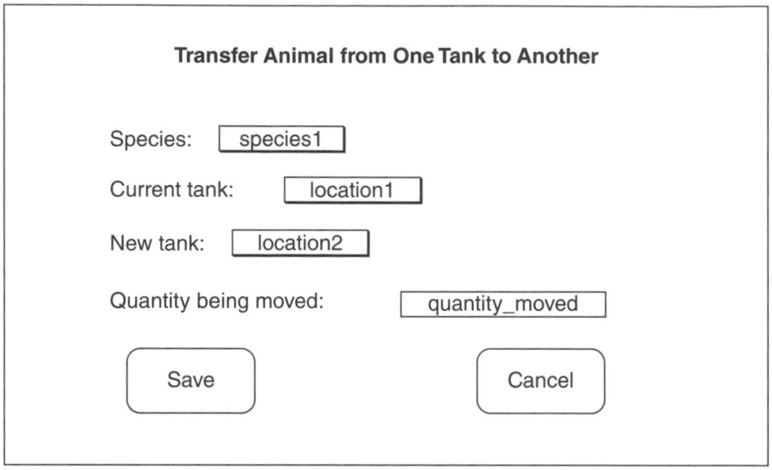

■ **FIGURE 12-23** Moving a species between tanks.

(Figure 12-23) therefore lets the user identify the species and its current location using pop-up menus. The user also uses a pop-up menu to identify the new location. To the database designer, this translates into the modification of one row (if the species is new to the exhibit tank) or the modification of one row and the deletion of another (if some of the species already live in the exhibit tank) in the table that represents the relationship between a species and a tank. All the database designer needs to do, however, is to provide the table; the application program will take care of managing the data modification.

Problem Analysis

Animal handlers are primarily concerned with the health of the animals in the aquarium. Therefore, it is important that they be able to detect any patterns while analyzing problems that occur in the tanks. Perhaps a single species is experiencing more problems than any other, or perhaps an animal handler is not paying as much attention to the condition of the tanks for which he or she is responsible.

The animal handlers want the information in Figure 12-24 included in the problem summary report. What cannot be seen from the summary screen created by the CASE tool is that the data will appear as a control-break layout. For example, each tank number will appear only once, and each type of animal will appear once for each tank in which it was the victim of a problem.

Problem Summary Report

starting_date *ending_date*

Tank	Head Keeper	Date	Species	Problem Description	Problem Resolution

■ **FIGURE 12-24** Problem summary report.

By the same token, each type of problem will appear once for each tank and species it affected. Only the problem solutions will contain data for every row in the sample output table.

To a database designer, the form in Figure 12-24 suggests the need for five entities:

- The species
- The tank
- The type of problem
- A problem occurrence (a type of problem occurring in one tank and involving one species)
- Problem solutions (one or more solutions tried for one problem occurrence). There may be many solutions to a single problem occurrence.

One of the best ways to handle problems is to prevent them in the first place. For this reason, the animal handlers also want to include maintenance data in their database.

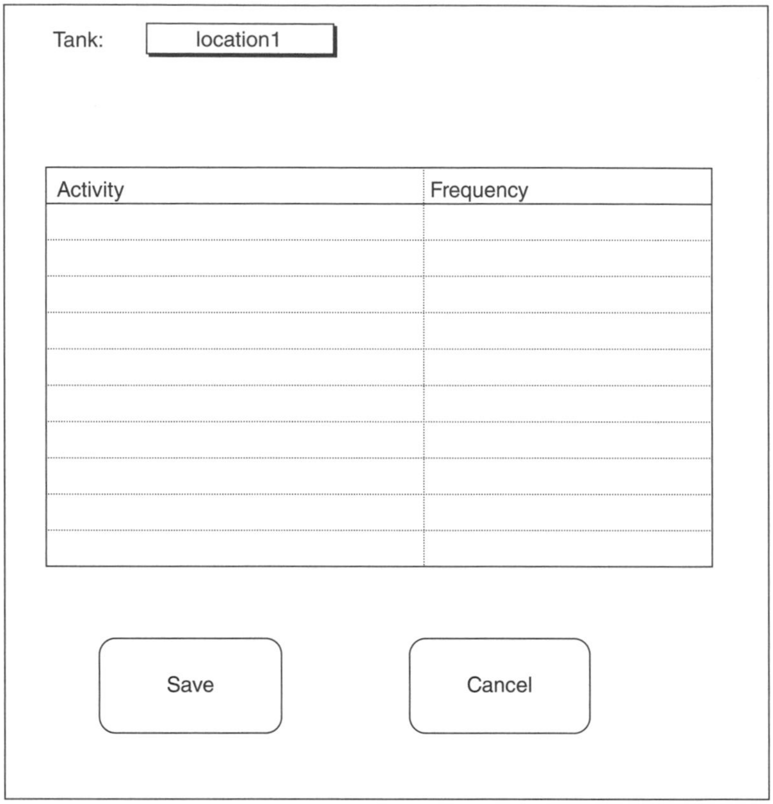

■ **FIGURE 12-25** Entering required maintenance.

To make data entry simpler for the end users, the form for entering required maintenance (Figure 12-25) lets a user select a tank and then enter as many maintenance activities as needed.

A database designer views such a form as requiring three entities: the tank, the maintenance activity, and the maintenance required for that tank (a composite entity between the tank and maintenance activity entities).

Creating the ER Diagram

After refining the entire application prototype, the database designers for the East Coast Aquarium generate a large interconnected ER diagram. (Part 1 is shown in Figure 12-26, and part 2 is shown in Figure 12-27.) As you can see when examining both figures, the centerpiece is the species entity, which participates in seven different relationships.

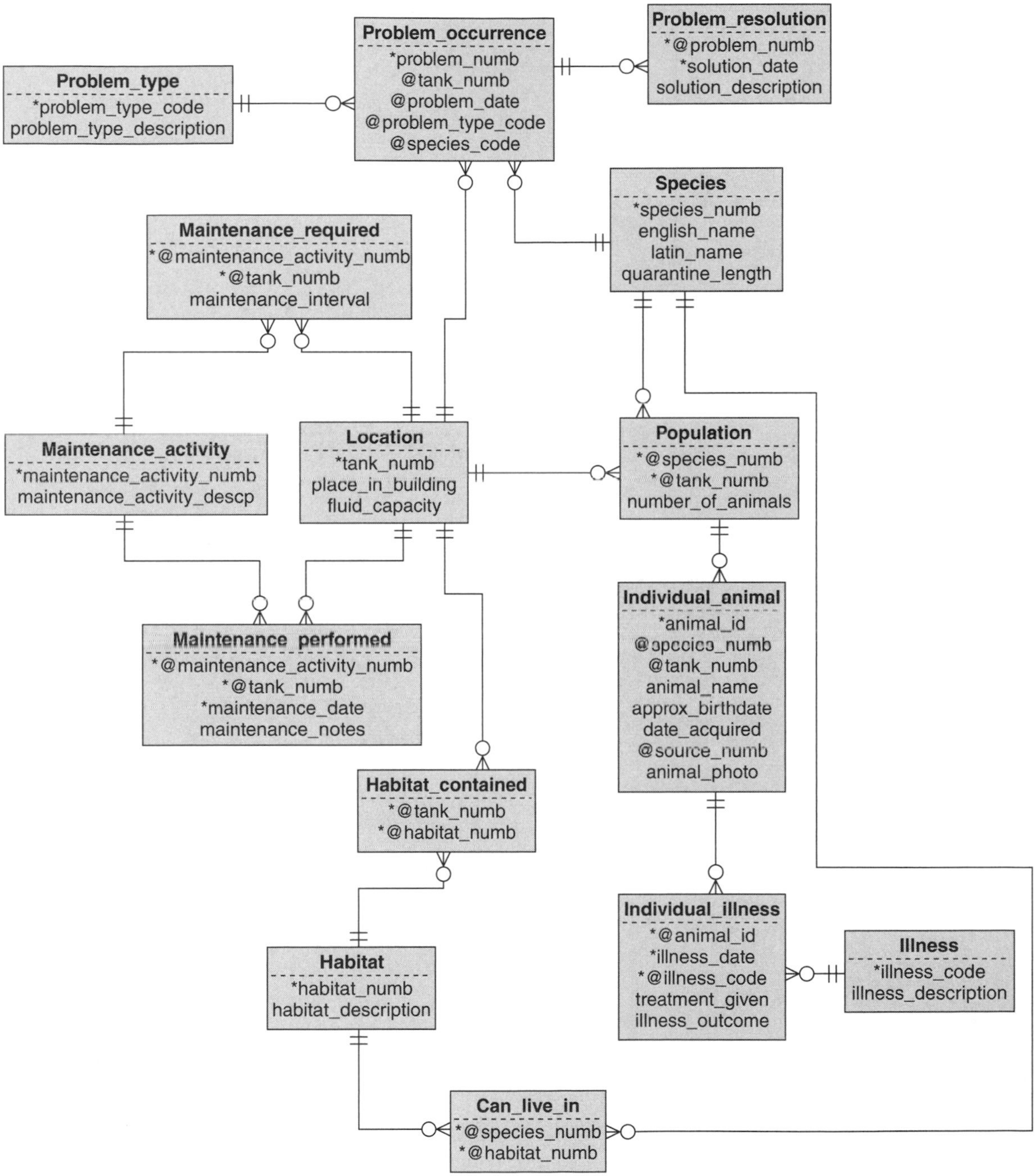

■ **FIGURE 12-26** Part 1 of animal handling ERD.

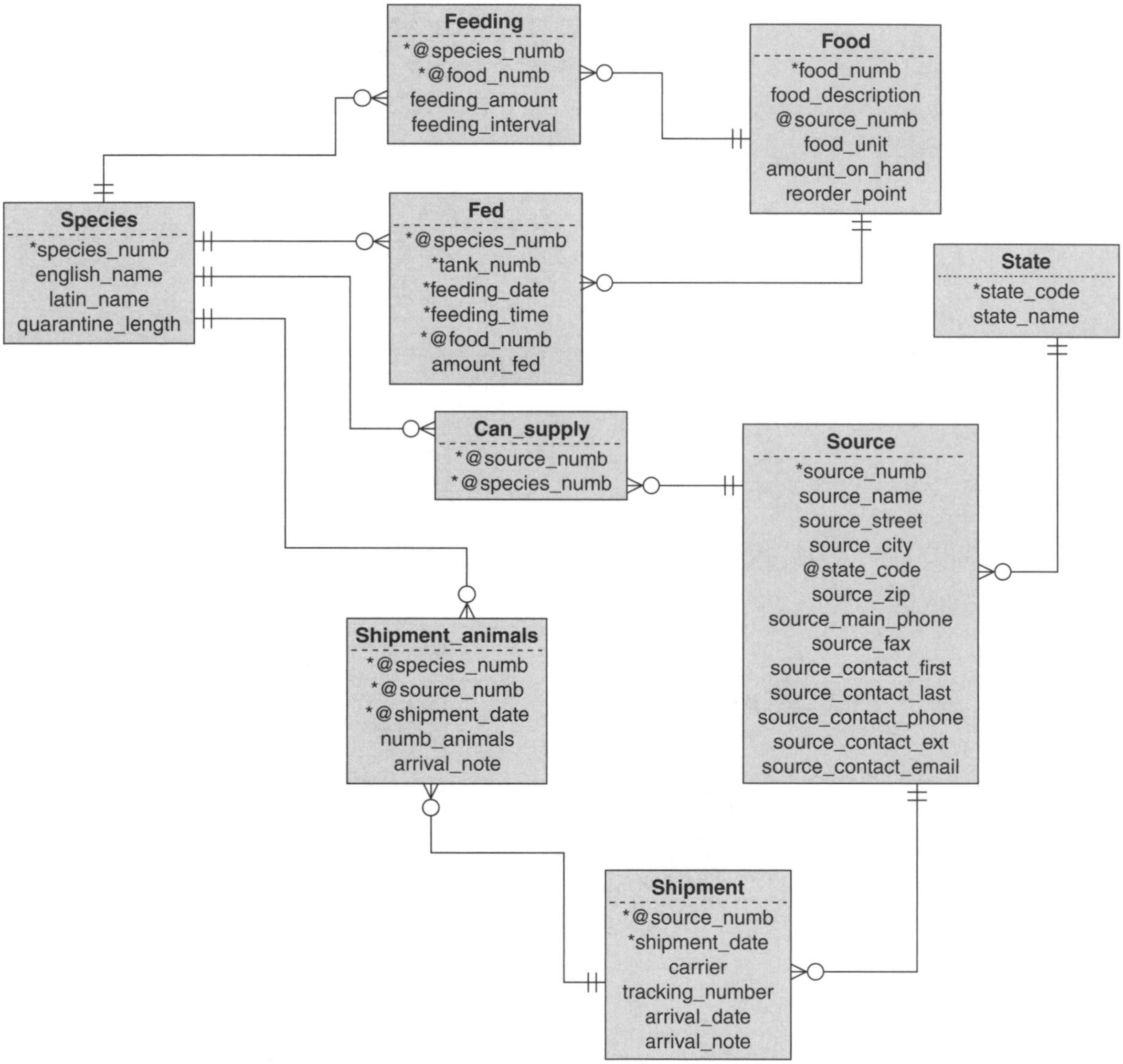

■ **FIGURE 12-27** Part 2 of animal handling ERD.

There are at least 11 many-to-many relationships represented by this design:

- Species to location
- Location to habitat
- Species to habitat
- Location to maintenance activity for required maintenance

- Location to maintenance activity for maintenance performed
- Location to problem
- Species to problem
- Species to food
- Species to source for ability of source to supply the species
- Shipment to species
- Illness to individual animal for tracking the condition of mammals and other large animals

The relationships involving location, problem, and species are particularly interesting. On the surface, there appears to be a many-to-many relationship between a tank and a type of problem. By the same token, there appears to be another many-to-many relationship between a species and a type of problem. The problem is that if the database maintained the two separate relationships, each with its own individual composite entity, then it will be impossible to determine which species was affected by which problem in which tank. To resolve the issue, the designer uses a three-way composite entity—problem_occurrence—that relates three parent entities (location, problem, and species) rather than the traditional two. Semantically, a problem occurrence is one type of problem affecting one species in one location, and therefore identifying it in the database requires all three parent entities.

In contrast, why is there no three-way composite entity among species, location, and habitat? As with the preceding example, there is a many-to-many relationship between species and location and a many-to-many relationship between habitat and location. The answer once again lies in the meaning of the relationships. Were we to create a single composite entity relating all three entities, we would be asserting that a given species lives in a given habitat in a given location. However, the animal handlers at the aquarium know that this type of data is not valid, particularly because if an animal lives in a tank with many habitats, it may move among multiple habitats. Instead, the relationship between species and habitat indicates *all* habitats in which a species can live successfully, and the relationship between location and habitat indicates the habitats present in a tank.

The remainder of the many-to-many relationships are the typical two-parent relationships that you have already seen in this book. The only aspect of these relationships that is the least bit unusual is the two relationships between maintenance activity and location. Each relationship has a different meaning (scheduled maintenance versus maintenance actually performed). The design therefore must include two composite entities, one to represent the meaning of each individual relationship.

> *Note:* There is no theoretical restriction to the number of relationships that can exist between the same parent entities. As long as each relationship has a different meaning, there is usually justification for including all of them in a database design.

Creating the Tables

The ER diagrams translate to the following tables:

```
species (species_numb, English_name, latin_name,
  quarantine_length)
location (tank_numb, place_in_building,
  fluid_capacity)
population (species_numb, tank_numb,
  number_of_animals)
individual_animal (animal_id, species_numb,
  tank_numb, animal_name, approx_birth_date,
  source_numb, animal_photo)
illness (illness_code, illness_description)
individual_illness (animal_id, illness_date,
  illness_code, treatment_given, illness_outcome)
habitat (habitat_numb, habitat_description)
habitat_contained (tank_numb, habitat_numb)
can_live_in (species_numb, habitat_numb)
problem_type (problem_type_code,
  problem_type_description)
problem_occurrence (problem_numb, tank_numb,
  problem_date, problem_type_code, species_code)
problem_resolution (problem_numb, solution_date,
  solution_description)
maintenance_activity (maintenance_activity_numb,
  maintenance_activity_desc)
maintenance_required (maintenance_activity_numb,
  tank_numb, maintenance_interval)
maintenance_performed (maintenance_activity_numb,
  tank_numb, maintenance_date, maintenance_notes)
```

```
food (food_numb, food_description, source_numb,
  food_unit, amount_on_hand, reorder_point)
feeding (species_numb, food_numb, feeding_amount,
  feeding_interval)
fed (species_numb, tank_numb, feeding_date,
  feeding_time, food_numb, amount_fed)
state (state_code, state_name)
source (source_numb, source_name, source_street,
  source_city, state_code, source_zip,
  source_main_phone, source_fax,
  source_contact_first, source_contact_last,
  source_contact_phone, source_contact_ext,
  source_contact_email)
can_supply (source_numb, species_numb)
shipment (source_numb, shipment_date, carrier,
  tracking_number, arrival_date, arrival_note)
shipment_animals (species_numb, source_numb,
  shipment_date, numb_animals, arrival_note)
```

Choosing a primary key for the problem occurrence table presents a bit of a dilemma. Given that a problem occurrence represents a relationship among a problem type, a tank, and a species, the theoretically appropriate primary key is a concatenation of the problem type, the tank number, the species number, and the problem date. However, this is an extremely awkward primary key to use as a foreign key in the problem_resolution table. Although it is unusual to give composite entities arbitrary unique keys, in this case it makes good practical sense.

There are several tables in this design that are "all key" (made up of nothing but the primary key). According to the CASE tool used to draw the ER diagram, this represents an error in the design. However, there is nothing in relational database theory that states that all-key relations are not allowed. In fact, they are rather common when they are needed to represent a many-to-many relationship that has no accompanying relationship data.

Generating the SQL

The SQL CREATE statements that generate the animal tracking database for East Cost Aquarium can be found in Figure 12-28. Because of the large number of composite entities, there are also a large number of foreign keys. Other than that, the SQL presents no unusual features.

```
CREATE TABLE state
(
    state_code char (2),
    state_name varchar (20),
    CONSTRAINT PK_STATE PRIMARY KEY (state_code)
);

CREATE TABLE source
(
    source_numb integer,
    source_name char (15),
    source_street varchar (500,
    source_city varchar (50),
    state_code char (2),
    source_zip char (10),
    source_main_phone char (10),
    source_fax char (10),
    source_contact_first char (15),
    source_contact_last char (15),
    source_contact_phone char (10),
    source_contact_ext char (5),
    source_contact_email varchar (256),
    CONSTRAINT PK_SOURCE PRIMARY KEY (source_numb),
    CONSTRAINT Relationstatesource1 FOREIGN KEY () REFERENCES STATE
);

CREATE TABLE shipment
(
    source_numb integer,
    shipment_date date,
    carrier varchar (30),
    tracking_number char (20),
    arrival_date date,
    arrival_note varchar (50,
    CONSTRAINT PK_SHIPMENT PRIMARY KEY (source_numb,shipment_date)
);

CREATE TABLE species
(
    species_numb integer,
    english_name varchar (256),
    latin_name varchar (256),
    quarantine_length integer,
    CONSTRAINT PK_species PRIMARY KEY (species_numb)
);
```

■ **FIGURE 12-28** SQL statements prepared by a CASE tool for the animal tracking database.

```
CREATE TABLE shipment_animals
(
    species_numb integer,
    source_numb integer,
    shipment_date date,
    numb_animals integer,
    arrival_note varchar (256),
    CONSTRAINT PK_SHIPMENTANIMALS PRIMARY KEY
    (species_numb,source_numb,shipment_date)
);

CREATE TABLE can_supply
(
    source_numb integer,
    species_numb integer,
    CONSTRAINT PK_CAN_SUPPLY PRIMARY KEY (source_numb,species_numb),
    CONSTRAINT Relationspeciescan_supply1 FOREIGN KEY ()
        REFERENCES species,
    CONSTRAINT Relationsourcecan_supply1 FOREIGN KEY () REFERENCES SOURCE
);

CREATE TABLE food
(
    food_numb integer,
    food_description varchar (256),
    source_numb integer,
    food_unit char (10),
    amount_on_hand integer,
    reorder_point integer,
    CONSTRAINT PK_food PRIMARY KEY (food_numb)
);

CREATE TABLE fed
(
    species_numb integer,
    feeding_date date,
    feeding_time time,
    tank_numb integer,
```

■ **FIGURE 12-28** Cont'd

```
    food_numb integer,
    amount_fed integer,
    CONSTRAINT PK_fed PRIMARY KEY
        (species_numb,tank_numb,feeding_date,feeding_time,food_numb),
    CONSTRAINT Relationspeciesfed1 FOREIGN KEY () REFERENCES species,
    CONSTRAINT Relationfoodfed1 FOREIGN KEY () REFERENCES food
);

CREATE TABLE feeding
(
    species_numb integer,
    food_numb integer,
    feeding_amount integer,
    feeding_interval interval,
    CONSTRAINT PK_feeding PRIMARY KEY (species_numb,food_numb),
    CONSTRAINT Relationspeciesfeeding1 FOREIGN KEY () REFERENCES species,
    CONSTRAINT Relationfoodfeeding1 FOREIGN KEY () REFERENCES food
);

CREATE TABLE location
(
    tank_numb integer,
    place_in_building char (6),
    fluid_capacity integer,
    CONSTRAINT PK_location PRIMARY KEY (tank_numb)
);

CREATE TABLE problem_type
(
    problem_type_code integer,
    problem_type_description varchar(256),
    CONSTRAINT PK_problem_type PRIMARY KEY (problem_type_code)
);

CREATE TABLE problem_occurrence
(
    problem_numb integer,
    tank_numb integer,
    problem_date date,
    problem_type_code integer,
    species_code integer,
    CONSTRAINT PK_problem_occurrence PRIMARY KEY (problem_numb),
```

■ **FIGURE 12-28** SQL statements prepared by a CASE tool for the animal tracking database—Cont'd

```
    CONSTRAINT Relationproblem_typeproblem_occurrence1 FOREIGN KEY ()
        REFERENCES problem_type,
    CONSTRAINT Relationproblem_occurrencelocation1 FOREIGN KEY ()
        REFERENCES location,
    CONSTRAINT Relationspeciesproblem_occurrence1 FOREIGN KEY ()
        REFERENCES species
);

CREATE TABLE problem_resolution
(
    problem_numb integer,
    solution_date date,
    solution_description varchar (256),
    CONSTRAINT PK_problem_resolution## PRIMARY KEY
        (problem_numb,solution_date),
    CONSTRAINT Relationproblem_occurrenceproblem_resolution1
        FOREIGN KEY () REFERENCES problem_occurrence
);

CREATE TABLE habitat
(
    habitat_numb integer,
    habitat_description varchar (256),
    CONSTRAINT PK_habitat PRIMARY KEY (habitat_numb)
);

CREATE TABLE can_live_in
(
    species_numb integer,
    habitat_numb integer,
    CONSTRAINT PK_can_live_in PRIMARY KEY (species_numb,habitat_numb),
    CONSTRAINT Relationhabitatcan_live_in1 FOREIGN KEY ()
        REFERENCES habitat
);

CREATE TABLE habitat_contained
(
    tank_numb integer,
    habitat_numb integer,
    CONSTRAINT PK_habitat_contained PRIMARY KEY (tank_numb,habitat_numb),
    CONSTRAINT Relationlocationhabitat_contained1 FOREIGN KEY ()
        REFERENCES location,
    CONSTRAINT Relationhabitathabitat_contained1 FOREIGN KEY ()
        REFERENCES habitat
);
```

■ **FIGURE 12-28** Cont'd

```
CREATE TABLE maintenance_activity
(
    maintenance_activity_numb integer,
    maintenance_activity varchar (256),
    CONSTRAINT PK_maintenance_activity
        PRIMARY KEY (maintenance_activity_numb)
);

CREATE TABLE maintenance_performed
(
    maintenance_activity_numb integer,
    tank_numb integer,
    maintenance_date date,
    maintenance_notes varchar (256),
    CONSTRAINT PK_maintenance_performed PRIMARY KEY
        (maintenance_activity_numb,tank_numb,maintenance_date),
    CONSTRAINT Relationmaintenance_activitymaintenance_performed1
        FOREIGN KEY () REFERENCES maintenance_activity,
    CONSTRAINT Relationlocationmaintenance_performed1 FOREIGN KEY ()
        REFERENCES location
);

CREATE TABLE maintenance_required
(
    maintenance_activity_numb integer,
    tank_numb integer,
    maintenance_interval interval,
    CONSTRAINT PK_maintenance_required PRIMARY KEY
        (maintenance_activity_numb,tank_numb),
    CONSTRAINT Relationmaintenance_requiredmaintenance_activity1
        FOREIGN KEY () REFERENCES maintenance_activity,
    CONSTRAINT Relationlocationmaintenance_required1 FOREIGN KEY ()
        REFERENCES location
);

CREATE TABLE illness
    (illness_code integer,
    illness_description varchar (256),
    CONSTRAINT PK_illness PRIMARY KEY (illness_code)
);
```

■ **FIGURE 12-28** SQL statements prepared by a CASE tool for the animal tracking database—Cont'd

```
CREATE TABLE population
(
    species_numb integer,
    tank_numb integer,
    number_of_animals integer,
    CONSTRAINT PK_population PRIMARY KEY (species_numb,tank_numb),
    CONSTRAINT Relationspeciespopulation1 FOREIGN KEY ()
        REFERENCES species,
    CONSTRAINT Relationlocationpopulation1 FOREIGN KEY ()
        REFERENCES location
);

CREATE TABLE individual_animal
(
    animal_id integer,
    species_numb integer,
    tank_numb integer,
    animal_name varchar (50),
    approx_birthdate char (10),
    date_acquired date,
    source_numb integer,
    animal_photo blob,
    CONSTRAINT PK_individual_animal PRIMARY KEY (animal_id),
    CONSTRAINT Relationpopulationindividual_animal1 FOREIGN KEY ()
        REFERENCES population
);

CREATE TABLE individual_illness
(
    animal_id integer
    illness_date date,
    illness_code integer,
    treatment_given varchar (256),
    illness_outcome varchar (256),
    CONSTRAINT PK_individual_illness
        PRIMARY KEY (animal_id,illness_date,illness_code),
    CONSTRAINT Relationindividual_animalindividual_illness1
        FOREIGN KEY () REFERENCES individual_animal,
    CONSTRAINT Relationillnessindividual_illness1
        FOREIGN KEY () REFERENCES illness
);
```

■ **FIGURE 12-28** Cont'd

Part III

Relational Design Practice

In this part of the book you will read about some of the practical techniques we use when working with relational database designs. You will be introduced to the SQL language statements needed to create relational schemes and their contents. You will also see how a CASE tool can help design and document a database. In addition, this part contains three complete relational design case studies to provide further examples of the database design process.

Chapter 13

Database Design Case Study 3: SmartMart

Many retail chains today maintain both a Web and a brick-and-mortar presence in the marketplace. Doing so presents a special challenge for inventory control because the inventory is shared between physical stores and Web sales. The need to allow multiple shipping addresses and multiple payment methods within a single order also adds complexity to Web selling. Online shopping systems also commonly allow users to store information about multiple credits.

To familiarize you with what is necessary to maintain the data for such a business, we'll be looking at a database for SmartMart, a long-established retailer with 325 stores across North America that has expanded into Web sales. SmartMart began as a local grocery store, but over the years it expanded to also sell clothes, sundries, home furnishings, hardware, and electronics. Some stores still have grocery departments; others carry just "dry" goods. In addition to the retail stores, SmartMart maintains four regional warehouses that supply the stores as well as ship products that are ordered over the Web.

THE MERCHANDISING ENVIRONMENT

SmartMart has three major areas for which it wants to an integrated database: in-store sales, Web sales, and some limited Human Resources needs. The sales data must be compatible with accounting systems to simplify data transfer. In addition, both the in-store sales and Web sales applications must use the same data about products.

Product Requirements

The products that SmartMart sells are stocked throughout the company's stores, although every store does not carry every product. The database must therefore include data about the following:

- Products
- Stores
- Departments within stores
- Products stocked within a specific department
- Current sales promotions for a specific product

The store and department data must be integrated with the database's Human Resources data.

In-Store Sales Requirements

The data describing in-store sales serve two purposes: accounting and inventory control. Each sale (whether paid with cash or credit) must decrement inventory and provide an audit trail for accounting. Retaining data about in-store sales is also essential to SmartMart's customer service reputation. The company offers a 14-day return period, during which a customer can return any product with which he or she is not satisfied. Store receipts therefore need to identify entire sales transactions, in particular which products were purchased during a specific transaction.

Because the company operates in several different states, there is a wide variety of sales tax requirements. Both which products are taxed and the sales tax rate vary among states. The database must therefore include sales tax where necessary as a part of an in-store transaction.

The database must distinguish between cash and credit transactions. The database will not store customer data about cash transactions, but it must retain credit card numbers, expiration dates, and customer names on credit sales.

Web Sales Requirements

Web sales add another layer of complexity to the SmartMart data environment. The Web application must certainly have access to the same product data as the in-store sales, but it must also integrate with a shopping cart application.

To provide the most flexibility, SmartMart wants to allow customers to store multiple shipping addresses, ship to multiple addresses on the same order, and store multiple credit card data from which a customer can choose when checking out. In addition, customers are to be given a choice as to whether to pick up their order or have it shipped. The Web application must therefore have access to data about which stores are in a customer's area and what products are available at each store, the same inventory information used by in-store sales.

Finally, the Web application must account for back orders and partial shipments. This means that a shipment is not the same as a Web order, whereas an in-store sale delivers its items at one time. (Should an in-store customer want to purchase an item that is not in stock, the item will be handled as if it were a Web sale.)

Personnel Requirements

Although a complete personnel database is beyond the scope of this case, SmartMart's management does want to be able to integrate some basic HR functions into the database, especially the scheduling of "sales associates" to specific departments in specific stores. The intent is to eventually be able use an expert system to analyze sales and promotion data to determine staffing levels and to move employees among the stores in a region as needed.

PUTTING TOGETHER AN ERD

As you might expect, the SmartMart ERD is fairly large. It has therefore been broken into three parts to make it easier to examine and understand.

Stores, Products, and Employees

As you can see in Figure 13-1 (the first third of the ERD), the SmartMart database begins with four "foundation" entities (entities that are only at the "one" end of 1:M relationships): employee, store, warehouse, and product.

The store and warehouse entities, at least at this time, have exactly the same attributes. It certainly would be possible to use a single entity representing any place products were kept. This would remove some of the complexity that arises when locating a product. However, there

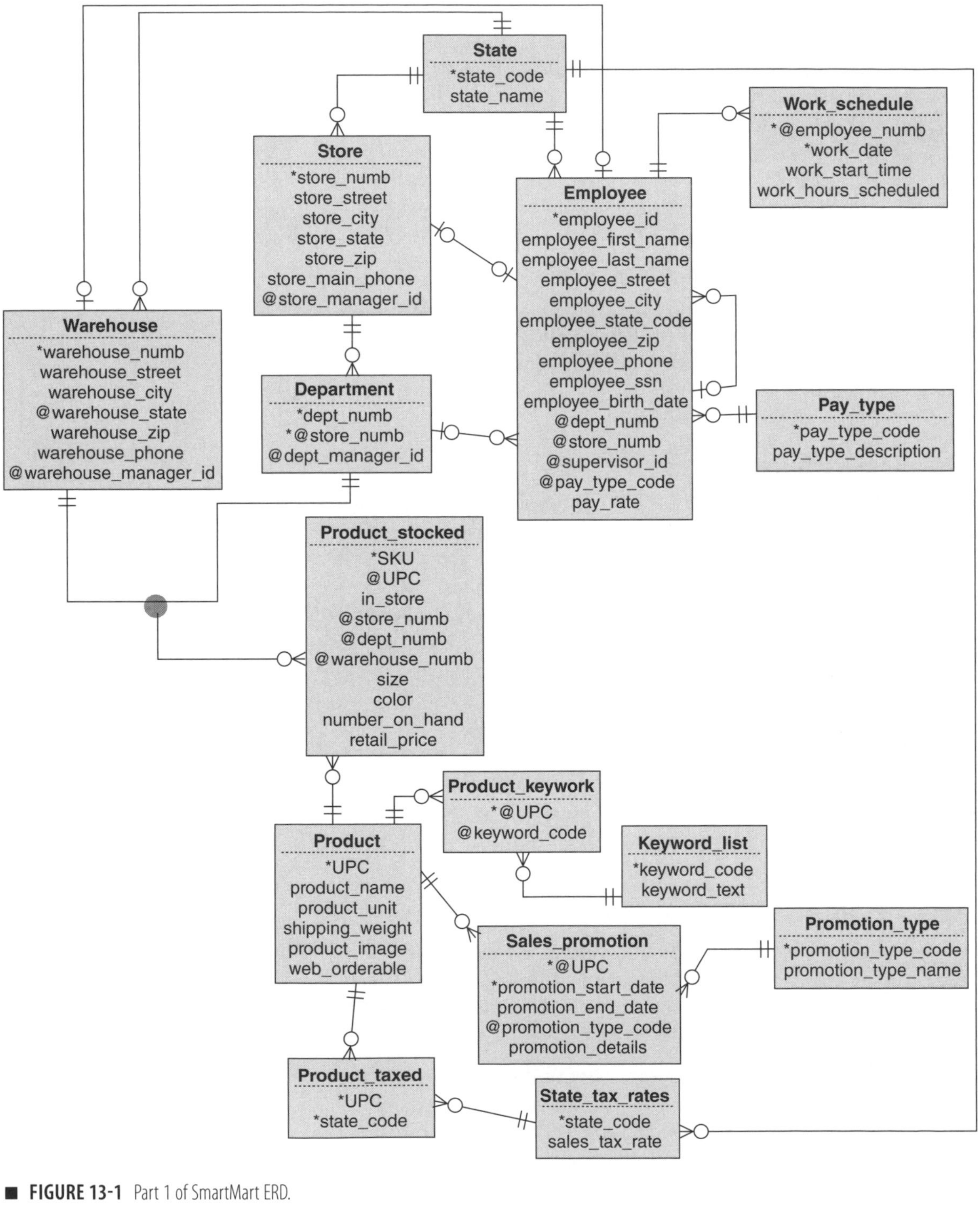

■ **FIGURE 13-1** Part 1 of SmartMart ERD.

is no way to be certain that the data stored about a store and a warehouse will remain the same over the life of the database. Separating them into two entities after the database has been in use for some time would be very difficult and time consuming. Therefore, the choice was made to handle them as two distinct entities from the beginning.

Reference Entities

There are also several entities that are included for referential integrity purposes (state, keyword_list, pay_type, promotion_type). These entities become necessary because the design attempts to standardize text descriptions by developing collections of acceptable text descriptions and then using a numbering scheme to link the descriptions to places where they are used. There are two major benefits to doing this.

First, when the text descriptions, such as a type of pay (e.g., hourly versus salaried), are standardized, searches will be more accurate. Assume, for example, that the pay types haven't been standardized. An employee who is paid hourly might have a pay type of "hourly," "HOURLY," "hrly," and so on. A search that retrieves all rows with a pay type of "hourly" will miss any rows with "HOURLY" or "hrly," however.

Second, using integers to represent values from the standardized list of text descriptions saves space in the database. Given the relative low price of disk storage, this usually isn't a major consideration.

The drawback, of course, is that when you need to search on or display the text description, the relation containing the standardized list and the relation using the integers representing the terms must be joined. Joins are relatively slow activities, but in this case, the reference relation containing the master list of text descriptions will be relatively small; the join uses integer columns, which are quick to match. Therefore, unless for some reason the reference relation becomes extremely large, the overhead introduced by the join is minimal.

Circular Relationships

If you look closely at the employee entity in Figure 13-1, you'll see a relationship that seems to relate the entity to itself. In fact, this is exactly what that circular relationship does. It represents the idea that a person who supervises other employees is also an employee: The supervisor_id attribute is drawn from the same domain as employee_id. Each supervisor is related to many employees, and each employee has only one supervisor.

It is always tempting to create a separate supervisor entity. Given that a supervisor must also be an employee, however, the supervisor entity would contain data duplicated from the employee entity. This means that we introduce unnecessary duplicated data into the database and run a major risk of data inconsistencies.

Note: To retrieve a list of supervisors and the individuals they supervise, someone using SQL would join a copy of the employee table to itself, matching the supervisor_id column in one table to the employee_id column in the other. The resulting table would contain data for two employees in each row (the employee and the employee's supervisor) that could be manipulated—in particular, sorted—for output as needed.

Mutually Exclusive Relationships

There is one symbol on the ERD in Figure 13-1 that has not been used before in this book: the small circle that sits in the middle of the relationships between a stocked product, a department (in a store), and a warehouse. This type of structure indicates a *mutually exclusive* relationship. A given product can be stocked in a store or in a warehouse but not both. (This holds true for this particular data environment because a product stocked represents physical items to be sold.)

The structure of the product_stocked entity reflects its participation in this type of relationship. In particular, it contains a Boolean column (in_store) that holds a value of true if the product is stocked in a store; a value of false indicates that the product is stocked in a warehouse. The value of the in_store attribute will then tell a user whether to use the warehouse_numb column or the concatenation of the store_numb column with the dept_numb attribute to find the actual location of an item.

One-to-One Relationships

Earlier in this book you read that true one-to-one relationships are relatively rare. There are, however, three of them visible in Figure 13-1. All involve employees that manage something: a store, a department within a store, or a warehouse. A corporate unit may have one manager at a time, or it may have no manager; an employee may be the manager of one corporate unit or the manager of none. It is the rules of this particular database environment that make the one-to-one relationships valid.

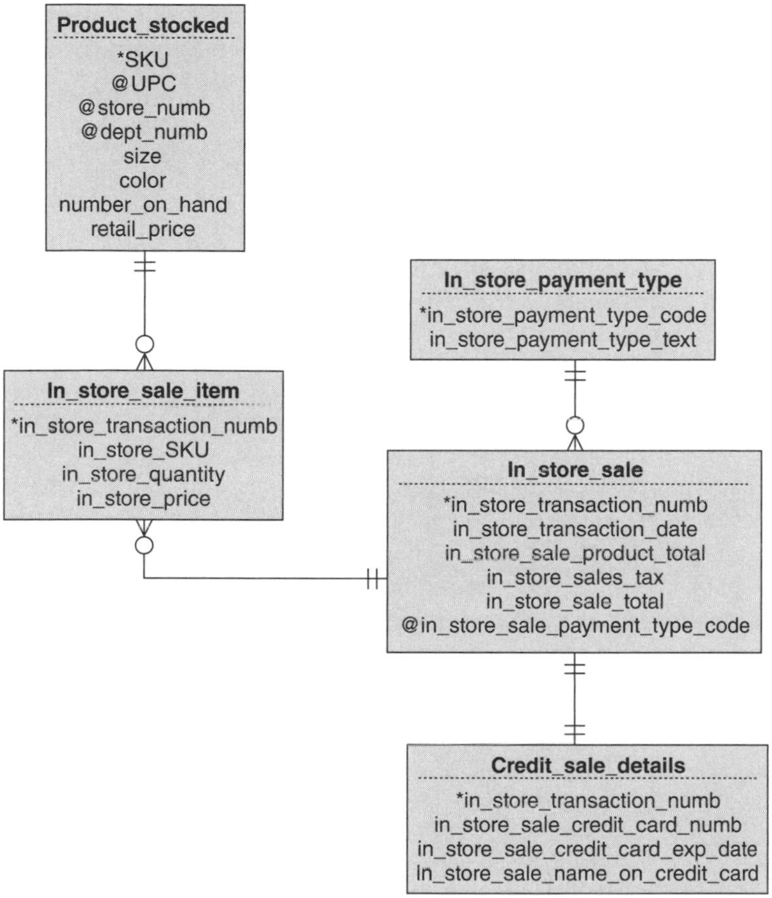

■ **FIGURE 13-2** Part 2 of SmartMart ERD.

In-Store Sales

The second part of the ERD (Figure 13-2) deals with in-store sales. The data that are common to cash and credit sales are stored in the in_store_sale entity. These data are all that are needed for a cash sale. Credit sales, however, require data about the credit card used (the credit_sale_details entity). Notice that there is therefore a one-to-one relationship between in_store_sale and credit_sale_details. The two-entity design is not required for a good database design, but it has been chosen for performance reasons with the assumption that there will be many more cash transactions than credit transactions. It therefore is a way of providing vertical partitioning to a single data set that is somewhat "unbalanced." In other words, a small proportion of the occurrences of the entity will have credit details, while others will not.

After SmartMart's database has been in production for some time, the database administrator can look at the actual relative proportion of credit and cash sales. If a large proportion of the sales are credit, then it may make sense to combine in_store_sale and credit_sale_details into a single entity and simply leave the credit details columns as null for cash sales. Although some space will be wasted, this combined design avoids the need to perform a lengthy join when retrieving data about a credit sale.

Web Sales

The third portion of the ERD (Figure 13-3) deals with Web sales. Each Web sale uses only one credit card, but a Web customer may keep more than one credit card number within SmartMart's database. A customer may also keep more than one shipping address; multiple shipping addresses can be used within the same order. (Multiple credit cards for a single order are not supported.)

At first glance, it might appear that the three relationships linking web_customer, web_sale, and web_customer_credit_card form a circular relationship. However, the meaning of the relationships is such that the circle does not exist:

- The direct relationship between web_customer and web_customer_credit_card represents the cards that a Web customer has allowed to be stored in the SmartMart database. The credit card data are retrieved when the customer is completing a purchase. He or she chooses one for the current order.
- The relationship between web_customer and web_sale connects a purchase to a customer.
- The relationship between web_customer_credit_card and web_sale represents the credit card used for a specific order.

It can be difficult to discern such subtle differences in meaning from a simple ERD. There are two solutions: define the meaning of the relationships in the data dictionary or add relationship names to the ERD.

The web_sale_shipping_address entity is used to display addresses from which a user can choose. However, because items within the

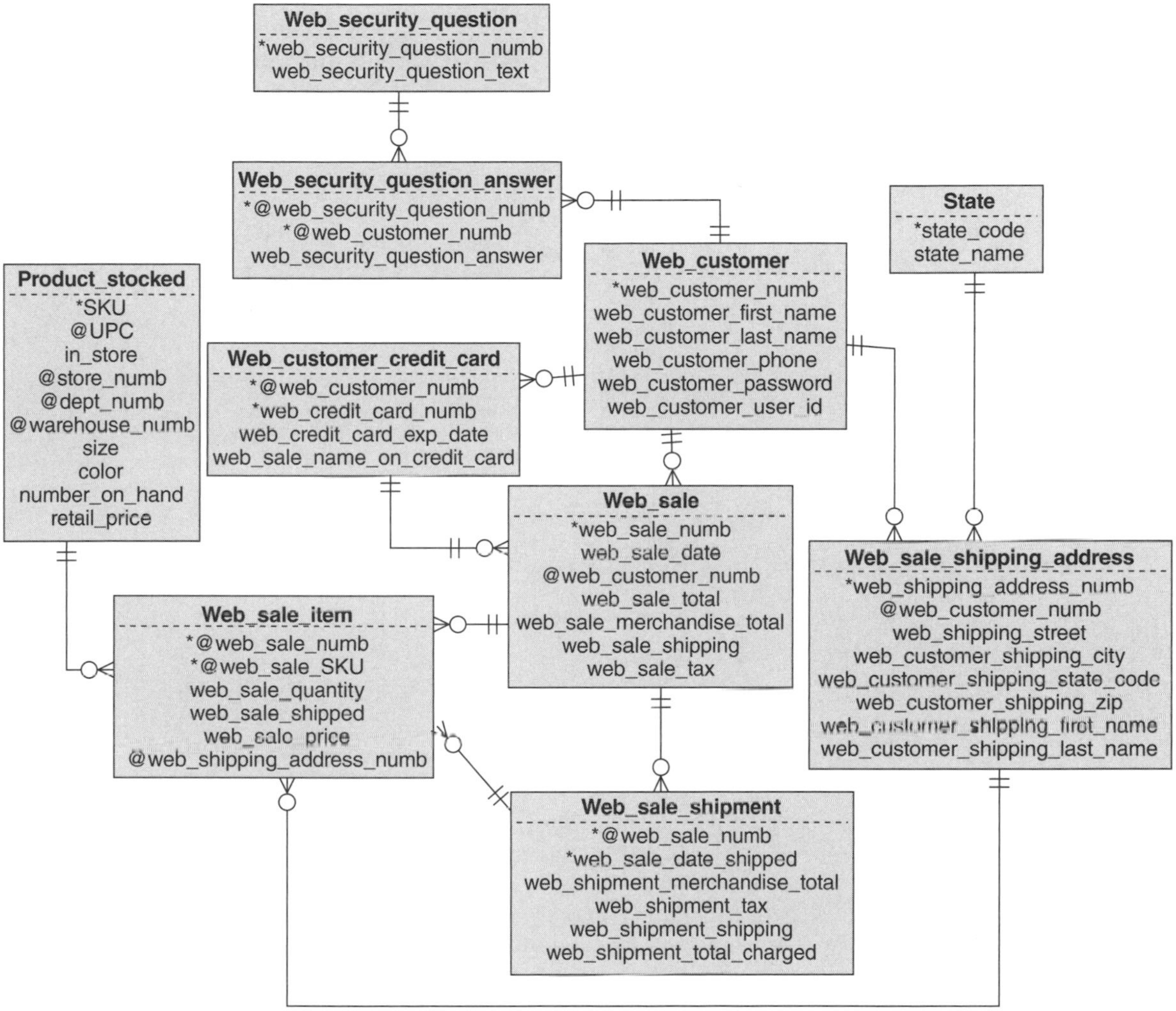

■ **FIGURE 13-3** Part 3 of SmartMart ERD.

same shipment can be sent to different addresses, there is a many-to-many relationship between web_sale and web_sale_shipping_address. The web_sale_item resolves that many-to-many relationship into two one-to-many relationships.

The relationship among web_sale, web_sale_item, and web_sale_shipment is ultimately circular, although at the time the order is placed, there are no instances of the web_sale_shipment entity. The circle is closed when items actually ship.

CREATING THE TABLES

The ERDs you have just seen produce the following tables, listed in alphabetical order:

```
credit_sale_details (in_store_transaction_numb,
  in_store_sale_credit_card_numb, in_store_exp_date,
  in_store_sale_name_on_credit_card)
department (dept_numb, store_numb, dept_manager_id)
employee (employee_id, employee_first_name,
  employee_last_name, employee_street,
  employee_city, employee_state_code, employee_zip,
  employee_phone, employee_ssn, employee_birth_date,
  dept_id, store_numb, supervisor_id, pay_type_code,
  pay_rate)
in_store_payment_type (in_store_payment_type_code,
  in_store_payment_type_text)
in_store_sale (in_store_transaction_numb,
  in_store_transaction_date,
  in_store_sale_product_total, in_store_sales_tax,in
  _store_total, in_store_payment_type_code)
in_store_sale_item (in_store_sale_transaction_numb,
  in_store_SKU, in_store_quantity, in_store_price)
keyword_list (keyword_code, keyword_text)
pay_type (pay_type_code, pay_type_description)
product (UPC, product_name, product_unit,
  shipping_weight, product_image,
  web_orderable)
product_keyword (UPC, keyword_code)
product_stocked (SKU, UPC, in_store, store_numb,
  dept_numb, warehouse_numb, size, color,
  number_on_hand, retail_price)
product_taxed (UPC, state_code)
promotion_type (promotion_type_code,
  promotion_type_name)
sales_promotion (UPC, promotion_start_date,
  promotion_end_date, promotion_type_code,
  promotion_details)
state (state_code, state_name)
state_tax_rates (state_code, sales_tax_rate)
store (store_numb, store_street, store_city,
  store_state_code, store_zip, store_main_phone,
  store_manager_id)
```

```
warehouse (warehouse_id, warehouse_street,
  warehouse_city, ware_house_state_code,
  warehouse_zip, warehouse_phone,
  warehouse_manager_id)
web_customer (web_customer_numb,
  web_customer_first_name, web_customer_last_name,
  web_customer_phone, web_customer_password,
  web_customer_user_id)
web_customer_credit_card (web_customer_numb,
  web_credit_card_numb, web_credit_card_exp_date,
  web_sale_name_on_credit_card)
web_sale (web_sale_numb, web_sale_date,
  web_customer_numb, web_sale_total,
  web_sale_merchandise_total,
  web_sale_shipping,web_sale_tax)
web_sale_item (web_sale_numb, web_sale_SKU,
  web_sale_quantity, web_sale_shipped,
  web_sale_price, web_shipping_address_numb)
web_sale_shipment (web_sale_numb,
  web_sale_date_shipped,
  web_shipment_merchandise_total, web_shipment_tax,
  web_shipment_shipping, web_shipment_total_charged)
web_sale_shipping_address (web_shipping_address_numb,
  web_customer_numb, web_shipping_street,
  web_shipping_city, web_shipping_state_code,
  web_customer_zip, web_customer_shipping_first_name,
  web_customer_shipping_last_name)
web_security_question (web_security_question_numb,
  web_security_question_text)
web_security_question_answer
  (web_security_question_numb, web_customer_numb,
  web_security_answer_text)
work_schedule (employee_id, work_date,
  work_start_time, work_hours_scheduled)
```

Because of the circulation relationship between a supervisor, who must be an employee, and an employee being supervised, the employee table contains a foreign key that references the primary key of its own table: supervisor_id is a foreign key referencing employee_id. There is nothing wrong with this type of design. The definition of a foreign key states only that the foreign key is the same as the primary key of some table; it does not rule out the foreign key referencing the primary key of its own table.

GENERATING THE SQL

The case tool that generated the SQL misses some very important foreign keys—the relationships between employees and various other entities—because the two columns don't have the same name (see Figure 13-4). Therefore, the database designer must add the constraints manually to the foreign key tables' CREATE TABLE statements:

```
employee table: FOREIGN KEY (supervisor_id)
  REFERENCES employee (employee_id)
warehouse table: FOREIGN KEY (warehouse_manager_id)
  REFERENCES employee (employee_id)
department table: FOREIGN KEY
  (department_manager_id) REFERENCES employee
  (employee_id)
store table: FOREIGN KEY (store_manager_id)
  REFERENCES employee (employee_id)
```

The manual foreign key insertions could have been avoided had the manager IDs in the warehouse, department, and store tables been given the name employee_id. However, it is more important in the long run to have the column names reflect the meaning of the columns.

There is also one foreign key missing of the two needed to handle the mutually exclusive relationship between a product stocked and either a department (in a store) or a warehouse. The foreign key from product_stocked to the department is present but not the reference to the warehouse table. The database designer must therefore add the following to the product_stocked table:

```
FOREIGN KEY (warehouse_numb) REFERENCES warehouse
  (warehouse_numb)
```

You may be wondering whether there could be a problem with including the two constraints if only one can be valid for any single row in product_stocked. There won't be, because, as we saw before, referential integrity constraints are used only when the foreign key is not null. Therefore, a product stocked in a warehouse will have a value in its warehouse_numb column but null in the store_numb and dept_numb columns. The reverse is also true: A product stocked in a store will have values in its store_numb and dept_numb columns but null in the warehouse_numb column.

The foreign key relationships to the state reference relation must also be added manually because the foreign key columns do not have the

```
CREATE TABLE state
(
    state_code char (2),
    state_name char (15),
    CONSTRAINT PK_state PRIMARY KEY (state_code),
    CONSTRAINT RelationstateState_tax_rates1 FOREIGN KEY ()
        REFERENCES state_tax_rates
);

CREATE TABLE warehouse
(
    warehouse_id integer,
    warehouse_street char (50),
    warehouse_city char (3),
    warehouse_state_code char (2),
    warehouse_zip char (10),
    warehouse_phone char (12),
    warehouse_manager_id integer,
    CONSTRAINT PK_warehouse PRIMARY KEY (warehouse_id)
);

CREATE TABLE state_tax_rates
(
    state_code char (2),
    sales_tax_rate number (5,20),
    CONSTRAINT PK_state_tax_rates PRIMARY KEY (state_code),
    CONSTRAINT RelationstateState_tax_rates1 FOREIGN KEY ()
        REFERENCES state
);

CREATE TABLE product
(
    UPC char (15),
    product_name varchar (256),
    product_unit char (10),
    shipping_weight integer,
    product_image blob,
    web_orderable boolean,
    CONSTRAINT PK_product PRIMARY KEY (UPC)
);

CREATE TABLE product_taxed
```

■ **FIGURE 13-4** SQL CREATE statements for the SmartMart database.

```
(
    UPC integer,
    state_code integer,
    CONSTRAINT PK_product_taxed PRIMARY KEY (UPC,state_code),
    CONSTRAINT RelationProductProduct_taxed1 FOREIGN KEY ()
        REFERENCES product,
    CONSTRAINT RelationState_tax_ratesProduct_taxed1 FOREIGN KEY ()
        REFERENCES state_tax_rates
);

CREATE TABLE in_store_payment_type
(
    in_store_payment_type_code integer,
    in_store_payment_type_text char (10),
    CONSTRAINT PK_in_store_payment_type PRIMARY KEY
        (in_store_payment_type_code)
);

CREATE TABLE web_customer
(
    web_customer_numb integer,
    web_customer_first_name char (15),
    web_customer_last_name INTEGER,
    web_customer_phone char (12),
    web_customer_password char (15),
    web_customer_user_id char (15),
    CONSTRAINT PK_web_customer PRIMARY KEY (web_customer_number)
);

CREATE TABLE web_sale_shipping_address
(
    web_shipping_address_numb integer,
    web_customer_numb integer,
    web_shipping_street char (50),
    web_customer_shipping_city char (50),
    web_customer_shipping_state_code char (2),
    eb_customer_shipping_zip char (10),
    web_customer_shipping_first_name char (15),
    web_customer_shipping_last_name char (15),
    CONSTRAINT PK_web_sale_shipping_address
        PRIMARY KEY (web_shipping_address_numb),
    CONSTRAINT RelationWeb_customerWeb_sale_shipping_address1
```

FIGURE 13-4 SQL CREATE statements for the SmartMart database—Cont'd

```
        FOREIGN KEY () REFERENCES web_customer,
    CONSTRAINT RelationstateWeb_sale_shipping_address1
        FOREIGN KEY () REFERENCES state
);

CREATE TABLE web_customer_credit_card
(
    web_customer_numb integer,
    web_credit_card_numb char (16),
    web_credit_card_exp_date date,
    web_sale_name_on_credit_card varchar (50),
    CONSTRAINT PK_web_customer_credit_card
        PRIMARY KEY (web_customer_numb,web_credit_card_numb),
    CONSTRAINT RelationWeb_customerweb_customer_credit_card1
        FOREIGN KEY () REFERENCES web_customer
);

CREATE TABLE web_sale
(
    web_sale_numb integer,
    web_sale_date date,
    web_customer_numb integer,
    web_sale_total number (7,2),
    web_sale_merchandise_total number (6,2),
    web_sale_shipping number (6,2),
    web_sale_tax number (6,2),
    CONSTRAINT PK_web_sale PRIMARY KEY (web_sale_numb),
    CONSTRAINT RelationWeb_customerWeb_sale1 FOREIGN KEY ()
        REFERENCES web_customer,
    CONSTRAINT Relationweb_customer_credit_cardWeb_sale1
        FOREIGN KEY () REFERENCES web_customer_credit_card
);

CREATE TABLE web_sale_shipment
(
    web_sale_numb integer,
    web_sale_date_shipped date,
    web_shipment_merchandise_total number(7,2),
    web_shipment_tax number (6,2),
    web_shipment_shipping number (6,2),
    web_shipment_total_charged number (6,2),
    CONSTRAINT PK_web_sale_shipment PRIMARY KEY (web_sale_numb),
```

■ **FIGURE 13-4** Cont'd

```
    CONSTRAINT RelationWeb_saleWeb_sale_shipment1
        FOREIGN KEY () REFERENCES web_sale
);

CREATE TABLE pay_type
(
    pay_type_code integer,
    pay_type_description varchar (10),
    CONSTRAINT PK_pay_type PRIMARY KEY (pay_type_code)
);

CREATE TABLE employee
(
    employee_id integer,
    employee_first_name varchar (15),
    employee_last_name integer,
    employee_street varchar (50),
    employee_city varchar (50),
    employee_state_code char (2),
    employee_zip char (10),
    employee_phone char (12),
    employee_ssn char (11),
    employee_birth_date date,
    dept_id integer,
    store_numb integer,
    supervisor_id integer,
    pay_type_code integer,
    pay_rate number (10,2),
    CONSTRAINT PK_employee PRIMARY KEY (employee_id),
    CONSTRAINT RelationEmployeeDepartment1
        FOREIGN KEY () REFERENCES department,
    CONSTRAINT Relationpay_typeEmployee1
        FOREIGN KEY () REFERENCES pay_type,
    CONSTRAINT RelationEmployeestate1
        FOREIGN KEY () REFERENCES state
);

CREATE TABLE department
(
    dept_numb integer,
    store_numb integer,
    dept_manager_id integer,
```

■ **FIGURE 13-4** SQL CREATE statements for the SmartMart database—Cont'd

```
    CONSTRAINT PK_department PRIMARY KEY (dept_numb,store_numb),
    CONSTRAINT RelationStoreDepartment1 FOREIGN KEY () REFERENCES Store
);

CREATE TABLE store
(
    store_numb integer,
    store_street char (50),
    store_city char (50),
    store_state_code char (2),
    store_zip char (10),
    store_main_phone char (12),
    store_manager_id integer,
    CONSTRAINT PK_Store PRIMARY KEY (store_numb)
);

CREATE TABLE work_schedule
(
    employee_numb integer,
    work_date date,
    work_start_time time,
    work_hours_scheduled integer,
    CONSTRAINT PK_work_schedule PRIMARY KEY (employee_numb,work_date),
    CONSTRAINT RelationEmployeeWork_schedule2
        FOREIGN KEY () REFERENCES employee
);

CREATE TABLE credit_sale_details
(
    in_store_transaction_numb integer,
    in_store_sale_credit_card_numb char (16),
    in_store_exp_date date,
    in_store_sale_name_on_credit_card varchar (50),
    CONSTRAINT PK_credit_sale_details
        PRIMARY KEY (in_store_transaction_numb)
);

CREATE TABLE promotion_type
(
    promotion_type_code integer,
    promotion_type_name INTEGER,
    CONSTRAINT PK_Promotion_type PRIMARY KEY (promotion_type_code)
);
```

■ **FIGURE 13-4** Cont'd

```
CREATE TABLE keyword_list
(
    keyword__code integer,
    keyword_text varchar (50),
    CONSTRAINT PK_keyword_list PRIMARY KEY (keyword__code)
);

CREATE TABLE product_keyword
(
    UPC char (15),
    keyword_code integer,
    CONSTRAINT PK_product_keyword PRIMARY KEY (UPC),
    CONSTRAINT RelationKeyword_listProduct_keyword1
        FOREIGN KEY () REFERENCES keyword_list
);

CREATE TABLE sales_promotion
(
    UPC char (15),
    promotion_start_date date,
    promotion_end_date date,
    promotion_type_code integer,
    promotion_details char (50),
    CONSTRAINT PK_sales_promotion PRIMARY KEY (UPC,promotion_start_date),
    CONSTRAINT RelationProductSales_promotion1
        FOREIGN KEY () REFERENCES product
);

CREATE TABLE in_store_sale
(
    in_store_transaction_numb integer,
    in_store_transaction_date date,
    in_store_sale_product_total number (8,2),
    in_store_sales_tax number (6,2),
    in_store_sale_total number (8,2),
    in_store_sale_payment_type_code integer,
    CONSTRAINT PK_in_store_sale PRIMARY KEY (in_store_transaction_numb),
    CONSTRAINT Relationin_store_salecredit_sale_details1
        FOREIGN KEY () REFERENCES credit_sale_details,
    CONSTRAINT Relationin_store_payment_typein_store_sale1
```

■ **FIGURE 13-4** SQL CREATE statements for the SmartMart database—Cont'd

```
        FOREIGN KEY () REFERENCES in_store_payment_type
);

CREATE TABLE product_stocked
(
    SKU char (15),
    UPC char (15),
    in_store boolean,
    store_ numb integer,
    dept_numb integer,
    warehouse_numb integer,
    size char (10),
    color char (15),
    number_on_hand integer,
    retail_price number (7,2),
    CONSTRAINT PK_product_stocked PRIMARY KEY (SKU),
    CONSTRAINT RelationProductProduct_stocked1
        FOREIGN KEY () REFERENCES product,
    CONSTRAINT RelationDepartmentProduct_stocked1
        FOREIGN KEY () REFERENCES department
);

CREATE TABLE in_store_sale_item
(
    in_store_transaction_numb integer,
    in_store_SKU integer,
    in_store_quantity integer,
    in_store_price number (7,2)0,
    CONSTRAINT PK_in_store_sale_item
        PRIMARY KEY (in_store_transaction_numb,in_store_SKU),
    CONSTRAINT RelationProduct_stockedin_store_sale_item1
        FOREIGN KEY () REFERENCES product_stocked,
    CONSTRAINT Relationin_store_salein_store_sale_item1
        FOREIGN KEY () REFERENCES in_store_sale
);

CREATE TABLE web_sale_item
(
    web_sale_numb integer,
    web_sale_SKU char (15),
    web_sale_quantity integer,
```

■ **FIGURE 13-4** Cont'd

```
    web_sale_shipped boolean,
    web_sale_price number (6,2),
    web_shipping_address_numb integer,
    CONSTRAINT PK_web_sale_item PRIMARY KEY (web_sale_numb,web_sale_SKU),
    CONSTRAINT RelationProduct_stockedWeb_sale_item1
        FOREIGN KEY () REFERENCES product_stocked,
    CONSTRAINT RelationWeb_saleWeb_sale_item1
        FOREIGN KEY () REFERENCES web_sale,
    CONSTRAINT RelationWeb_sale_shipmentWeb_sale_item1
        FOREIGN KEY () REFERENCES web_sale_shipment,
    CONSTRAINT RelationWeb_sale_shipping_addressWeb_sale_item1
        FOREIGN KEY () REFERENCES web_sale_shipping_address
);

CREATE TABLE web_security_question
(
    web_security_question_numb integer,
    web_security_question_text varchar (256),
    CONSTRAINT PK_web_security_question PRIMARY KEY
        (web_security_question_numb)
);

CREATE TABLE web_security_question_answer
(
    web_security_question_numb integer,
    web_customer_numb integer,
    web_security_question_answer_text varchar (256),
    CONSTRAINT PK_web_security_question_answer PRIMARY KEY
        (web_security_question_numb,web_customer_numb)
    CONSTRAINT RelationWeb_security_questionWeb_security_question_answer1
        FOREIGN KEY () REFERENCES web_security_question
    CONSTRAINT RelationWeb_customerWeb_security_question_answer1
        FOREIGN KEY () REFERENCES web_customer
);
```

■ **FIGURE 13-4** SQL CREATE statements for the SmartMart database—Cont'd

same name as the primary key column in the state table. Whether to use the same name throughout the database (state_name) is a design decision. If all of the tables that contain a state use the same name, foreign keys will be added automatically by the CASE tool. However, depending on the way the states are used, it may be difficult to distinguish among them if the column names are all the same.

Part IV

Database Implementation Issues

When the time comes to implement your relational database, you will probably discover that there are other decisions you need to make besides the design of the tables. You will need to worry about concurrency control and database security; you may have to send your data to a data warehouse or exchange data with another system that requires an XML document as the transfer medium. In this final part of this book, we will examine all of those topics to round out your understanding of relational databases.

Chapter 14

Concurrency Control

For the most part, today's DBMSs are intended as shared resources.[1] A single database may be supporting thousands of users at one time. We call this type of use *concurrent use*. However, although many users are working with the same database, it does not mean that more than one user is (or should be) working with exactly the same data as another at precisely the same moment.

It is physically impossible for two users to read or write exactly the same bit on a disk at precisely the same time. Operating systems and hardware disk controllers work together to ensure that only one read or write request is executed for any given disk location. This type of *concurrency control* is distinct from what occurs within a database environment. Database concurrency control is concerned with the logical consistency and integrity of a database; the physical concurrency control offered by the OS and the hardware is assumed to be in place.

In this chapter we begin by looking at the multiuser environment and then turn to the consistency and integrity problems that can occur when multiuser access is not controlled. Then we explore several solutions to those problems.

THE MULTIUSER ENVIRONMENT

Any time you have more than one user interacting with the same database at the same time, you have a multiuser environment. The DBMS must be able to separate the actions of one user from another and group them into a logical whole. It must also be able to ensure the integrity of the database while multiple users are modifying data.

---

[1] As mentioned earlier in this book, a major exception to this statement is Microsoft Access, which is designed for a single user at a time.

Transactions

A *transaction* is a unit of work submitted to a database by a single user. It may consist of a single interactive command, or it may include many commands issued from within an application program. Transactions are important to multiuser databases because they either succeed or fail as a whole. For example, if you are entering data about a new customer and an order placed by that customer, you won't be able to save any of the information unless you satisfy all the constraints on all the tables affected by the modification. If any validation fails, the customer data, the order data, and the data about the items on the data cannot be stored.

A transaction can end in one of two ways: If it is successful, then the changes it made are stored in the database permanently—the transaction is *committed*—or if the transaction fails, all the changes made by the transaction are undone, restoring the database to the state it was in prior to the start of the transaction (a *rollback*). A transaction is an all-or-nothing unit. Either the entire transaction succeeds or the entire transaction fails and is undone. We therefore often call a transaction the *unit of recovery*. A transaction may fail for several reasons:

- A transaction may be unable to satisfy constraints necessary for modifying data.
- A transaction may time out. (See the discussion later in this chapter on Web database issues.)
- The network connection between the user and the database may go down.
- The server running the database may go down for any reason.

> *Note:* In the interests of efficiency, some DBMSs commit all transactions that perform only data retrieval, even if the retrievals requested by the transactions returned no data.

Logging and Rollback

To effect transaction rollback, a DBMS must somehow save the state of the database *before* a transaction begins. As a transaction proceeds, the DBMS must also continue to save data modifications as they are made. Most DBMSs write this type of transaction audit trail to a *log file*. Conceptually, a log file looks something like Figure 14-1.

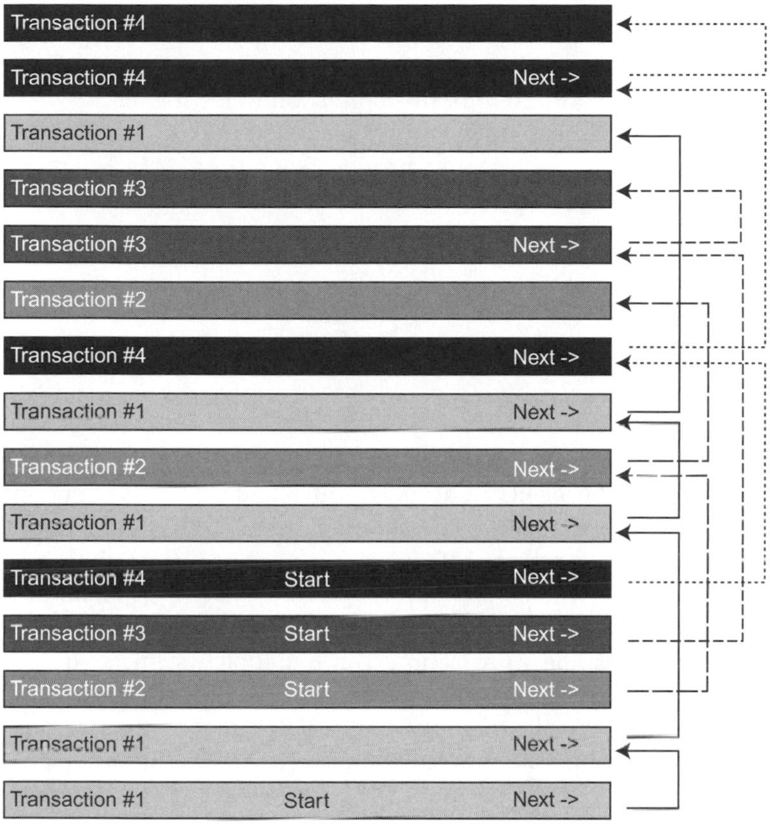

■ **FIGURE 14-1** The conceptual structure of a database log file.

> *Note:* Throughout this section, we will describe several things as "conceptual." This is because the exact procedure for performing some actions or the specific file structure in use depends on the DBMS. However, the effect of actions and/or file structures is as described.

When a transaction begins, it is given a number. Each time the transaction makes a change, the values prior to the change are written to a record in the log file. Records for transactions running concurrently are intermixed in the file. Therefore, the records for each transaction are connected into a linked list, with each record pointing to the next.

When a transaction commits, its changes are written to the database, and its records are purged from the log file. If a transaction fails for any reason, however, a rollback occurs conceptually in the following way:

1. Find the last record for the transaction in the log file.
2. Replace current values with the values in the log record.
3. Follow the pointer to the previous log record.
4. Repeat steps 2 and 3 until reaching the record that marks the start of the transaction.

> *Note:* Committing a transaction is final. By definition, a committed transaction is never rolled back.

There is one major problem with maintaining a log file: ensuring that all changes to the log file are actually written to disk. This is important because it is more efficient for a computer to wait until it has a complete unit of data to write before it actually accesses the disk than to write each time data are modified. Operating systems maintain disk I/O *buffers* in main memory to hold data waiting to be written. When a buffer is full, the write occurs. The buffering system is efficient because while memory—which is one of the computer's fastest components—fills several buffers, the disk may be taking its time with the writing. Once it finishes a write, the disk empties the next buffer in line. In this way, the slower device, the disk, is kept busy. However, a problem occurs when the computer fails for any reason. (Even a power outage can be at fault.) Whatever data were in the buffers at that time, waiting to be written, are lost. If those lost buffer contents happen to contain database log records, then the database and the log may well be inconsistent.

> *Note:* The number and size of a computer's I/O buffers depend on both the hardware and the operating system. Typically, however, the buffers in today's machines are between 1 and 4 K.

The solution is something known as a *checkpoint*. A checkpoint is an instant in time at which the database and the log file are known to be consistent. To take a checkpoint, the DBMS forces the OS to write the I/O buffers to disk, even if they aren't full. Both database changes and log file changes are forced to disk. The DBMS then writes a small file (sometimes called the "checkpoint file" or the "recovery file") that contains the location in the log file of the last log record when the checkpoint was taken.

There will always be some unit of time between checkpoints during which log records are written to the log file. If a system failure occurs, anything after the checkpoint is considered to be suspect because there is no way to know whether data modifications were actually written to disk. The more closely spaced the checkpoints, the less data that will be lost due to system failure. However, taking a checkpoint consumes database processing and disk I/O time, slowing down overall database processing. It is therefore the job of a database administrator to find a checkpoint interval that balances safety and performance.

Recovery

Recovering a database after a system failure can be a tedious process. It must not only take into account the transactions that were partially completed but those that were committed after the last checkpoint was taken and whose records haven't yet been purged from the log file. Conceptually, a recovery would work like this:

1. Find the latest checkpoint file.
2. Read the checkpoint file to determine the location of the last log record known to be written to disk in the log file.
3. Set up two lists for transactions: one for those that need to be *undone* and one for those that need to be *redone*.
4. Starting at the last verified log file record, read from the back of the file to the front of the file, placing each transaction found in the *undo* list.
5. Stop at the beginning of the file.
6. Now read each record from the front to the back. Each time you encounter a commit record, you'll know that you've discovered a transaction that completed yet didn't have its log records purged from the log file. Because almost all of these transactions will be after the last checkpoint record, there is no way to ensure that any changes made by these transactions were written to the database. Therefore, move these transactions to the *redo* list.
7. Undo any transactions for which there are no commit records.
8. Redo the suspect committed transactions.

No normal database processing can occur while the recovery operation is in progress. For large operations with many transactions in the log file, recovery may therefore take some time.

PROBLEMS WITH CONCURRENT USE

As mentioned earlier, the computer hardware and OS take care of ensuring that only one physical write occurs to a given storage location at one time. Why, then, might a database need additional concurrency control? The answer lies in the need for logical, in addition to physical, consistency of the database. To understand what can occur, let's look at some examples.

Lost Update #1

Assume, for example, that a small city has four community centers, each of which receives a single shipment of publicity materials for each city-wide event from the city's printer. To keep track of what they have received and what is already in their storage rooms, each community center has a table in the database like the following:

```
publicity_materials (event_name, event_date,
  numb_posters_received, numb_brochures_received)
```

West Side Community Center has been accidentally left out of the delivery of posters for a special event on Saturday. The community center sends e-mail to all of the other community centers in the area and requests 10 to 20 posters. Someone at the East Side Center calls in to say that they have 15 posters they can send. The West Side staff member who takes the call checks to see how many posters have been received, sees a 0, and then enters the 15 in the publicity_materials table.

About the same time, another call comes in from the North Side Center and is answered by a different staff member. North Side Center has 12 posters to offer. The second staff member queries the database and sees that there are 0 posters (the 15 posters from East Side Center haven't been stored yet) and therefore enters the 12 into the database. However, in the few seconds that elapse between viewing 0 posters and entering 12 posters, the 15 posters are stored in the database. The result is that the 12 overwrites the existing value, wiping out the number 15 that was just stored. West Side Community Center will be receiving 27 posters, but they don't know it. The second update wiped

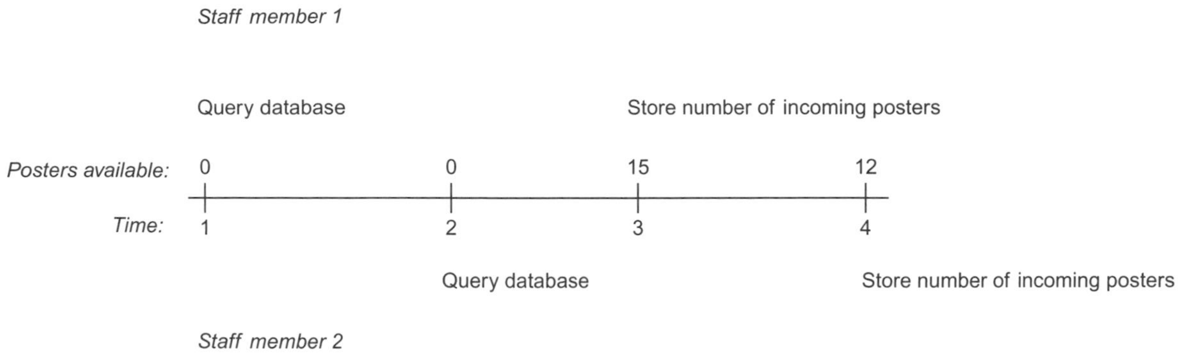

■ **FIGURE 14-2** Lost update.

out the first. The unintentional loss of data when data are replaced by a newer value is the *lost update*.

You can see exactly how the first update to the database was lost if you look at the timeline in Figure 14-2. Notice first that the actions of the transactions (one for each user) overlap in time. We therefore say that the transactions are *interleaved*. The goal of concurrency control is to ensure that the result of interleaved transaction is the same as if the transactions ran one after the other (the transactions are *serializable*)

In this particular example, regardless of which transaction runs first, the correct answer should be 27: The second staff member should retrieve something other than 0 from the database and know that he or she would need to add the second group of posters to the first. But that's not what happens without concurrency control. Instead, at time 4—when the second staff member stores 12 posters—the 0 that the staff member retrieved at time 2 is old data, so the lost update occurs because the second transaction was based on old data.

Lost Update #2

A more subtle type of lost update occurs when an existing database value is modified rather than merely replaced. As an example, consider two travel agents, one in Philadelphia and the other in Boston. Both use the same airline reservations database. A customer calls the Boston travel agency and, as a part of a cross-country trip, needs to reserve three seats on a flight from Chicago to Denver on a specific date and at a specific time. The travel agent queries the database and discovers that exactly three seats are available on a flight that meets the customer's criteria and informs the customer, who is waiting on the phone.

Meanwhile, a customer calls the travel agent in Philadelphia. This customer also needs three seats from Chicago to Denver on the same date and at the same time as the Boston customer. The travel agent checks the database and discovers that there are exactly three seats available, but they are the same three seats the Boston travel agent just offered to his customer.

While the Philadelphia travel agent is talking to her customer, the Boston travel agent receives the go-ahead from the other customer to book the seats. The number of available seats on the flight is modified from three to zero.

The Philadelphia travel agent has also received consent to reserve the seats and proceeds to issue a command to do so. The problem, however, is that the Philadelphia travel agent is working from old information. There may have been three seats available when the database was queried, but they are no longer available at the time the reservations are made. As a result, the flight is now overbooked by three seats.

> *Note:* Let's not get too carried away here. We all know that airlines often overbook flights intentionally, but for the purposes of this example, assume that zero seats available means no more seats—period.

A summary of what is happening in this situation can be found in Figure 14-3. This lost update—just like the previous example—occurs because the Philadelphia travel agent is working with old data at time 4 when he or she books three seats.

There are two general strategies for handling the lost update problem:

- Prevent a second transaction from viewing data that have been viewed previously and that might be modified.
- Prevent a second transaction from modifying data if the data have been viewed by another transaction.

The first can be accomplished using locking and the second with timestamping, both of which will be discussed shortly.

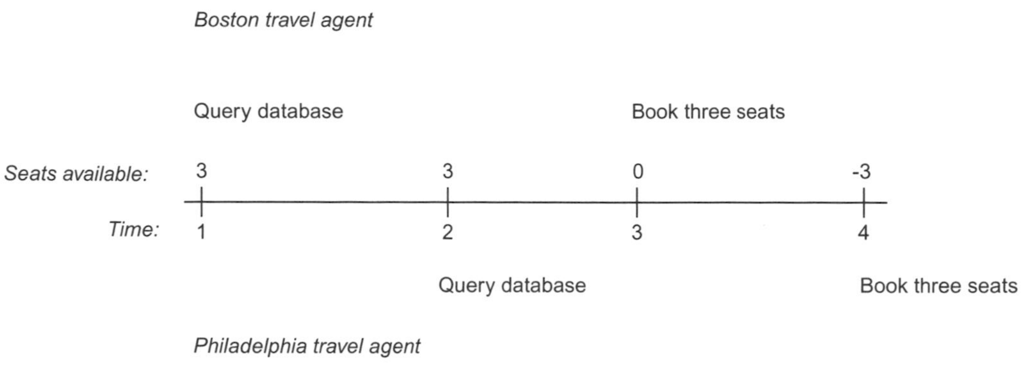

■ **FIGURE 14-3** A second lost update example.

event_name	event_date	total_attendance
Knitting	10-1-10	15
Basketball	10-1-10	20
Open swim	10-1-10	30
Story hour	10-2-10	40
Soccer	10-2-10	35
Open swim	10-2-10	20
Knitting	10-3-10	20
Swim meet	10-3-10	80
Paper making	10-3-10	10
Book club	10-4-10	25
Open swim	10-4-10	20
Kids gym	10-5-10	10
Open swim	10-5-10	30
Handball tournament	10-6-10	50
Open swim	10-6-10	15
Story hour	10-7-10	35
Open swim	10-7-10	40

■ **FIGURE 14-4** The events table at the start of the attendance summary report transaction.

Inconsistent Analysis

The other major type of concurrency control problem is known as *inconsistent analysis*. As an example, assume that the West Side Community Center database contains the following relation to store data about attendance at special events:

```
Events (event_name, event_date, total_attendance)
```

A staff member needs to produce a report that totals the attendance for all events during the past week. As she starts running the report, the table looks something like Figure 14-4. If the report were to run without being interleaved with any other transaction, the sum of the total_attendance column would be 495.

A second staff member needs to make some modifications to the attendance figures in the events table, correcting two errors. He changes the attendance at the basketball practice on 10-1-10 from 20 to 35. He also changes the attendance at the handball tournament on 10-6-10 from 50 to 55.

After the modifications are made, the attendance total is 515. If the report runs before the modifications, the result for the attendance total is 495. Either one of these results is considered correct because both represent the result of running the transactions one after the other.

However, look at what happens when the transactions are interleaved. As you can see in Figure 14-5, the report transaction begins running first. After accessing each of the first 10 rows, the interim total is 295. At time 2, the update transaction begins and runs to completion. At time 4, the report completes its computations, generating a result of 500. Given our definition of a *correct result,* this is definitely incorrect.

The problem occurred because the update transaction changed the basketball practice attendance figure *after* the report had processed that row. Therefore, the change is never reflected in the report total. We can solve the inconsistent analysis problem by

- Preventing the update because another transaction has viewed the data.
- Preventing the completion of the view-only transaction because the data have been changed.

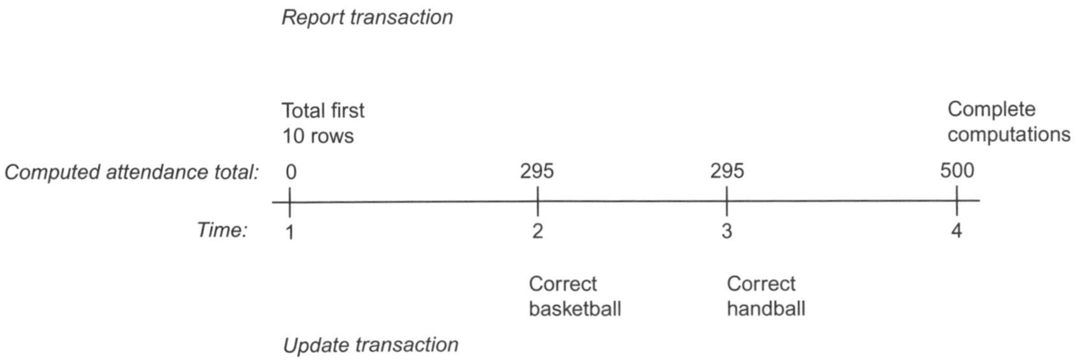

■ **FIGURE 14-5** An inconsistent analysis.

The first solution can be done with locking, and the second with timestamping.

Dirty Reads

A *dirty read* occurs when a transaction reads and acts on data that have been modified by an update transaction that hasn't committed and is later rolled back. It is similar to an inconsistent analysis, but the update transaction doesn't commit. To see how this might happen, consider Figure 14-6.

The report generating the transaction starts first. It retrieves and totals the first 10 rows. Then the update transaction begins, making changes to both the basketball and handball totals. The report transaction runs again at time 4, reading the modified totals written to the database by the update transaction. The result, as it was with the inconsistent analysis example in the preceding section, is 500. However, at time 5, the update transaction is rolled back, restoring the original values in the table. The correct result, however, should be 495.

As with an inconsistent analysis, a dirty read can be handled by preventing the update transaction from making its modifications at times 2 and 3, using locking or timestamping to prevent the report from completing because the data "may" have been changed.

Nonrepeatable Read

A *nonrepeatable read* occurs when a transaction reads data for the second time and determines that the data are not the same as they were from the first read. To help understand how this occurs, let's

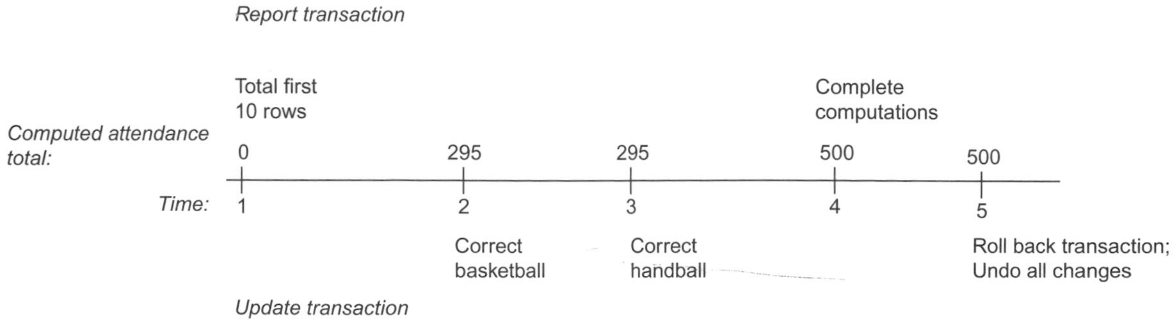

■ **FIGURE 14-6** A dirty read.

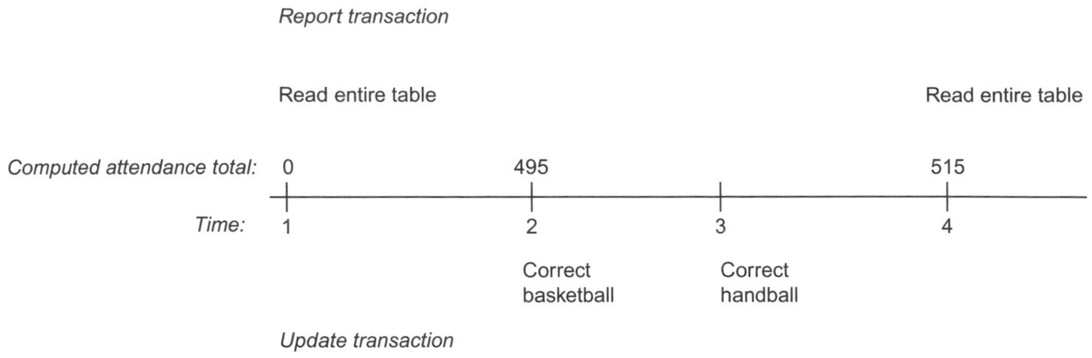

■ **FIGURE 14-7** A nonrepeatable read.

change the community center reporting scenario just a bit. In this case, the report transaction must output two tables with events and their attendance, one ordered by date and one ordered by the name of the event. It will access the events table twice. When the update transaction runs between the two retrievals, the problem appears (Figure 14-7).

Notice that the total attendance for the first read by the report transaction is correct at that time (495). However, when the transaction reads the table again, the total is correct for the data as modified but not for the first read of the data.

The nonrepeatable read can be handled by preventing the update transaction from making its modifications because another transaction has already retrieved the data or by preventing the report transaction from completing because the data have been modified.

Phantom Read

A *phantom read* is similar to a nonrepeatable read. However, instead of data being changed on a second retrieval, new rows have been inserted by another transaction. For this example, the update transaction inserts a new row into the events table:

Open swim 10-8-10 25

Assuming that the report transaction is once again creating two output tables, the interaction might appear as in Figure 14-8. The report transaction's second pass through the table once again produces an

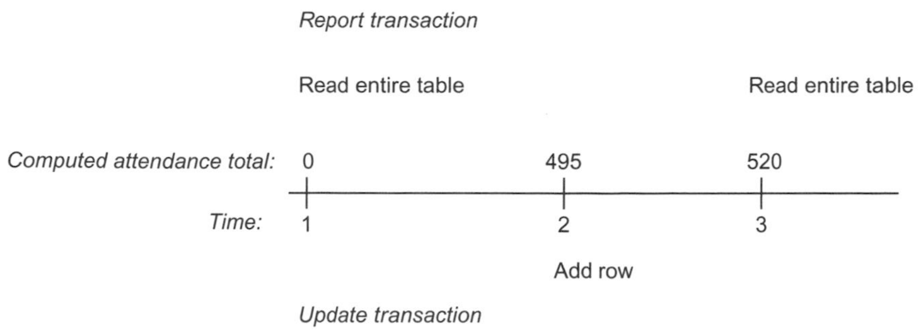

■ **FIGURE 14-8** A phantom read.

incorrect result, which is caused by the row inserted by the interleaved update transaction.

As with other concurrency control issues that involve the interaction of update and retrieval transactions, the phantom read problem can be solved by preventing the insertion of the new row at time 2 or preventing the report transaction from completing at time 3 because the needed data have been changed.

SOLUTION 1: CLASSIC LOCKING

Locking is a method for giving a transaction control over some part of a database. It is the most widely used concurrency control practice today.

The portion of the database locked (the *granularity* of the lock) varies from one DBMS to another and depends to some extent on exactly what type of operation is being performed. The granularity can vary from a single row in a table to the entire database, although locking of single tables is very common.

Read or Exclusive Locks

To handle lost updates with locking, we need to prevent other transactions from accessing the data viewed by an update transaction because there is the possibility that the update transaction will modify everything it has retrieved.

Operation of Write/Exclusive Locks

The strongest type of lock is an *exclusive lock* (also known as a *write lock*). A transaction is given a write lock on a data element when it retrieves that element. Then, by definition, no other transaction can obtain a write lock on that element until the transaction holding the lock releases its lock. If a transaction needs a piece of data that is locked by another transaction, it must wait until it can obtain the exclusive lock.

To see how this solves the lost update at the West Side Community Center, look at Figure 14-9. At time 1, the first staff member queries the database to see how many posters are on hand. She not only sees that there are no posters, but her transaction also receives an exclusive lock on the poster data. Now, when staff member 2's transaction attempts to query the database, the transaction must wait because it can't obtain the lock it needs to proceed. (Transaction 1 already holds the single possible write lock.)

Staff member 1 enters the 15 posters, and her transaction commits, releasing the lock. Transaction 2 can now continue. It queries the database and now retrieves 15 for the second staff member. He is now working with current data and can decide not to accept the additional 12 posters or to add them to the existing 15, producing the correct result of 27. The write lock has therefore solved the problem of the lost update.

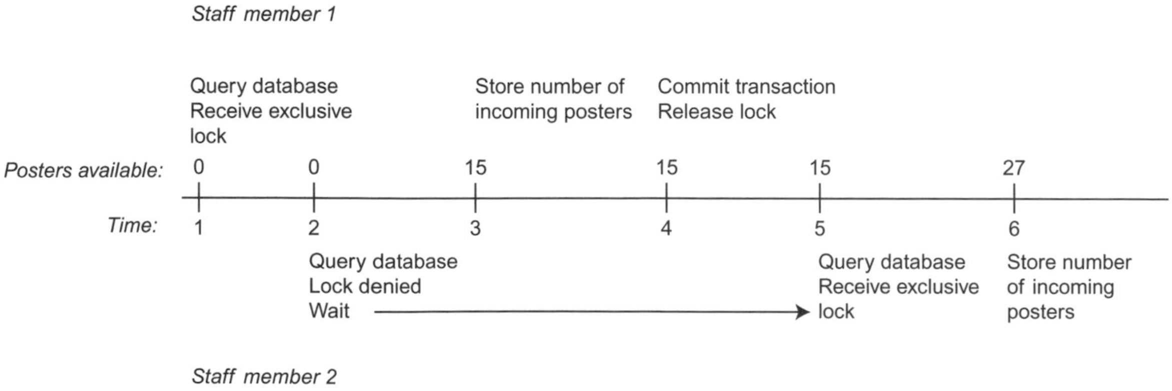

■ **FIGURE 14-9** Using exclusive locks to solve a lost update problem.

Problem with Write/Exclusive Locks: Deadlock

Although write locks can solve a lost update problem, they generate a problem of their own: a condition known as *deadlock*. Deadlock arises when two transactions hold locks that each other needs, so neither can continue. To see how this happens, let's look again at the two travel agents, this time one in Boston and one in Los Angeles. The Boston travel agent is attempting to book a round trip from Boston to Los Angeles. The Los Angeles travel agent is trying to book a trip from Los Angeles to Boston and back.

You can see the actions and locks of the two transactions in Figure 14-10. At time 1, the Boston travel agent retrieves data about the flights to Los Angeles, and her transaction receives an exclusive lock on the data. Shortly thereafter (time 2), the Los Angeles travel agent queries the database about flights to Boston, and his transaction receives an exclusive lock on the Boston flight data. So far so good.

The trouble begins at time 3 when the Boston travel agent attempts to look for return flights from Los Angeles to Boston. The transaction cannot obtain a lock on the data and therefore must wait. At time 4, the Los Angeles travel agent tries to retrieve return flight data and cannot obtain a lock, so the second transaction must wait as well. Each transaction is waiting for a lock on data that the other has locked, and neither can continue. This is the deadlock.

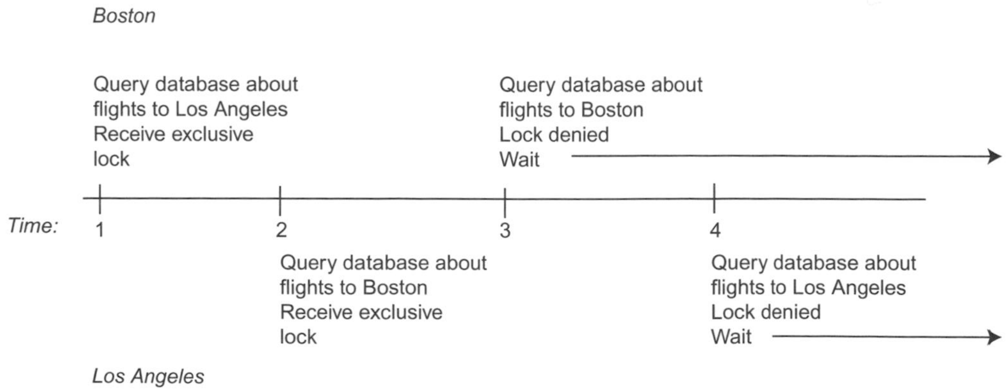

■ **FIGURE 14-10** Deadlock.

In busy database systems, deadlock is inevitable. This means that a DBMS must have some way of dealing with it. There are two basic strategies:

- *Detect and break:* Allow deadlock to occur. When the deadlock is detected, choose one transaction to be the "victim" and roll it back, releasing its locks. The rolled-back transaction can then be restarted. The mix of transactions will be different when the victim is restarted, and the same deadlock is unlikely to occur in the near future. In this case, all transactions start, but not every transaction runs to completion.
- *Predeclare locks:* Require transactions to obtain all necessary locks before beginning. This ensures that the deadlock cannot occur. Not all transactions start immediately, but every transaction that starts will finish.

Predeclaration of locks is very difficult to implement because it is often impossible to know what a transaction will need to lock until the transaction is in progress. In contrast, detecting deadlock is actually quite straightforward. The DBMS maintains a data structure known as a *graph* to keep track of which transaction is waiting for the release of locks from which other transaction, as in Figure 14-11a. As long as the graph continues in a downward direction, everything is fine (the graph is *acyclic*). However, if a transaction ends up waiting for another transaction that is higher in the graph (the graphic become *cyclic*), as in Figure 14-11b, deadlock has occurred.

In Figure 14-11a, T2 is waiting for something locked by T3; T5 is waiting for something locked by T3. When T5 completes and releases its locks, T3 can continue. As soon as T3 finishes, it will release its locks, letting T2 proceed. However, in Figure 14-11b, T5 is waiting for something locked by T2. T2 can't complete and release what T5 needs because T2 is waiting for T3, which in turn is waiting for T5, which is

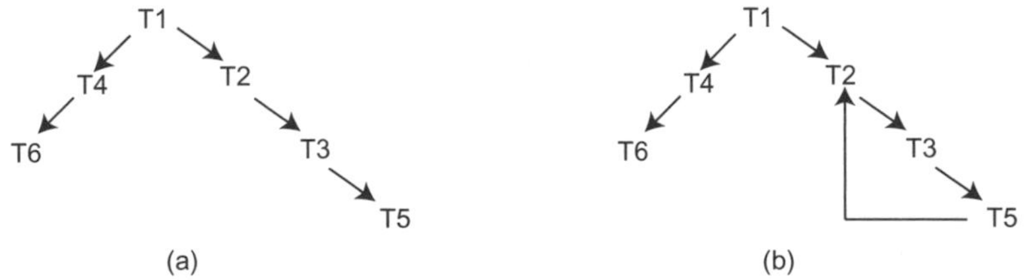

■ **FIGURE 14-11** Graphs to monitor transaction waits.

waiting for T2, and so on endlessly. This circle of locks is the deadlock.

Because detecting deadlock is so straightforward, most DBMSs that use classic locking for concurrency control also use the detect-and-break deadlock handling strategy.

Read or Shared Locks

Although a DBMS could use exclusive locks to solve the problem of inconsistent analysis presented earlier in this chapter, exclusive locks tie up large portions of the database, slowing performance and cutting down on the amount of concurrent access to the database. There is no reason, however, that multiple transactions can't view the same data, as long as none of the transactions attempt to update the data. A lock of this type—a *shared*, or *read*, lock—allows many transactions to read the same data but none to modify it. In other words, as long as there is at least one shared lock on a piece of data, no transaction can obtain an exclusive lock for updating.

Let's look at how shared locks can solve the inconsistent analysis problem. Figure 14-12 diagrams the situation in which the report transaction begins first. The transaction retrieves 10 rows to begin totaling attendance and receives a shared lock on the table. At time 2, the update transaction begins. However, when it attempts to obtain

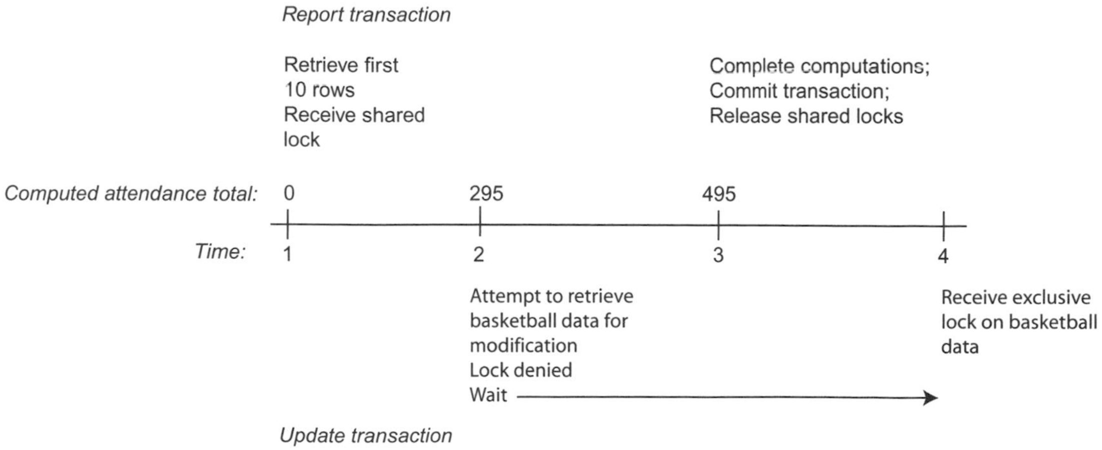

■ **FIGURE 14-12** Using shared locks to prevent inconsistent analysis.

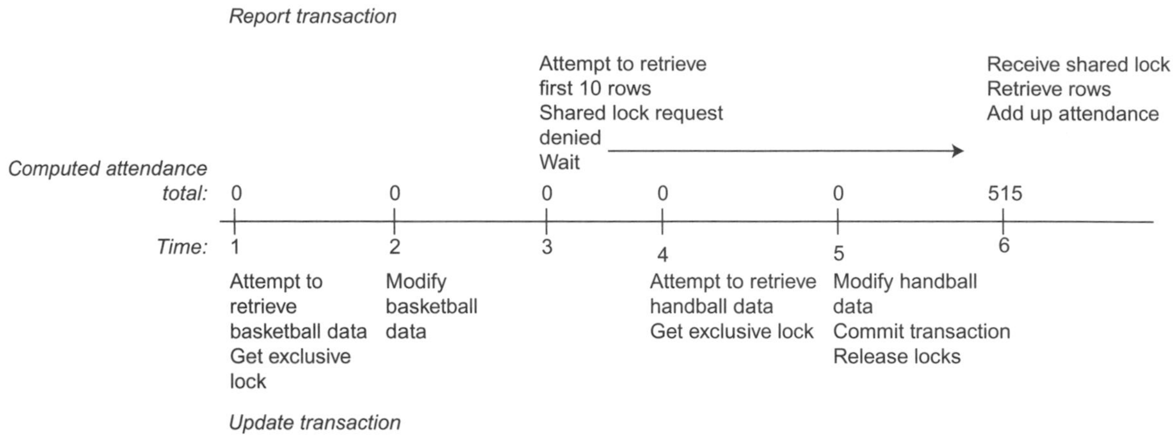

■ **FIGURE 14-13** The transaction from Figure 14-9 starting in the opposite order.

the exclusive lock it needs for data modification, it must wait because at least one other transaction holds a shared lock on the data. Once the report transaction completes (generating the correct result of 495), the shared locks are released and the report transaction can obtain the locks it needs.

Now consider what happens if the update transaction starts first. In this case, it is the report transaction that must wait because it cannot obtain shared locks as long as the modification has exclusive locks in place. As you can see from Figure 14-13, the report transaction produces a result of 515. However, under our rules of correctness for serializable transactions, this is as correct a result as the 495 that was produced when the report transaction started first.

Two-Phase Locking

In practice, the way locks are applied is a bit more complex than what you have just read. Some DBMSs use a variation of the exclusive and shared locking scheme known as *two-phase locking*. The intent is to allow as many shared locks as possible, thus increasing the amount of concurrent use permitted by a database.

Two-phase locking works by giving an update transaction a shared lock when it retrieves data and then upgrading the lock to an exclusive lock when the transaction actually makes a data modification. This helps increase the amount of concurrent use by keeping the amount of data tied up in exclusive locks to a minimum and by minimizing the time that exclusive locks are in place. The trade-off is that an update transaction may not be able to obtain an exclusive lock for data on which it holds a shared lock because other transactions hold shared locks on the same data. The update transaction may then be rolled back, causing it to release all its locks. It can then be restarted. Alternatively, it may wait for the exclusive lock to become available.

One major drawback to two-phase locking is that some processes may need to wait a long time before obtaining the exclusive locks they need to complete processing. This is not an issue for most business databases. However, real-time systems, such as those that monitor oil refineries, nuclear plants, and chemical factories, cannot tolerate delays in transaction processing. Therefore, many real-time databases cannot use two-phase locking.

Locks and Transaction Length

For locking to be effective, locks must be held until the end of the transaction, releasing only when a transaction either commits or is rolled back. For interactive commands—for example, SQL commands being entered singly—a transaction usually lasts only a single command. However, application programs can control the length of a transaction.

Some SQL implementations contain statements to indicate the start of a transaction (for example, START TRANSACTION). All, however, provide both COMMIT and ROLLBACK commands to terminate a transaction. The application program must intercept and interpret SQL return codes to determine whether actions against the database have been successful.

The combination of the need to hold locks until a transaction ends and programmer control over the length of an embedded SQL transaction means that a poorly written application program can have a major negative impact on database performance. A transaction that is too long or that unnecessarily locks database resources will impede the execution of concurrent transactions. It is therefore the responsibility of application developers to test their programs under concurrent use conditions to ensure that excessive locking is not occurring.

SOLUTION 2: OPTIMISTIC CONCURRENCY CONTROL (OPTIMISTIC LOCKING)

A database that is used primarily for retrieval with few updates can also take advantage of a variation on locking known as *optimistic locking*. It is based on the idea that when there are few updates performed, there are relatively few opportunities for problems such as lost updates to occur.

An update transaction in an optimistic locking environment proceeds in the following manner:

- Find the data to be modified, and place a copy in the transaction's work area in main memory.
- Make the change to data in the transaction's work area.
- Check the database to ensure that the modification won't conflict with any other transaction (e.g., cause a lost update).
- If no conflicts are detected, write the modified data back to the database. If a conflict is detected, roll back the transaction and start it again.

The core of the process is determining whether there are conflicting transactions. An update transaction must therefore check all other transactions, looking for instances of retrieval of the same data. Therefore, optimistic locking performs well when there aren't too many other transactions to check and the number of conflicts is low. However, performance suffers if there are many concurrent update transactions and/or update conflicts.

SOLUTION #3: MULTIVERSION CONCURRENCY CONTROL (TIMESTAMPING)

Multiversion concurrency control, or *timestamping*, is a concurrency control method that does not rely on locking. Instead, it assigns a timestamp to each piece of data retrieved by a transaction and uses the chronological ordering of the timestamps to determine whether an update will be permitted.

Each time a transaction reads a piece of data, it receives a timestamp on that data. An update of the data will be permitted as long as no other transaction holds an earlier timestamp on the data. Therefore, only the transaction holding the earliest timestamp will be permitted to update, although any number of transactions can read the data.

Timestamping is efficient in environments where most of the database activity is retrieval because nothing blocks retrieval. However, as the proportion of update transactions increases, so does the number of transactions that are prevented from updating and must be restarted.

TRANSACTION ISOLATION LEVELS

The SQL standard makes no determination of what concurrency control method a DBMS should use. However, it does provide a method for specifying how tight concurrency control is in the face of the three "read phenomena" (dirty read, nonrepeatable read, phantom read). The inclusion of the relaxing of tight concurrency control is in response to the performance degradation that can occur when large portions of a database are locked. Despite the performance advantages, relaxing concurrency control can place a database at risk for data integrity and consistency problems.

There are four *transaction isolation levels* that provide increasingly strict concurrency control and solutions to the read phenomena:

- *Serializable:* Transactions must be serializable, as described in this chapter. This is the tightest isolation level.
- *Read committted:* This prevents a dirty read but allows nonrepeatable reads and phantom reads. This means that a transaction can retrieve all data from all committed transactions, even if the read may be inconsistent with a previous read.
- *Repeatable read:* This prevents dirty reads and nonrepeatable reads, but it does not control for phantom reads.
- *Read uncommitted:* This has virtually no concurrency control, making all three read phenomena possible.

The SQL standard allows a user to set the isolation level with one of the following:

```
SET TRANSACTION LEVEL SERIALIZABLE
SET TRANSACTION LEVEL READ COMMITTED
SET TRANSACTION LEVEL REPEATABLE READ
SET TRANSACTION LEVEL UNCOMMITTED
```

Some major DBMSs do not necessarily adhere to the standard exactly. Oracle, for example, provides only three isolation levels: serializable, read committed, and read only. The read-only level restricts transactions to retrieval operations; by definition, a read-only transaction cannot modify data. The DB2 syntax uses SET CURRENT ISOLATION; with SQL Server, the statement is SET TRANSACTION ISOLATION LEVEL. None uses the precise syntax just specified. The moral to the story is that if you are going to manipulate isolation levels, check your DBMSs documentation for the specific syntax in use.

WEB DATABASE CONCURRENCY CONTROL ISSUES

Databases that allow access over the Web certainly face the same issues of concurrency control that a non-Web database faces. However, it also has another problem: The length of a transaction will vary considerably, the results of both the Web's inconsistent performance and the tendency of Web users to walk away from the computer for periods of time. How long should a transaction be kept open? When should a partially completed transaction be aborted and rolled back?

One way Web DBMSs handle the situation is by working with a unit known as a *session*. A session may contain multiple transactions, but a transaction is confined to only one session. The length of a session will vary, but usually it will have a limit on the amount of time the session can remain idle. Once the limit has passed, the DBMS will end the session and abort any open transactions. This does not mean that the user necessarily loses all information generated during such a rolled-back transaction. For example, some shopping cart applications store the items added to the cart as they are added. Even if the session is terminated by the DBMS, the items remain in the database (associated with the user's login name) so the shopping cart can be reconstructed should the user visit the site again. Alternatively, a database application could use a cookie to store the contents of a shopping cart prior to ending a session, although a cookie may not be large enough to hold even part of the data from a transaction.

Optimistic locking also works well over the Web. A transaction works with a copy of data to be modified that has been downloaded to the client computer over the Internet. The client communicates with the database only when it is time to write the update. A transaction that never completes leaves no dangling locks because no locks are placed until the DBMS determines that an update does not conflict with other transactions.

DISTRIBUTED DATABASE ISSUES

Distributed databases add yet another layer of complexity to concurrency control because there are often multiple copies of data, each kept at a different location. This presents several challenges:

- To use classic locking, locks must be placed on all copies of a piece of data. What happens if some of the locks can be placed and others cannot?
- What happens if an instruction to commit a transaction modifying copies of the same data doesn't reach all parts of the database? Some transactions may commit, while others hang without an end. Should the committed transactions be rolled back to keep the database consistent? That violates a basic precept of concurrency control: A committed transaction is *never* rolled back.

Early distributed DBMSs attempted to use timestamping for concurrency control. The overhead required to maintain the timestamps, however, was significant.

Today most distributed DBMSs use some type of two-phase locking. To lessen the chance of needing to roll back a committed transaction, distributed databases also add a *two-phase commit*. During the first phase, the transaction that initiated the data modification sends a "prepare to commit" message to each copy that is locked. Each copy then responds with a "ready to commit" message. Once the transaction receives a "ready" message from each copy, it sends a "commit" message (the second phase). If some copies do not respond with a "ready" message, the transaction is rolled back at all locations.

Whichever type of concurrency control a distributed DBMS employs, the messages needed to effect the concurrency control can significantly increase the amount of network traffic among the database sites. There is also the issue of locks that aren't released by the local DBMS because no commit message was received from the remote DBMS placing the lock. Most distributed DBMSs therefore allow database administrators to set a limit on the time a transaction can sit idle. When a transaction "times out," it is rolled back and not restarted.

FOR FURTHER READING

Bernstein, Philip A., and Nathan Goodman. "Concurrency Control in Distributed Database Systems." *ACM Computing Surveys*, 13(2), 185–221, 1981.

Bernstein, Philip A., Vassos Hadzilacos, and Nathan Goodman. *Concurrency Control and Recovery in Database Systems*. Addison-Wesley, 1987.

"How Oracle Manages Concurrency Control"; available at *http://download.oracle.com/docs/cd/B10501_01/server.920/a96524/c21cnsis.htm#2570*

Thomasian, Alexander. *Data Concurrency Control: Methods, Performance, and Analysis*. Springer, 1996.

Chapter 15

Database Security

In our current computing environment, we usually think that the instant world-spanning access provided by the Internet is a good thing. However, that access has a dark side: those who would inadvertently or purposefully violate the security of our data. Security has always been a part of relational database management, but now it has become one of the most important issues facing database administrators.

Another way to look at security is to consider the difference between *security* and *privacy*. Privacy is the need to restrict access to data, whether it be trade secrets or personal information that by law must be kept private. Security is what you do to ensure privacy.

Many people view network security as having three goals:

- *Confidentiality:* Ensuring that data that must be kept private stay private.
- *Integrity:* Ensuring that data are accurate. For a security professional, this means that data must be protected from unauthorized modification and/or destruction.
- *Availability:* Ensuring that data are accessible whenever needed by the organization. This implies protecting the network from anything that would make it unavailable, including such events as power outages.

One thing that makes data theft such a problem is that data can be stolen without anyone knowing about it. A good thief can get into a target system, copy the data, and exit without leaving a trace. Because copying digital data does not affect the source, examining the data won't reveal that any copying has taken place. An accomplished thief will also modify system log files, erasing any trace of the illegal entry.

The popular media would have you believe that the source of most computer security problems is the "hacker." However, if you ask people actually working in the field, they will tell you that nearly half the security breaches they encounter come from sources internal to an organization, and, in particular, employees. This means that it won't be sufficient to secure a network against external intrusion attempts; you must pay as much attention to what is occurring within your organization as you do to external threats. Databases in particular are especially vulnerable to internal security threats because direct access is typically provided only to employees.

SOURCES OF EXTERNAL SECURITY THREATS

The Internet has been both a blessing and a curse to those who rely on computer networks to keep an organization in business. The global network has made it possible for potential customers, existing customers, and employees to reach an organization through its Web site. But with this new access have come the enormous problems caused by individuals and groups attempting illegal entry into computer networks and the computer systems they support.

Physical Threats

We are so focused on the security issues that come over a network that we tend to ignore physical threats to our database installation. Certainly, we need to worry about a disgruntled employee with a hammer, but there is more to physical security risks than that. The major issue today is physical access to a server by a knowledgeable data thief.

All servers have at least one user account that has access rights to the entire computer. When the servers are housed in a locked location, operators tend to leave the privileged user account logged in. It makes administration just a bit easier. The operators rely on the security on the server room door to keep unauthorized people out. The problem with this strategy is that sometimes physical barriers aren't sufficient; a knowledgeable data thief will be able to circumvent whatever lock has been placed on the server room door and gain physical access to the servers. If the privileged accounts are left logged in, all the thief needs to do is sit down at a machine and start extracting data.

Hackers and Crackers

External threats are initiated by people known in the hacking community as *crackers*. Initially, the term *hacker* referred to someone who could write an ingenious bit of software. In fact, the phrase "a good hack" meant a particularly clever piece of programming. Outside of the hacking community, however, anyone who attempts illegal access to a computer network is called a hacker.

Hacking often involves becoming intimate with the details of existing software to give the hacker the knowledge necessary to attempt an unauthorized system break-in. Nonetheless, those who adhere to the original definition of *hacker* wanted to differentiate themselves from those who perform illegal activities, thus the term *cracker*.

There are many ways to classify those who break into computer systems, depending on which source you are reading. However, most lists of the types of hackers include the following (although they may be given different names):

- *White hat hackers*: This group considers itself to be the "good guys." Although white hat hackers may crack a system, they do not do it for personal gain. When they find a vulnerability in a network, they report it to the network owner, hardware vendor, or software vendor, whichever is appropriate. They do not release information about the system vulnerability to the public until the vendor has had a chance to develop and release a fix for the problem. White hat hackers might also be hired by an organization to test a network's defenses.

  White hat hackers are extremely knowledgeable about networking, programming, and existing vulnerabilities that have been found and fixed. They typically write their own cracking tools.

- *Script kiddies*: The script kiddies are hacker "wannabes." They have little, if any, programming skill and therefore must rely on tools written by others. Psychological profiles of script kiddies indicate that they are generally male, young (under 30), and not socially well adjusted. They are looked down upon by most other hackers.

  Script kiddies do not target specific networks but, instead, scan for any system that is vulnerable to attack. They might try to deface a Web site, delete files from a target system, flood network bandwidth with unauthorized packets, or in some other way commit what amounts to cyber vandalism. Script kiddies typically don't want to keep their exploits secret. In fact, many of those who are caught are trapped because they have been bragging about what they have done.

- *Black hat hackers*: Black hat hackers are motivated by greed or a desire to cause harm. They target specific systems, write their own tools, and generally attempt to get in and out of a target system without being detected. Because they are very knowledgeable and their activities often undetectable, black hat hackers are among the most dangerous.
- *Cyberterrorists*: Cyberterrorists are hackers who are motivated by a political, religious, or philosophical agenda. They may propagate their beliefs by defacing Web sites that support opposing positions. Given the current global political climate, there is also some fear that cyberterrorists may attempt to disable networks that handle utilities such as nuclear plants and water systems.

Types of Attacks

When a hacker targets your network, what might you expect? There are a number of broad categories of attacks.

- *Denial of service*: A denial of service attack (DoS) attempts to prevent legitimate users from gaining access to network resources and, by extension, any database that uses the network. It can take the form of flooding a network or server with traffic so that legitimate messages can't get through, or it can bring down a server. If you are monitoring traffic on your network, a DoS attack is fairly easy to detect. Unfortunately, it can be difficult to defend against and stop without disconnecting your network from the Internet.
- *Buffer overflow*: A buffer overflow attack takes advantage of a programming error in an application or system program. The hacker can insert his or her own code into a program and from there take control of a target system. Because they are the result of a programming error, buffer overflow conditions are almost impossible for a network engineer to detect. They are usually detected by hackers or the software vendor. The most common defense is a patch provided by that vendor.

  Closely related to the more general buffer overflow vulnerability, an *SQL injection attack* occurs when a hacker uses openings in SQL statements to insert and execute malicious code from a database application. Such attacks can be prevented by following specific syntax forms when embedding SQL in high-level programming languages. It is therefore important that application coding syntax rules be documented, updated, and readily accessible to application programmers.

- *Malware*: Malware includes all types of malicious software, such as viruses, worms, and Trojan horses. The goal of a hacker in placing such software on a computer may be simple maliciousness or to provide access to the computer at a later date. Although there is a constantly escalating battle between those who write malware and those who write malware detection software, a good virus checker goes a long way to keeping network devices free from infection.
- *Social engineering*: A social engineering attack is an attempt to get system access information from employees using role playing and misdirection. It is usually the prelude to an attempt to gain unauthorized access to the network.
- *Brute force*: One way to gain access to a system is to run brute force login attempts. Assuming that a hacker knows one or more system login names, he can attempt to guess the passwords. By keeping and monitoring logs of who is attempting to log into a system, a network administrator can usually detect brute force break-in attacks.

> *Note:* There is no gender discrimination intended with the use of the pronoun "he" when referring to hackers. The fact is that most hackers are male.

SOURCES OF INTERNAL THREATS

Most internal threats come from two sources: employees and accidents. Employee threats may be intentional or accidental.

Employee Threats

In most cases, employees know more about a network and the computers on it than any outsider. At the very least, they have legitimate access to user accounts. IT personnel, of course, have various levels of increased access. Intentional employee security threats include the following:

- Personnel who employ hacking techniques to upgrade their legitimate access to root/administrator, allowing them to divulge trade secrets, steal money, and so on for personal or political gain.

- Personnel who take advantage of legitimate access to divulge trade secrets, steal money, and so on for personal or political gain.
- Family members of employees who are visiting the office and have been given access to company computers to occupy them while waiting.
- As mentioned earlier, personnel who break into secure machine rooms to gain physical access to mainframe and other large-system consoles.
- Former employees, especially those who did not leave the organization willingly, who want revenge. Attacks may be physical—actually damaging equipment—or traditional hacking attacks that result in damaged data.

As dangerous as the intentional employee security threat may be, employees can also cause a great deal of damage unintentionally, such as the following:

- Becoming the victim of a social engineering attack, unknowingly helping a hacker gain unauthorized network access.
- Unintentionally revealing confidential information.
- Physically damaging equipment, resulting in data loss.
- Misusing a system, introducing inaccurate and/or damaged data, or accidentally deleting or modifying data.
- Installing personal equipment on a network (for example, a wireless access point) that isn't included in the organization's security measures.

Most unintentional employee threats theoretically can be handled through employee education. For example, it seems logical that instructing employees not to write passwords on sticky notes that are then fixed to monitors would help prevent compromised passwords. However, when you are dealing with human beings, even the best education can be forgotten in the stress of getting a job done on time.

Employees certainly can unintentionally damage a network. In addition, true accidents also occur. A security plan should guard against data damage and loss caused by

- Electrical power fluctuations
- Hardware failures
- Natural disasters such as fire and flood

Guarding against accidental network damage includes power protection—for example, surge protectors and UPSs—and comprehensive backup schemes. When done well, backup takes significant planning and disaster recovery rehearsals.

EXTERNAL REMEDIES

External security measures are typically outside the responsibility of database administrators. However, you should be aware of what security protections external to the database are in place and, if they appear inadequate, know how to make your concerns and recommendations heard. In this section we'll therefore look at security strategies that should be in place external to the database to provide a first line of defense.

Securing the Perimeter: Firewalls

A *firewall* is a piece of software that filters incoming and outgoing network traffic and stops messages that violate the rules that define allowable traffic. It is typically placed between the Internet and an internal network. Its primary job is to eliminate as much undesirable network traffic as possible.

> *Note:* You may hear a firewall spoken of as a piece of hardware. However, a firewall device is really a special-purpose computer that runs firewall software. Because the device is dedicated to the firewall application, it may be more powerful than firewall software that is added to a router or other network interconnection device.

If you look at Figure 15-1, you'll notice that the network looks very much like something that might be used by SmartMart from Chapter 13. Specifically, it includes a Web server that is exposed to the Internet through a router and a database server that is isolated from the Web server by a second firewall.

The first firewall—the one connected to the edge router—allows specific messages to pass, including those intended for the Web server and for destinations that represent legitimate network traffic (for example, e-mail and remote employees).

The edge router will send all Web traffic to the Web server, preventing it from getting onto the internal network. However, because Web users

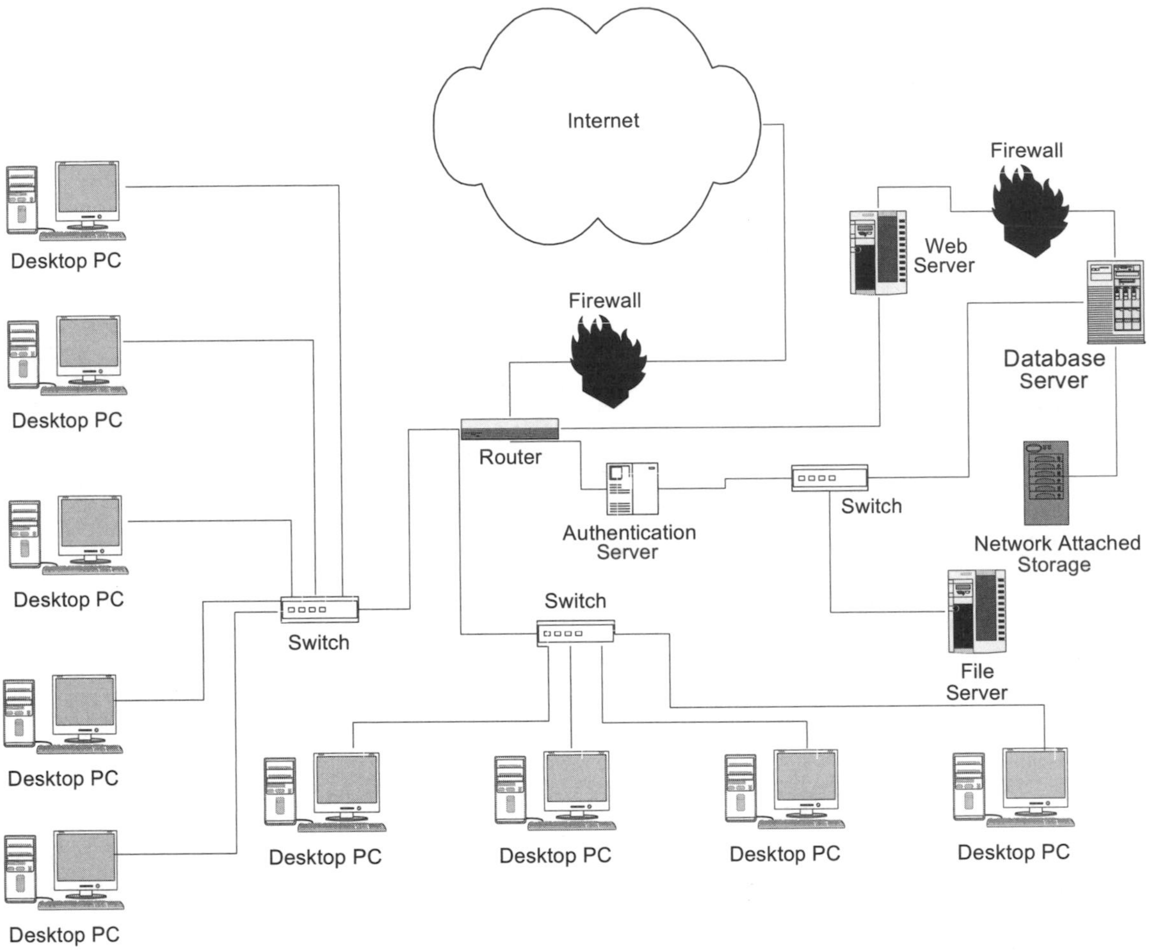

■ **FIGURE 15-1** Using firewalls to secure a network and create a DMZ to protect the database server.

need access to data stored on the database server, simply routing that traffic to the Web server doesn't provide protection for the database.

To protect the database, only messages from the Web server are permitted to interact with the database. A second firewall has therefore been placed between the two servers. The Web server is said to reside in a DMZ, a part of the network that is walled off from the internal network.

A Web transaction that involves access to the database server proceeds as follows:

1. User's browser generates a request for data stored in the database (for example, a page from a retail catalog) and transmits it to the company network.
2. The edge router passes the request to the Web server.
3. The Web server requests data from the database.
4. The firewall between the Web server and the database server passes the message because it comes from the database server.
5. The database server retrieves the requested data and sends it back through the firewall to the Web server.
6. The Web server formats the data and sends a response to the user, whose browser displays the new Web page.

Notice that internal users have direct access to the Web server without having to pass through the DMZ. The assumption is that internal users will be authorized for direct database access.

Handling Malware

When a database server is infected by malware, it can be a serious problem. The result may be loss of data, loss of access to the database, or loss of control of the database server's hardware. Protection against malware is typically provided by "virus protection" software running on firewalls and the servers themselves.

Most current virus protection software handles worms, Trojan horses, and bots as well as viruses. The most important thing to keep in mind, however, is that there is an ever-escalating battle between those who write malware and those who produce the virus protection software. As soon as a new threat is identified, the software developers rush to add the new malware to their protection database; the malware producers then write new malware that is typically more powerful and more sophisticated than previous releases. You can never be completely safe from malware because there is always a lag, however brief, between the detection of a new piece of malware and the updating of virus protection software to handle that malware. The best thing you can do is update the database that accompanies your virus protection software regularly.

Buffer Overflows

Because a buffer overflow problem is a flaw in the way software is written, there is really nothing an organization without access to the source code and a staff of programmers can do to fix it. An organization must rely on the software developer to release updates (*patches*) to the code.

Patching is a cooperative operation in that once the vendor has released a patch, it is up to organizations using the software to install the patch. Nonetheless, the best defense against buffer overflow vulnerabilities (and any other vulnerabilities caused by bugs in software) is to apply all available patches.

Patch management can become a nightmare for an IT staff. There are so many patches released for some types of software (for example, Microsoft Windows in all its myriad versions) that it is difficult to know which patches are important and stable and, in a large organization, which patches have been applied to which machine. Nonetheless, to protect your database server (both the operating system and the DBMS), you must work with IT to ensure that all necessary patches have been applied.

Physical Server Security

Physical security requires a two-pronged approach: preventing physical access to the server and, should that fail, securing the administrative accounts. Actual physical methods include any or all of the following:

- Security cameras outside machine/server room doors to record everyone who enters, exits, and loiters in the area.
- Smart locks on machine/server room doors that store the code of each individual who enters and exits, along with the date and time of an entry or exit. Smart locks can be equipped with biometric identification devices if desired. (These will be discussed shortly.)
- Removal of signs from machine/server room doors and hallways so no one can locate hardware rooms by simply walking the hallways of the building.

The recording produced by security cameras and smart locks must be examined regularly to determine if any unusual access patterns appear.

Should an unauthorized person manage to defeat the physical security, he will probably want to gain software access to a computer. (We are assuming that physical damage to the equipment is a rare goal of an intruder.) This means that the administrative accounts for each server must be secured. First, the accounts should never be left logged in. It may be more convenient for operators, but it makes the servers vulnerable to anyone who happens to walk by. Second, login attempts to the administrative accounts should be limited. For example, after three failed attempts to log in, the server should disallow further login attempts for some predetermined length of time.

User Authentication

Any user who is permitted direct access to a database must first be authenticated for access to the local area network. The forms that such authentication takes depend on the size and security risks of the network. Positive user identification requires three things:

1. Something the user knows
2. Something the user has
3. Something the user is

The first can be achieved with passwords, the second with physical login devices, and the third with biometrics.

User IDs and Passwords (What the User Knows)

The first line of defense for any network authentication scheme is the user ID and password. User IDs in and of themselves are not generally considered to be private; in fact, many are based on user e-mail addresses. The security therefore resides in the password. General security practice tells us the following about passwords:

- Long passwords are better than short passwords.
- Passwords with a combination of letters, numbers, and special characters (for example, punctuation) are more secure than passwords that are all letters or all numbers.
- User education is needed to ensure that users don't share their passwords with anyone or write them down where others may see them.
- Passwords should be changed at regular intervals.

Although "general wisdom" dictates that passwords should be changed regularly, there are some problems with that policy. When users are forced to change their passwords, they often forget which password they have used. The solution is to write the password down, sometimes placing it in an insecure location such as the center drawer of a desk or even on a sticky note affixed to a monitor.

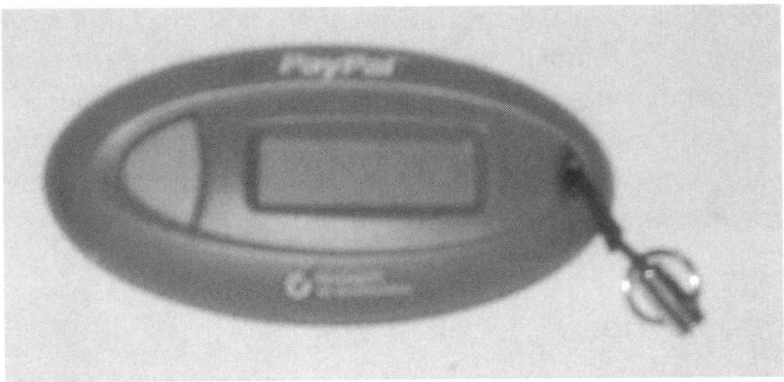

■ **FIGURE 15-2** The PayPal security token.

Login Devices (What the User Has)

The second layer of user authentication is requiring that someone attempting to log in present a physical device that only an authorized user will have. The device has some way of making it unique to the user ID.

Login devices include access cards that a user must scan in some way before entering a password and devices that issue one-time passwords that the user enters in addition to a regular password. For example, for $5, PayPal will send you a small device that generates a one-time password (Figure 15-2). To log on, the user must first enter the standard user ID and password. Then, however, the authentication application asks for a code from the device. The device is for those users who are concerned about the security of their accounts, but it is not required.

Some authentication tokens require that the token be physically inserted into a computer connected directly to the network. For example, the eToken series from Aladdin Systems consists primarily of devices that are to be plugged into a USB port to authenticate both the user and the user's location.[1]

The advantage of a login device is that it is small—usually small enough to attach to a keychain—so it is easy for the user to keep the device handy. However, if the user doesn't have the device and needs access, there must be an alternative form of authentication available. PayPal, for example, provides several alternatives, such as answering

[1] See *www.aladdin.com/etoken/devices/default.aspx*.

security questions or providing a financial account number that is linked to the PayPal account.

Biometrics (What the User Is)

Biometric identification—identification based on certain characteristics of a person's body—has long been a part of science fiction. The idea of retina prints, thumbprints, palmprints, and facial scans doesn't seem particularly far-fetched. Today you can purchase a mouse with a thumbprint reader that sends the print to a computer for authentication. The computer won't unlock unless it recognizes the thumbprint, making this a seemingly good way to secure laptops and desktops in sensitive areas.

VPNs

Remote access to a database is typical today. Users travel; users work from home. The days are long gone where remote users dialed into their work network using a modem and a standard telephone line. Most remote access reaches an internal network over the Internet. The problem facing a database administrator is ensuring that the data remain safe while traveling on the external network.

One commonly applied solution is a *virtual private network* (VPN). VPNs provide encryption for data transmissions over the Internet. Although there are several types of VPNs, many use a security protocol known as *IPSec,* including the VPNs that are built into desktop operating systems such as Windows and Mac OS X.

IPSec encrypts the data, turning it into something that is meaningless to anyone who does not have the secret encryption keys. Even if data are intercepted while traveling over the Internet, they will be useless. We say that IPSec provides a secure *tunnel* for data (see Figure 15-3). One type of tunneling encrypts data only when it is actually on the Internet; the other provides *end-to-end* encryption where data are encrypted from the sending computer to the destination network.

To operate a VPN, the destination network must have a VPN server, a machine that receives all incoming VPN traffic and handles authenticating the VPN user. The VPN server acts as a gatekeeper to the internal network. Once authenticated, VPN users can interact with the destination network as if they were physically present at the network's location.

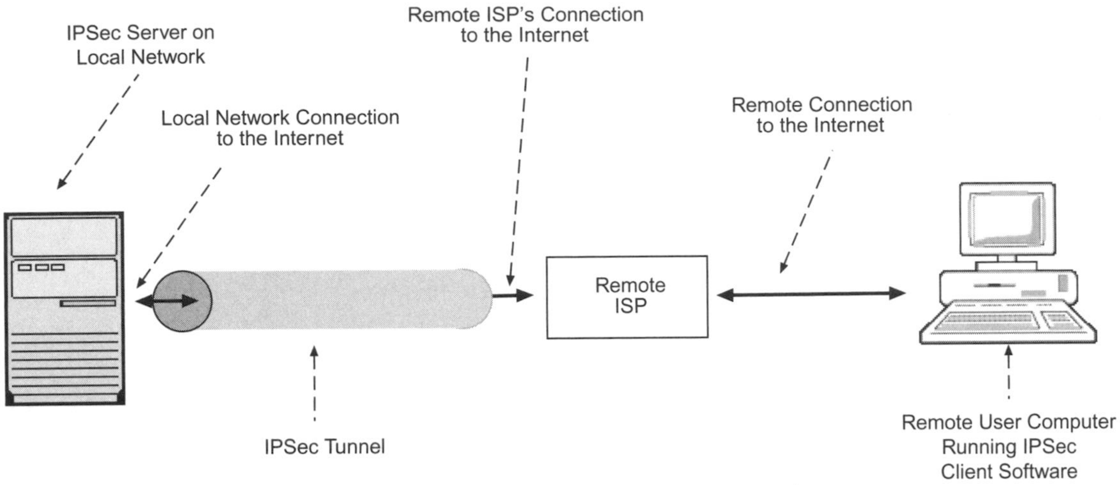

■ **FIGURE 15-3** The architecture of an IPSec VPN.

Combating Social Engineering

Social engineering isn't a technical attack at all but a psychological/behavior attack, so it can't be stopped by technical means. It requires employee education to teach employees to recognize this type of attack and how to guard against it.

As an example, consider the following scenario: Jane Jones is the secretary for the R&D department of a high-tech firm. Her boss, John Smith, often works at home. Ms. Jones has been with the company for many years, and she is a trusted employee. She knows the user names and passwords for her computer, Mr. Smith's desktop and laptop, and Mr. Smith's mainframe account.

One morning, Ms. Jones receives a telephone call. "Ms. Jones, this is James Doe from IT. I have some upgrades that I need to install on your computer and Mr. Smith's computer. I don't need to come to your office. I can do it over the network if I have the user IDs and passwords."

"Oh, that sounds fine," says Ms. Jones. "I hate it when IT has to come by and interrupt my work to fix something. My user ID is . . ." (she gives Mr. Doe the user names and passwords).

Unfortunately, the man who claims to be James Doe isn't who he says he is. He's a hacker, and with just a little research and a phone call, he has received access to two corporate desktops. First, he checked the corporate directory online. It was simple to find the name of an IT employee, as well as the names of the head of R&D and his secretary. Then all he had to do was place a phone call to Ms. Jones. She cooperated, and he was in business.

The phony James Doe does install a file or two on each of the compromised computers. However, the files are actually a Trojan horse that he can activate later when he needs control of the compromised machines.

Ms. Jones made one critical error: She revealed user names and passwords. She felt comfortable doing so because she knew that someone named James Doe worked for IT. She had never thought that there would be a problem trusting someone from that department; the idea of an impersonator never crossed her mind.

There is no technological solution to a social engineering attack of this type. The best prevention is employee awareness. Training sessions with role playing to demonstrate how such attacks are perpetrated can be very helpful. A few simple policies will also go a long way:

- Never reveal your user ID or password to *anyone,* no matter who that person claims to be.
- If someone claims to be a corporate employee and asks for your user name and password, take his or her name, a supervisor's name, and an extension. Then hang up and call the supervisor to report the attempt to obtain a user ID and password.
- If someone claims to be a vendor representative (or anyone else who is not an employee) and asks for a user ID and password, hang up and notify IT security immediately.

An organization should also take steps to restrict the information that it makes public so it becomes more difficult for a hacker to develop a convincing social engineering attack. For example, employee directories should not be available publicly. Instead, use titles (such as "IT Manager") in any contact lists that are accessible to nonemployees. Organizations with registered Internet domain names should also restrict the information available to those who issue a "whois" command on the domain name.

Handling Other Employee Threats

There are many things an organization can do to guard against other employee threats:

- Develop and enforce policies that forbid employees to install their own hardware and software on corporate machines and networks. Use network discovery and mapping software to monitor network hardware and detect any unauthorized equipment.
- Conduct employee training sessions to familiarize employees with the organization's policies on the release of information.
- Document all organizational security policies, distribute them to employees, and require employees to sign, indicating that they have read and accepted the policies.
- Require employees to take two consecutive weeks of vacation at least once every two years. If an employee is hacking the organization's information systems and covering up the unauthorized access, an absence of two weeks is likely long enough to expose what is occurring.
- When an employee is going to be fired, disable all of the employee's computer accounts prior to telling the employee about the termination.

INTERNAL SOLUTIONS

Up to this point, the security measures we've discussed have all been applied outside the DBMS. They are put in place by network administrators rather than database personnel. There are, however, at least two layers of security that a relational DBMS adds to whatever is supplied by the network.

Internal Database User IDs and Passwords

The user IDs and passwords we discussed earlier in this chapter are used to give a user access to a network. They do not necessarily (and probably shouldn't) give access to a database. Most of today's relational DBMSs provide their own user ID and password mechanism. Once a user has gained access to the network, he or she must authenticate again to gain direct access to the database (either at the command line or with an application program).

It is important to distinguish between direct access to the database and account access by Web customers. Someone making a purchase on a Web site does not interact directly with the database; only the Web server has that type of access. A Web user supplies a user name and password, both of which are probably stored in the database. The Web server sends a query to the DBMS to retrieve data that match the user ID/password pair. Assuming that a matching account is found, the Web server can then send a query to retrieve the Web user's account data. Web customers cannot issue ad hoc queries using a query language; they can only use the browser-based application provided for them. Therefore, there is little that the typical Web user can do to compromise the security of the database.

However, internal database users have direct access to the database elements for which their accounts have been configured. They can formulate ad hoc queries at a command line to manipulate the tables or views to which they have access. The trick, then, is to tailor access to database elements based on what each user ID "needs to know." A relational database accomplishes this by using an authorization matrix.

Authorization Matrices

Most DBMSs that support SQL use their data dictionaries to provide a level of security. Originally known as an *authorization matrix*, this type of security provides control of access rights to tables, views, and their components.

Types of Access Rights

The typical SQL-based DBMS provides six types of access rights:

- *SELECT:* Allows a user to retrieve data from a table or view.
- *INSERT:* Allows a user to insert new rows in a table or updatable view. Permission may be granted to specific columns rather than the entire database element.
- *UPDATE:* Allows a user to modify rows in a table or updatable view. Permission may be granted to specific columns rather than the entire database element.
- *DELETE:* Allows a user to delete rows from a table or updatable view.

- *REFERENCES:* Allows a user to reference a table column as a foreign key in a table that he or she creates. Permission may be granted to specific columns rather than the entire database element.
- *ALL PRIVILEGES:* Gives a user all of the preceding rights to a table or view.

By default, granting access rights to another user does not give the user the right to pass those rights on to others. If, however, you add a WITH GRANT OPTION clause, you give the user the ability to grant his or her rights to another user.

Using an Authorization Matrix

Whenever a user makes a request to the DBMS to manipulate data, the DBMS first consults the authorization matrix to determine whether the user has the right to perform the requested action. If the DBMS cannot find a row with a matching user ID and table or view identifier, then the user has no right at all to the database element. If a row with a matching user ID and table identifier exists, then the DBMS checks for the specific rights that the user has to the table or view and either permits or disallows the requested database access. Because all database access begins with at least one search of a data dictionary table, we say that relational DBMSs are *data dictionary driven.*

Database Implementations

Access rights to tables and views are stored in the data dictionary. Although the details of the data dictionary tables vary from one DBMS to another, you will usually find access rights split between two system tables named something like Systableperm and Syscolperm. The first table is used when access rights are granted to entire tables or views and the second when rights are granted to specific columns within a table or view.

A Systableperm table has a structure similar to the following:

```
Systableperm (table_id, grantee, grantor,
  selectauth, insertauth, deleteauth, updateauth,
  updatecols, referenceauth)
```

The columns represent:

- table_id: An identifier for the table or view.
- grantee: The user ID to which rights have been granted.
- grantor: The user ID granting the rights.

- selectauth: The grantee's SELECT rights.
- insertauth: The grantee's INSERT rights.
- deleteauth: The grantee's INSERT rights.
- updateauth: The grantee's UPDATE rights.
- updatecols: Indicates whether rights have been granted to specific columns rather than the entire table or view. When this value is Y (yes), the DBMS must also look in Syscolperm to determine whether a user has the right to perform a specific action against the database.

The columns that hold the access rights take one of three values: Y (yes), N (no), or G (yes with grant option).

Granting and Revoking Access Rights

When you create an element of database structure, the user name under which you are working becomes that element's owner. The owner has the right to do anything to that element; all other users have no rights at all. This means that if tables and views are going to be accessible to other users, you must grant them access rights.

Granting Rights

To grant rights to another user, a user that either created the database element (and therefore has all rights to it) or has GRANT rights issues a GRANT statement:

```
GRANT type_of_rights ON table_or_view_name TO
  user_ID
```

For example, if the DBA of Antique Opticals wants to allow the accounting manager (who has a user ID of acctg_mgr) to access an order summary view, the DBA would type:

```
GRANT SELECT ON order_summary TO acctg_mgr
```

To allow the accounting manager to pass those rights on to others, the DBA would need to add one line to the SQL:

```
GRANT SELECT ON order_summary TO acctg_mgr WITH
  GRANT OPTION
```

If Antique Opticals wants to give some student interns limited rights to some of the base tables, the GRANT might be written:

```
GRANT SELECT, UPDATE (retail_price,
  distributor_name) ON item TO intern1, intern2,
  intern3
```

The preceding example grants SELECT rights to the entire table but gives UPDATE rights on only two specific columns. Notice also that you can grant multiple rights in the same command as well as the same group of rights to more than one user. However, a single GRANT applies to only one table or view.

In most cases, rights are granted to specific user IDs. You can, however, make database elements accessible to anyone by giving him or her the rights to the special use ID PUBLIC. For example, the following statement gives every authorized user the rights to see the order summary view:

```
GRANT SELECT ON order_summary TO PUBLIC
```

Revoking Rights

To remove previously granted rights, use the REVOKE statement, whose syntax is almost the opposite of GRANT:

```
REVOKE access_rights ON table_or_view_name FROM
  user_ID
```

For example, if Antique Opticals' summer interns have finished their work for the year, the DBA might want to remove their access from the database:

```
REVOKE SELECT, UPDATE (retail_price,
  distributor_numb) ON item FROM intern1, intern2,
  intern3
```

If the user from which you are revoking rights has the GRANT option for those rights, then you also need to make a decision about what to do if the user has passed on those rights. In the following case, the REVOKE option will be disallowed if the acctg_mgr user has passed on his or her rights:

```
REVOKE SELECT ON order_summary FROM acctg_mgr
  RESTRICT
```

In contrast, the syntax

```
REVOKE SELECT ON order_summary FROM acctg_mgr
  CASCADE
```

will remove the rights from the acctg_mgr ID along with any user IDs to which acctg_mgr granted rights.

Who Has Access to What

The internal database security measures we have discussed to this point assume that we know which users should have access to which data. For example, does a bookkeeper need access to data from the last audit or should access to those data be restricted to the comptroller? Such decisions may not be as easy as they first appear. Consider the following scenario (loosely based on a real incident).

The Human Relations department for a small private college occupies very cramped quarters. Personnel files have not been converted to machine-readable form but instead are stored in a half dozen locked four-drawer file cabinets in the reception area, behind the receptionist's desk. The receptionist keeps the keys to the file cabinets and gives them to HR employees as needed.

The problem with this arrangement is that the receptionist, who is a long-time college employee, has a habit of peeking at the personnel files. (She is known for having the juiciest gossip in the building at break times.)

One day the receptionist comes in to work and sees that the file cabinets are being moved out of the reception area. In their place, a PC has been placed on her desk. The new HR system is online, and an IT staff member has come to train the receptionist. She has a word processor, access to the college faculty/staff directory, and an appointment scheduling application.

> "How do I get to the personnel files?" she asks at the end of the training session.
>
> "You don't have the application," the IT employee responds.
>
> "Why not?"
>
> The IT staff member shrugs. "You'll have to ask the database administrator."
>
> The receptionist is immediately out the door, headed for the IT department. She finds the database administrator in his office.
>
> "Why didn't I get the personnel application?" she asks.
>
> "Because you don't need access to that information to do your job, and legally we have to ensure the privacy of those data."

> At this point, the receptionist is furious. "But I've always had access to the personnel files!" she shouts.

The scene degenerates from there.

The problem would appear to be that the HR receptionist should never have had access to the personnel files in the first place. However, it's a bit more complicated than that. Access to information makes people feel powerful. It's the "I know something you don't know" syndrome. Remove or restrict access, and many people feel that they have lost power and status in the organization.

Some organizations have solved this problem by appointing a committee to handle the decisions about who has access to what. Users who feel that they need additional access must appeal to the committee rather than to a single individual. This protects the staff members who are making the decisions and provides broader input to the decision-making process.

The other side of this issue is data sharing. Occasionally you may run into employees who have control of data that have to be shared, but the employee is reluctant to release the data. Whether it is a researcher who controls survey data, a district manager who handles the data about the sales department, or a salesperson who guards the data he collects when in the field, psychologically the issue is the same as determining data access: Access to data and controlling data can make people feel powerful and important.

Data sharing can be mandated by a supervisor (if necessary, as a condition to continued employment). However, it is often better to try to persuade the data owner that there is benefit to everyone if the data are shared. By the same token, the committee that makes decisions about data access must also be willing to listen to the data owner's arguments in favor of keeping the data restricted and be willing to agree if the arguments are compelling.

BACKUP AND RECOVERY

Every discussion about database security should include at least a few words about preparing for catastrophic failures. Disk drives develop bad sectors, making it impossible to read or write data; natural disasters can fill the server room with water. Earthquakes and fires happen. When such failures occur, there is only one thing you can do: revert to a backup copy. In this section we'll look at making backups and how they fit into a disaster recovery scheme.

Backup

We don't usually think of backups as a part of a security strategy, but in some circumstances it can be the most effective way to recover from security problems. If a server becomes so compromised by malware that it is impossible to remove (perhaps because virus protection software hasn't been developed for the specific malware), then a reasonable solution is to reformat any affected hard disks and restore the database from the most recent backup. Backups are also your only defense against physical damage to data storage, such as a failed hard disk.

A backup copy is a usable fallback strategy only if you have a backup that isn't too old and you are certain that the backup copy is clean (in other words, not infected by malware).

How often should you make backup copies? The answer depends on the *volatility* of your data. In other words, how much do your data change? If the database is primarily for retrieval, with very little data modification, then a complete backup once a week and incremental backups every day may be sufficient. However, an active transaction database in which data are constantly being entered may need complete daily backups. It comes down to a decision of how much you can afford to lose versus the time and effort needed to make backups often.

Assuming that you have decided on a backup interval, how many backups should you keep? If you back up daily, is it enough to keep a week's worth? Do you need less or more than that? In this case, it depends a great deal on the risk of malware. You want to keep enough backups that you can go far enough back in time to obtain a clean copy of the database (one without the malware). However, it is also true that malware may affect the server operating system without harming the database, in which case the most recent backup will be clean. Then you can fall back on the "three generations of backups" strategy, where you keep a rotation of "child," "father," and "grandfather" backup copies.

It used to be easy to choose backup media. Hard disk storage was expensive; tape storage was slow and provided only sequential retrieval, but it was cheap. We backed up to tape almost exclusively until recently, when hard disk storage became large enough and cheap enough to be seen as a viable backup device. Some mainframe installations continue to use tape cartridges, but even large databases are quickly being migrated to disk backup media. Small systems, which once could back up to optical drives, now use disks as backup media almost exclusively.

The issue of backup has a psychological as well as a technical component: How can you be certain that backups are being made as scheduled? At first, this may not seem to be something to worry about, but consider the following scenario (which is a true story).

In the mid-1980s, a database application was installed for an outpatient psychiatric clinic that was affiliated with a major hospital in a major northeastern city. The application, which primarily handled patient scheduling, needed to manage more than 25,000 patient visits a year, divided among about 85 clinicians. The database itself was placed on a server in a secured room.

The last patient appointment was scheduled for 5 PM, which was when most staff left for the day. However, the receptionist stayed until 6 PM to close up after the last patient left. Her job during that last hour included making a daily backup of the database.

About a month after the application went into day-to-day use, the database developer who installed the system received a frantic call from the office manager. There were 22 unexplained files on the receptionist's computer. The office manager was afraid that something was terribly wrong.

Something was indeed wrong, but not what anyone would have imagined. The database developer discovered that the unidentified files were temporary files left by the database application. Each time the application was launched from the server, it downloaded the structure of the database and its application from the server and kept them locally until the client software was shut down. The presence of the temporary files meant that the receptionist wasn't quitting the application but only turning off her computer. If she wasn't quitting the database application properly, was she making backup copies?

As you can guess, she wasn't. The only backup that existed was the one the database developer made the day the application was installed and the data were migrated into the database. When asked why the backups weren't made, the receptionist admitted that it was just too much trouble. The solution was a warning from the office manager and additional training in backup procedures. The office manager also monitored the backups more closely.

The moral of this story is that just having a backup strategy in place isn't enough. You need to make certain that the backups are actually being made.

Disaster Recovery

The term *disaster recovery* refers to the activities that must take place to bring the database back into use after it has been damaged in some way. In large organizations, database disaster recovery will likely be part of a broader organizational disaster recovery plan. However, in a small organization, it may be up to the database administrator to coordinate recovery.

A disaster recovery plan usually includes specifications for the following:

- Where backup copies will be kept so they will remain undamaged even if the server room is damaged
- How new hardware will be obtained
- How the database and its applications are to be restored from the backups
- Procedures for handling data until the restored database is available for use
- Lists of those affected by the database failure and procedures for notifying them when the failure occurs and when the database is available again

The location of backup copies is vitally important. If they are kept in the server room, they risk being destroyed by a flood, fire, or earthquake along with the server itself. At least one backup copy should therefore be stored off-site.

Large organizations often contract with commercial data storage facilities to handle their backups. The storage facility maintains temperature-controlled rooms to extend the life of backup media. They may also operate trucks that deliver and pick up the backup media so that the off-site backup remains relatively current.

For small organizations, it's not unheard of for an IT staff member to take backups home for safekeeping. This probably isn't the best strategy, given that the backup may not be accessible when needed. Some use bank safe deposit boxes for offsite storage, although those generally are only accessible during normal business hours. If a small organization needs 24/7 access to off-site backup copies, the expense of using a commercial facility may be justified.

When a disaster occurs, an organization needs to be up and running as quickly as possible. If the server room and its machines are damaged, there must be some other way to obtain hardware. Small organizations can simply purchase new equipment, but they must have a plan for where the new hardware will be located and how network connections will be obtained.

Large organizations often contract with *hot sites,* businesses that provide hardware that can run the organization's software. Hot sites store backup copies and guarantee that they can have the organization's applications up and running in a specified amount of time.

Once a disaster recovery plan has been written, it must be tested. Organizations need to run a variety of disaster recovery drills, simulating a range of system failures. It is not unusual to discover that what appears to be a good plan on paper doesn't work in practice. The plan needs to be modified as needed to ensure that the organization can recover its information systems should a disaster occur.

THE BOTTOM LINE: HOW MUCH SECURITY DO YOU NEED?

Many of the security measures described in this chapter are costly, such as adding user authentication measures beyond passwords and user IDs and contracting with a hot site. How important are high-end security measures? Should your organization invest in them?

The answer depends on a number of factors but primarily on the type of data being protected:

- Are there laws governing the privacy of the data?
- Could the data be used as the basis for identity theft?
- Do the data represent trade secrets that could seriously compromise the organization's market position should they be disclosed?

The final question you must answer is how much risk you are willing to tolerate. Assume that it is affordable to install enough security to protect against about 80 percent of security threats. However, it may well cost as much as that entire 80 percent to achieve an additional 10 or 20 percent of protection. If you are willing (and able) to tolerate a 20 percent chance of a security breach, then the 80 percent security is enough. However, if that is too much risk, then you will need to take more security measures, regardless of cost.

FOR FURTHER READING

Bond, Rebecca, Kevin Yeung-Kuen See, Carmen Ka Man Wong, and Yuk-Kuen Henry Chan. *Understanding DB2 9 Security*. IBM Press, 2006.

Clarke, Justin. *SQL Injection Attacks and Defense*. Syngress, 2009.

Davis, Michael. *Hacking Exposed Malware and Rootkits*. McGraw-Hill Osborne Media, 2009.

Gertz, Michael, and Sushil Jajodia. *Handbook of Database Security: Applications and Trends*. Springer, 2007.

Kenan, Kevin. *Cryptography in the Database: The Last Line of Defense*. Addison-Wesley Professional, 2005.

Litchfield, David. *The Oracle Hacker's Handbook: Hacking and Defending Oracle*. Wiley, 2007.

Litchfield, David, Chris Anley, John Heasman, and Bill Grindlay. *The Database Hacker's Handbook: Defending Database Servers*. Wiley, 2005.

Natan, Ron Ben. *Implementing Database Security and Auditing*. Digital Press, 2005.

Thuraisingham, Bhavani. *Database and Applications Security: Integrating Information Security and Data Management*. Auerbach Publications, 2005.

Welsh, Thomas R. *A Manager's Guide to Handling Information Security Incidents*. Auerbach, 2009.

Chapter 16

Data Warehousing

A *data warehouse* is a repository of transaction and nontransaction data used for querying, reporting, and corporate decision making. The data typically come from multiple sources. They are not used for day-to-day corporate operations, and therefore once data have been stored, the data generally don't change as much as the databases we have used as examples up to this point.

Because of the cost associated with creating and maintaining a data warehouse, only very large organizations establish their own. Tables can grow to hold millions of rows; storage capacities have now moved into the petabyte range. Full-fledged data warehouses therefore require mainframe processing capabilities or clusters of smaller servers.

> *Note:* Who has data warehouses that large? Wal-Mart, for one. By the third quarter of 2007, its data warehouse was 4 petabytes in size. To put that much data into perspective, consider that all the data in U.S. academic research libraries could be stored in 2 petabytes.

The software that manages a data warehouse is typically a relational DBMS.[1] However, data modeling is somewhat different because the goals of the data warehouse are different from an operational transaction-based database. The purpose of this chapter is to acquaint you with how data warehouses fit into the information strategy of large organizations, as well as how and why their designs differ from the relational data model as it has been presented throughout this book.

[1] Most data warehouse software is commercial. However, Infobright has released an open-source product. For details, see *http://pcworld.about.com/od/businesscenter/Infobright-Releases-Open-sourc.htm.*

SCOPE AND PURPOSE OF A DATA WAREHOUSE

To better understand the difference between a data warehouse (or its smaller sibling, a *data* mart), let's return to SmartMart, the retailer whose operational database was presented in Chapter 13. SmartMart's operational system performs the following data management activities for the organization:

- Tracks the location and stock level of inventory items
- Stores in-store and Web sales data, including promotions applied at the time of purchase
- Handles employee scheduling and work assignments (feeds into the payroll system)

The applications that run against the database answer queries such as the following:

- Where is a specific product in stock, and how many are available?
- What promotions apply to a product being purchased?
- What items were ordered on a specific Web order?
- Where and when is a specific employee working?

The queries provide information necessary for the day-to-day operations of the business. However, they aren't intended to provide the types of information that upper-level management needs to make strategic decisions, such as which products sell well in which parts of country, and to evaluate the results of previous decisions, such as which promotions generated a significant rise in sales and should be repeated. Although an operational database can provide summary reports for a district manager showing how the stores in her territory performed over various time periods, such reports are typically limited to only a few years, and the content of the reports is fixed when the report application is developed.

Strategic planning and reviews of the implementation of strategic plans must be able to "slice and dice" the data in a variety of ways. In other words, the queries need to allow data to be grouped by a variety of descriptions—sales by state, sales by promotion type, sales by zip code, sales by date, and so on—in an ad hoc manner. The data in an operational database may be offloaded to archival storage after a year or so to keep the database from becoming too large, but the data in a data warehouse are usually kept indefinitely.

Operational systems are usually accompanied by a variety of prewritten applications, such as those that run on point of sale terminals and management summary reports such as that described earlier. Very few users have ad hoc query access to the database. In contrast, there are few (if any) prewritten applications for the data in a data warehouse. Users work with a query tool that makes it possible to explore data groupings however they choose and however the data might lead them.

The primary activity performed using a data warehouse is *data mining*, through which a user analyzes data to look for patterns in the data. For example, data mining can identify which products sell best in which parts of a company's market. The results can be used to tailor marketing campaigns to the location or to shift inventory levels to better match demand.

A data mining activity conducted by the 7-Eleven Corporation, for example, indicated that around 8 PM in the evening, sales of beer and diapers went up. When you think about it, this makes sense: Fathers are sent to the convenience store to get diapers in the early evening, and while they are there, they decide to pick up some beer. The corporation relocated merchandise in the stores so that diapers were placed next to the beer coolers. As a result, beer sales went up significantly.

You have to be carefully when data mining, because statistically you are bound to find "something" sooner or later. For example, a data mining activity discovered that individuals with higher incomes tended to own more expensive houses than those with lower incomes. This type of fact is certainly true but of little practical use to anyone.

Because we continually add data to a data warehouse and rarely delete data, data warehouses tend to be extremely large databases, with tables containing millions and tens of millions of rows. The sheer volume of the data and the processing power needed to perform ad hoc queries against them require a mainframe rather than a desktop server. Although many desktop servers do rival mainframes in raw processing power, they can't handle the high volume of I/O that data warehouses require.

Note: Data marts, the smaller versions of full-fledged data warehouses, can and often run on desktop servers.

Most of the large data warehouses today use relational DBMSs such as DB/2 and Oracle, two of the few products capable of handling the data volume.

OBTAINING AND PREPARING THE DATA

Early in the evolution of data warehousing, general wisdom suggested that the data warehouse should store summarized data rather than the detailed data generated by operational systems. Experience has shown, however, that the data warehouse needs as much detail as the operational system. Storing the detail makes the data warehouse more flexible, allowing users to query in any way they choose. You can always produce summaries if you have the details, but if you only have summarized data, such as totals and averages, you can't recreate the detail should you need it.

Most, but not all, of the data come from operational systems. Data may also come from outside sources. For example, a company such as SmartMart might want to include demographic data about geographic regions and would be more likely to purchase such data from a government entity rather than attempt to collect those data itself.

Although a data warehouse may store much of the same data as an operational database, there are some significant differences in the way the data are handled:

- Operational databases are generally updated in real time. For example, a sales transaction is entered into the database as the sale occurs. In contrast, data warehouses are typically loaded in batches at regular intervals, such as once a day.
- Operational systems are interested in the latest or current values of many data elements, such as a customer's current address and telephone. Data warehouses, however, want to see how data have changed over time and therefore need to keep historical data. This means that there may be multiple values for a customer's address; each value will then be associated with the dates that the address was valid. (See the section "Dates and Data" later in this chapter for more information.)
- Missing values are acceptable in an operational database. For example, if the attribute color doesn't apply to an inventory item, then the value for that column in the product's row can simply be left null. However, nulls in a data warehouse can produce unpredictable or inaccurate results. Assume that we want to know the percentage of products sold over the Web that aren't shipped, such as software that is downloaded. Such items have no shipping weight and in the operational database, they produce no problems when the shipping weight column remains null. But when the data warehouse software is counting the number of items that aren't shipped,

the nulls aren't specific enough. A null might represent an item that isn't shipped but might also represent a shipped item for which we don't know the shipping weight. Therefore, nulls in a data warehouse need to be replaced with specific values, such as "doesn't ship" in our example of the nonshipping inventory items.

Data warehouses typically obtain their data from multiple sources, be they operational systems or data obtained from outside the company. This generates a significant problem when the data sources don't represent duplicated data in the same way. For example, two operational systems (say, one from sales and one from marketing) may use different transaction identifiers, although many transactions appear in both databases. The software that loads the data warehouse must recognize that the transactions are the same and merge the data into a single entity.

Before they are loaded into a data warehouse, data must be modified so that they match whatever format is used in the data warehouse. In addition, duplicated data must be identified and coalesced; nulls must be replaced with specific values. These activities, along with the procedures for cleaning the data (removing errors), are performed before the data are loaded.

The process of getting data into the data warehouse is known as *extract-transform-load* (ETL). It is virtually impossible to purchase complete software that will perform ETL processing because the sources of data for each data warehouse are so different. In most cases, such software must be custom-developed for each warehouse. Much of the expense in setting up a data warehouse therefore comes from the writing and testing of the ETL software. Running data through the ETL software and maintaining the ETL software also consume a large portion of IT staff effort in maintaining the data warehouse. This work takes place out of the user's sight in the "back room" where the data are prepared.

Note: When all or most of the data that go into a data warehouse come from within an organization, the changes necessary to make data formatting consistent can be made either in the feeder systems or during the ETL process. If the organization has many operational systems—and, in particular, is working with legacy software—then it may not be feasible to modify the operational systems. However, many organizations can benefit from a project that makes data formatting consistent across multiple databases. The effort to make the changes may be worthwhile in and of itself, even without the benefits to the ongoing ETL process.

DATA MODELING FOR THE DATA WAREHOUSE

Because the purpose of a data warehouse differs from that of an operational system, there are differences in the types of tables that make up the design. The most commonly used data model used in data warehouses is *dimensional modeling*. As you will see, it takes its basic precepts from the relational data model, such as tables and a variety of keys. However, the tables are generally not normalized. In fact, they are really only in first normal form because many tables contain data about multiple entities. They are nonetheless legal relations because they are two-dimensional tables without repeating groups.

Dimensional Modeling Basics

Dimensional modeling uses two major types of tables: *fact tables* and *dimension tables*. Fact tables hold numeric data that can be summarized as needed; dimension tables hold the descriptive criteria by which a user can organize the data. As a first example, consider Figure 16-1.

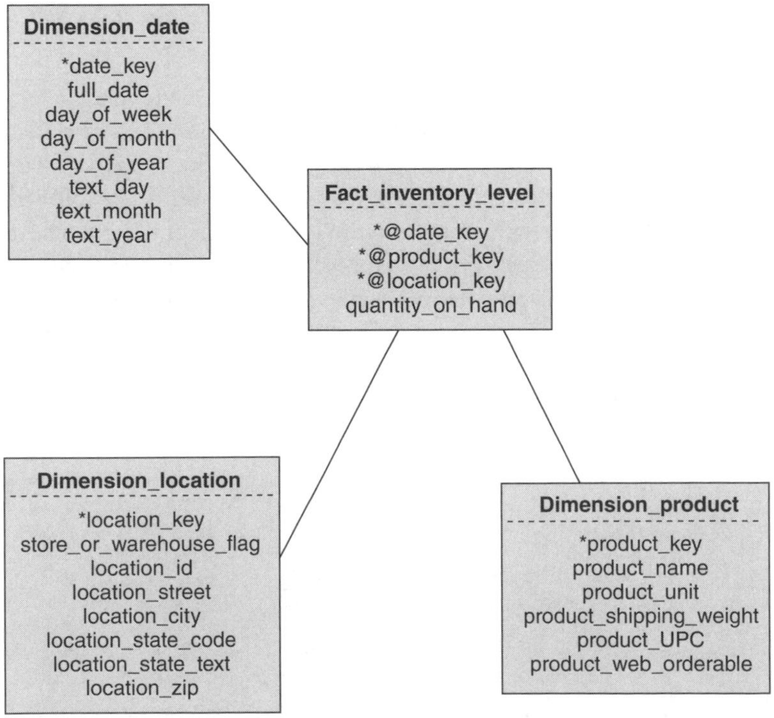

■ **FIGURE 16-1** Dimension and fact tables to capture inventory levels at a given point in time.

These tables support querying the data warehouse about inventory levels of products on any given date. They illustrate several of the characteristics of dimensional modeling that are different from pure relational design.

Natural keys, such as UPCs, ISBNs, or invoice numbers, are not used as all or part of the primary keys. Instead, each row in a table is given a unique integer key. These keys speed up joins between the fact and dimension tables. For example, the primary key of the dimension_date table is an arbitrary integer rather than the date itself. When the natural keys are included in a table, they are known as *deprecated dimensions*. (Although they are natural keys, they are not referenced by any foreign keys in the data warehouse.)

Fact tables contain foreign keys and data that can be summarized. For example, the fact_inventory_level table contains foreign keys to the date, location, and product dimension tables. The summarizable data item is the quantity in stock. The primary key of the table is the concatenation of two or more of the foreign keys (all of which are arbitrary integer keys). Data warehouses use referential integrity to ensure that the arbitrary foreign keys used in the fact tables reference existing dimension table rows. However, unlike true relational databases, the dimensional model foreign keys are always meaningless. Data warehouses also enforce non-null, unique primary keys.

Dimension tables contain descriptive data. The dimension_date table, for example, has its unique integer key along with attributes for the many ways in which a person might want to use a date in a query. There will be one row in a date dimension table for each date that might be used by any query against the data warehouse.

What can a user do with the dimensional model of the inventory levels? There are a variety of analyses that the model can satisfy, including the following:

- How do the inventory levels of product X vary from month to month?
- How do the inventory levels of product X vary from month to month and store to store?
- Which stores show the greatest/least inventory of product X after the winter holiday shopping season?
- Which products had more inventory in the warehouses for product X than in stores during the winter holiday season?
- Which warehouses had the total lowest inventory at the end of each month?

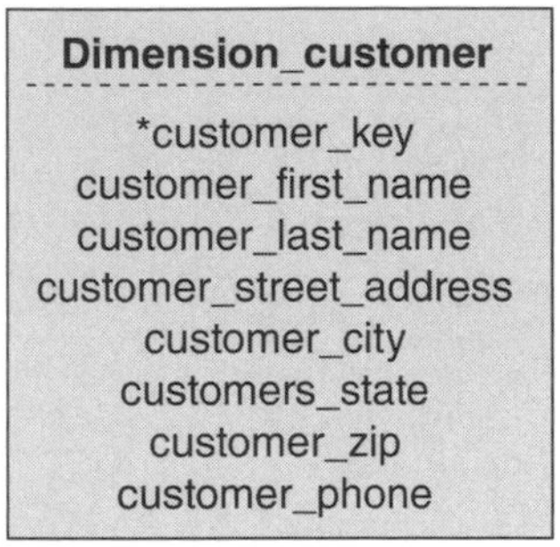

■ **FIGURE 16-2** A simple customer dimension.

Dates and Data

Unlike operational databases, data warehouses keep track of data changes over time. For example, the SmartMart operational database is concerned about inventory levels at the current time; inventory levels a week ago aren't particularly relevant. However, the design in Figure 16-1 takes a snapshot of inventory levels at some specified date. The data warehouse will therefore contain many snapshots, making possible the analysis of inventory levels over time.

In some circumstances, this can present some problems to the data warehouse designer, especially where human data such as addresses are concerned. Consider, for example, the simple customer dimension in Figure 16-2. The problem with this design is that over time, customers change their addresses and phone numbers. An analysis based on customer location during a specific time period may be incorrect if there are multiple addresses for the same customer.

One solution is to include only the most recent address for a customer in the data warehouse. However, this makes it impossible to analyze sales by location, given that the address in the related customer row may not have been the address when the sale was made. Another solution is to add the dates during which an address was valid to the customer dimension table, as was done in Figure 16-3. There will then be one row in the table for each address used by a customer when making purchases. Because each sale is related to the customer based on an arbitrary customer key rather than a concatenation of customer data, there will be no problem determining the correct address for a specific sale (see Figure 16-4). Queries based on location and date will then need to include logic to ensure that an address was valid during the time period of the analysis.

DATA WAREHOUSE APPLIANCES

During the early 1980s, when relational databases were supplanting those based on older data models, several hardware vendors tried to sell special-purpose computers called *database machines*. The idea was to take a minicomputer and use it to run just a DBMS (with an OS that was specifically tailored to that purpose). It would be connected to another computer in a master-slave relationship. Requests for database processing came first to the master machine, which passed them to the database machine. The database machine completed all database activity and sent the results back to the master computer, which in turn sent the data to the user.

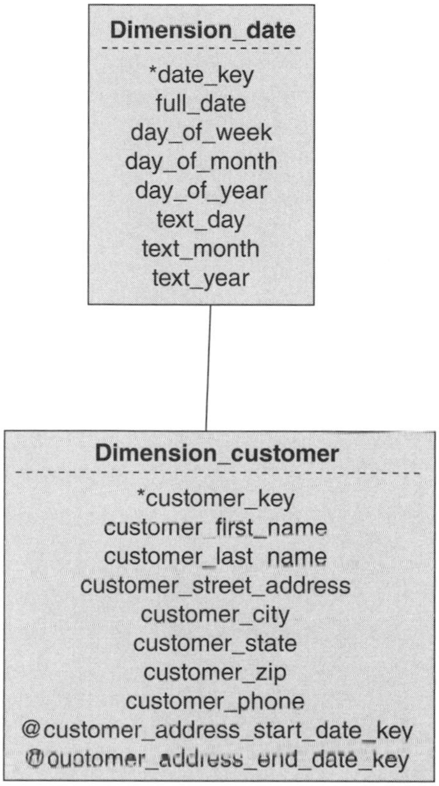

■ **FIGURE 16-3** Including valid dates for an address.

In theory, by offloading database processing to a dedicated machine, overall system performance (including database performance) would improve. In practice, however, only database applications that were severely CPU-bound showed significant performance improvements when running on a database machine. The overhead needed to move queries and data to and from the database machine erased any performance gains that occurred from relieving the master computer's CPU of database work. By 1990, almost no one had heard of a database machine.

The rise of data warehouses has seen the reappearance of computers dedicated to database work. Today the situation is very different because a dedicated database computer is really a special-purpose server that is connected directly to a network.

One such hardware configuration, for example, is being offered by Dell, EMC, and Oracle. The appliance includes a Dell rack server and

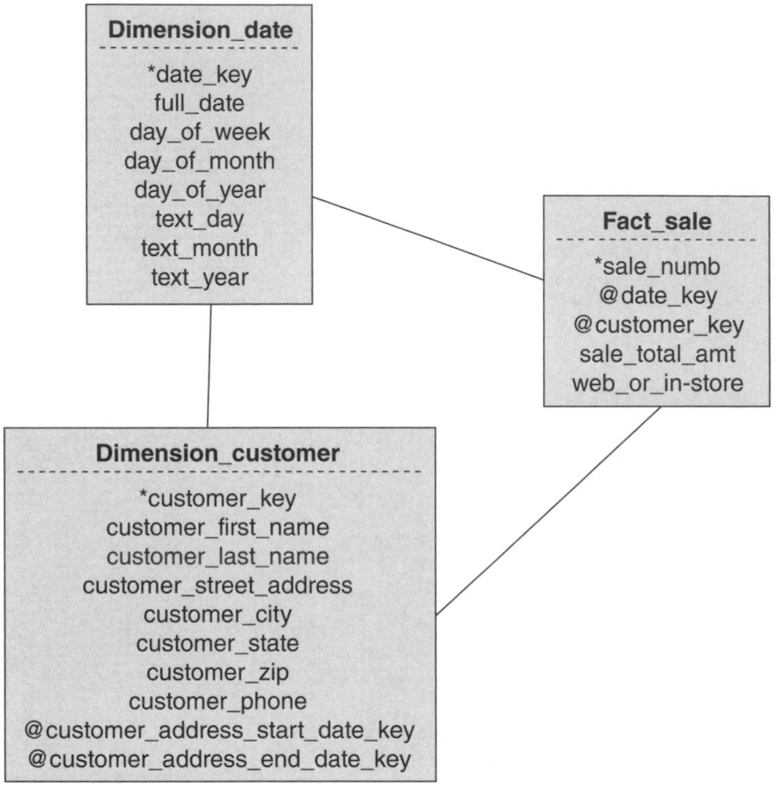

■ **FIGURE 16-4** Relating a customer with a time-sensitive address to a sale.

an EMC networked storage array loaded with Oracle's data warehouse software.[2] Terradata also provides a server-class data warehouse appliance (hardware and Terradata's data warehouse software) that scales to 170 Tb. It is designed for relatively small data warehouses and data marts.[3]

The benefit of such a preconfigured solution is that it simplifies setting up the data warehouse. An appliance such as Terradata's also means that the entire data warehouse infrastructure is supported by a single vendor, which many organizations prefer.

---

[2] For details, see *www.intelligententerprise.com/showArticle.jhtml?articleID=210603924*.
[3] More details can be found at *www.intelligententerprise.com/channels/business_intelligence/showArticle.jhtml?articleID=212101077*.

FOR FURTHER READING

Golfarelli, Matteo, and Stefano Rizzi. *Data Warehouse Design: Modern Principles and Methodologies*. McGraw-Hill Osborne, 2009.

Hammergren, Thomas C. *Data Warehousing for Dummies*, 2nd ed. For Dummies, 2009.

Imhoff, Claudia, Nicholas Galemmo, and Jonathan G. Geiger. *Mastering Data Warehouse Design: Relational and Dimensional Techniques*. Wiley, 2003.

Kimball, Ralph, and Joe Caserta. *The Data Warehouse ETL Toolkit: Practical Techniques for Extracting, Cleaning*. Wiley, 2004.

Kimball, Ralph, and Margy Ross. *The Data Warehouse Toolkit: The Complete Guide to Dimensional Modeling*, 2nd ed. Wiley, 2002.

Kimball, Ralph, Margy Ross, Warren Thornwaite, Joy Mundy, and Bob Becker. *The Data Warehouse Lifecycle Toolkit*, 2nd ed. Wiley, 2008.

Pyle, Dorian. *Data Preparation for Data Mining*. Morgan Kaufmann, 1999.

Rainardi, Vincent. *Building a Data Warehouse: With Examples in SQL Server*. Apress, 2007.

Tan, Pang-Ning, Michael Steinbach, and Vipin Kumar. *Introduction to Data Mining*. Addison-Wesley, 2005.

Westphal, Christopher. *Data Mining for Intelligence, Fraud & Criminal Detection: Advanced Analytics & Information Sharing Techniques*. CRC, 2008.

Chapter 17

Data Quality

As early as the 1960s, there was an expression in computing that most people in the field agreed was true: "Garbage in, garbage out." (It was abbreviated GIGO and was pronounced "guy-go.") We worried about the effect of the quality of input data on the output of our programs. In the intervening years, during the rise of databases, GIGO was largely forgotten. Today, however, with some data warehouses approaching a petabyte of data, the quality of that data has become extremely important once again.

Exactly what do we mean by "data quality"? To be useful, the data in a database must be accurate, timely, and available when needed. Data quality ensures the accuracy and timeliness of data and, as you will see, it is much easier to ensure data quality *before* data get into a database than after they are stored.

> *Note:* Much of what we do to ensure data quality is just plain common sense. In fact, you may find yourself saying, "Well, that's obvious" or "Of course you would do that" as you read. The truth is, however, that as logical as many data quality procedures seem to be, some organizations simply overlook them.

WHY DATA QUALITY MATTERS

Why do we care so much about data quality? Because we need to be confident that what we retrieve from a database is reliable. We will be making both operational and strategic decisions based on what we retrieve from a database. The quality of those decisions is directly related to the quality of the data that underlies them.

Consider, for example, the decisions that a buyer makes for the clothing department of a retail chain such as SmartMart. Choices of what to stock for the winter holiday shopping season are made nine to 12 months in advance, based on what sold the previous year and the buyer's knowledge of clothing styles. The buyer therefore queries the operational database to create a report showing how much of each style sold at each store and on the Web. She can see that jeans sell well in one particular store in a region, while another store sells more dress pants. She will then adjust her orders to reflect those sales patterns.

However, if the sales data are incorrect, she runs the risk of ordering the wrong type of merchandise for each store. SmartMart can certainly move inventory from one store another, but during the holiday shopping season, customers are often unable to wait for merchandise to arrive. They will either purchase a different item or go to another retailer. In the long run, SmartMart will lose sales.

We can probably come up with hundreds of scenarios in which inaccurate data cause problems for businesses: customers who can't be contacted because of out-of-date phone numbers or e-mail addresses, orders missing items that are never shipped, customers who aren't notified of recalls, and so on. The bottom line is that when we have problem data, business suffers.

Note: It is often better to have a database application crash than it is to have a report that contains inaccurate results. In the former case, it's clear that you have a problem; in the latter case, there may be no indication that the report is invalid, so you'll go ahead and use it, bad data and all.

Data quality problems arise from a wide range of sources and have many remedies. Throughout the rest of this chapter we will look at a variety of data quality ills, how they are likely to occur, and what you can do to prevent them, or at least minimize their occurrence.

RECOGNIZING AND HANDLING INCOMPLETE DATA

One source of data quality problems is missing data. There are two general sources: data that are never entered into the database and data that are entered but deleted when they shouldn't be.

Missing Rows

Missing rows occur for a number of reasons. One common reason is that someone has been using low-level data manipulation tools to "maintain" the database and in the process either deleted rows or missed rows when copying data from one table to another.

> *Note:* The ability to manipulate rows in this way with a low-level tool violates one of Codd's rules for a relational database, which states that it should not be possible to circumvent integrity rules with low-level tools.

Missing rows can be very hard to detect if their absence doesn't violate referential integrity constraints. For example, it's impossible to detect that an item is missing from an order—until the customer contacts you about not receiving the item. It's not necessarily obvious, however, where the error has occurred. Any of the following might have happened:

- An item was lost in transmission from the customer's computer to the vendor's computer (Internet order), or a customer service representative didn't enter the item (phone or mail order).
- An error in one of the vendor's application programs missed entering the row.
- Someone maintaining the database with a low-level data manipulation tool accidentally deleted the item.

It's a relatively easy matter to enter the missing item and ship it to the customer. But what is to prevent the error from occurring again? To do that, we have to find the cause of the error and fix it, and because the possible causes are so diverse, it will be a long, difficult process. Ultimately, we can fix a bug in an application program and put policies in place that control the use of maintenance languages. We can even conduct additional training for data entry personnel to make them more careful when they enter ordered items. We cannot, however, control packets lost on the Internet.

Missing Column Data

SQL is based on what we call three-valued logic. The result of a logical comparison between data and a search criterion can be true, false, or maybe. The maybe occurs when a column contains null because no determination can be made. Sometimes nulls are harmless—we don't care that the data are missing—but in other situations we wish we had the data. Currently there is no way to distinguish between the two types of null, but some database theorists have proposed that DBMSs should support four-valued logic: true, false, maybe and it's okay, and maybe and it's not okay. It's the nulls that fall into the last category that cause problems with missing data. For example, assume that a customer table has a column for the customer's country. If the customer is in the country where the company is based, a null in the country column doesn't really matter. However, if the customer is in another country, then we need to know the country, and leaving that value null leads to problems of undeliverable marketing mailings.

Missing column data can be prevented relatively easily by disallowing nulls in those columns that must have values.

Missing Primary Key Data

A relational database with tight integrity controls prevents data from entering a database because part of a primary key is null. From the viewpoint of data retrieval, this is a positive result because it ensures that every piece of data that makes it into the database is retrievable. However, the lack of a primary key may mean that a set of data are never stored in the database, despite the data being important to the business operating the database.

One situation in which this problem occurs is when entities that are only at the "one" end of relationships have no obvious primary key attribute and no arbitrary key has been created. The primary key is therefore created from the concatenation of two or more columns. For example, if an employee entity has no employee number attribute, then a primary key might be constructed of first name, last name, and phone number. If a phone number isn't available, the data can't be entered because there isn't a complete primary key; the data are never stored. In this case, the solution lies in the database design. Those "top" entities that do not have inherent primary keys should be given arbitrary primary keys. Those arbitrary keys then filter down through the design as parts of foreign keys and ensure that primary key values are available for all instances of all entities.

RECOGNIZING AND HANDLING INCORRECT DATA

Incorrect data are probably the worst type of problems to detect and prevent. Often the data aren't detected until someone external to an organization makes a complaint. Determining how the error occurred is equally difficult because sometimes the problems are one of a kind.

Wrong Codes

Relational databases make significant use of coded data. The codes are defined in tables related to the tables where they are used through primary key–foreign key relationships. For example, we often store the names of U.S. states as two-letter abbreviations and then use a table that contains the abbreviation and the full state name for validation and output (when the full state name is needed).

Coding, however, is a two-edged sword. Consider the following scenario: A company divides its products into categories, each of which is represented by a three-letter code. The codes are stored in a table with the code and a description of the product category (e.g., PEN and "custom imprinted pens," WCP and "white cups," and so on). When the company decides to carry a new product, the application program used by the staff allows the user to make up a code and enter the code and its description. To make things easier for the user, the user doesn't need to explicitly enter the new code. During data entry, the application captures a failed referential integrity check, automatically asks the user for the code description, and creates the new row in the code table. The problem here, however, is if the user mistypes a code for an existing product, the application handles it as a new product. Therefore, many codes for the same product could exist in the database. Searches on the correct code will not retrieve rows containing the incorrect codes.

The solution is to restrict the ability to enter new codes. In some organizations, only database administrators have the right to modify the master code tables. If a new product needs to be entered, the DBA assigns and enters the code prior to a clerical worker entering product data. Application programs then retrieve the list of codes and make it available to data entry personnel.

Wrong Calculations

One of the decisions that a database designer makes is whether to include calculated values in a database or to compute them as needed on the fly. The decision depends on many factors, including the overhead to perform the calculations and how often they are used. We often, for example, compute and store line costs in a line items table:

```
line_items (order_numb, item_numb, quantity_ordered,
  line_cost)
```

The line cost is computed by retrieving the cost for each item from the items table (item number is the foreign key) and then multiplying it by the quantity ordered. The lookup of the price is quick and the computation is simple.

What happens, however, if the formula for computing the line cost is incorrect? Primarily, the total amount of the order (which is also often stored) will be incorrect. It is much more likely that someone will notice that the order total is incorrect, but it may require a bit more investigation to find the specific error and track down its source.

Many of the automatic calculations performed by a DBMS when data are modified are performed using *triggers*, small procedures stored in the database whose executions are triggered when specific actions occur (for example, storing a new row). An error in an automatic calculation therefore means examining not only application programs but all relevant database triggers. Nonetheless, once an error in a computation has been identified and corrected, it is unlikely that exactly the same problem will occur again.

Wrong Data Entered into the Database

We humans are prone to typing errors. Despite all our best efforts at integrity constraints, we are still at the mercy of simple typos. If a user types "24 West 325th Street" instead of "325 West 24th Street," you can be sure that the customer won't receive his or her order. The transposition of a pair of letters or digits in a post code or zip code is all it takes to separate a customer from his or her purchase!

The typographical error is the hardest error to detect because we rarely know about it until a customer complains. The fix is usually easy: edit the data and replace the error with the correct values. However, determining how the error occurred is even tougher than finding the source of missing rows. Was it simply a one-time typing error, in which case an apology usually solves the problem, or is there some underlying application code problem that is causing errors?

The best strategy for separating typos from system errors is to keep logs of errors. Such logs should include the table, row, and column in which the error was detected, when the error was reported, and who was responsible for entering the erroneous data. The intent here is not to blame an employee but to make it possible to see patterns that may exist in the errors. When multiple errors are in the same column in the same table, the evidence points toward an underlying system problem. When many errors are made by the same employee, the evidence points to an employee who needs more training. However, a random pattern in the errors points to one-of-a-kind typographical errors. (Whether the random errors are at a level that suggests the need for more training for all data entry personnel depends, of course, on the organization and the impact of the errors on the organization.)

Violation of Business Rules

A business often has rules that can be incorporated into a database so that they can be enforced automatically when data are modified. For example, a book club that bills its customers after shipping may place a limit on customer accounts. The orders table includes a trigger that adds the amount of a newly stored order to the total amount owed in the customer table. If the customer table has no constraint to limit the value in the total amount owed column, a customer could easily run up a balance beyond what the company allows.

It is certainly possible to enforce such constraints through application programs, but there is no guarantee that all data modification will be made using the application program. In all cases where business rules can be implemented as database constraints, you should do so. This relieves application programmers of the responsibility of enforcing constraints, simplifies application program logic, and ensures that the constraints are always enforced.

RECOGNIZING AND HANDLING INCOMPREHENSIBLE DATA

Incomprehensible data are data we can't understand. Unlike incorrect data, it is relatively easy to spot incomprehensible data, although finding the source of the problem may be as difficult as it is with incorrect data.

Multiple Values in a Column

Assume that you are working with a personnel database. The dependents table has the following structure:

```
Dependents (employee_ID, child_first_name,
  child_birth_date)
```

The intent, of course, is that there will be one row in the table for each dependent of each employee. However, when you issue a query to retrieve the dependents of employee number 12, you see the following:

Employee_ID	child_first_name	child_birth_date
12	Mary, John, Sam	1-15-00

Clearly, something is wrong with these data. As we discussed earlier in this book, putting multiple values in the same column not only violates the precepts of the relational data model but makes it impossible to associate data values accurately. Does the birth date apply to the first, second, or third dependent? Or does it apply to all three? (Triplets, perhaps?) There is no way to know definitively from just the data in the database.

Character columns are particularly vulnerable to multiple data values, especially where names are concerned, because they must be left without constraints other than a length. You can't attach constraints that forbid blanks or commas because those characters may be part of a legitimate name. The only solution to this type of problem is user education: You must teach the people who are doing the data entry that multiple values mean multiple rows.

Orphaned Foreign Keys

Much of the querying we do of a relational database involves joins between primary and foreign keys. If we delete all of the foreign key references to a primary key, then the row containing the primary key simply doesn't appear in the result of a join. The same thing occurs if the primary key referenced by a foreign key is missing: The rows with the foreign keys don't appear in the result of a join. The former may be a problem, but the latter *always* is. For example, a customer with no orders in a database may be just fine, but orders that can't be joined to a customer table to provide customer identification will be a major headache.

A relational database must prevent these "orphaned" foreign keys from existing in the database, and the solution should be provided when the foreign keys are defined. As you will remember from Chapter 9, the definition of a foreign key can contain an ON DELETE clause.

Its purpose is to specify what should happen to the row containing a foreign key when its primary key reference is deleted. The DBMS can forbid the deletion, set foreign key values to null, or delete the foreign key row. Which you choose, of course, depends on the specific needs of your database environment. Nonetheless, an ON DELETE clause should be set for every foreign key so that orphans never occur.

RECOGNIZING AND HANDLING INCONSISTENT DATA

Inconsistent data are those that are correct and make sense, but when they are duplicated throughout the database and/or organization, they are not the same. We normalize relations to help eliminate duplicated data, but in large organizations there are often multiple databases that contain information about the same entities. For example, a retail company might have one database with customer information for use in sales and another for use in customer service. If the data are to be consistent, then the name and address of a customer must be stored in exactly the same way in both databases.

> *Note:* The best way to handle inconsistent data is the same regardless of the type of inconsistent data. The solution is therefore presented at the end of this section.

Inconsistent Names and Addresses

When names and addresses are repeated throughout an organization, it's tough to keep the data consistent. By their very nature, name and address columns have few constraints because the variation of the data in those columns is so great. Adding to the problem is the difficulty of detecting when such data are inconsistent: You rarely know until someone complains or you have to match data between databases.

Inconsistent Business Rules

Some business rules can be implemented as database constraints. When there are multiple data stores within an organization, those constraints may not be applied consistently. Assume, for example, that the highest salary paid by an organization is $125,000 annually. There is a central personnel database and smaller personnel databases at each of six satellite offices. The central database contains all personnel data, but the satellite databases contain data only for the site at which they are installed. The satellite databases were designed and installed at the same time. The salary column in the employee table has the correct CHECK clause to limit the salary value. However, IT ran into a problem with that check clause at headquarters because the CEO's salary was $1,500,000. Their solution was simply to modify the check clause to allow for the higher salary. The CEO is an exception to the rule, but once the CHECK clause was modified, *anyone* who was entered into the central database could be given a higher salary without violating a table constraint.

Now assume that the CEO hires a new manager for one of the satellite offices at a salary of $150,000. Someone on the Human Resources staff enters the new employee's information into the database. Because the constraint on the salary limit has been removed, the data are stored. However, when the update is propagated to the appropriate satellite database, the constraint on the employee table prevents the update. The organization is left with a distributed database in an inconsistent state.

Inconsistent Granularity

Granularity is the level of detail at which data are stored in a database. When the same data are represented in multiple databases, the granularity may differ. As an example, consider the following table:

```
order_lines (order_numb, item_numb, quantity, cost)
order_lines (order_numb, item_numb, cost)
```

Both tables contain a cost attribute, but the meaning and use of the columns are different. The first relation is used in the sales database and includes details about how many of each item were ordered and the amount actually charged for each item (which may vary from what is in the items table). The second is used by marketing. Its cost attribute is actually the line cost (quantity × cost from the sales database). Two attributes with the same name therefore have different granularities. Any attempt to combine or compare values in the two attributes will be meaningless.

This type of problem needs to be handled at an organizational level rather than at the single database level. See the last part of this section for details.

Unenforced Referential Integrity

In the preceding section we discussed the problem of orphaned foreign keys. They represent a violation of referential integrity that occurs *after* the data have been stored and can be handled with strict foreign key definitions when the tables are created. However, what happens if foreign key constraints are never added to a table definition? Foreign keys may then be orphaned as soon as they are added to the database because there is nothing to ensure that they reference existing primary keys.

As you might expect, the solution to this problem is straightforward: Ensure that referential integrity constraints are present for all foreign keys. Make it a policy that everyone who has the right to create tables in the database must follow this rule.

Inconsistent Data Formatting

There are many ways to represent the same data, such as telephone numbers and dates. Do you surround an area code with parentheses, or do you put a hyphen after it? Do you store the area code in the same column as the rest of the phone number, or is it stored in its own column? Do dates have two- or four-digit years, and which comes first, the month, the day, or the year? How are months represented (numbers, codes, full words)? There are so many variations for telephone numbers and dates that unless there is some standard set for formatting throughout an organization's data management, it may be nearly impossible for queries to match values across databases.

Preventing Inconsistent Data on an Organizational Level

There is no easy solution to preventing inconsistent data through an organization. It requires planning at the organizational level and a commitment by all those who are responsible for databases to work together and, above all, to communicate.

A large organization with multiple databases should probably be involved in *data administration*, a process distinct from *database administration*. Data administration keeps track of where data are used throughout an organization and how the data are represented. It provides oversight for data at an organizational level rather than at the database level. When the time comes to use the data in a database or application program, the developers can consult the *metadata* (data about data) that have been identified through the data administration process and then determine how the data should be represented to ensure consistency.[1]

It is important to keep in mind, however, that even the best data administration can't totally protect against inconsistent names and addresses. Although organizational metadata can specify that the abbreviation for street is always "St." and that the title for a married woman is always stored as "Mrs.," there is no way to ensure that names and addresses are always spelled consistently. Human error will always be a factor. When that occurs, the best strategy may be just to smile sweetly to the complaining customer and fix the problem.

EMPLOYEES AND DATA QUALITY

One recurrent theme throughout this chapter is that many data quality problems are the result of human error. They may be attributable to a single individual or to a group of employees as a whole. But how do you know? The database needs to keep track of who enters data. The easiest way to implement such audit trails is to add a column for an employee ID to each table for which you want to keep data entry data. Assuming that an employee must log in to the system with a unique user name before running any application programs, the application programs can tag rows with the employee ID without any employee intervention.

If you need to keep more detailed modification information—in particular maintaining an audit trail for each modification of a table—then you need a further modification of the database design. First, you give each row in each table a unique numeric identifier:

```
customer (customer_numb, customer_first_name,
  customer_last_name, customer_street,
  customer_city, customer_zip, customer_phone,
  row_ID)
```

The row ID is an integer that is assigned when a row is created. It is merely a sequence number that has no relationship to the row's posi-

[1] A discussion of data administration is beyond the scope of this book. If you would like to learn more, see the Inmon title in the For Further Reading section at the end of this chapter.

tion in the table or to the customer number. The row ID continues to get larger as rows are entered to the table; row IDs for deleted rows are not reused.

Note: Should a table be old enough or large enough to run out of row IDs, row IDs for deleted rows can be reused, or row IDs can be reassigned to the entire table in a contiguous sequence (perhaps using a larger storage space, such as a 64-bit rather than a 32-bit integer). This is a rather lengthy process because all foreign keys that reference those row IDs must be updated as well.

The design must then include a table to hold the audit trail:

```
customer_mods (row_ID, modification_date,
  column_modified, employee_ID)
```

A search of this table will indicate who made a change to which column on which date in the customer table. Alternatively, row IDs can be unique throughout the database (rather than within each table) and all audit information kept in one table:

```
modifications (table_name, row_ID, modification_date,
  column_modified, employee_ID)
```

An even more detailed audit trail could include columns for the old value in the modified column and the new value.

FOR FURTHER READING

Arkady, Maydancik. *Data Quality Assessment*. Technics Publications, 2007.

Batini, Carlo, and Monica Scannapieco. *Data Quality: Concepts, Methodologies and Techniques*. Springer, 2006.

English, Larry P. *Improving Data Warehouse and Business Information Quality: Methods for Reducing Costs and Increasing Profits*. Wiley, 1999.

Fisher, Craig, Eitel Lauria, Shobha Chengalur-Smith, and Richard Wang. *An Introduction to Data Quality*. M.I.T. Information Quality Program, 2006.

Inmon, William H., Bonnie O'Neil, and Lowell Fryman. *Business Metadata: Capturing Enterprise Knowledge*. Morgan Kaufmann, 2007.

McGilvray, Danette. *Executing Data Quality Projects: Ten Steps to Quality Data and Trusted Information*. Morgan Kaufmann, 2008.

Olson, Jack E. *Data Quality: The Accuracy Dimension*. Morgan Kaufmann, 2003.

Redman, Thomas C. *Data Quality: The Field Guide*. Digital Press, 2001.

Chapter 18

XML

XML (Extensible Markup Language) is a cousin of HTML that has become important as a data management tool. XML documents are text files marked with tags that indicate the structure of the content of the files. XML is software and platform independent, which means that it provides an excellent environment for transferring data between database systems.

XML has been accepted by the Word Wide Web Consortium (W3C) and has become a de facto standard for cross-platform data transfers. Because it is an open source specification, a number of application programming languages have been built on top of it, such as XHTML, RSS, MathML, GraphML, Scalable Vector Graphics, and MusicXML.

Major DBMSs handle XML in two ways. Some store XML documents as binary objects. The documents are not searchable and therefore may be accompanied by keywords assigned to the documents for search purposes. The documents are stored and retrieved as complete units. Other DBMSs store XML data in standard character columns and then generate complete documents for output. Although incorporating XML still isn't a "typical" relational DBMS activity, its use is expanding, and you may well encounter an organization that uses it.

XML SYNTAX

Like HTML, XML documents contain tags that identify elements in the document. However, each markup language has a different purpose. HTML tags communicate with a Web browser, telling the browser how to display the page. XML tags, however, identify data elements and how they are related to one another. HTML tags are defined as part of the language specification. In contrast, almost all XML tags are defined by the person or software writing the XML.

```
<?xml version="1.0"?>
<!Product entity data!>

<entities>
   <product>
      <UPC>1234567890123</UPC>
      <manufacturer>Soup Company</manufacturer>
      <product_name>Pea soup</product_name>
      <product_unit>can</product_unit>
      <shipping_weight>16 oz.</shipping_weight>
      <product_image>http://private.smartmart.com/images/
         1234567890123.jpg</product_image>
      <web_orderable>F</web_orderable>
   </product>
</entities>
```

■ **FIGURE 18-1** An XML instance of the SmartMart product entity.

To see how it works, consider the XML in Figure 18-1, which contains data for an instance of SmartMart's Product entity. Notice first that tags are surrounded by < and >, just as they are in HTML. Most tags are paired, with the closing tag beginning with /. The data are text. (Because there is no provision for storing binary images, the product image is supplied as the URL of a server where all the images are stored. An application program will be needed to resolve the URL, retrieve the image file, and store the image in the database.)

The tags in Figure 18-1 are also nested. The <entities> tag is known as the *root tag* because it represents the top of the tag hierarchy. The <product> tag is nested underneath it, with all of the product's attributes nested inside the product. Nested paired tags work just like parentheses in programming languages: The last opened tag must also be the first tag closed. To transfer all of SmartMart's product data from one database to another, an XML document would contain multiple <product> tags, each with different data. Elements that have no data can be handled as solo tags that contain only an opening tag that ends with /.

Elements can also have attributes. In this case, the term is used somewhat differently from how it is used in a database environment. Here it is used for data values that apply to a specific element as "children" of that element. In Figure 18-2, for example, you can see a modified version of the product entity instance. The product entity and shipping weight elements now have attributes.

XML also supports something known as an entity that has nothing to do with the entities represented in a database. Instead, XML entities are placeholders for special characters that have meaning to an XML parser, making it possible to include those characters in data. The five predefined entities can be found in Table 18-1. Additional entities can be created as needed.

```
<?xml version="1.0"?>
<!Product entity data!>

<entities>
   <product>
      <UPC>1234567890123</UPC>
      <manufacturer>Soup Company</manufacturer>
      <product_name>Pea soup</product_name>
      <product_unit pack_size="48"
         packaging="carton">can</product_unit>
      <shipping_weight unit=oz">16</shipping_weight>
      <product_image>http://private.smartmart.com/images/
         1234567890123.jpg</product_image>
      <web_orderable>F</web_orderable>
   </product>
</entities>
```

FIGURE 18-2 The XML instance from Figure 18-1 with element attributes.

Table 18-1 XML Predefined Entities

Character	Entity
&	&
<	<
>	>
'	'
"	"

XML DOCUMENT CORRECTNESS

XML documents may be examined by XML *conforming parsers* to determine if they meet basic standards for correctness. At the lowest level, an XML document needs to be *well formed*, in which case it adheres to the basic syntax rules, such as having a </> tag for each < > tag. XML documents that are *valid* also conform to rules governing their content. For example, a valid document contains only those elements that appear in a related XML schema. (See the next section for more information.)

Well-formed documents must meet a number of rules, including the following:

- Elements that have content must have a start tag and an end tag (*<tag_name>data</tag_name>*).
- Elements that may be empty can use a single tag as a shorthand for the paired tags required by elements that have content (*<tag_name/>*).
- Attribute values must be surrounded by quotes (either single or double).
- Characters used to delimit items in an XML document must be represented within data by entities.
- Like parentheses and braces in computer programs, tags can be nested but must not overlap. In other words, the last opened tag must be the next tag closed.

> *Note:* Conforming parsers for checking the correctness of XML documents are available as stand-alone tools. However, XML-enabled Web browsers such as Firefox can also do the job. Simply attempt to open the XML document in the browser. If the browser can't interpret the document, it will let you know.

XML SCHEMAS

The syntax in Figures 18-1 and 18-2 is designed to transfer data, but it isn't suited for defining the structure of an XML document. XML has therefore been extended to support several schema languages. XML schemas are intended to specify the structure of XML documents that contain data. Documents can then be validated against the schema to ensure that they adhere to the format that the DBMS expects. XML schemas can also be used to specify the format for an XML document generated as output by a DBMS.

> *Note:* XML schemas are the more modern equivalent of XML Data Type Definitions (DTDs).

The first schema language to be recommended by the W3C was XML Schema, an example of which appears in Figure 18-3. As you can see, the product relation is defined as a complex data type.

Keep in mind that an XML schema is not precisely the same as a relational schema, although you could include the same structural elements (and the same relationships) in an XML schema as you do in a relational schema. An XML schema specifies the layout of data in a text document. In contrast, a relational schema specifies the structure of relations and constraints on those relations. XML schemas, although able to include elements that represent primary and foreign keys, have no provision for constraints on data. If constraints are to be applied, they must be enforced once the data have been loaded into a relational database as normal relational data rather than XML documents.

```
<?xml version="1.0" encoding="utf-8" ?>
<xs:schema elementFormDefault="qualified" xmlns:xs="http://www.w3.org/2001/XMLSchema">
  <xs:element name="product">
    <xs:complexType>
      <xs:sequence>
        <xs:element name="UPC" type="xs:string" />
      <xs:element name="manfacturer" type="xs:string" />
        <xs:element name="product_name" type="xs:string" />
        <xs:element name="product_unit" type="xs:string" />
        <xs:element name="shipping_weight" type="xs:string" />
        <xs:element name="product_image" type="xs:string" />
      <xs:element name="web_orderable" type="xs:string" />
    </xs:sequence>
  </xs:complexType>
</xs:element>
```

■ **FIGURE 18-3** An XML schema definition for the product entity.

XML SUPPORT IN RELATIONAL DBMSS

Although XML itself is defined by a standard, the way in which a specific DBMS supports XML is not. To give you an overview of the nature and extent of such support, this section looks at DB2 and Oracle, two of the most widely used DBMSs.

DB2

DB2 supports the storage of XML with an XML column data type. A data type of XML can be assigned to a column in any relation and can then store one XML document in that column for each row of the table. The syntax for including an XML column in a table is the same as creating a table using any other SQL data type (for example, Figure 18-4).

To store a document, an application program sends the text (for example, Figure 18-5) to the DB2 server. The server then checks the document to see that it is correct (well formed and valid) and then converts it into a hierarchical representation such as that in Figure 18-6. This hierarchy is stored separately from the rest of the table,

```
CREATE TABLE stocked_products
(
    store_numb int PRIMARY KEY,
    UPC char (13) PRIMARY KEY,
    Product_details XML);
```

■ **FIGURE 18-4** The definition of a table for DB2, including an XML column.

```
<product_details>
    <product_name>gel pen</product_name>
    <product_dept>Office Supplies</product_dept>
    <product_desc>
        <color>black</color>
        <unit>box</unit>
        <numb_per_pack>12</numb_per_pack>
    </product_desc>
</product_details>
```

■ **FIGURE 18-5** Sample XML for loading into a DB2 XML column.

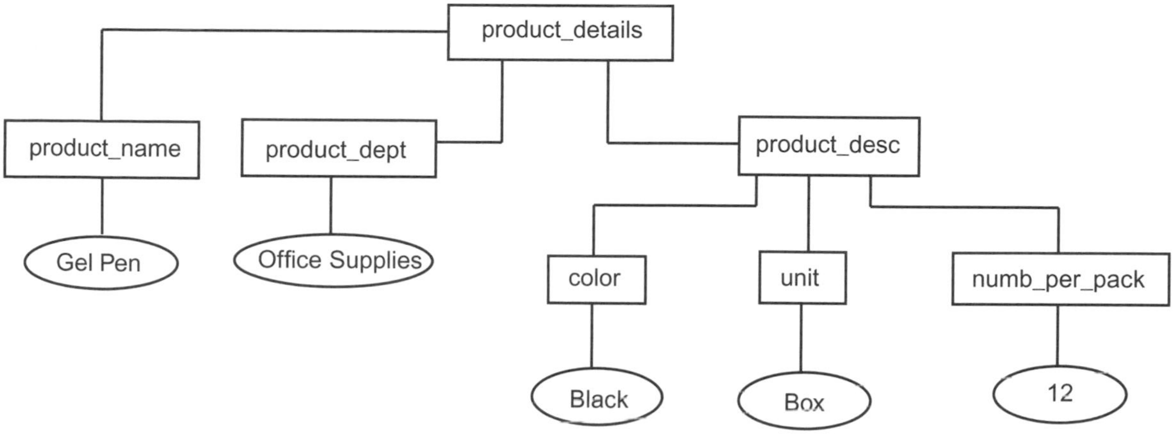

■ **FIGURE 18-6** The hierarchical representation of and instance of the XML column specified in Figure 18-5.

although an internal data structure links the relational and XML storage structures.

DB2's XML column data type does not need to be linked to an XML schema. However, schemas can be applied to documents to check their correctness.

As you know, indexing can significantly speed up database query performance. XML documents, however, bury their data within the document (and thus within a single DB2 column). The hierarchical storage structure, such as that in Figure 18-6, however, makes indexing possible. To create an index on a specific element, the user must supply the path through the hierarchy to reach the desired data. For example, to create an index on the product name from Figure 18-6, someone might type:

```
CREATE INDEX idx_product_name ON products
  (product_details) GENERATE KEY USING XML PATTERN
  '/product_details/product_name' AS SQL VARCHAR
  (50);
```

Notice that the key for the index is indicated by the path to the data element and that it must be given an SQL data type for use in the index. If a value in an XML document can't be transformed into the index data type, the value won't be included in the index.

DB2 supports manipulation of XML data through two extensions: SQL/XML and XQuery. Both are query languages, although support for data modification using XQuery is still under development.[1] SQL/XML is an extension of the SQL standard, although, as with most DBMSs, the implementation is proprietary. XQuery is also an open standard.

SQL/XML contains extensions to standard SQL to retrieve either entire XML documents or specific elements from a document. When referencing specific elements in an XML document, you include the path through the document storage hierarchy to reach the element, just as it was done with creating an index on a single data element.

Oracle

Oracle provides three storage options for XML documents:

- Store an entire XML document as a character large object (CLOB). Because the document is stored as a whole, it cannot be validated against an XML schema and provides slow performance on relational queries. CLOB storage also uses the most disk space.
- Parse the document with an XML schema (including validation) and store the data in binary form. This is the easiest storage method to use, and although its performance on relational queries isn't optimal, it does outperform CLOB storage.
- Store parsed data in an object-relational format, a combination of relational and object-oriented data modeling. The result is slow performance when an XML document is added to the database but the best query performance and minimal use of disk space.

Like DB2, Oracle provides a data type for a column in a relation to store XML data (XMLType). An XMLType column in a relation can accept data from a previously stored CLOB, a character column (VARCHAR2), a correctly formatted SQL INSERT statement, or the query of another XMLType column.

An SQL INSERT statement to add a row to the stocked products table in Figure 18-4 might look like Figure 18-7. Notice that the XML specification is preceded by the data type to alert the DBMS that what follows is in XML format.

Oracle's SQL implementation allows querying of XMLType columns using the standard SQL SELECT command. The product also supports

[1] At the time this book was written, the most recent update of the XQuery standard seemed to be from August 2008. You can find it at *www.w3.org/TR/xqupdate/*.

```
INSERT INTO stocked_products
{
    3,
    '1010101010101',
    XMLType (<product_details>
        <product_name>gel pen</product_name>
        <product_dept>Office Supplies</product_dept>
        <product_desc>
            <color>black</color>
            <unit>box</unit>
            <numb_per_pack>12</numb_per_pack>
        </product_desc>
        </product_details>)
);
```

■ **FIGURE 18-7** Using SQL to insert data into an Oracle XMLType column.

SQL/XML for querying relational data to produce XML documents as output and provides an XQuery implementation.

FOR FURTHER READING

Chaudhri, Akaml B, Awais Rashid, and Roberto Zicari. *XML Data Management: Native XML and XML-Extended Database Systems*. Addison-Wesley Professional, 2003.

IBM Redbooks. *Integrating XML with DB2 XML Extender and DB2 Text Extender*. IBM, 2000.

Melton, Jim, and Stephen Buxton. *Querying XML: XQuery, XPath, and SQL/XML in Context*. Morgan Kaufmann, 2006.

Powell, Galvin. *Beginning XML Databases*. Wrox, 2006.

Quin, Liam. *Open Source XML Database Toolkit: Resources and Techniques for Improved Development*. Wiley, 2000.

Scardina, Mark, Ben Chang, and Jinyu Wang. *Oracle Database 10g XML & SQL*. McGraw-Hill Osborne Media, 2004.

Williams, Kevin, Michael Brudage, Patrick Dengler, Jeff Gabriel, Andy Hoskinson, Michael Kay, Thomas Maxwell, Marcelo Ochoa, Johnny Papa, and Mohan Vanmane. *Professional XML Databases*. Wrox, 2000.

Appendix

Historical Antecedents

In the beginning, there were data files ... and from the need to manage the data stored in those files arose a variety of data management methods, most of which preceded the relational data model and, because of their shortcomings, paved the way for the acceptance of relational databases.

This appendix provides an overview of data management organizations used prior to the introduction of the relational data model. Although you do not need to read this appendix to understand the main body of this book, some of the concepts discussed here were introduced in the case studies in Part III.

FILE PROCESSING SYSTEMS

The first commercial computer—ENIAC—was designed to help process the 1960 Census. Its designers thought that all computers could do was crunch numbers; the idea that computers could handle text data came later. Unfortunately, the tools available to handle data weren't particularly sophisticated. In most cases, all the computing staff had available was some type of storage (at first tapes and later disks) and a high-level programming language compiler.

Early File Processing

Early file processing systems were made up of a set of data files—most commonly text files—and application programs that manipulated those files directly without the intervention of a DBMS. The files were laid out in a very precise, fixed format. Each individual piece of data (a first name, a last name, street address, and so on) was known as a

0	John	Smith	25 W. Main Street …
1	Jane	Johnson	120 Elm Lane …
2	Edward	Smith	44 Pine Heights …
3	Louis	Johnson	250 W. Main Street …
4	John	Jones	RR1 Box 250B …
5	Theresa	Jones	Anderson Road …
6	Thomas	Smith	12589 Highway 25 South …
7	Jan	Smith	48 Roxbury Court …
8	Edward	Jones	10101 Binary Road …
9	Emily	Johnson	202 Somerset Blvd …
10	Thomas	Johnson	25 N. Main Street …
11	Louis	Smith	918 Bayleaf Terrace …

■ **FIGURE A-1** A portion of a fixed field length data file.

field. The data that described a single entity were collected into a *record*. A data file was therefore made up of a collection of records.

Each field was allocated a specific number of bytes. The fixed field lengths meant that no delimiters were required between fields or at the ends of records, although some data files did include them. A portion of such a data field might appear like Figure A-1.

The programs that stored and retrieved data in the data files located data by their byte position in the file. Assuming that the first record in a file was numbered 0, a program could locate the start of any field with the computation:

```
record_number * record_length +
  starting_position_of_field
```

This type of file structure therefore was very easy to parse (i.e., separate into individual fields). It also simplified the process of writing the application programs that manipulated the files.

If the file was stored on tape, then access to the records was sequential. Such a system was well suited to batch processing *if* the records were in the order in which they needed to be accessed. If the records were stored on disk, then the software could perform direct access reads and writes. In either case, however, the program needed to know exactly where each piece of data was stored and was responsible for issuing the appropriate read and/or write commands.

> *Note:* Some tape drives were able to read backward to access data preceding the last written or read location. However, those that could not read backward needed to rewind completely and then perform a sequential scan beginning at the start of the tape to find data preceding the previous read/write location. Understandably, random access to data was unacceptably slow for interactive data processing.

These systems were subject to many problems, including all of those discussed in Chapter 3. In addition, programmers struggled with the following situations:

- Changing the layout of a data file (e.g., changing the size of a field or record) required changing all of the programs that accessed that file as well as rewriting the file to accommodate the new layout.
- Access was very fast when processing all records sequentially in the physical order of the file. However, searches for specific records based on some matching criteria also had to be performed sequentially, which was a very slow process. This held true even for files stored on disk.

The major advantage to a file processing system was that it was cheap. An organization that installed a computer typically had everything it needed: external storage and a compiler. In addition, a file processing system was relatively easy to create in that it required little advance planning. However, the myriad problems resulting from unnecessary duplicated data, as well as the close coupling of programs and physical file layouts and the serious performance problems that arose when searching the file, soon drove data management personnel of the 1950s and 1960s to search for alternatives.

ISAM Files

Prior to the introduction of the database management system, programmers at IBM developed an enhanced file organization known as *indexed sequential access method* (ISAM), which supported quick sequential access for batch processing but also provided indexes to fields in the file for fast access searches.

An ISAM file must be stored on disk. It is written initially to disk with excess space left in each cylinder occupied by the file. This allows records to be added in sequential key order. When a cylinder fills up, records are written to an overflow area and linked back to where they appear in the sequence in the file's primary storage areas (see Figure A-2).

Note: Hard drives write files to a single track on a single surface in a disk drive. When the track is full, then the drive writes to the same track on another surface. The same tracks on all the surfaces in a stack of platters in a disk drive are known as a cylinder. By filling a cylinder before moving to another track on the same surface, the disk drive can avoid moving the access arm to which read/write heads are attached, thus saving time in the read or write process.

When the overflow area fills up, the file must be *reblocked.* During the reblocking process, the file size is increased and records are rewritten, once again leaving expansion space on each cylinder occupied by the file. No data processing can occur using the file while reblocking is in progress.

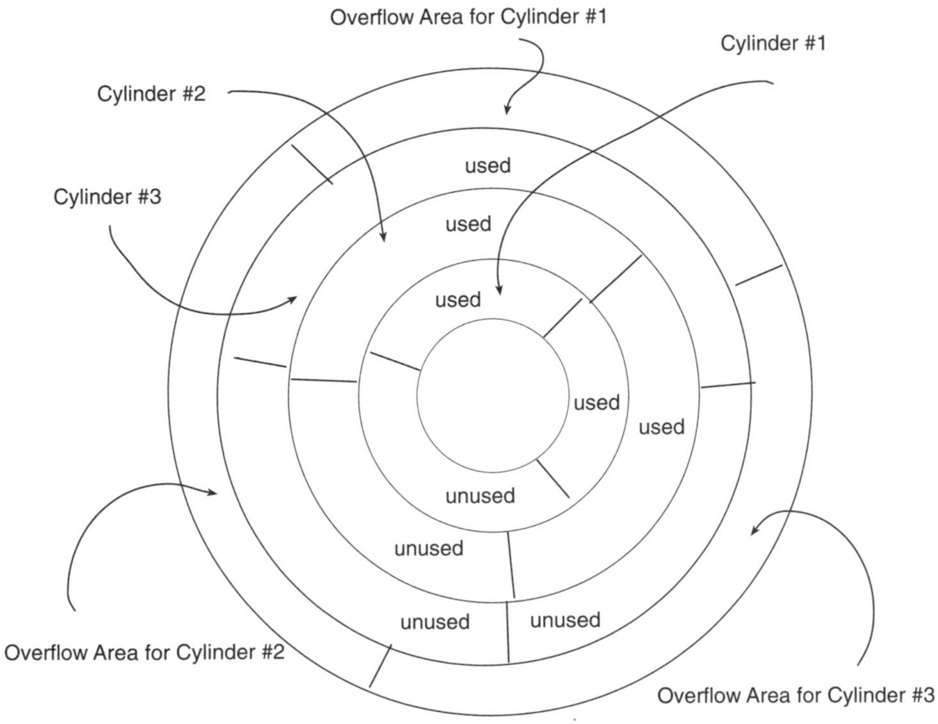

■ **FIGURE A-2** ISAM file organization.

Depending on the implementation, indexes to ISAM files may be stored in the same file as the data or in separate files. When the data files are stored separately, the functions that manipulate the files treat the indexes and data as if they were one logical file.

> *Note:* Although ISAM files have largely fallen into disuse, the DBMS Informix (now owned by IBM) continues to use its own version of ISAM—c-isam—for data storage.

Limitations of File Processing

File processing, regardless of whether it uses simple data files or ISAM files, is awkward at best. In addition to the problems mentioned earlier in this section, there are two more major drawbacks to file processing.

First, file processing cannot support ad hoc queries (queries that arise at the spur of the moment, cannot be predicted, and may never arise again). Because data files are created by the organization they are using, there is no common layout to the files from one organization to another. There is therefore no reasonable way for a software developer to write a language that can query any data file. A language that could query file A probably wouldn't work with file B because there is no similarity between the layout of the files. Therefore, access is limited to preplanned queries and reports that are provided by application programs.

So much of today's data access requires ad hoc querying capabilities. Consider, for example, an ATM machine, perhaps the penultimate ad hoc query device. When you walk up to the machine, there is no way for the machine's software to predict which account you will access. Nor is there any way to predict who will use a particular machine or what that person will request from the machine. Therefore, the software must be able to access data at any time, from any location, from any account holder, and perform any requested action.

Second, when a file processing system is made up of many files, there is no easy way to either validate cross-references between the files or perform queries that require data from multiple files. This cross-referencing issue is a major data integrity concern. If you store customer data in file A and orders in file B, you want the customer data in file B (even if it's only a customer number) to match the customer data in file B. Whenever data are duplicated, they must remain consistent. Unfortunately, when data are stored in multiple files, there is no easy way to perform this type of validation. The only way is to write a program that uses both files and explicitly verifies that the customer data in file B matches the data in file A. Although it can be done, file processing systems rarely perform this type of validation.

By the same token, queries or reports that require data to be extracted from multiple files are difficult to prepare. The application program that generates the output has to be created to read all the necessary files, resulting in a program that is difficult to debug and maintain due to its complexity.

The solution is to look for some way to separate physical storage structures from logical data access. In other words, the program or user who is manipulating data shouldn't have to be concerned about physical placement of data in files but should be able to express data manipulation requests in terms of how data logically relate to one another. This separation of logical and physical data organization is the hallmark of a database system.

File Processing on the Desktop

One of the problems with data management software written for PCs has been that both developers and users often didn't understand the exact meaning of the term *database*. As a result, the word was applied to any piece of software that managed data stored in a disk file, regardless of whether the software could handle logical data relationships.

This trend began in the early 1980s with a product called pfs:File. The program was a simple file manager. You defined your fields and then used a default form for entering data. There was no way to represent multiple entities or data relationships. Nonetheless, the product was marketed as a database management system, and thus the confusion in the marketplace began.

A number of products have fallen into this trap. One is FileMaker Pro, which began as a file manager and has been upgraded to database status. The FileMaker company introduced a product named Bento in 2008, which it advertises as a "personal database manager." Bento is a rather nice piece of software, but it isn't a database management system; it's a file manager. After nearly 30 years, the confusion about and the misuse of the term *database* persist.

You may often hear products such as those in the preceding paragraph described as "flat-file databases," despite the term "database" being a misnomer. Nonetheless, desktop file managers can be useful tools for applications such as maintaining a mailing list, a customer contact list, and so on.

The issue here is not to be a database snob but to ensure that consumers actually understand what they are buying and the limitations that actually accompany a file manager. This means that you must pay special attention to the capabilities of a product when you are considering a purchase.

THE HIERARCHICAL DATA MODEL

The first true database model to be developed was the *hierarchical data model,* which appeared as the basis of a commercial product in 1966. Like the two network data models that followed, it was a *navigational data model,* meaning that access paths were constrained by predeclared pointer structures in the schema.

Characteristics of the Hierarchical Data Model

A database that is designed to use the hierarchical data model is restricted to one-to-many relationships. In addition, no child entity may have more than one parent entity. The implications of this last restriction are significant.

As an example, consider the ER diagram in Figure A-3, which contains two hierarchies, or *trees*. The first relates departments to their employees and their projects. The second relates employees to projects. There is a one-to-many relationship between an employee and a department but a many-to-many relationship between projects and employees. The relationship between department and project is one-to-many.

Ideally, we would like to be able to use a composite entity to handle the many-to-many relationships. Unfortunately, the hierarchical data model does not permit the inclusion of composite entities. (There is no way to give a single entity two parent entities.) The only solution is to duplicate entity occurrences. This means that a project occurrence must be duplicated for every employee who works on the project. In addition, the project and employee entities are duplicated in the department hierarchy as well.

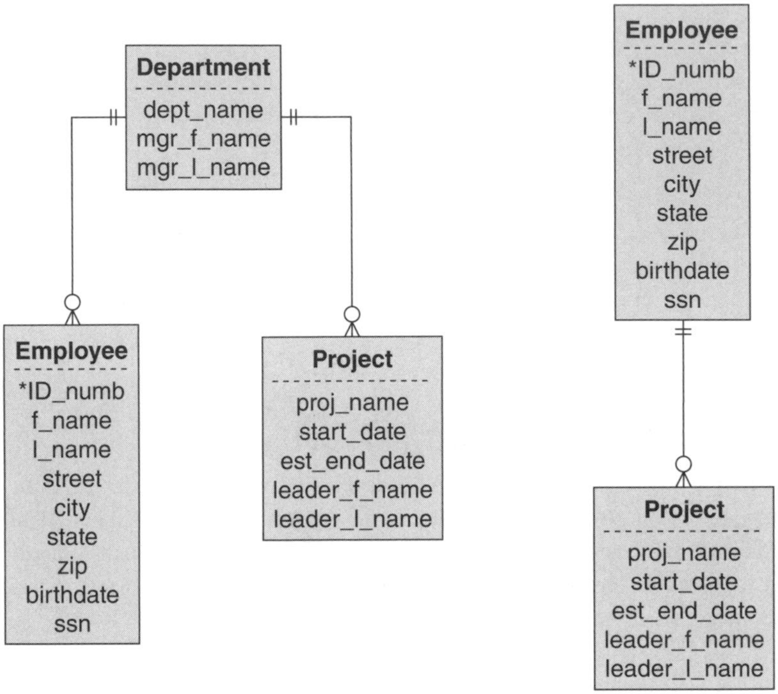

■ **FIGURE A-3** Sample hierarchies.

By their very nature, hierarchies include a great deal of duplicated data. This means that hierarchical databases are subject to the data consistency problems that arise from unnecessary duplicated data.

There is another major limitation to the hierarchical data model. Access is only through the entity at the top of the hierarchy, the *root*. From each root occurrence, the access path is top to bottom and left to right. This means that the path through the department hierarchy, for example, is through a department, to all its employees, and only then to the projects. For example, Figure A-4 contains two occurrences of the department/employee/project hierarchy. The arrows on the dashed lines represent the traversal order.

The relationships among the entities in an occurrence of a hierarchy are maintained by pointers embedded in the data. As a result, traversing a hierarchy in its default order is very fast. However, if you need random access to data, then access can be extremely slow because you must traverse every entity occurrence in the hierarchy preceding a needed occurrence to reach the needed occurrence. Hierarchies are

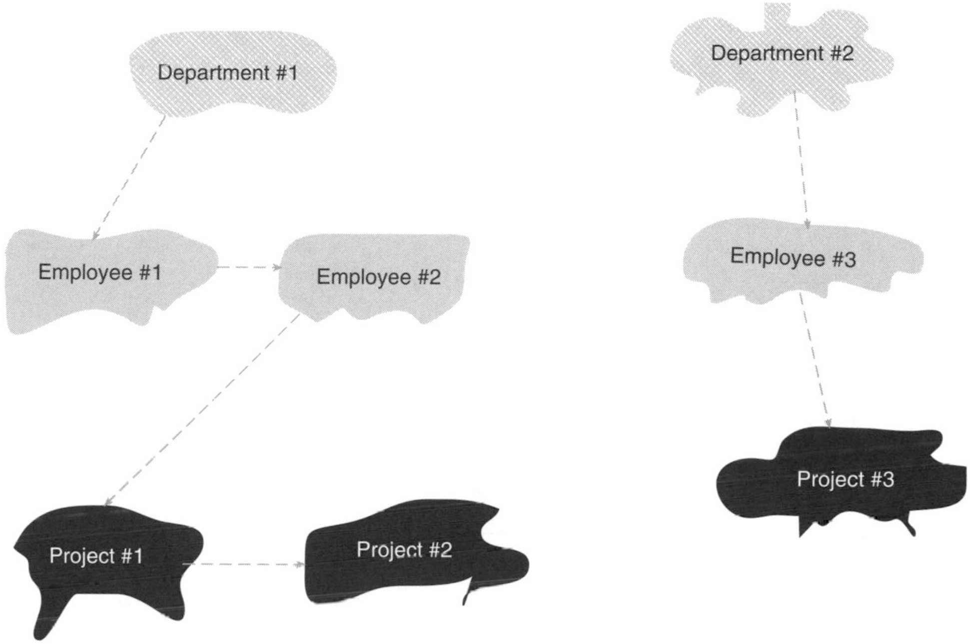

■ **FIGURE A-4** Tree traversal order in two occurrences of a hierarchy.

therefore well suited to batch processing in tree traversal order but are not suitable for applications that require ad hoc querying.

The hierarchical model is a giant step forward from file processing systems, including those based on ISAM files. It allows the user to store and retrieve data based on logical data relationships. It therefore provides some independence between the logical and physical data storage, relieving application programmers to a large extent of the need to be aware of the physical file layouts.

IMS

The most successful hierarchical DBMS has been IMS, an IBM product. Designed to run on IBM mainframes, IMS has been handling high-volume transaction-oriented data processing since 1966. Today, IBM supports IMS legacy systems but actively discourages new installations. In fact, many tools exist to help companies migrate from IMS to new products or to integrate IMS into more up-to-date software.

IMS does not adhere strictly to the theoretical hierarchical data model. In particular, it does allow multiple parentage in some very restrictive

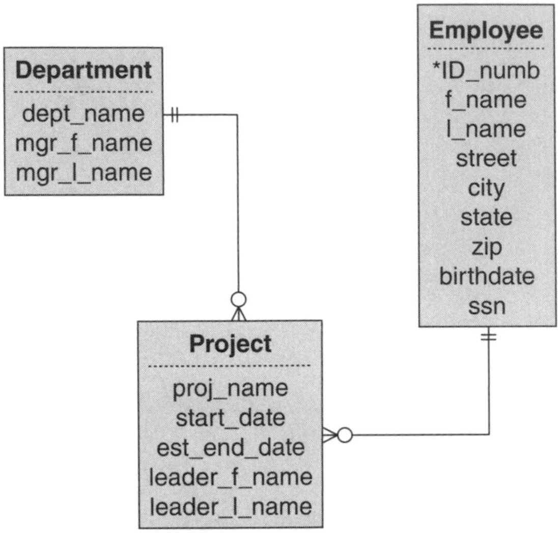

■ **FIGURE A-5** Two IMS hierarchies with permitted multiple parentage.

situations. As an example, consider Figure A-5, which actually contains two hierarchies: the department-to-project hierarchy and the hierarchy consisting of just the employee.

Note: IMS refers to each hierarchy as a database and each entity as a segment.

The multiple parentage of the project entity is permitted because the second parent—the employee entity—is in another hierarchy and is at a higher level in the hierarchy. Despite the restrictions on multiple parentage, this easing of the rules goes a long way to removing unnecessary duplicated data.

IMS does not support a query language. All access is through application programs that are usually written in COBOL. Like a true hierarchical DBMS, it is therefore best suited to batch processing in tree traversal order. It has been heavily used in large businesses with heavy operational transaction processing loads, such as banks and insurance companies.

THE SIMPLE NETWORK DATA MODEL

At the same time IBM was developing IMS, other companies were working on DBMSs that were based on the simple network data model. The first DBMS based on this model appears in 1967 (IDS from GE) and was welcomed because it directly addressed some of the limitations of the hierarchical data model. In terms of business usage, simple network databases had the widest deployment of any of the prerelational data models.

Note: The network data models—both simple and complex—predate computer networks as we know them today. In the context of a data model, the term network refers to an interconnected mesh, such as a network of neurons in the brain or a television or radio network.

Characteristics of a Simple Network

A simple network database supports one-to-many relationship between entities. There is no restriction on multiple parentage, however. This means that the employees/departments/projects database we have been using as an example could be designed as in Figure A-6. In this example, the project acts as a composite entity between department and employee. In addition, there is a direct relationship between department and employee for faster access.

Given the restrictions of the hierarchical data model, the simple network was a logical evolutionary step. It removed the most egregious limitation of the hierarchical data model: no multiple parentage. It

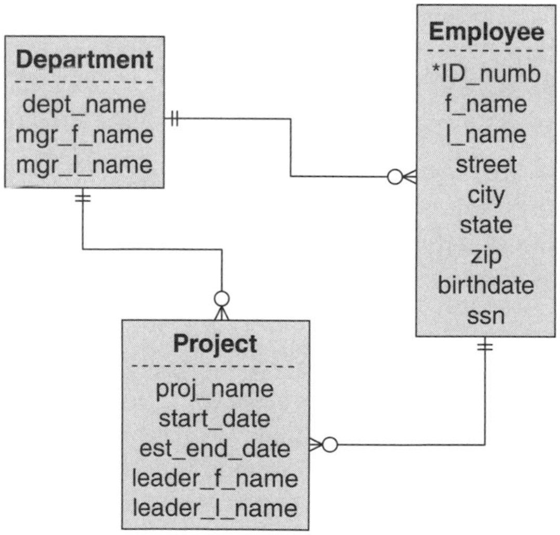

■ **FIGURE A-6** A simple network data model.

also further divorced the logical and physical storage, although as you will see shortly, simple network schemas still allowed logical database designers to specify some physical storage characteristics.

Simple network databases implement data relationships either by embedding pointers directly in the data or through the use of indexes. Regardless of which strategy is used, access to the data is restricted to the predefined links created by the pointers unless a fast access path has been defined for a particular type of entity. In this sense, a simple network is navigational, just like a hierarchical database.

There are two types of fast access paths available to the designer of a simple network. The first—*hashing*—affects the strategy used to place entity occurrences in a data file. When an entity occurrence is hashed into a data file, the DBMS uses a key (the value or one or more attributes) to compute a physical file locator (usually known as the *database key*). To retrieve the occurrence, the DBMS recomputes the hash value. Occurrences of related entities are then *clustered* around their parent entity in the data file. The purpose of this is twofold: It provides fast access to parent entities and puts child entities on the same disk page as their parents for faster retrieval. In the example we are using, a database designer might choose to hash department occurrences and cluster projects around their departments.

Note: An entity occurrence can either be clustered or hashed; it can't be both because the two alternatives determine physical placement in a data file.

Note: For an in-depth explanation of indexing, see "Indexing" in Chapter 7.

The second type of fast access path is an index, which provides fast, direct access to entity occurrences containing secondary keys. If occurrences are not hashed and have no indexes, then the only way to retrieve them is by traversing down relationships with parent entity occurrences.

To enable traversals of the data relationships, a simple network DBMS must keep track of where it is in the database. For every program running against the database, the DBMS maintains a set of *currency indicators*, each of which is a system variable containing a database key of the last entity occurrence accessed of a specific type. For example, there are currency indicators for each type of entity, for the program as a whole, and so on. Application programs can then use the contents of the currency indicators to perform data accesses relative to the program's previous location in the database.

Originally, simple network DBMSs did not support query languages. However, as the relational data model became more popular, many vendors added relational-style query languages to their products. If a simple network database is designed like a relational database, then it can be queried much like a relational database. However, the simple network is still underneath, and the database is therefore still subject to the access limitations placed on a simple network.

Simple network databases are not easy to maintain. In particular, changes to the logical design of the database can be extremely disruptive. First, the database must be brought offline; no processing can be done against it until the changes have been made. Once the database is down, then the following process occurs:

1. Back up all data or save the data in text files.
2. Delete the current schema and data files.
3. Compile the new database schema, which typically is contained in a text file, written in a *data definition language* (DDL).
4. Reallocate space for the data files.
5. Reload the data files.

In later simple network DBMSs, this process was largely automated by utility software, but considering that most simple network DBMSs were mainframe-based, they involved large amounts of data. Changes to the logical database could take significant amounts of time. There are still simple network databases in use today as legacy systems. However, it would be highly unusual for an organization to decide to create a new database based on this data model.

CODASYL

In the mid-1960s, government and industry professionals organized into the Committee for Data Systems Languages (CODASYL). Their goal was to develop a business programming language, the eventual result of which was COBOL. As they were working, the committee realized that they had another output besides a programming language: the specifications for a simple network database. CODASYL spun off the Database Task Group (DBTG), which in 1969 released its set of specifications.

The CODASYL specifications were submitted to the American National Standards Institute (ANSI). ANSI made a few modifications to the standard to further separate the logical design of the database from its physical storage layout. The result was two sets of very similar, but not identical, specifications.

> *Note:* It is important to understand that CODASYL is a standard rather than a product. Many products were developed to adhere to the CODASYL standards. In addition, there have been simple network DBMSs that employ the simple network data model but not the CODASYL standards.

A CODASYL DBMS views a simple network as a collection of two-level hierarchies known as *sets*. The database in Figure A-6 requires two sets: one for department → employee and department → project and the second for employee → project. The entity at the "one" end of the relationship is known as the *owner* of the set; the entities at the "many" end of relationships are *member* of the set. There can be only one owner entity but many member entities in any set. The same entity can be an owner of one set and a member of another, allowing the database designer to build a network of many levels.

As mentioned in the previous section, access is either directly to an entity occurrence using a fast access path (hashing or an index) or in traversal order. In the case of a CODASYL database, the members of a set have an order that is specified by the database designer.

If an entity is not given a fast access path, then the only way to retrieve occurrences is through the owners of some set. In addition, there is no way to retrieve all occurrences of an entity unless all of those occurrences are members of the same set, with the same owner.

Each set provides a conceptual linked list, beginning with the owner occurrence, continuing through all member occurrences, and linking back to the owner. Like the occurrences of a hierarchy in a hierarchical database, the occurrences of a set are distinct and unrelated, as in Figure A-7.

> *Note:* Early CODASYL DBMSs actually implemented sets as linked lists. The result was complex pointer manipulation in the data files, especially for entities that were members of multiple sets. Later products represented sets using indexes, with database keys acting as pointers to the storage locations of owner and member records.

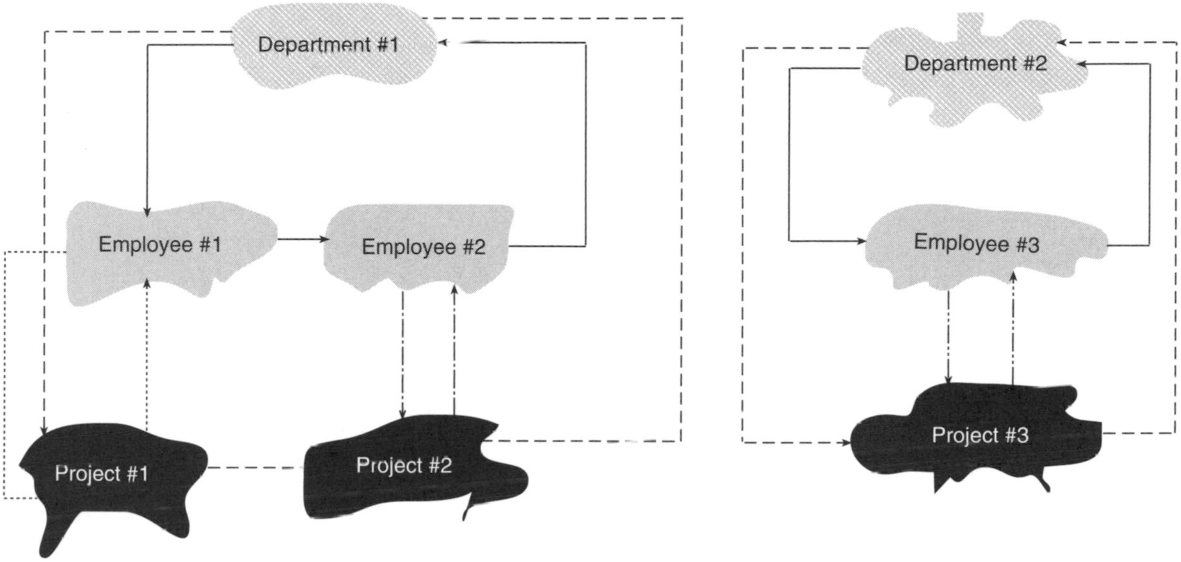

■ **FIGURE A-7** Occurrences of CODASYL sets.

The independence of set occurrences presents a major problem for entities that aren't a member of any set, such as the department occurrences in Figure A-7. To handle this limitation, CODASYL databases support a special type of set—often called a *system set*—that has only one owner occurrence: the database system itself. All occurrences of an entity that is a member of that set are connected to the single owner occurrence. Employees and projects would probably be included in a system set also to provide the ability to access all employees and all projects. The declaration of system sets is left up to the database designer.

Any DBMS that was written to adhere to either set of CODASYL standards is generally known as a CODASYL DBMS. This represents the largest population of simple network products that were marketed.

Arguably, the most successful CODASYL DBMS was IDMS, originally developed by Cullinet. IDMS was a mainframe product that was popular well into the 1980s. As relational DBMSs began to dominate the market, IDMS was given a relational-like query language and marketed as IDMS/R. Ultimately, Cullinet was sold to Computer Associates, which marketed and supported the product under the name CA-IDMS.

> *Note:* Although virtually every PC DBMS in the market today claims to be relational, many are not. Some, such as FileMaker Pro, are actually simple networks. These are client–server products, robust enough for small business use. They allow multiple parentage with one-to-many relationships and represent those relationships with preestablished links between files. These are simple networks. As you become familiar with the relational data model, you will understand why such products aren't relational. It doesn't mean that they aren't good products but simply that they don't meet the minimum requirements for a relational DBMS.

THE COMPLEX NETWORK DATA MODEL

The complex network data model was developed at the same time as the simple network. It allows direct many-to-many relationships without requiring the introduction of a composite entity. The intent of the data model's developers was to remove the restriction against many-to-many relationships imposed by the simple network data model. However, the removal of this restriction comes with a steep price.

As you will remember from Chapter 4, there are at least two major problems associated with the inclusion of direct many-to-many relationships. Consider first the database segment in Figure A-8. Notice that there is no place to store data about the quantity of each item being ordered. The need to store relationship data is one reason why we replace many-to-many relationships with a composite entity and two one-to-many relationships.

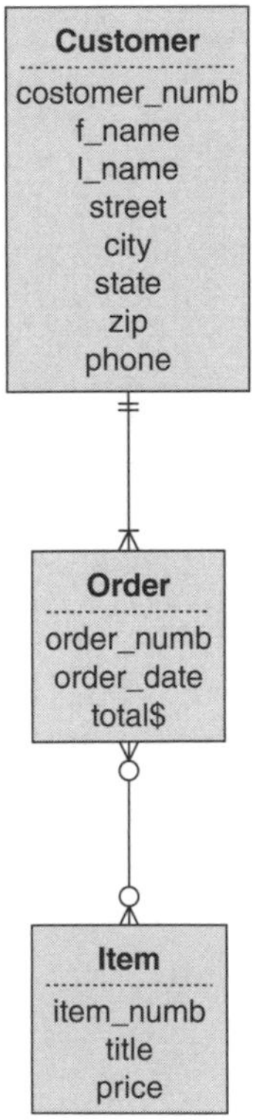

■ **FIGURE A-8** A complex network lacking a place to store relationship data.

Nonetheless, if we examine an occurrence diagram for Figure A-8 (see Figure A-9), you can see that there is no ambiguity in the relationships. However, assume that we add another entity to the design, as in Figure A-10. In this case, each item can appear on many shipments, and each shipment can contain many items.

The problem with this design becomes clear when you look at the occurrences in Figure A-11. Notice, for example, that it is impossible to determine the order to which Shipment #1 and Shipment #2 belong. After you follow the relationships from the shipment occurrence to Item #1, there is no way to know which order is correct.

There are two solutions to this problem. The first is to introduce an additional relationship to indicate which shipment comes from which

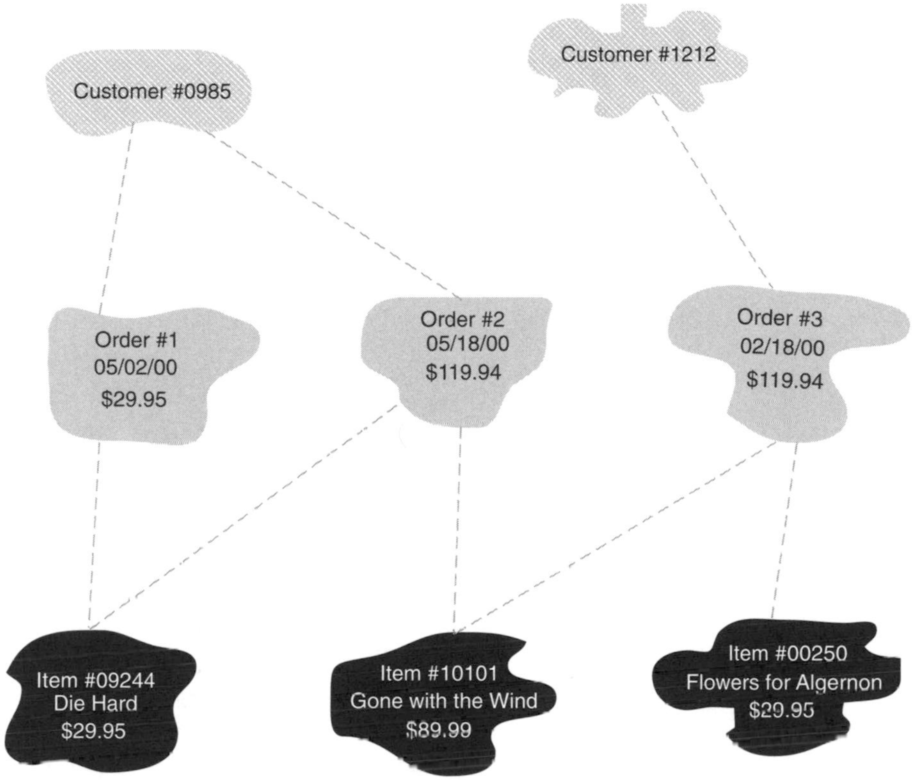

■ **FIGURE A-9** Sample occurrences for the design in Figure A-8.

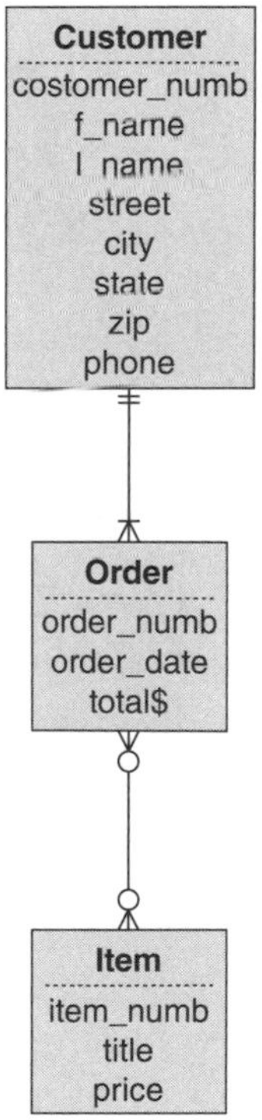

■ **FIGURE A-10** A complex network with ambiguous logical relationships.

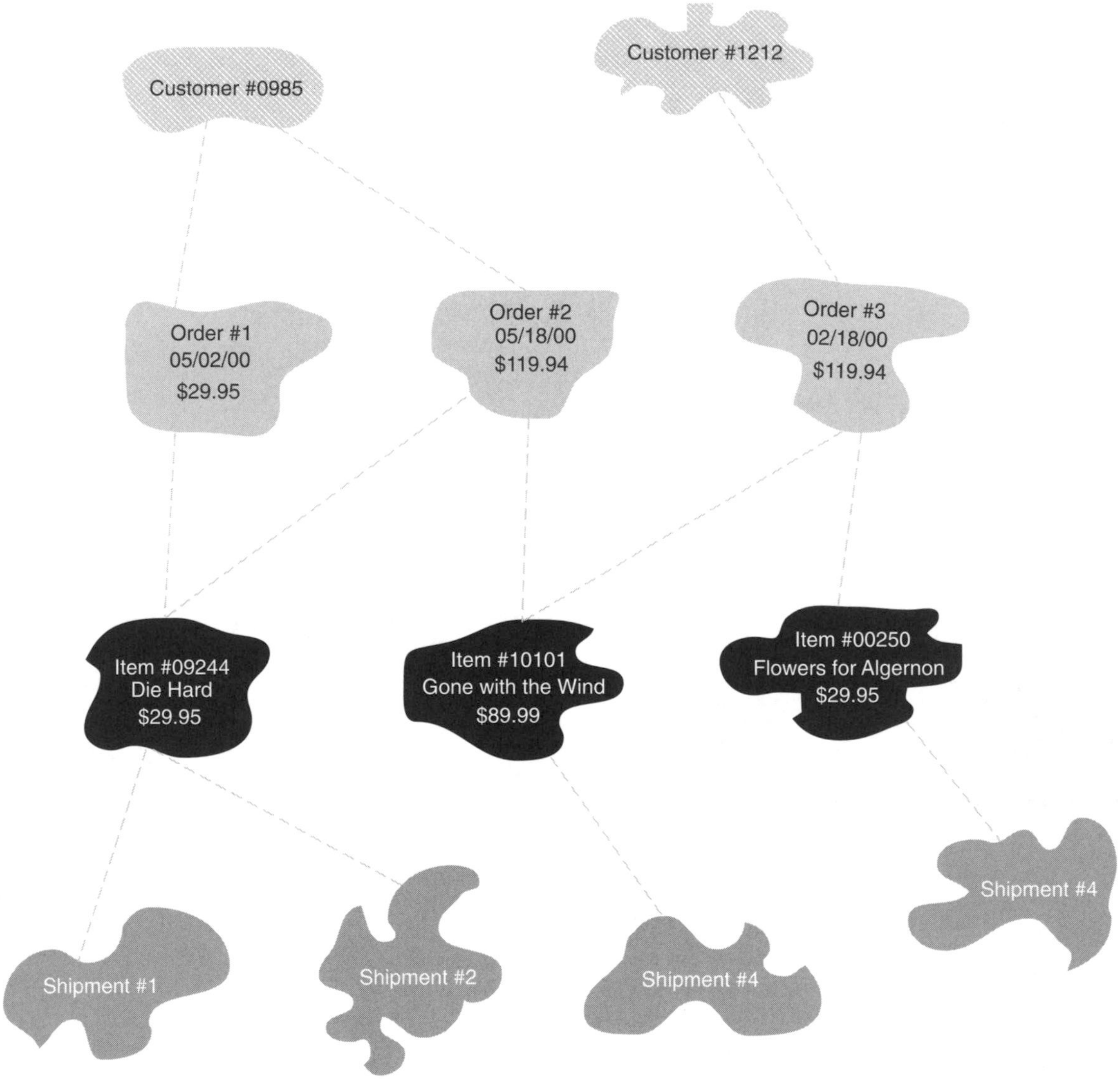

■ **FIGURE A-11** Occurrences of the complex network in Figure A-10 containing ambiguous logical relationships.

order, as in Figure A-12. Although this is certainly a viable solution, it results in increased complexity for storing and retrieving data.

The other solution is to abandon the use of the complex network altogether and introduce composite entities to reduce all the many-to-many relationships to one-to-many relationships. The result, of course, is a simple network.

Note: As discussed in Chapter 5, a relational DBMS can represent all the relationships acceptable in a simple network—including composite entities—but it does so in a nonnavigational manner. Like a simple network, it can capture all of the meaning of a many-to-many relationship and still avoid data ambiguity.

Because of the complexity of maintaining many-to-many relationships and the possibility of logical ambiguity, there have been no widely successful commercial products based on the complex network data model. However, the data model remains in the literature and provides some theoretical completeness to traditional data modeling.

Note: In terms of the sequence of the development of data models, the relational data model followed the network data models. Since the development of the relational data model, two additional data models have appeared: the object-oriented data model and multidimensional databases (usually known as online analytical processing [OLAP] or star schema databases). Multidimensional databases are designed primarily for use with data warehouses.

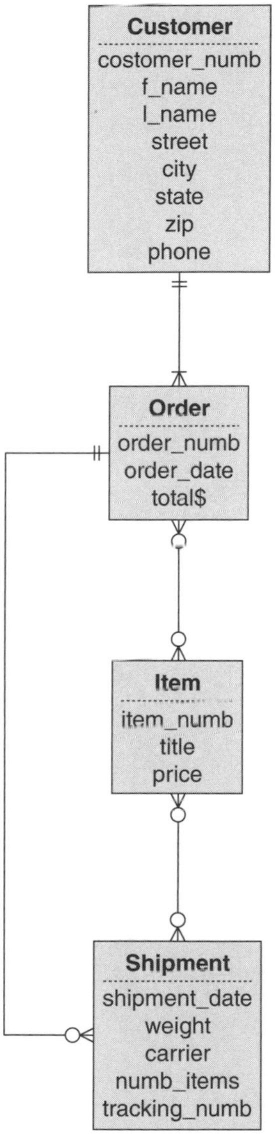

■ **FIGURE A-12** Using an additional relationship to remove logical ambiguity in a complex network.

Glossary

All-key relation: A relation in which every column is part of the primary key.

Attribute: Data that describe an entity; the formal term for a column in a relation.

Authorization matrix: A database system table that contains information about which users have access to which parts of the database. The DBMS consults the authorization matrix before performing user data manipulation requests.

Base table: Relations whose data are physically stored in a database.

Binary large object (BLOB): A column data type specifying that the column will show the contents of a file (text and/or graphics) in its binary representation, without being searchable or readable in any way by the DBMS.

Black hat hackers: Hackers who break into a computer system for profit or with a desire to do harm.

Buffer overflow attack: An attempt to gain unauthorized control over a computer system by exploiting a programming error in an application or system program.

Candidate key: A column or combination of columns that can be used as the primary key of a relation.

Cardinality (of a relationship): The type of relationship (one-to-one, one-to-many, or many-to-many).

Catalog: Another term for a data dictionary.

Circular inclusion constraint: A constraint on a relation that specifies that if a row is added to a specific table, rows must be added to one or more other tables.

Client/server architecture: System architecture where processing tasks are shared between server and client computers.

Clustering: Physically storing foreign key rows close to the primary key rows they reference to improve database performance.

CODASYL database: A database that adheres to the Committee on Data Systems Languages (CODASYL) database standard.

Column homogeneous: A property of a relation stating that all the values in a given column are taken from the same domain.

Commit (a transaction): End a transaction by making its changes permanent.

Committee on Data Systems Languages (CODASYL): A committee of government and industry technologists that developed the COBOL programming language and a standard for a simple network database.

Complex network data model: A navigational data model that permits direct many-to-many relationships as well as one-to-many and one-to-one relationships.

Composite entity: An entity that exists to represent the relationship between two other entities. It may have relationship data as attributes.

Computer-aided software engineering (CASE) tool: A software package that provides specialized tools for software and database modeling diagrams.

Concatenated identifier: An entity identifier made up of a combination of values from multiple attributes.

Concurrency control: Mechanisms to ensure that a database remains consistent and accurate during concurrent use.

Concurrent use: Multiple users working with the same database at the same time.

Conforming parser: Software that can read an XML document to determine whether the document is well formed.

Constraint: A rule to which data in a database must adhere.

Context diagram: The top-level diagram in a data flow diagram that shows the environmental context in which the information system exists.

Currency indicator: A system value kept by a navigational database to indicate a transaction's current position in the database hierarchy.

Cyberterrorists: Hackers who are motivated by a political, religious, or philosophical agenda.

Cylinder: The same track on all surfaces in a stack of platters in a hard disk.

Database: A collection of data and information about the relationships among those data.

Database administrator (DBA): A person who has the responsibility for maintaining a database.

Database key: In a CODASYL database, an internal pointer to the physical storage location of a record occurrence in a file.

Database management system (DBMS): Software that manages the storage and retrieval of data stored in a database.

Data definition language: A special-purpose computer language used to define the schema of a navigational database.

Data dictionary: A repository that describes the data stored in a database along with definitions of data relationships.

Data dictionary driven: A property of relational databases in which all access to stored data is preceded by access to the data dictionary to determine if the requested data elements exist and if the user has the access rights to perform the requested action.

Data flow: The path taken by data as they are processed throughout an organization.

Data flow diagram (DFD): A graphic method for documenting the flow of data within an organization.

Data mart: A small data warehouse.

Data model: The formal way of expressing relationships in a database.

Data store (in a DFD): A place where data are stored.

Data warehouse: A repository of transaction and nontransaction data used for querying, reporting, and corporate decision making.

Deadlock: A problem that occurs as a result of exclusive/writing locking where two or more transactions become stalled waiting for the release of locks held by each other.

Deletion anomaly: A problem with the design of a relation such that deleting data about one entity in a row causes a part of the primary key to become null, requiring the deletion of the entire row, which may contain data that must be retained.

Denial of service attack: An attack on a computer system that attempts to prevent legitimate users from gaining access to network resources and, by extension, any database that uses that network.

Determinant: An attribute on which other attributes are functionally dependent.

Dimensional modeling: The most frequently used data model for data warehouses.

Dimension table: A table in a data warehouse that contains descriptive information for grouping data stored in fact tables.

Dirty read: A problem with uncontrolled concurrent use of a database where a transaction acts on data that have been modified by an update transaction that hasn't committed and is later rolled back.

Disaster recovery: Activities that must take place to bring the database back into use after it has been damaged in some way.

Distributed database: A database where portions of the database are stored on computers at physically distributed locations. The entire database is the sum of all the parts.

Distribution independence: A constraint on a distributed database that specifies that the database should look and act like a centralized database to users.

Domain: A specification of permissible values for an attribute.

Domain constraint: A rule that requires that all values of an attribute come from a specified domain.

Entity: Something about which we store data.

Entity identifier: A value (or combination of values) that uniquely identifies each occurrence of an entity in a database.

Entity integrity: A constraint on a relation that states that no part of the primary key can be null.

Entity-relationship diagram (ERD): A graphic technique for representing entity relationships.

Entity-relationship (ER) model: A technique for representing entity relationships that is independent of any specific data model and any specific software.

Equi-join: A join based on matching identical values.

Evolutionary prototyping: A form of prototyping in which successive prototypes of the software are modified based on user feedback, eventually converging on the production system.

Exclusive lock: A lock that gives the transaction holding the lock the exclusive right to read and write a portion of the database.

Extensible markup language (XML): A platform-independent markup language for specifying the structure of data in a text document used for both data storage and the transfer of data.

Extract-transform-load: The process of taking data from operational databases (and optionally external sources), modifying the data to meet the requirements of a data warehouse, and loading the data into the warehouse.

Fact table: A table used in dimensional modeling to contain summarizable facts.

Field: In a file processing system, the smallest unit of meaningful data, such as a first name or street address.

File processing system: A system that handles data by storing them in data files and then manipulating the files through application programs.

Firewall: A piece of software that filters incoming and outgoing network traffic and stops messages that violate the rules that define allowable traffic.

Foreign key: An attribute (or combination of attributes) in a relation that is the same as the primary key of another relation. A foreign key may be a non-key attribute in its own relation, or it may be part of a concatenated primary key.

Functional dependency: A relationship between two attributes (or two combination of attributes) in a relation such that for every unique value of the second attribute, the table contains only one value of the first attribute. The first attribute, however, may be associated with multiple values of the second attribute.

Granularity (of a lock): The size of the portion of a database to which a lock is applied.

Hashing: A technique for providing fast access to data based on a key value by determining the physical storage location of those data.

Hierarchical data model: A legacy data model where all relationships are one-to-many or one-to-one, and entities at the "many" end of a relationship can be related to only one entity at the "one" end of the relationship.

Horizontal portioning: Splitting the rows of a table between multiple tables with the same structure to improve database performance.

Inconsistent analysis: A problem that occurs from uncontrolled concurrent use of a database where a transaction produces incorrect output because another transaction was concurrently modifying data being retrieved.

Index: A data structure in a database that provides a logical ordering of data based on key values.

Indexed sequential access method (ISAM): A physical file storage technique that also provides indexes to data based on a key for fast access on that key.

Inner join: An equi-join.

Insertion anomaly: A problem with the design of a relation such that all data for a complete primary key are not available, preventing data from being stored in the relationship.

Instance (of an entity): A group of attributes that describes a single real-world occurrence of an entity.

Instance (of a relation): A relation that contains at least one row of data.

Interleaved execution: The interweaving of the actions of two or more concurrent database transactions.

IPSec: A type of security used by a virtual private network.

Join: A relational algebra operation that combines two relations horizontally by matching values between the two tables. Most valid joins involve matching primary key values to foreign key values.

Join dependency: The most general form of dependency between attributes in a relation such that a table can be put together correctly by joining two or more tables, all of which contain only attributes from the original table.

Legacy database: A database using a pre-relational data model that is still in use.

Locking: Restricting access to parts of a database to specific transactions to provide concurrency control.

Logging: The process of keeping an audit trail of changes made by a transaction to be used to undo the transaction should it need to be rolled back.

Lost update: A problem that occurs during uncontrolled concurrent use of a database where an update made by one transaction wipes out the effect of an update made by a concurrent transaction.

Malware: Unwanted software—such as a virus, worm, or Trojan horse—that is inadvertently loaded onto a computer and causes disruption or distribution of computer functioning.

Mandatory relationship: A relationship between two entities in a database such that an instance of the second entity cannot exist in the database unless it is related to an instance of the first entity.

Many-to-many relationship: A relationship between two entities in a database such that each instance of the first entity can be related to many instances of the second and each instance of the second entity can be related to many instances of the first.

Metadata: Data about data; the data stored in a data dictionary.

Modification anomaly: A problem that occurs when duplicated data become inconsistent when not all occurrences of the same value are modified at the same time.

Multivalued attribute: An attribute that can contain more than one value at a time.

Multivalued dependency: A general case of a functional dependency where a determinant determines a small group of values (as opposed to a single value) for two unrelated attributes.

Multiversion concurrency control: A concurrency control method in which data retrievals and modifications are marked with the time they occur. Modifications are allowed if no other transaction holds an earlier timestamp on the data.

Mutually exclusive relationship: A relationship between entities such that an instance of an entity can be related to an instance of either a second or third entity, but not both.

Natural identifiers: Entity identifiers that are unique by nature, such as invoice numbers.

Navigational data model: A data model where relationships between entities are represented by physical data structures (for example, pointers or indexes) that provide the only paths for data access.

Nonrepeatable read: A problem with uncontrolled concurrent use of a database that occurs when a transaction reads data for the second time and determines that the data are not the same as they were from the first read.

Normal form: A set of theoretical rules to which a relation must conform.

Normalization: The process of designing relations to adhere to increasingly stringent sets of rules to avoid problems with poor database design.

Null: A database value, distinct from a blank or zero, meaning "unknown."

Object-oriented analysis: A method for viewing the interaction of data and manipulations of data that is based on the object-oriented programming paradigm.

One-to-many relationship: A relationship between two entities in a database such that one instance of an entity can be related to many instances of a second entity and the second entity can be related to only one instance of the first.

One-to-one relationship: A relationship between two entities in a database such that each instance of an entity is related to no more than one instance of the other entity.

Optimistic locking: A concurrency control method that allows all modifications but then rolls back transactions if other transactions have modified the data.

Page: The size of the block of data that a computer (and therefore a database) transfers between disk and main memory at one time.

Performance tuning: Making changes to the design of a database to enhance database performance.

Phantom read: A problem with uncontrolled concurrent use of a database that occurs when a transaction reads data for the second time and determines that new rows have been inserted by another transaction.

Physical schema: The underlying physical storage of a database, managed by the DBMS.

Precision: The number of digits to the right of a decimal point in a number.

Predicate: A statement of logical criteria against which data are evaluated during a query.

Primary key: A column or combination of columns whose value uniquely identifies each row in a relation.

Process (in a DFD): Something that is done to data.

Product: The relational algebra operation that combines two tables by forming all possible combination of rows; the Cartesian product of two tables.

Project: The relational algebra operation that creates a projection of a relation.

Projection: A subset of a relation created by copying selected columns and all rows in those columns.

Prototyping: A form of system development where developers prepare models of a system that are not fully functional. User feedback is used to modify the prototype or to develop a final system.

Query optimizer: A portion of a DBMS that determines the most efficient sequence of relational algebra operations to use to satisfy a query.

Read lock: Control over a portion of the database given to one or more transactions that prevents other transactions from modifying the data while the locks are in place.

Reblocking: In an ISAM file, rewriting the file to leave physical space on each track occupied by the file to allow the addition of records in key sequence order.

Record: In a file processing system, a collection of data that describes one instance of an entity.

Recovery: The process of restoring a database from a damaged or inconsistent state so it becomes operational again.

Referential integrity: A constraint on a relation that states that every non-null foreign key value must match an existing primary key value.

Relation: The definition of a two-dimensional table with columns and rows. There is no more than one value at the intersection of each column and row (no repeating groups).

Relational algebra: The set of theoretical operations used to manipulate data in a relation.

Relational data model: A paradigm for describing the structure of a database in which entities are represented as tables, and relationships between the entities are represented by matching data.

Relationship data: Data that apply to the relationship between two entities rather than to the entities themselves.

Repeating group: A multivalued attribute that must be removed before the data in the group can be stored in a relational database.

Requirements document: A document prepared as the output of a systems analysis that describes the information requirements of a new or modified information system.

Restrict: The more recent term for the relational algebra operation that chooses rows from a table based on evaluating data against logical criteria (a *predicate*).

Roll back (a transaction): Undo the changes made by a transaction, restoring the database to the state it was in before the transaction began.

Schema: The overall logical plan of a database.

Script kiddies: Hackers who use prewritten software to break into computer systems.

Select: The original relational algebra term for *restrict*; the SQL command to retrieve data from a database.

Serializable: A condition in which interleaved transactions produce the same result that they would have produced if they had run in a series.

Service-oriented architecture (SOA): A method for organizing a company's entire information system functions so all information components are viewed as services that are provided to the organization.

Set: In a CODASYL database, a two-level hierarchy representing one or more one-to-many relationships.

Shared lock: Control over a portion of the database given to one or more transactions that prevents other transactions from modifying the data while the locks are in place.

Simple network data model: A legacy data model where all relationships are one-to-many or one-to-one; a navigational data model where relationships are represented with physical data structures such as pointers.

Single-valued attribute: An attribute that contains only one value at any given time.

Social engineering: A nontechnological method for gaining unauthorized access to a computer system by tricking people into revealing access information.

Sorting: Physically reordering the rows in a table based on the values in one or more columns.

Spiral methodology: A more formal form of prototyping that uses a gradual process in which each cycle further refines the system, bringing it closer to the desired end point.

SQL injection attack: An attack against a database system launched through an application program containing embedded SQL.

Structured design life cycle: The classic model for developing an information system. It involves a sequence of activities that defines and develops a new or modified system. It works best in environments where information needs are well known.

Systems analysis: Conducting a needs assessment to determine what a new or modified information system should do.

System set: In a CODASYL database, a special set with only one owner occurrence that is used to collect all occurrences of a single entity.

Table: A term used synonymously with *relation* in the *relational data model*.

Three-schema architecture: A view of a database environment in which the logical schema provides an interface between the physical schema and user views of the database.

Three-valued logic: A set of logical truth tables that include the values true, false, and unknown.

Throwaway prototyping: A type of prototyping in which the prototype software is demonstrated and evaluated and then discarded. The production system is developed from scratch based on feedback to the prototype.

Timestamping: A concurrency control method in which data retrievals and modifications are marked with the time they occur. Modifications are allowed if no other transaction holds an earlier timestamp on the data.

Transaction: A unit of work presented to a database.

Transitive dependency: A set of functional dependencies where an attribute that is a candidate key for its relation determines a second attribute, and the second attribute determines a third, producing a functional dependency between the first and third as well.

Tree: In the hierarchical data mode, a single entity hierarchy.

Tuple: The formal term for a row in a relations.

Two-phase locking: A concurrency control method that begins by giving transactions shared/read locks on data and then upgrades the locks to exclusive/write locks only when the transaction is ready to modify data.

Unified modeling language (UML): A style of ER diagramming.

Unit of recovery: A transaction,, called so because a transaction either succeeds or fails as a whole.

Update anomaly: A problem that occurs when duplicated data become inconsistent when not all occurrences of the same value are modified at the same time.

Vertical partitioning: Storing a relation as two or more tables that are projections of the original relation to improve database performance.

View: A virtual table that is constructed by executing a named query that is stored as part of a database.

Virtual private network (VPN): A method that provides remote access to local area networks that uses the Internet and encrypts transmissions for security.

Virtual table: A table whose data exist only in main memory rather than being stored physically in the database.

Waterfall method: An alternative name for the traditional structured systems development life cycle based on the idea that one step falls into another.

Weak entity: An entity whose instances cannot exist in a database unless a related instance of another entity is present and related to it.

Well-formed (XML document): An XML document that conforms to the syntax rules for a correct document.

White hat hackers: Hackers who break into computer systems and then report vulnerabilities to the software owner or developer. Their motives are usually to help make systems more secure.

Write lock: A lock that gives the transaction holding the lock the exclusive right to read and write a portion of the database.

XML schema: A document without data that specifies the structure of an XML document.

Index

D

E